To Pastor (

I hope you enjoy A.T.

Best Wishes,

[signature]

A. T.

A.T.

**Michael M. Poinski
LTC, USAR (Ret.)**

Word Association Publishers
www.wordassociation.com

ISBN: 978-1-59571-248-6
Library of Congress Control Number: 2008920206

Word Association Publishers
205 5th Avenue
Tarentum, PA 15084
www.wordassociation.com

Special Thanks

To my daughter Megan for help with editing and story development. Thanks sweetie! Love ya!

To my dear friend John Dabrowski for his review and endorsement. My sincerest thanks.

To Mark Baker for the cover artwork. Mark, your cartoons are the best. Pvt. Murphy is alive and well and assigned to every military unit.

To all whom serve this great nation in the military, and those who serve the common good. God bless you all!

PREFACE

Africans, Asians, Europeans, Latinos, Native Americans, all of them... Americans.

They all share a common bond: a love of country and a willingness to serve and defend our cherished freedoms. May we always remember and give thanks and praises to those Americans who served, are serving, and will serve in the military to preserve our nation and Constitutional rights.

Those who serve in the military have three choices:
1) Active Component
2) National Guard
3) Reserve Component

The National Guard and Reserves serve one weekend a month and two weeks of active duty service per year. The two weeks of active duty service is called annual training, or more commonly referred to as A.T.

Why two weeks of annual training on active duty? A great American had the following philosophy on training:

"IN NO OTHER PROFESSION ARE THE PENALTIES FOR EMPLOYING UNTRAINED PERSONNEL SO APPALLING OR SO IRREVOCABLE AS IN THE MILITARY"

GENERAL DOUGLAS MACARTHUR

FOREWORD

"I bump it a quarter", mused the poker player holding a pair of sevens and nines as he threw a quarter into the pot. Every player at the table saw the raise, knowing they had a good chance to win. "I'll bump it another quarter", replied Bobo, the card shark of the Phi Sig house. When the Bo re-raised the bet, there was one of two possibilities, he had an excellent hand, or crap. Dave Marshall took another swig from his can of Stroh's. Time to fold. As he tossed his cards aside, the other members of his college frat gathered around the TV in the dining room. The volume was turned up high enough for everyone to hear. Time to check out what's happening, he thought to himself as he got up from the table.

December was the month of changing weather in Ohio. In 1969, this first day of December was going to be a big change for all males from 19 to 26 years of age, including all the brothers of the Phi Sig house at Akron University. This was the day the Selective Service Commission re-instituted the draft lottery.

Every able-bodied American male had to register for the draft when they turned 18 years of age. If one was healthy and available, they were given the status of 1-A. The waiting game would then commence. For many, a letter would come informing the candidate to report for a physical. From there, they would be examined for mental and physical well-being. For those who were in school or college working toward a degree, a deferment was granted until graduation. They would then be eligible like all the rest, unless they could prove hardship or other reasons they could not serve in the military. Congressman Alexander Pirnie was the official lottery drawer, as he reached into a large glass receptacle and grabbed a blue plastic capsule that contained a date. In all, there were 366 capsules, to include the leap year date of February 29th. Congressman Pirnie handed the blue capsule to Colonel Daniel Omer, who read aloud the first lottery number picked, "September 14...September 14 is 001". Shouts of disbelief rang out from the men watching the TV in the dining room. One of the brothers, Ken Matuney, a soon-to-graduate senior and a R.O.T.C. cadet, had his birth date pulled as number 001. He was going into the Army no matter what, but that wasn't what upset everyone in the room. Ken also won the lottery pool, in which every Phi Sig had thrown a dollar into. Ken just won $142.

The other members of the frat were keeping a close eye on the lottery drawing, and everyone's birthday was being written down a large calendar by one of the members. Marshall knew he would be alerted when his number arrived. He was in Army R.O.T.C. as well. He figured it was better to choose one's destiny, rather than have it randomly chosen for you.

"Bo, who won that last pot?" asked Marshall as he sat back down in his seat at the poker table. Bobo smiled as he took another drag on his cigarette. "You're lookin' at him," replied the Bo as he began to deal the cards and called the game, "follow the queen, high low, and one repair card for a quarter." The cards were getting better for Marshall. One queen in the hole, and one on top. Maybe this is a good omen, he thought as the cards kept coming.

As the poker game continued, one of the frat brothers at the table with a low lottery number commented it was time to take a hiatus to Canada. Another from the dining room yelled, "Dave, they just pulled your date. You're number 40." Marshall shook his head. He knew he was going in, only this time it was official. "Well boys, looks like I better not drop out of R.O.T.C.," sighed Marshall as he looked at his cards, smirked, and tossed a quarter into the pot.

INTRODUCTION

While driving through the rural countryside east of Ravenna, Ohio, motorists whiz past the grounds of a mothballed government ammunition plant.

The rusted fencing, the desolate grounds, and the few structures with peeling paint visible from the road made the place look deserted—except for the contracted civilian security forces manning the gated access road from a small wooden booth. Inside the compound, the ramshackle structures—built during World War II—stood like a formation of old soldiers. The wood framed structures were like a pair of combat boots after several years of hard wear and tear: Well worn, but serviceable. No matter the season or the government dollars trickling down for improvements, the buildings were perpetually in desperate need of a coat of paint

But one weekend a month, the old compound came to life. Well, sort of.

The U.S. Army Reserve's 683rd Heavy Equipment Maintenance Company spent one weekend a month filling the grounds of the old ammunition plant with fatigues, servitude and work for the good of the nation.

The Army Reservists' freedom of movement within the complex was highly restricted due to the secretive—and possibly hazardous nature of what it was used for. The aging ammunition bunkers and storage sheds were off limits to everyone, especially the curious Reservists. There were few places the Reservists could go, with only one route of travel to and from the maintenance shops, located three miles from the 683rd Orderly Room, where the company headquarters section was located.

As a maintenance company, the 683rd rebuilt starters, alternators, engines, transmissions, tanks, artillery, weapons and generators, relined brake shoes, and repaired canvas and metal fabrication. The unit's motto was "If we can't fix it, it ain't broke," and its members were experts in repairing everything the Army had—except electronics, aviation equipment, and public relations debacles. There were other Reserve units created to take care of those areas.

The maintenance shops consisted of two old railroad repair buildings deep inside the government complex. However, the maintenance shops saw as little action as the restricted ammunition bunkers. Because the Reservists met just two days out of each month, not much maintenance—what they called their "mission work"—was done. All the 683rd vehicles stayed parked outside and were covered in dirt, leaves, or buried under a foot of snow, depending on the season.

When the Reservists arrived to perform their weekend drill, half of their time was spent working on other Reserve units' vehicles, not their own. That was their primary mission – to repair everyone else's broken down equipment. Whatever time was left was devoted to training of basic military skills. Time was a scarce commodity. The Reservists were allotted one weekend a month to cram in as much training as possible.

Despite its relative inaction, the 683rd Maintenance Company was more than 250 soldiers strong and one of the larger company-sized units in the Army Reserve. In 1982, a diverse band of citizen soldiers made up the ranks of the company. The veteran members were the non-commissioned officers, normally referred to as NCOs, and chief warrant officers, whom were usually called chiefs. Many of them had served in Vietnam, and later joined the Army Reserves to pursue a civilian career and still be eligible for the Army's retirement benefits. After 20 years of service, the U.S. government gave them an incredible 60th birthday present: A retirement pension and medical care for the rest of their lives. Before turning 60, the drill pay they received at the end of every month was another incentive to stay in the Army Reserve Program as a drilling Reservist.

The bulk of the 683rd was made up of young soldiers. Many were fresh out of high school and joined the Army Reserve for the college benefits and extra money. Some of these Reservists had served on active duty and wanted to decrease their involvement after finishing their two-year commitment.

The 683rd lieutenants were newly commissioned officers. Most had not been to their basic training course due to an early commissioning experiment for Reserve Officer Training Corps (ROTC) cadets. The ROTC was established to attract young college educated people to serve in the military. After four years of classroom instruction, numerous field exercises and an eight-week officers' boot camp—in addition to a college degree—Uncle Sam gave all graduating ROTC cadets a commission in the Army Reserve after they successfully completed all educational and military requirements. The newly commissioned lieutenants got to choose their branch assignments, picking from specialties such as infantry, artillery, armor, military police, ordnance, etc. Some opted to fulfill their military service obligation all at once and do a two-year tour on active duty and four years in the Ready Reserve. Others chose to hone their military experience and their civilian career simultaneously, with a six-year stint in the Army Reserves.

Many of the lieutenants in the 683rd were still living the college student's life, sleeping in late, subsisting on a diet of pizza and beer, and trying to figure out what to do when they graduated. At least one weekend a month, they hauled out their fatigues—and in doing so put away their thoughts about the pending responsibilities in the civilian world.

The 683rd was a tough bunch to get a handle on. Three commanding officers had come and gone in two years. The unit was in chaos. Infighting became commonplace. Unit morale had reached a low point as the internal power struggles began to affect the younger soldiers.

At the end of 1981, everything around the Ravenna Army Ammunition Plant was crackling with optimism. Cleveland had just hosted Major League Baseball's All-Star Game. MTV had started round-the-clock broadcast of music videos—an excellent waste of time for non-drill weekends. A woman sat on the bench of the U.S. Supreme Court. President Reagan had promised a tax cut and to rebuild the military of the United States.

The world around the 683rd was changing. It was high time they changed as well.

JANUARY DRILL, 1982

Before the sun came up on a frigid Saturday, Dave Marshall woke up early. The first thought in his head was to scrape the new layer of ice off the windshield of his car. As his eyes popped open, he looked at his bedside clock. 0534, the blaring red numbers told him. He'd set his alarm for 0535. He chuckled to himself as he pulled up a pair of sweatpants and synched them tightly as he kissed his still slumbering wife Linda on the head. He silently switched off his alarm clock so his wife could get a little more sleep.

With a light spring in his step, he went downstairs to put on his boots, make a pot of coffee, and get his car started and warmed up. Despite the early hour and the layer of ice that was sure to be clinging to everything outside, Marshall whistling to himself, had been looking forward to this day.

From the outside, Marshall seemed to have everything a young man could want. He had a beautiful home, a burgeoning career, an adoring wife and a cute little girl. He was still young—just 31—and successful.

Marshall was happy, but something was missing. Before he started his own business of selling commercial heating equipment, he was a full-time soldier in the U.S. Army. He had left behind the excitement and daily challenges of being a soldier for civilian life years ago.

A year ago, he returned to the military on a part-time basis as a member of the Army Reserves. He lived only 20 minutes away from the Ravenna Army Ammunition Plant, which was home to several Reserve units.

His first assignment was with the 694th Maintenance Battalion Headquarters. The 694th Battalion Headquarters was staffed with 50 highly trained officers and sergeants with a great deal of military experience. The 694th Battalion Headquarters' job was, in short, to make sure that all units below them did what they were supposed to do, and that they did it well.

Marshall was the battalion adjutant, otherwise referred to as the battalion S-1. The S-1 was responsible for all administrative and personnel functions within the battalion, such as new assignments for personnel, promotions, orders, pay problems, and taking care of all sorts of personnel matters. The 694th Maintenance Battalion was comprised of six companies with an overall assigned strength of nine hundred and sixty four personnel.

Marshall marched from the porch in his unlined combat boots and onto his driveway to a drum cadence in his head. He held the ice scraper at right shoulder arms, like the M16 rifle he was taught to properly carry in basic training.

Today was an Army Reserve drill weekend, but not just any drill. Today he would be a company commander.

When Lieutenant Colonel Ralph Finder asked Marshall to be the new commander of the 683rd Maintenance Company, Marshall was surprised. He was not expecting a command position for another year or so.

Finder was the commander of the 694th Maintenance Battalion and an imposing figure of a man in a quiet sort of way. He taught history at a nearby university and with his tall and powerful build, he towered over most people—except Marshall. Finder, who had served in more units than most of his subordinates during his long military career, was careful and calculated in his decision-making.

It was obvious that Finder wanted his own military career to blossom. A successful two-year stint serving as a battalion commander would assure him of a promotion to colonel. However, one bad company commander might be disastrous for his Army Reserve career. Finder knew his responsibilities were great, and whatever transpired with his subordinate units would directly affect his chances of promotion.

After weighing his options, Captain Dave Marshall agreed to take the helm of the 683rd. He enjoyed working within the battalion headquarters, but knew that the only way to advance to the rank of major was to have a successful three years as a company commander. Marshall also enjoyed getting his hands dirty and getting into the action. Troop units, like the 683rd, did the work. Staff and headquarters people, like those in the 694th Maintenance Battalion Headquarters, sat behind desks and provided administrative support and direction. Besides, Finder had decided to take a gamble on him. A stint as the 683rd commander would make or break Marshall's career as well. Marshall, a beacon of optimism, knew that Finder's trust was well-placed.

Marshall surveyed his car, partially blanketed under some fresh snow that had fallen the night before, and tried to transfer his optimism there. As he began brushing the moist and heavy snow off of his car, Marshall thought back to when he joined the Army in the first place. Ironically, Marshall thought with a smile, it wasn't his choice to join up—Uncle Sam gave him some gentle persuasion.

Twelve years earlier, the Vietnam War was raging and Marshall was a draftable 19-year-old college student. The U.S. Army needed more soldiers to fill its ranks. All males age 19 and older were required to register for the draft. In 1969, Congress reinstated the draft. Birth dates were pulled out of a large bowl and assigned a sequential number. The people born on the days that were drawn first would be promptly drafted into the military. Marshall and his fraternity brothers knew that people with draft lottery numbers below 180 were destined for the military sooner or later. Marshall's lucky draft lottery number was 40.

He had a decision to make. Attending college gave him a valid draft deferment—Marshall wondered what to do. His number would not change, the war in Vietnam was not at an end, and his deferment only lasted until he received his degree. He did not have an indefinite draft deferment. Those were only given to people who were a family's sole surviving son, people with medical or mental problems, and those with criminal records.

Marshall decided to enroll in ROTC (Reserve Officer Training Corps) and serve his country after graduation. Once he had his bachelor's degree, he also received a second lieutenant commission from the Army's ROTC program. ROTC helped prepare him for Army life. How to be an effective leader would have to be learned on the job.

Marshall did not join the Army alone. He married Linda, his college sweetheart, who received an Army nursing scholarship and put her talents to work in military service. Linda Marshall may have been a beautiful young blonde woman, but her aptitude and skill brought her a higher military rank than her husband. She was commissioned a first lieutenant in the Army Nurse Corps, and assigned to the Army hospital in Fort Bragg, N.C. Dave Marshall endured all of the jokes from his friends and family about being out-ranked by his wife, and served in the Ordnance Branch of the Army with the 503d Heavy Equipment Maintenance Company at Fort Bragg.

After three years of full-time military service in North Carolina, Dave Marshall—and his wife Linda—rose to the rank of captain. They grew wise beyond their years with the responsibilities and challenges the Army offered. Then the Army handed them something very unexpected: New duty assignments. The new assignments would have transplanted the Marshalls thousands of miles from home and from each other. They agreed to shelve their fatigues and move back home to Ohio to rejoin civilian life, having successfully fulfilled their active duty military obligations.

As he finished scraping the last bit of ice from the windshield, Dave Marshall thought fondly of the warm North Carolina winters he'd grown to love in Fort Bragg, and wondered why he and Linda had decided to move back up north. He looked at his watch. 5:43. With a gasp, he jumped into the driver's seat, started up the car's engine and ran inside to take a hot shower, change into his Army fatigue uniform and grab a cup of coffee for the road. It was his first day on the job and he wanted to be at the Army Reserve Center extra early. If he didn't hurry now, he ran the risk of being just on time.

As he blessed the snowplow drivers of northeast Ohio for clearing the roads so well, Marshall pulled into the Reserve Center with seven minutes to spare. Entering the soothingly warm building, Marshall made a beeline for Lieutenant Colonel Finder's office to formally report in for duty. He entered the cigar-perfumed office where the battalion commander was waiting for him, stopping about three feet from his desk.

"Captain Dave Marshall reports!" he exclaimed, snapping his right hand with fingers extended and joined to the edge of his right eyebrow in a perfect salute. As all good soldiers, Marshall could quickly summon perfect and exacting military protocol.

Finder smiled and returned the salute with the same precision.

"Have a seat, Captain Marshall," he said, gesturing toward an ancient brown stuffed chair at the side of the room. "We've got a few things to cover regarding the 683rd for its soon-to-be new commander."

Marshall relaxed slightly, dropping his salute and sitting stiffly in the chair. It was coated in vinyl, about as old as he was, and had the same smell as the office, reminiscent of an old musty, tobacco-permeated basement.

Finder opened a drawer and retrieved a cigar. As he tapped it on the desk, he told Marshall what, exactly, he was in for.

"Well Dave, looks like you're gonna have your hands full with that unit," he began. "My staff informs me there's an internal power struggle goin' on. The previous commander couldn't keep a handle on it. I'm looking for someone who can." He bit the tip of his cigar and spat the end into a trash can. "Up to it?"

As Finder pulled out a well worn lighter to ignite his cigar, Marshall soaked all the information in and weighed it in his mind. Internal power struggles were the result of inadequate supervision and a lack of guidance from above. Someone had to fill the void before total chaos entered in. Marshall thought back to his first assignment on active duty when there was racial strife among the soldiers. He quickly resolved it by getting all parties to work together as a team. Marshall could do this. He looked straight into the superior officer's eyes.

"Sir, I've had some experience with difficult situations before on active duty," Marshall said. "Getting everyone to work together as a team is the answer. I'm pretty confident I can do that."

Finder smiled to himself and blew a cloud of pungent cigar smoke in the air. This was the kind of confidence that was sorely needed to mend the 683rd. If Marshall could keep this attitude and desire for the job, the unit's problems would be over.

Finder looked at the captain and started filling him in on the details of his new responsibilities.

"Dave, let me give you a bit of information about the upcoming annual training for the 683rd." Marshall couldn't help but find himself momentarily hypnotized by the clouds of smoke that filled the room. He pulled a small notebook out of his breast pocket, which he carried on the suggestion of his newspaper reporter brother-in-law, and jotted down the details about the 683rd's upcoming annual training at Fort Knox, Kentucky.

Annual training was a new term to be experienced for Marshall. Reserve units would spend two weeks at an Army base and be formally evaluated on how well they performed their assigned mission. This evaluation would be used to determine the overall readiness and capability of a unit.

As he took notes, Marshall's thoughts began to spin. He hadn't even formally assumed command and already he was feeling slightly overwhelmed. No matter, Marshall told himself. This was just the kind of challenge he was ready for.

Finder coughed as he finished briefing Marshall on the upcoming A.T., interrupting Marshall's thoughts.

"Good luck, Dave," he said, placing his hands on the armrests of his worn leather desk chair and leaning forward like he was planning to stand up. "If you need the help of my staff, just let me know. Is there anything that you need before we do the change-of-command ceremony?"

Marshall stirred in his seat, unconsciously trying to find a more comfortable position. The cigar smoke had filled the office and was making it difficult for Marshall to keep his focus on the matters at hand. He thought for a few moments and carefully chose his words.

With so much infighting in the unit, Marshall wondered if the soldiers were following the rule of using the chain of command. The process was developed to resolve problems at the lowest level possible. A soldier with a problem would go to his next superior to resolve it. If the immediate superior couldn't resolve the problem, it would go to the next individual up the chain. If it went all the way to the top, it landed on the President's desk. Problems rarely got that far.

"I'm a strong advocate for using the chain of command, Sir," Marshall said. "I would appreciate you letting me know when one of my soldiers violates the chain."

Finder stood up and smiled at Marshall while finishing his cigar. "You got it Dave. I don't like people doin' the end-around on any of my commanders," he said. Finder glanced at his watch and gestured toward his office's open door.

"Now how about you and I take a stroll outside so we can officially put you in command, shall we?"

Finder led the way through the wide hallway of the old building, which led to a large wood planked landing with steps leading down to the rear parking area. The 683rd was patiently waiting in formation with all their personnel assembled for the formal change-of-command ceremony.

A large rectangle had been shoveled out of the ankle-deep snow for the soldiers to stand in formation, but the snow continued to fall with white flakes dotting their olive drab fatigue uniforms. The soldiers were bundled up in their standard-issue field jackets, scarves, gloves, and ball caps—though several were wearing red ball caps.

As he saw his superiors exit the building, First Sergeant Bill Tisher, the highest-ranking sergeant of the 683rd, called the formation to attention. Everyone snapped to attention in unison. Finder and Marshall both marched up to the front of the formation, taking their positions in front of Tisher.

Captain Reginald VanSkeegan, the newly assigned Battalion Adjutant who took over Marshall's recently vacated position, read aloud the change-of-command orders, which confirmed Captain Dave Marshall as the new company commander of the 683rd Maintenance Company. "Captain David Marshall, hereby assumes command of the 683rd Maintenance Company. Effective this day, January 9th, 1982. Signed Ralph D. Finder, Lieutenant Colonel, 694th Maintenance Battalion, commanding."

When the adjutant was done, Tisher did an about-face movement and took the company gidon (a burgundy flag with the gray unit numbers stitched across the top with an ordnance bomb below, attached to a wooden pole measuring 8 feet in length) from the gidon bearer at the front of the formation, directly behind the first sergeant. Tisher turned again and presented the gidon to Finder. The battalion commander took the gidon from Tisher and turned 90 degrees to his right, handing it to Marshall. Before Finder let go of the gidon, he uttered these pearls of wisdom.

"Captain Marshall, this gidon is light, but the responsibilities that go with it are very heavy. May you be successful in your new command," Finder said.

Marshall thanked the battalion commander and handed the gidon back to Tisher, who gave it back to the gidon bearer. Finder and Tisher exited from the front of the formation while Marshall, the newly installed company commander of the 683rd Heavy Equipment Maintenance Company, remained in place. The battalion chaplain, Captain William Dillon, provided a word of prayer for the new commander and the unit as everyone removed their caps and bowed their heads.

After the chaplain finished his prayer and had blessed the unit, Marshall gave the formation his first official command.
"At ease," Marshall barked. Everyone relaxed and began to brush off the newly fallen snow from their clothes as they shivered in place. As was the custom, the new commander introduced himself to the troops.

"I've heard a lot of good things about the 683rd. I've been assigned to this unit to make it better. Change has come, starting today," Marshall said, surveying the faces of the soldiers that looked back at him. Some were young, some wore more experience in their faces. Some looked very interested in what he had to say. Some, who were wearing the red caps, looked bored. He made a mental note to himself to check more into that later. Showing no emotion, he went on.

"Let me share with you my philosophy about the Army. First of all, we work together as a team. Teamwork is essential to mission accomplishment. Without it, we fail."

"Secondly, I'm a by-the-book commander, and I expect you to

be by-the-book soldiers. People with experience and know-how wrote Army doctrine for all of us to follow."

"Thirdly, we're all human and we make mistakes, but let's not make the same mistake twice. This is a place to learn your job, and develop your skills."

"Finally, let me tell you what my mission is with the 683rd. My mission is to get this unit ready to go to war. The Army Reserve, National Guard, and the active duty forces are this country's deterrent to war. If we are prepared for war, those enemies of the United States will think long and hard about picking a fight with us."

A few soldiers nodded their heads as Marshall spoke. Good, he thought, I'm getting through to them. Now here comes the kicker, he thought—it's time for them to work together.

"Annual training is only six months away, which means we've got six weekends to get ready. I want to see all the officers and platoon sergeants in the conference room in 15 minutes. Ten-hut!"

Marshall called for the first sergeant. Tisher quickly marched to the front of the formation.

"Top, take charge of the company and have the section sergeants and troops report to their duty stations," Marshall said, addressing 1SG Tisher as Top, the Army's shorthand version for the highest ranking sergeant in the unit. Tisher saluted Marshall and took over the formation. Marshall left to go into his new office while Tisher gave out the information of the day, consisting of the required training, priorities and what was going on for the weekend to the troops.

Thirteen minutes later in the Reserve Center conference room, Tisher called the assembled officers and NCOs to attention as Marshall walked in. He glanced briefly at the assembled personnel, staring at him with great anticipation. Marshall calmly addressed them.

"Take your seats," Marshall said. He paused as the room filled with clangs, scrapes and scratches as the soldiers sat in metal folding chairs. Taking a deep breath, Marshall began the speech he'd practiced in his car as he drove to the Reserve center that morning.

"I've been given command of this unit to get it up to Army standards. I'm not here to make friends. I'm here to get this unit ready for its wartime mission." His voice was stern, and the soldiers were silent. No one dared whisper or make any type of subtle comment while Marshall spoke.

"One of the first things I will insist on is that everyone in this room will set an excellent example. That includes wearing the proper uniform and headgear." Those with red hats gazed coldly towards their new commander. Marshall pretended not to notice. "That will commence immediately. If I see anyone not in proper uniform tomorrow, they'll be sent home without pay and receive a written reprimand."

Marshall ignored the murmuring and continued his speech.

"I expect professionalism and adherence to the principles of military conduct and discipline from all of you here in this room. I expect every section to focus on their wartime missions. If your section doesn't have a mission, one will be found for you."

Sergeant First Class Schmoot raised his hand to ask a question. Marshall saw the hand out of the corner of his eye and thought, sheesh, they're already testing me. Marshall did not recognize Schmoot for his question, and instead fired off a fast response to the raised hand.

"Sergeant, this is not an open discussion, nor is it a question and answer period," Marshall said tersely. "I want all of you to use the chain of command. Get used to it. Go through the chain instead of directly going to me for answers. Everyone in this room will function together as a team. There will be no more inner-company rivalry. That is finished as of today."

Chief Warrant Officer McCarthy and Schmoot were visibly uncomfortable as Marshall continued with his command guidance. Marshall changed the subject.

"We have six months to get this unit ready for annual training. I've been informed our training site will be Mount Eden Base Camp, Fort Knox, Kentucky. Our mission has not been formally provided, but I can assure you we will provide maintenance support to all units in our sector. We will be under the command of the 168th Support Group out of Columbus,

Ohio. Colonel Biggs will be the overall commander. I do not have a list of the other units we will be with, but there'll be a large combination of different units. We've got one commercial bus for transportation, which means this unit will have to take every piece of rolling stock we have, plus additional trucks and tractors to haul all the trailers. In others words, nearly everyone will be a driver, assistant driver or a passenger with every piece of equipment this unit has that is not bolted down to the shop floor."

"That means that every section will start getting their equipment ready and loading their vehicles with what they need to perform their mission in the field. This afternoon I will be in the motor pool to check on the status of every section's equipment. A.T. is six months away, which means we've got twelve drill days to get ready."

Silence filled the room. All eyes and mouths were open in amazement. Some of their equipment had not moved since the Nixon administration. Marshall finished his instructions.

"All right everybody, now you know what I expect from you. This unit will be able to perform its wartime mission, so let's get going."

Sergeant First Class John Lemasters was smiling, though many of the NCOs and officers were shaking their heads, having a hard time comprehending what they were just told. Higher headquarters had thrown down the gauntlet. It was time for the 683rd to perform above expectations.

"That is all," concluded Marshall, giving a nod to Tisher.

"Ten hut!" the first sergeant yelled as Marshall left the room—and left nobody but himself to answer the soldiers' questions.

After they were dismissed from the conference room, McCarthy and Schmoot walked out together. They had been close with their previous commander, Captain Smith. Before Smith had been relieved and reassigned, McCarthy and Schmoot used to sip a couple shots of Tennessee's finest whiskey in Smith's office after drill, laughing and make jokes about the other soldiers in the battalion. Eventually they headed to their favorite watering hole, the Double Z Tavern, for a game of pool and a few pitchers of beer. Smith gave McCarthy and

Schmoot the red hats and ascots to show everyone else that they were his favorites—and to symbolize the Bloody Marys they would have to drink the morning after to sober up. The practice spread to other members of the unit who participated in the monthly gathering at the Double Z. One or two new initiates were "red-hatted" every drill.

"Well Chief, looks like I'll have to dig out my old OD (olive drab) ball cap for tomorrow," said Schmoot, who wanted to go along with the new commander.

McCarthy shot him a withering look and responded in a serious and quiet voice. "Not so fast Denny. I think its time to pay our respects to the battalion commander."

Schmoot had become close friends with McCarthy through the years of carousing through drills, and looked up to him for guidance. Schmoot, who was in his thirties, always tried to be a good soldier. He relied on McCarthy as his personal mentor.

McCarthy was in his mid-fifties, and frustration was affecting him in his personal and military life. He was grossly overweight, had high blood pressure, arthritis, and other medical aliments, which hampered his ability to enjoy the moment. He drank more than he should have—and always seemed to have the foulest insults. He never had anything nice to say about the other soldiers, the people he knew through his civilian job, his wife, her family, and everyone who drove on the road at the same time he did. If things did not go McCarthy's way, he would take it as a personal affront. This made McCarthy bitter and melancholic, and he often griped that nobody seemed to like him. Most of the unit personnel tried to avoid him if possible. They all knew McCarthy was full of piss and vinegar.

Later that morning at the motor pool, Chief Warrant Officer Robert James and Marshall met up for the first time. Marshall wanted to find out as much as he could about the condition of the trucks and equipment, as well as meet James, an active duty warrant officer recently assigned to the unit.

James was a southern gentleman in his late fifties and near retirement. He had a kind face and demeanor, and silvery gray eyes and hair. Setting a good example for the soldiers to follow was always foremost in his mind. He maintained a personal standard of excellence by exercising regularly. He had no bad habits, and he was always able to keep his composure regardless of the circumstance. He never cursed and would not tolerate those around him that did. He never demanded respect. He earned it.

Marshall walked through the main shop area and strode into the motor pool office. Inside the small, drafty room, three soldiers sat in the middle of what looked like the aftermath of an explosion at the IRS. James gave a long, disapproving look to the soldiers, who were trying to file new records—and find old ones—in a badly tended file cabinet. The soldiers scrambled to pick up the papers as James turned his gaze on the unit's new commander.

"Sir, glad to have you on board," James said, standing up and giving Marshall a friendly salute.

"Thanks Chief," said Marshall, returning both the salute and the smile.

Chief James looked a bit embarrassed and said, "Sorry about the mess; these files haven't seen much daylight for a long while and nobody's quite sure where to find things."

Marshall noticed that since he walked in, the three soldiers had picked up all of the papers, organized them into neat stacks, and placed them on James' desk.

Marshall was visibly impressed. "I'm very glad to see this unit has a pro in charge of the motor pool. I understand you were assigned to the unit a couple of months ago."

"Yes, Sir. My wife is still movin' our household items from Fort Campbell to Akron. It's been rather stressful on her lately," replied James.

James turned the conversation to more important matters than neglected and incomprehensible file cabinets, or the daily stresses of moving. "The grapevine tells me you've had some active duty experience."

Marshall was also impressed that the chief had done his homework on the new commander.

Marshall told him. "Well Chief, I hope things go smoothly with regards to moving into your new home. As for me, your sources tell the truth. My first three years were spent at Fort

Bragg in the 503rd Heavy Equipment Maintenance Company, the same type of unit as this one. We had lots of work to keep up with." Marshall stopped. He might as well not sanitize the reality of his former workload. "Actually, there were times we'd have to set up 24-hour operations due to the large backlogs."

James smiled at Marshall with a twinkle in his eye.

"Well, you won't have that situation here," he said. "The motor pool mechanics are skilled in minor repairs to vehicles and generators, but their work has nothing to do with the maintenance shop's easy workload. Most of the time the main shop has so little work scheduled the automotive maintenance sections have nothing to do."

Marshall sat down in one of the old steel folding chairs that had seen better days, trying to both make himself comfortable and ignore the chair's constant groaning under his weight.

"That's going to have to change Chief," said Marshall. "I'll get with battalion maintenance operations and see if they can help get us some mission work these troops can use after we get back from annual training."

Marshall glanced around the room. The three soldiers were flipping through the papers, quietly and neatly reordering them. In the main shop, Marshall could hear the tune of the Motown classic "Sugar Pie Honeybunch" filling the air. He leaned close to the chief warrant officer and spoke softly.

"You've been in this unit for a little while. I'd like to know your feelings on the weakness and strengths of this company," he said.

James sat back in his chair and chuckled. He lifted his right hand and gestured to the three soldiers in the room to leave. Clutching their stacks of paperwork and some empty folders, they filed out of the room. The last one to leave grabbed the doorknob and started to pull the door closed. In her arms, she balanced the stack of papers, a stapler, and a foam cup of coffee. As the door was inches from closing, her wrist slipped and papers flew everywhere. As she watched the papers fall, she gracefully grabbed her coffee cup and steadied it. Not a drop of coffee spilled on the floor. Her face turned bright red.

"Oh sh…" she started under her breath, squatting on the floor to pick up the paper. James glared. She looked frightened and stood up straight. "I mean, oops, Sir." James shook his head slowly as she pulled the door closed.

After several seconds, he began speaking. "Did you see that example of well-meaning carelessness just now?" James asked Marshall. The commander nodded. "That's pretty much the unit in a nutshell. They try awfully hard, but can't seem to get a grip on the most important thing they're carrying.

"The unit has a good NCO corps and a couple of bad apples just like every unit. You'll find out who they are pretty soon," James started to get into it. "The lieutenants are about as green as they come. Most of 'em never been to the basic officer's course yet. Heck, I believe three of them are in their senior year of college. They got their butter-bars from that early commissioning program. They try hard, but they've needed a commander to teach 'em how to be officers. That's a big problem from what I've been able to see. Not enough experienced officers comin' in."

"As for the younger soldiers, they seem to be pretty motivated when they come back from their basic and advanced individual training courses, but when they get here and find nothin' to do, they get disillusioned, even after they start getting college benefits and drill pay."

"And since there's so little for 'em to do, a lot of the time they do their own thing," James went on. "Some of the ladies paint their nails. Rumor has it that one of the automotive mechanics owes one of the clerical staff somewhere in the neighborhood of $250 from money lost in a never-ending pinochle game that goes on every drill. Oh, and there's probably at least one person dancing to the music on the radio in the shop right now."

Marshall was horrified. His 3-year-old daughter had more discipline than some of this crew. He tried to suppress his shock and his realization of how big of a job he really had.

"Thanks Chief, I, uh, appreciate your candor," Marshall replied. "I kinda figured this job wasn't going to be a cakewalk. Looks like there's nowhere to go but up."

He stood up and hoped that the unit's own equipment was in good enough condition the soldiers at least had good reason to turn drill into a pinochle tournament. Banishing doubts, which crept into his mind, Marshall turned on his unflagging optimism.

"How about we go take a look at the unit vehicles, shall we?" he said to James, hoping he wouldn't regret it.

As they opened the office door, they noticed that the music had been turned way up. Two of the soldiers who had been filing papers looked a bit nervous. Their stacks of papers were nowhere to be seen. As the door opened, they gave the officers a quick salute. The woman who had dropped the papers earlier was pensively rearranging them and gulping down the coffee that she'd saved from spilling.

Marshall felt confident Chief James would mentor his soldiers well and make on-the-spot corrections with regards to proper military protocol. No need for unnecessary saluting indoors, even though they were taught: when in doubt...salute!

Marshall and James walked in the fresh snow to the vehicle motor park, which was one hundred yards away from the main shop building. The 683rd Motor Park was nothing more than a bare spot of snow-covered ground where all the unit's motor vehicles and trucks were parked. Marshall noticed the vehicles were scattered about in no particular order. Most other units group their vehicles by size and type so they can more easily account for them. Surveying the mess of vehicles in the lot, Marshall got a slight sinking feeling in his stomach.

"Chief, are these vehicles exercised every drill period?" Marshall asked, though he was pretty sure he already knew the answer.

"No sir, they're not." Chief James replied in a lowered voice. "I've been after the section leaders to pull PM (preventative maintenance) on 'em, but they always come back with an excuse about limited time or personnel."

That can't be right, Marshall thought. He started searching in his field jacket pockets for his copy of the unit training schedule (a detailed list of events and times with references) to double-check. It had been a while since he'd cleaned out his field jacket, Marshall thought, finding an extra pair of gloves, a clean handkerchief, a folded military map and an old stick of gum in the four pockets. The training schedule, he remembered, was in his pants pocket. He pulled it out unfolded it and took a good look. Just as he thought.

"According to the training schedule, there is one hour dedicated to motor stables right after morning formation, right?" Marshall asked the Chief. Motor stables was an old Army term for working on every piece of mechanical equipment the unit had, in which the assigned operator would check fluid levels, tire pressure, and clean the equipment before starting it up. Every piece of mechanical equipment the Army has comes with an operator's manual and lists the things the operator must do during motor stables before starting up the equipment.

James grinned. He knew what the new commander was getting at.

"Yes sir," James began, "but not all of 'em comply." Marshall motioned with his head to follow as he began strolling through the motor park looking at the unit vehicles. He noticed many trucks had no canvas to cover their cabs and beds. Some of the deuce-and-a-half trucks were missing cargo bows that held up the canvas, and many were littered with trash inside the driver's compartment and truck beds. Fall leaves were matted around the tires, like the vehicles had not moved since summer. Out of the corner of his eye, Marshall spotted a 1 1/2 ton cargo trailer, with a locust tree growing up through the towing fork. It hadn't been used or moved in quite a while.

Marshall gave the vehicles a critical look. After giving the tires a piercing gaze, he quickly looked away. The tires were old and badly dry-rotted, with deep cracks and crevices on the sidewalls. Marshall felt one wrong look, word, or thought could burst them as they sat.

Marshall searched for the most polite way to address the condition of the trucks.

"These vehicles look pretty sick," Marshall mentioned carefully. "And I think I've seen daylight coming through these tires. How old are they?"

Nobody had ever asked that question before, James reflected. Marshall must be genuinely concerned about the welfare and safety of the 683rd soldiers. Or, at least, the roadworthiness of its equipment. James hoped that Marshall would be able to handle the answer.

"Sir, these are the original tires that came with the vehicles," he replied. "Some of 'em are older than the soldiers assigned to drive 'em."

Marshall groaned inwardly. That was not what he wanted to hear. He opened the door of one of the trucks, tossed an empty crumpled up McDonald's bag that was sitting on the seat to Chief James, and climbed inside. The vehicle registration plate on the dashboard showed a manufactured dated of 1961. Marshall took a moment to reflect on the quality tires that were manufactured in his hometown, then did some quick math.

"These tires are over twenty years old," said Marshall. "Twenty years ago, we didn't even know where Vietnam was on a map. Twenty years ago, I was struggling with math and rushing home to watch cartoons on TV. Is there any policy on replacing tires in the command?"

James folded his hands, rolled his eyes, and recited the policy of the 83rd Army Reserve Command Headquarters.

"No change-out until they fail and can't be repaired."

Marshall stroked his chin. This is a bigger problem than anyone had realized, he thought. These vehicles have to make it to Fort Knox for A.T., and the tires did not look as if they would last half way to Cincinnati. He tried to figure out how many tires he needed for these vehicles to be roadworthy. Four, 12, 28, what? He shook his head.

He and James walked through the motor park and looked at every tire on every truck. No such luck. Many were showing excessive signs of tire wear and severe dry rot around the sidewalls.

Because of their excellent design, Army trucks had dual tires on both rear axles. The dual tires helped with traction, but they also made life easier for the driver. If one tire blew, the other would handle the load until the driver pulled over and changed the tire. The Army's 2½-ton truck, commonly referred to as a "deuce-and-a-half," could go just about anywhere. Most drivers never experienced changing a flat. Obviously, Marshall thought, most drivers in the 683rd had never had that experience. It was high time that they started performing preventative maintenance, he decided.

"Well Chief," Marshall said to James, "I want the best tires on the front of every vehicle we're taking to Fort Knox, with a new tire on the driver's side." James nodded in agreement as Marshall continued. "The spare tire will have to be good rubber also. I'd like you to pull a few strings to get the tire pipeline flowing. Do you have any strings to pull?"

James did, though it might take some work. "I've got some buddies at the tire exchange center in Columbus. I'll get working on it right away and see what can be done." James hoped that his buddies at the tire exchange would forget about the bets they put on the Browns/Bengals game last month.

Marshall couldn't help but chuckle. "Chief, do you realize this unit is just twenty miles away from Akron, the tire capital of the world?" James smiled. "And here we are with a motor park full of old dry-rotted tires." Marshall gave a hard kick to one of the badly dry-rotted tires as he spoke. He jumped back as he heard a loud hiss from the tire, then a dying wheeze as it flattened. "Well Chief, looks like I found your first candidate for the tire exchange program."

Marshall and James laughed all the way back to the motor pool office. Once they got there, they thawed out from the cold and Marshall stated the obvious.

"Chief, I'm going to start enforcing motor stables from now on," Marshall said. James smiled. He liked what he was hearing.

Marshall continued. "No more bad canvas, trashed up vehicles, and lack of operator maintenance."

"I'm giving you full authority to honcho this. I want you to inform me of anyone not toeing the line. This equipment is going to make it to Fort Knox. I just hope and pray we'll all arrive safely. Now who's the commo (electronic communications) chief?"

"That'll be Sergeant Jackie Mooney," James replied. "He's another active duty type assigned to the unit. He's also the unit supply sergeant."

James looked at Marshall's face. It was expressionless. Marshall was in deep thought trying to make sense of all he had just learned and come up with a plan of attack to get things moving in the right direction.

James knew that the new commander had a lot to worry about, but Mooney wasn't among them.

"You can trust him, sir," James said. "He's a squared away NCO that likes to soldier."

Marshall nodded and sighed. "Thank goodness," he said. James knew exactly how he felt.

Both Marshall and James walked back into the office and noticed the soldiers seemed to have at least put the paperwork in more organized piles.

Marshall looked at his watch. Oh no! He was supposed to meet Tisher in 10 minutes. Marshall hated showing up late. That was too close to late for him. He preferred being about 15 minutes early for everything. That made it easier to handle life's little surprises.

"Chief, I need to get back to the orderly room, and it's a five-minute drive through the snow," Marshall said, shaking James' hand. James nodded.

"You're going to see a change starting tomorrow," Marshall said. It was partially a resolution, partially reassurance that things were going to change. "Any section that is not working on their assigned equipment during motor stables, I want to know about it."

Marshall sprinted to his Buick Electra he drove to the motor pool. He took a close look at the tires. Groaning, he realized they were the same as those on the rest of the equipment—very little tread left. He shook his head, made a mental note to buy some new tires later that evening, and whispered a prayer that he'd make the three-mile drive back safely and not slide off the snow-covered road.

After a drive that wasn't as harrowing as it could have been, Marshall arrived back at the orderly room. He looked at his watch. Three minutes to spare! He wiped the half-melted snow off the top of his boots and poured himself a cup of coffee from the still-hot percolator.

No sooner had Marshall sat down behind his desk than he heard a soft knock on his door. First Sergeant Tisher was lurking in the open doorway. Tisher's silhouette filled much of the door frame—he was a big, burly man—but his kind face and balding head softened his tough looking frame. Tisher was in his mid forties and well liked and still respected by all the unit soldiers.

Tisher was glad to see Marshall take command of the 683rd. As first sergeant, his duties included take caring of the soldiers and advising the company commander, to include operational details within the unit. Tisher was always busy trying to get the unit to straighten up and become more effective, much like Marshall's plan for the unit.

"Come on in," Marshall said, motioning to Tisher. He responded with a smile. Tisher entered the office, closed the door behind him and sat down in one of Marshall's vinyl-covered spare chairs.

"You want some coffee?" Marshall asked. Tisher shook his head.

"So how's your first day been?" Tisher asked.

"Top, I spoke with Chief James, who tells me we've got problems with motor stables," Marshall said. "Anything you can add?"

Tisher responded enthusiastically.

"Yes, sir. The previous commander didn't know too much about preventative maintenance, so there was never any emphasis placed on it," Tisher said. "None of the sections bothered to fix their own equipment, and well, you've seen the result."

"I have," Marshall said. "Are these soldiers aware that they're in a maintenance unit?" Tisher laughed with his commander.

"It's a perfect example of the old saying: A mechanic works on everyone's car but his own," Tisher said.

Marshall nodded his head and made up his mind. This was going to change. The 683rd was going to get back to basics. It would be a painful process, but Marshall hoped that in a short amount of time, the soldiers would begin to take pride in the unit and themselves.

Marshall switched from being thoughtful to command mode.

"Top, this afternoon I want you to have a meeting with the NCOs and let them know this commander's highest priority is to get this unit ready," he told Tisher. "That means equipment and personnel. Everyone will be pulling motor stables as shown on the training schedule. No excuses."

Tisher smiled.

"Music to my ears. Yes sir!" he responded. Tisher's hand snapped to his forehead, saluting his commander to show that he knew an order when he heard one.

Marshall continued with his other "command decisions" he made that day.

"Tomorrow, I'm going to have a meeting with all the officers prior to the morning formation. The officers' meeting will be in my office at 0630 hours." Tisher opened his mouth to ask about the timing of his meeting with the non-commissioned officers. Marshall answered the question before Tisher even had the chance to ask it.

"Top, there would be no problem if you have your meeting at the same time, but you and I need to get together at 0615 hours to go over the day's agenda and establish priorities for the drill." Tisher nodded as Marshall continued.

"We'll start planning staff meetings with key personnel on the Wednesday before the scheduled drill. The meeting will start at 1900 hrs in the conference room. Key personnel will get paid if additional funds for staff meetings are available. Lowest rank gets paid first, highest last."

Tisher grinned and looked at the new commander.

"Looks like you'll be doing a lot of God and country, sir," he said, inferring that Marshall would be dedicating a great deal of time and effort without pay.

Marshall returned the smile.

"Well Top, I'm not in it for the money," Marshall said. "The others will be sacrificing for this unit, so we might as well reward them for the dedication. Who knows? After a while, they might even do it for just the sake of getting out of the house."

Both men chuckled and Marshall changed the subject.

"Now, is there any way we can get some good coffee that doesn't taste like dirty motor oil?" Marshall asked.

"Sir, I think it's something to do with your coffee maker," Tisher said. "The last commander didn't believe in cleaning things. Like I said, he didn't know about preventative maintenance."

Marshall laughed, hoping that Tisher was just kidding.

Noon chow was being held outside the shop area. The cooks were shivering in place while they served cold catered meals to the troops in an unheated tent next to the motor park. Marshall came down to have lunch and scratched his head, puzzled at the setup. Most units have a dining facility, or mess hall, to prepare and serve meals. He walked up to the mess sergeant, who was assisting the other cooks as they ladled portions onto paper plates and cups as the soldiers stood in a single file line in the cold. He looked like your average greasy spoon chef: skinny, rumpled clothes, West Virginia accent thicker than maple syrup, and a lit cigarette dangling from the corner of his mouth.

"Sergeant Adkins, why are your cooks serving catered meals in an unheated tent in January?" Marshall asked him. Sergeant Lonnie Adkins blushed. Originally, Adkins was a mechanic in the one of the automotive repair sections. Six months earlier, he decided to help out with the mess section when no one wanted to fill the head cook vacancy. Unfortunately, his own skill and resources had not yet advanced him past the boil-a-pot-of-water stage of cooking.

"Sir, I only have two cooks, no mess hall, no heated tent and over two hundred troops to feed," Adkins answered slowly.

Marshall pondered his answer.

"I see your point," said Marshall. "What kind of training do you and your people need in order to get up to speed for annual training?"

Adkins answered immediately.

"Sir, in order to do an adequate job, I'll need four more cooks, two cooks helpers, and another two years to train 'em up." He paused. "And, um, a cooking class for me."

Marshall hoped that Adkins was joking about the cooking class. He realized that for someone who doesn't much like being the brunt of jokes, he had spent much of his day at the 683rd hoping they were all kidding about everything.

"Well, I can't enroll you in Cordon Bleu Culinary Institute, but I've got some good news," Marshall said. "We're supposed to have some units co-located with us during annual training. I'll see what's available to supplement your section."

Adkins smiled. "Sounds great, sir. Thanks!"

Marshall responded with a scowl. "By the way, no one smokes in the chow line or behind it," he said. Adkins could feel his face turning red. He was violating an Army field sanitation directive by smoking a cigarette while serving food. Way to impress the new commander, he thought. He dropped his cigarette in the snow and stomped it out, stammering an apology.

"That's better," Marshall said. "Ashes don't taste very good. Carry on, Sarge." Marshall walked back inside.

"I am such an idiot!" Adkins said to himself.

Private Huck Hudson was standing in front of Adkins with an empty and expectant plate and Styrofoam cup glared at him.

"Yeah, and I'm hungry!" he said. "Come on Sarge, give me some of that piping hot, ice-cold soup!"

Marshall managed to obtain one of Sergeant Adkins' renowned icebox lunches, and poked his food with his fork, searching for ashes as he walked to the orderly room to meet with the first sergeant. He walked in and saw several office personnel eating sack lunches at their desks. One of the soldiers took a close look at the paper plate heaped with potato salad, fried chicken and biscuits that Marshall brought in.

"Darn it!" she said, snapping her fingers. "Adkins' crew is servin' up Kentucky Fried Chicken today! I wish I hadn't brought my lunch. I thought that he was gonna get lunch from that greasy spoon down the road. I hate that place!"

Marshall gave the soldier a quizzical look. She took her eyes off of his plate and gasped when she noticed the person carrying it was the new commander. She blushed, stood up and clumsily saluted.

"Um, sorry for the food commentary, sir," she said, stammering. "I'm Lieutenant Meglynn, I'm your new food critic," she smiled as she held her salute.

Marshall nodded and smiled back at the soldier, enjoying her sense of humor.

"Nice to meet you, Lieutenant," he said. "It's good to know my soldiers are passionate about lunch."

Marshall knocked on Tisher's doorframe.

"Afternoon, Top," he said. Tisher looked up and grinned, inviting the new commander –and his plate full of Colonel Sanders' finest – into his office. Tisher was eating a pile of homemade spaghetti off of a foam plate.

"It was my turn to cook last night, and spaghetti's always easy," Tisher told Marshall. "It usually tastes better than what the mess section can come up with, but I do love the Colonel's secret recipe."

Marshall chewed his defrosted potato salad.

"While I like fried chicken as much as anyone, it's quite obvious we're short some trained cooks for annual training," Marshall said. "I don't think there are any fast food joints out in the woods at Fort Knox. Is there anything in the personnel pipeline with the right MOS?"

Tisher smiled from ear to ear. He had wonderful news for the commander.

"Sir, I just found out we're going to have the mess section of the 646th Supply & Service Company attached to us for annual training. The mess sergeant is none other than Sergeant Ralph Emery, the owner of Ralph's Taj Mahal Restaurant in Youngstown. And, you could say that Ralph's culinary skills are really extra special."

Marshall couldn't hold back his delight, and laughed out loud with relief. At least one thing was going perfectly right.

"Top, that is the best news I've heard all day," Marshall said. "Things are beginning to look up already. I take it you've worked with Sergeant Emery before," Marshall said.

"Sir, he's the best!" Tisher responded enthusiastically. "We will be eating like kings out in the field on Uncle Sam's dime. The only problem we'll have is watching that we don't gain too much weight. My wife might become a little too suspicious."

"Sounds great, Top," said Marshall. "Make sure Sergeant Adkins knows what's happening. I want his section to learn as much as they can with Sergeant Emery being their mentor for two weeks."

First Sergeant Tisher's smile quickly faded.

"Well Sir, I don't mean to ruin the moment, but we've got a problem," he said. "Sergeant Schmoot went to the battalion commander to complain about you."

Marshall shook his head and rolled his eyes towards the ceiling,

"It looks like my detractors are already showing themselves," he said. "Anything else?"

"Well, it wasn't just Schmoot," Tisher said. "Chief McCarthy was with him too."

Marshall began to chuckle. He hadn't even had a full day in command and two of the top troublemakers just broadcast their intentions to make his job difficult. That's one less thing I have to figure out, Marshall thought.

"Thanks, Top. Those two just made my day," Marshall replied.

Tisher laughed nervously with the commander, relieved to see that Marshall took the news so well. Many commanders would have been angered at such gross insubordination. Tisher was expecting to see him to loose his cool, but Marshall, the seasoned veteran, took it all in stride.

Only one question remained, Tisher thought. What would McCarthy and Schmoot be up to next?

Marshall deposited his nearly finished lunch dans le plat en papier into an empty steel wastebasket next to Tisher's desk and walked to his office. He picked up his rotary dial phone and called the battalion commander.

"Afternoon, Colonel," Marshall said.

"Good afternoon, Commander," Finder responded. "I trust your first day has been interesting."

"Interesting is one way to put it," Marshall said. "I understand a couple of my unit malcontents stopped by to see you, I hope it wasn't a total waste of your time."

Lieutenant Colonel Finder held back a laugh.

"Not at all Captain Marshall," he said. "They were very concerned about the way you're conducting yourself as the new commander."

"I'm sure they were, Sir," Marshall said. "Of course, they conveniently forgot how the chain of command works. Or maybe there was an extenuating circumstance. I did see a bright light in the sky over your office today. Did they bring offerings of gold, frankincense and myrrh like I instructed them?"

Finder laughed.

"Well, they did have some pretty nice sacrificial red hats," Finder said. "Anyway, I told 'em to accept you as the new commander or find another unit."

Relieved to hear that Finder was backing him up, Marshall slowly let out the breath that he did not realize he had been holding.

"Thank you, Sir. I appreciate that," Marshall said.

Finder continued speaking.

"On a completely different note, Dave, I like planning ahead. Don't you?"

Marshall nodded, then realized that the battalion commander could not see him.

"Yes, Sir," Marshall said.

"Good," Finder replied. "Stop by my office after drill and give me a rundown of what you've found and what your plans are for A.T."

Marshall accepted.

"Be glad to, Sir," he said. "See you then."

Marshall hung up the phone and smiled wryly. It was time to deal with his newly revealed fan club.

Immediately after the telephone conversation, Chief McCarthy and Sergeant Schmoot were summoned to report immediately to the company commander's office in the orderly room. Within ten minutes, both men were sitting quietly in Marshall's office, while Marshall was reading over an Army regulation in the orderly room. Neither one dared to speak, but squirmed quietly in their seats. The office was a cramped space with pale green walls. The walls were the same color as in all Army buildings, a pea-green sort of shade that the Army seems to buy by the tanker-load. The color was intended to have a calming effect. It was not doing its job for McCarthy and Schmoot.

Marshall walked into his office reviewing his copy of The Uniformed Code of Military Justice Manual of Courts Marshal. Both McCarthy and Schmoot looked worried. This was not a good sign. Silence hung heavily in the office as he shut the door behind him.

Marshall sat down behind his desk, looked straight at the soldiers, and broke the silence in a calm but serious voice. "Both of you just violated my chain of command policy," Marshall said.

The soldiers glanced at each other and shrugged their shoulders. Marshall cleared his throat and continued speaking, "Sergeant Schmoot, report to the first sergeant," Marshall ordered. "He wants to have a heart-to-heart talk with you." Schmoot gave a silent sigh of relief. He stood up and gave McCarthy a thumbs-up sign behind his back as he left. McCarthy began to stand up to leave.

"Mr. McCarthy, please stay," Marshall ordered, annoyance obvious in his voice. McCarthy groaned and sat back down. Schmoot shook his arms in front of his body as if to celebrate getting off easy and departed the commander's office without saluting. Marshall shook his head. Failing to salute one's commander before leaving the room was an obvious –and quite insulting—infraction of military protocol.

Turning his attention to the senior warrant officer taking up a large amount of space in his office, Marshall looked directly into McCarthy's eyes. McCarthy, who was old enough to be Marshall's father, stared right back at him.

Marshall pulled no punches as he spoke to McCarthy. "Mr. McCarthy, it's been how long? Five, maybe six hours since I've taken command?" McCarthy's glare grew angrier. Marshall continued speaking. "Already you've violated one of my command directives."

· McCarthy responded with a grunt.

"Listen Chief, you don't have to be here," Marshall said, growing more annoyed by the second. "I want your support, or I want you out of this unit. It's as simple as that. I don't need you running to the battalion commander's office every time you hear something that you don't like or agree with."

Marshall leaned forward from his desk, closer to McCarthy.

"It's your choice," Marshall said. "Are you in or out?"

McCarthy didn't look at the new commander. His eyes wandered around the room, looking for a place to hide.

McCarthy knew he had been caught in the act and there was no escape.

"I'm not leaving this unit," He finally responded in a low voice.

Marshall looked directly at the embarrassed and overweight warrant officer, who kept squirming in his seat.

"Then I have your support?" Marshall asked him.

Sheepishly, McCarthy looked at Marshall and replied.

"Yes, Sir," he said in a small voice.

"I'm glad to hear that, Mr. McCarthy," Marshall said. "Now, since you're a seasoned veteran, I don't want to insult your intelligence by explaining something so basic as the chain of command to you, but you leave me no choice."

McCarthy grunted. Marshall ignored him.

"Your immediate supervisor is Lieutenant Burks," Marshall said. "Speak to her if you've got a problem. No more of this B.S., Chief. You know better. This will not happen again. That's all I've got to say on this matter. You may go."

McCarthy rolled forward out of his chair, struggled to get to his feet, and marched out of the new commander's office without saluting.

Marshall shook his head and pulled out his small notebook. "The unit needs training on military conduct and discipline, cooking, maintenance, and proper uniform," he scribbled.

Although he did little dances the entire way there, Schmoot was not having any easier of a time in the first sergeant's office. Tisher was completely disgusted with Schmoot. The first sergeant wanted the 683rd to pick itself up from the quagmire of infighting and low morale. But the unit had too many prima donnas.

"Dennis, what the hell has gotten into you?" Tisher asked. Schmoot grunted in response. Tisher ignored him.

"You've been in the Army long enough to know better," Tisher said. "The Old Man is trying to pull this unit together and you and McCarthy are tryin' to pull it apart. You're lucky it's his first day. He's got a lot of other fish to fry besides you and your sidekick."

The term Old Man was coined after World War I, when company commanders were in there thirties and forties. Officer promotions to the next higher rank were slow due to the reduction in size of the Army, hence the company commander was usually one of the oldest men in the unit.

Schmoot's eyes focused on the doorway and he shrugged his shoulders. Tisher continued.

"Just whose bright idea was it to go to the battalion commander anyway?" he asked.

Schmoot sat quietly, looking rather despondent and worried, as well as deep in thought. After a moment, he quietly responded.

"Top, Mr. McCarthy thought it best that I come along and add the NCO's perspective why Captain Marshall shouldn't be the new commander."

Tisher looked Schmoot squarely in the eye.

"Oh? Why shouldn't he be the new commander?" Tisher asked.

"He took our red hats away!" Schmoot defiantly blurted out.

Tisher stifled a laugh.

"Don't worry, Sergeant," Tisher said. "You can always wear those stupid red hats when you're dressed in your civvies if you want. Dismissed!"

Later that day in Marshall's office, he and Tisher were discussing unit capabilities, strengths and weakness of each section.

"Top," said Marshall, "I got a feeling I already know who we can count on in this unit. I think we'll both have to keep a close eye on our problem children. They've got way too much free time."

Tisher nodded.

"You mean the soldiers shouldn't be practicing their pinochle skills – and winning each others' pay—during drill?" Tisher asked Marshall with a wry grin.

"They can do that on Friday nights before coming to drill," Marshall said. "It's time to get 'em busy every minute of every drill period. That should keep everyone including McCarthy and Schmoot occupied. Too much idle time causes morale problems. It's best to keep soldiers busy and focused on their work."

Marshall thought of his day and smiled.

"Besides, Top, I think there's a lot of work that hasn't been done," Marshall said.

Tisher's mood changed. Marshall had hit on one of the things that vexed him the most about the unit.

"Yes, I know," Tisher said. "The tech supply section hasn't had a mission since I've been with the unit. That's six years and counting."

The 683rd Tech Supply mission was to provide repair parts and components (complete engines, transmissions, starters, etc.) for the maintenance mission of the 683rd. This was a daunting task, considering the Army was continually phasing out old equipment and replacing it with newer and upgraded models.

Obtaining funding to purchase these needed parts was another difficult issue, which had to be constantly justified. Maintaining an adequate parts stock took expertise and dedication. Thousands of repair parts had to be properly identified, ordered, stored, maintained and monitored. Stockage levels (what was needed to be on hand) were critical to successful accomplishment of the maintenance mission.

One can't fix a tank with duct tape and bailing wire. On the other hand, if you didn't have a maintenance mission, you didn't need repair parts. The dilemma facing the military was peacetime versus wartime requirements and the budgets needed for both. Training and maintaining, however, was a top priority.

"Top, that's gonna change!" Marshall replied confidently, grinning at First Sergeant Fisher. "I'm going to get with the battalion maintenance operations officer and see what he and his people can do for us."

"That's great news, but good luck doing it," Tisher said. Marshall ignored Tisher's seemingly negative attitude and continued speaking.

"Colonel Finder and I are getting together after drill," said Marshall. "Do any other sections need more work?"

"Sir, Mr. Farley's the shop officer. He's in charge of the entire maintenance shop," Tisher replied. "I know for a fact he is eager to talk to you on that subject."

Marshall nodded in agreement, picking up on the First Sergeant's cue. "Yeah Top, I was going to drop by and see him next. Thanks for the suggestion."

After Tisher left Marshall's office, Marshall headed out to the shop office in the 683rd Maintenance Facility to meet with the unit's shop officer, Chief Warrant Officer Jim Farley. Marshall smiled to himself as he realized that the selection of the shop officer was nontraditional – like most of the procedures in the 683rd. Most units would only give the position of shop officer to a seasoned commissioned officer, not a warrant officer. But, as Marshall had already seen in abundance, the 683rd lieutenants had no experience and barely knew how act like an officer, much less run shop operations.

Chief Farley was waiting outside his office for Marshall, and saluted the commander while he was still a ways off. Farley looked like a modern day Viking in fatigues. He was in his late thirties with short curly blond hair and a handlebar mustache. He towered over most of the soldiers at a height of six feet tall. Farley had years of experience in Army maintenance, and knew practically all there was to know in that regard.

Despite all his skills and his imposing physique, Farley wasn't much of a leader. He was soft spoken and thoughtful, but tended to be a micro-manager. Keeping soldiers in line and barking commands wasn't the job of the shop officer anyway, but Farley made up for his timidity with his technical acumen. Farley could conduct symphonies with his mastery of a toolbox, and was an expert in all facets of maintenance.

Farley was glad to see someone willing to lay down the law take command. He also felt there was no place to go except forward. The 683rd had been marching backwards for quite a while.

While Marshall was still about 25 feet from the office, he noticed Farley's salute. With snappy precision, he returned the gesture. After a moment's pause, he walked into the shop office.

"Welcome to my home away from home, Captain," Farley said with a smile. "Please, help yourself to some coffee."

Marshall shivered in the poorly insulated building and took Farley up on his offer, pouring hot coffee in a foam cup.

"Thank you, Mr. Farley," Marshall said. "Nothing like Army coffee to keep you on your toes." He sipped the top layer of coffee from the steaming cup.

As Marshall took another sip, a loud metallic crash reverberated through the shop area. Startled, Marshall spilled a little bit of coffee on Farley's mahogany-colored desk. Farley smiled.

"It's OK, Sir," Farley said. "Do you like this dark wooden desk? It was white pine when they first brought it in here. Too many times, I was sitting here doing paperwork and 'CRASH!' like the building's falling down around me. And whoops, there goes my coffee. I reckon I've spilled at least 10 gallons of coffee on this desk."

Marshall started to chuckle. Then he realized that Farley's desk did have a stale coffee sort of smell to it.

"Um, glad I could help with your furniture refinishing then," Marshall said. "Let's take a walk around the shop."

The shop was full of soldiers working on equipment in the bay areas. Marshall and Farley couldn't speak to each other while on the floor because of a cacophony of clangs, bangs, crashes and shouts from the soldiers. The main shop had eight maintenance bays and the second shop building next door had six.

Hmmm, the shop's floor is clean with clear markings showing each work area, thought Marshall as he toured the area. The overhead crane was an added bonus whenever a heavy-lift of a truck engine was required.

When they were far enough from the din to hear their own thoughts –and to be sure that they wouldn't be overheard by the soldiers—Marshall delved into some of the pertinent shop issues.

"Chief Farley, how many sections need mission work?" Marshall asked.

Farley was surprised at Marshall's quick and direct question. He spent a moment thinking about his response.

"Sir, for the time we have allotted every drill, we've got to be careful what we take into the automotive shop," Farley said.

"If the sections can't finish the job within the two-day drill period, we'll have to evacuate it by 5-ton wrecker to the civilian maintenance shop in Canal Fulton, which is 60 miles away. Another concern is that the owning unit of that piece of equipment won't be mission-capable on their unit readiness report."

The unit readiness report was a detailed report sent to higher (and higher) headquarters that gave the overall status of a unit. The report took into account, the number of unit personnel assigned, versus vacancies, their skill levels and if they were qualified to military standards to do their job, as well as the status of the equipment, what was on hand and operational, what was missing, and what was being repaired.

Marshall nodded. He knew the importance of getting the job in, repaired, and back to the customer unit within two days. It was extremely hard to do, especially if repair parts were needed and not on hand to finish the job. It was a typical conundrum within the military: Do more with less. One had to train the soldiers with very little or no funding, and not lower unit readiness. Officers and NCOs had to be creative, and make due with what was available without violating Army directives, or any civil laws as well.

"I understand the issue, Chief," Marshall said. "What about the other sections besides automotive?"

Chief Farley paused a moment, trying to find the right words.

"Well Sir, all the sections need more jobs in-shop to train on," he said. "The only way these guys will ever get proficient and raise their skill levels is to work on the equipment we'll see during wartime. And that includes that repair parts to fix'em."

The armament section was responsible for fixing everything that shoots, from a .45 caliber pistol to a self-propelled artillery piece. The service and recovery section had vast capabilities, which included canvas repair, bodywork, machining and recovery all types of Army equipment including tanks. Lastly, the tech supply section provided all the repair parts and materials needed to fix the Army's huge inventory of equipment. All of them needed more work to train their personnel.

"I'll be getting with Major Breedlow later on to discuss additional missions for the sections," Marshall said. "I'll make sure that he knows which sections need more work,"

"Thank you, Sir," Farley responded.

Although A.T. was still months away and it seemed like the soldiers had a difficult time performing simple maintenance tasks like changing tires, Marshall was optimistic that their skills would blossom in the coming months.

"Chief, I've got an idea for some of our soldiers during A.T.," Marshall said. "The Fort Knox Boatwright Maintenance Facility will be full of track vehicles to work on, including the new M1 Abrams and M2 Bradley. This is the equipment we're supposed to be able to fix if this unit gets activated. Although it's rather unlikely that we'll invade Nicaragua or anything like that, we need to learn how it all works and become experts in those tanks' inner workings. We should contact Fort Knox and see if they'll be able to help us."

Chief Farley was delighted. He would love to get his wrench on some of those newly fielded tanks, and he knew that the rest of the soldiers in the tank automotive and armament section would feel the same way. Or, he thought, at least they should.

"Yes Sir, I'll get on it right away," Farley said with a smile. "The people to talk to will be in their offices on Monday. I'll give 'em a call and start the ball rolling."

"Wonderful!" Marshall responded. He glanced at his watch. Thirteen minutes to final formation, where the soldiers line up one last time before being sent home. The shop was nearly empty, except for Chief Farley and several of the shop office NCOs working on some paperwork.

Oh no, Marshall thought. It would take him seven minutes to get back to the orderly room, which would leave him just six minutes to spare before final formation. He hated cutting things close like this.

"Chief, thank you for the quick tour," Marshall said. "I have to run. I don't want to be late for final formation. See you there!"

The men shook hands and Marshall dashed away. Farley started jogging after him, then glanced at his watch. There were 13 minutes to final formation! Plenty of time, he thought.

Thanks to Marshall's sprinting, he made it to the orderly room with seven minutes to spare.

Miraculously, all were standing in formation in the outdoor assembly area for final formation at 1700 hours. Marshall dismissed the formation and sent them home for the night and told them he would see them again at 0700 hours the following day. As the soldiers made their way to their cars in the parking lot adjacent to the headquarters building, Marshall silently thanked the Lord for getting through the day virtually unscathed.

Marshall breathed a deep sigh of relief as he walked to the battalion commander's office for their meeting. The first day is supposed to be the toughest, and it was over.

Lieutenant Colonel Finder was waiting for Marshall outside his office.

"Well Dave, how was your first day as commander of the 683rd Maintenance Company?" Finder asked knowingly.

Marshall paused. There were many things he could say, but he searched for the most diplomatic and honest response.

"Sir, it was definitely an eye-opener," Marshall finally replied. "We've got an anti-authority faction that surfaced early, mission work that needs to be brought in to keep the troops busy and trained up, A.T. coming in less than six months, and every truck has dry rotted tires. Oh, and Colonel Sanders is apparently in charge of our mess operations."

Finder's voice and expression turned serious.

"That's why we picked you to command the unit," he told Marshall. "The feeling around the headquarters is that if anyone can get that unit back on track, you can."

Well, Marshall thought, at least he knew he was going to have the needed support from Finder to help get things back on track. He just hoped that the unit wasn't beyond all hope.

"Thank you for your confidence in me, Sir," Marshall replied earnestly. "I won't let the command down."

"I know you won't, Captain," Finder said.

"By the way, Major Breedlow may be able to help you with some mission work for the unit," he continued. "I've asked him to get together with you and see if there's anything his section can do."

Marshall's outlook brightened.

"Thank you Sir," he said to Finder.

Major John Breedlow was the OIC, or officer in charge, of the 694th Maintenance Operations Section. He was an experienced officer with a good sense of humor, and he enjoyed working with other professional officers and NCOs.

Breedlow was also quite the storyteller. Many times when Marshall walked by the maintenance operations section, he would hear a roar of laughter from those listening to Breedlow's tales. From the antics of the young lieutenants in Vietnam he was in charge of, to the misadventures of him and his crazy brother-in-law, he kept everyone in stitches.

Despite Breedlow's jovial stories, he was a serious workhorse. Marshall felt if anyone could help increase the 683rd's maintenance workload, it was Breedlow. After all, Breedlow did command the 683rd four years earlier.

Finder smiled at Marshall.

"By the way, I hope you've talked to your two problem children," he said. "I don't want to see them hanging around my door without clearance from you first."

Marshall laughed, glad to know that Finder didn't like soldiers going behind their commander's back.

"Already counseled both culprits, Sir," Marshall said. "It won't happen again."

"Good," said Finder. "Now let me talk to you about what I've been able to glean from divisional headquarters about your annual training at Fort Knox."

Marshall sat up a little straighter and pulled out his notebook.

"First of all, be prepared to be the overall commander of the northern Ohio convoy of all Reserve units. The normal tasking goes to the largest company to handle that. You'll receive formal tasking within the next few months. From what I've been told you'll be supporting a multitude of reservists at Mount Eden Base Camp, deep in the hills and woods of Fort Knox."

Marshall stopped writing. That sounded like a lot of responsibility. Finder noticed his apprehension.

"Dave, don't worry," Finder said. "These other units are well trained. If you can handle the 683rd, you can handle a few hundred more."

Finder took another look at the young – and overwhelmed – captain who sat in his office.

"You should call it a night too," Finder said. "Enjoy a quiet evening at home with the wife, get some rest, and I'll see you back here tomorrow morning.

"Let me know how things progress. Dismissed."

Marshall came to attention and rendered a salute to his boss then departed the battalion commander's office with a renewed hope that things would continue to go well.

Major Breedlow met Marshall in the hallway.

"Hey Dave, I hear that Mutt and Jeff already tried to shoot you down on your first day," chuckled Breedlow. "I forgot to tell you to watch your back when you're around those two clowns. Both think they can run a unit without a commander."

"Thanks. I've noticed," Marshall replied. "Would you like to have them in your section? I have a feeling they're making plans to find a new home."

"Hell no, Captain! I don't want those dirty birds anywhere near me," Breedlow said. "Just watch your backside with those two, Dave."

"Well, most of my unit seems to have nothing to do except watch their backsides," Marshall said. "What the unit really needs is more mission work in several sections, especially the tech supply and armament sections. I'm focused on getting the unit ready for A.T. and we'll need all the time we have left to prepare. After A.T. is over – and I hope I'm still around as commander – we sure could use a lot more mission work."

Breedlow agreed with Marshall that more mission work before A.T. was not needed. When the 683rd returned from Fort Knox, it would be the starting point for more productive drills.

"That'll give my staff plenty of time to work on it for you," said Breedlow. "Just send me a formal type-written request. We'll do the rest."

"Thank you, Sir," Marshall said. "Is there a special form that we need to fill out, or should we just write a formal letter? And is it addressed to you, or to Colonel Finder as a formality?"

Breedlow shook his head.

"Captain, I have only one thing to say to you at this point," Breedlow said. "It's 1800 hours. Your soldiers left an hour ago. You've just finished your first day in a rough job. Leave the Army behind for a few hours. Go home. Eat a homemade dinner. Watch a video with your wife. Get rested up and come back tomorrow. We'll pick up this conversation then."

Marshall couldn't argue with anything the major said. He saluted him. "Yes Sir!" Marshall said. He spun on his heel and walked to his car for a night of rest.

JANUARY DRILL, SUNDAY

At 0623 hrs, Captain Marshall was dusting the snow off of his jacket and stomping his feet on the rubber entrance mat to get the wet slushy snow off of his boots. He was back in his new office, and he shuffled toward the coffee pot. He'd barely slept a wink the night before. Visions of soldiers playing cards, red hats and flat tires kept wandering through his head every time he closed his eyes.

Exhilaration for his new post – mixed with trepidation at the monumental task before him – buoyed Marshall's spirits. That and an insulated metal travel mug full of coffee, which his wife thoughtfully made for him as he ran through the door. Marshall completely drained the metal mug during the 20-minute drive to the Ravenna Army Ammunition Plant and needed another caffeine jolt so he wouldn't lose his edge.

As he plugged in the coffee maker, which began to percolate, the 683rd's officers started trickling into Marshall's office for the new commander's first meeting with all of them.

"Good morning, Sir!" shouted a young female lieutenant with her hair pulled back in a tight bun, so she could tuck it under her hat.

Marshall had no time to respond.

"Morning, Captain!" interrupted a skinny man with red hair walking through the door.

"Sir, happy Sunday!" The soldier who introduced herself as Second Lieutenant Meglynn the day before strode through the office.

It was 0628 hours. The meeting would begin in two minutes. Marshall walked through the crowd accumulating in his office to pour himself a cup of coffee. The chorus of greetings continued.

"Good morning, Captain!"

"Good day, Sir!"

"Top of the morning, Sir. Um, where am I supposed to sit?"

Marshall filled his cup three-quarters full and turned around. His office had become standing-room only, with about 10 officers crowded inside. Several more were on the way. One young officer had even taken the commander's desk chair.

Marshall smiled. If nothing else, he thought, having officers' call in his office was a good way to keep warm in the barely heated Reserve Center.

Two of the young lieutenants decided to enjoy a morning smoke with their coffee, which immediately began to choke everyone in the room as the second-hand smoke permeated the air. Marshall was not pleased that they failed to ask permission first. With his head starting to spin from the degraded environmental conditions, and the clashing of smells of aftershave, coffee, and cigarettes, Marshall made his first command decision of the day, and decided to move the meeting to the conference room so everyone would have a little more space and breathing room.

A crush of soldiers moved toward the door. Marshall shook his head.

Suddenly, someone crashed into his right arm, jostling his hand and spilling Marshall's coffee onto the floor. He turned and saw Lieutenant Meglynn, a horrified look on her face and a rosy blush creeping into her cheeks.

"Sir, oh my goodness, I'm um, so sorry," she stammered. "I wasn't looking where I was going. I'll clean it up, Sir."

The lieutenant reached into her pocket, searching for her travel-sized package of tissues. She grabbed a plastic-wrapped package and pulled it out of her pocket. Marshall watched in amusement.

"Sir, I'll get it all clean," she said, struggling with the package to pull out a tissue. Marshall touched her shoulder.

"I don't think you'll have much luck cleaning the floors with that," he said.

Meglynn looked at the plastic package in her hand. It was a sanitary napkin. The blush in her cheeks became fluorescent.

"Sir, I'm not usually this clumsy, Sir," she said in a quiet voice.

Marshall handed her a roll of paper towels from his desk and told her to carry on.

Several minutes later, the young lieutenants and veteran warrant officers were relaxing in the conference room, smoking what was left of their cigarettes and enjoying their coffee as Marshall walked in and greeted everyone.

"Good morning everyone," he said in his command voice. "From now on, this meeting will take place here, on the Saturday morning drill day at 0645 hours. Priorities for the drill weekend will be given out. That'll include requirements from higher headquarters and what we must accomplish with training and mission work." Everyone at the meeting nodded attentively.

"For those of us who do not smoke, smoking will no longer be allowed during this meeting, or any future meetings. The smoking lamp is now out, except for those designated smoking areas. Get used to it." Marshall was firm in his proclamation. As an ex-smoker, he had a very low tolerance for secondhand smoke.

Marshall stood up and began to walk over to the chalkboard and write down a few of his key points. "I've discussed our mission requirements with the battalion commander and Major Breedlow, and requested that our missions be augmented after we return from A.T.. As for immediate priorities, my number one priority is to get our people and assigned equipment ready for A.T."

He quickly wrote down the first priority on the chalkboard. All present at the meeting did likewise on their notepads, which were opened and pens at the ready, frantically transcribing Marshall's guidance for annual training.

"All your equipment that isn't bolted to the shop floor needs to be loaded onto your trailers, trucks and vans. Get your vehicles ready for the trip to Fort Knox and your drivers and assistant drivers trained on the vehicles you have, and what you'll need to borrow to haul everything to A.T.."

The assembled officers mouths began to open, they couldn't believe what they just heard. The gauntlet had been thrown. They had never been tasked to take everything with them to annual training before. This was going to be a very large undertaking.

A heavy silence filled the conference room. They all knew that this was a tall order and a lofty goal.

Second Lieutenant Kate Kiley, an attractive 25-year old who was married to one of the NCOs in the 683rd, broke the silence with a question.

"Sir, what will our A.T. mission be?" she asked.

Marshall was glad to have young lieutenants who could ask the right questions.

"Right now, I've been informed that we will be supporting a combat engineer company doing some road repair and environmental improvements in the Mount Eden area."

A smile went up from the warrant officers. They knew what some of the supposed environmental improvements were.

Marshall continued. "That'll also includes maintenance support for the other units that will be out there with us." Kiley nodded in agreement, having heard the word.

"I've also been tasked to be the overall convoy commander and coordinator for all northern Ohio units going to Mount Eden Base Camp," Marshall continued. "Looks like there will be over 500 troops in the field."

The floodgate of questions opened, and the officers raised their hands and shouted out questions like reporters at a press conference.

Marshall called on Second Lieutenant Stiles, who looked surprisingly comfortable sitting in a metal folding chair.

"Sir, what about the track and turret mechanics?" Stiles asked. "There won't be any work for them at the field site."

Another good question, Marshall thought. He had anticipated this problem and was already working toward a solution.

Marshall quickly replied, "Chief Farley is going to make coordination with the Boatwright Maintenance Facility on main post. He's going to find out if they can help with some of those hard to train specialties in the unit, such as the tank turret and track vehicle sections. We all know Fort Knox has plenty of the new M1 Abrams tanks, and possibly the M2 & M3 Bradley fighting vehicles. There's plenty of old M60 tanks around to keep them occupied as well."

Lieutenant Stiles' eyes gleamed with excitement as Marshall mentioned the state-of-the-art new tanks.

Marshall's tone became more serious and cautious as he spoke. "Unfortunately, working inside the M1 Abrams turret requires a secret security clearance. Working on the outside doesn't."

"Sir, I'll see how many of my turret folks already have a secret clearance," Stiles said. Everyone at the meeting knew it would take a miracle to obtain a secret security clearance before the start of annual training. Without the proper security clearance, turret mechanics could only work on the outside of the new M1.

Marshall directed his gaze towards both Farley and James with one raised eyebrow, trying to get their attention.

Chief Farley took the cue and spoke up. "Sir, as we discussed yesterday, I'll call the civilian director of Boatwright on Monday. He and I worked together years ago on active duty at Fort Knox. Coordination should not be a problem. Also, I'm sure they could use some additional manpower. Summer time is when most of the civilians take their 2-week vacation."

"Excellent news, Chief!" Marshall exclaimed.

Marshall looked at the remainder of the officers in the room. Some looked intently at him. Some half smiled. Some looked frightened. Marshall cleared his throat and switched to a serious tone of voice.

"I need to know if there are any other sections that need some specific training," he said. The room was silent.

"Speak up now," Marshall continued. "We're not going to have this opportunity again for quite a while."

The rest of the officers looked at each other, as if Marshall was speaking another language and they were afraid to tell him so. Marshall nodded in understanding. He had the distinct impression that prior to his arrival, annual training must not have been well planned in advance.

"All right. I'll give you until next month to think about it," Marshall said. "If you come up with anything you'd like to have your folks trained on during A.T., your input would be appreciated, so keep me posted.

"Chief Farley, what was the unit's policy with personnel working on main post while the rest of the unit is in the field?" Marshall asked.

Chief Farley replied, "Captain, in the past, we signed for some barracks and an orderly room on main post and requested those staying on main post be attached to one of the training units for admin support. They'll eat at one of the mess halls near their barracks. We'll need to put a request through the Reserve Affairs Office at Fort Knox."

Marshall stroked his chin, pondering the information. The assembled officers watched their new commander with bated breath. He started thinking aloud.

"Our people need technical training as well as field training," Marshall said. "When equipment is in constant use, it tends to break down, and I expect mission work will pick up rapidly during the second week of A.T.. When that happens, we may have to pull all the on-post soldiers to the field site to keep up with the maintenance backlog."

Many of the officers nodded in agreement. Some nodded in disbelief. The soldiers have a hard enough time keeping their own equipment in line when they've got two entire days a month to dedicate to it.

Marshall noticed the spaced-out look on some of his officers' faces.

"We've got more planning to do, folks," he said to them. "I expect input from everyone in this room. Time is not on our side."

Second Lieutenant Deborah Stiles was the armament platoon leader and the unit training officer. Despite her positions of authority, the Army was a new experience for her. She had never spent a night in a tent in the field—just in her own backyard.

Stiles was 22 and in her last year of college. She was studying to be a nurse. She enjoyed helping people and was an excellent student. She spent between two and four hours studying each night, taking very meticulous notes. Her notes were perfectly organized, color coded, and carefully memorized. When exams came around, Stiles became the most popular girl in her class, with everyone hoping to study with her.

Stiles had short curly brown hair and a husky build. Many of the soldiers in the unit said she looked like Peppermint Patty in the Peanuts cartoons, and the nickname stuck. It annoyed her. She never wore sandals, and unlike her cartoon namesake, she smoked like a chimney—especially when under stress.

Stiles was ready to put her top-of-the-line organizational skills to good use for the new commander. She raised her hand and Marshall called on her.

"Sir, as the unit training officer, I'll have the A.T. training schedule ready by next drill."

Marshall was a bit amused.

"Lieutenant Stiles, the training schedule is commonly referred to as a living document because it changes and evolves constantly," Marshall said. "Go ahead and begin to make a draft copy for my review. Let's not finalize it until two months before we go. Keep in mind, everything is going to change, so be flexible.

Marshall turned his gaze to the other soldiers in the meeting.

"That goes for everyone in this room," he said. "Be flexible, adapt and overcome. That should be everyone's motto."

Chief McCarthy raised his hand, and Marshall called on him.

"Captain, we know what the overall mission is going to be," McCarthy said. "What are your thoughts on the overall training objectives?"

Marshall liked how McCarthy didn't mince words and came straight to the point. Although he had covered certain facets of the overall plan section-by-section, the "big picture" needed to be addressed.

"Our training objectives are to use annual training to sharpen both the maintenance and soldier skills of everyone in the unit," Marshall said. "Keep in mind that every soldier has a primary MOS as an infantryman."

Surprise registered on the faces of several of the officers, many of whom had not picked up a weapon or completed an obstacle course since basic training.

"That's right," Marshall continued. "Everyone in this unit better know how to soldier first."

Lieutenant Rodriguez quickly interjected, "Sir, I'd like to assist in developing the tactical training plans for A.T.."

Marshall was glad to see he had a volunteer. "Excellent", said Marshall. "Your expertise will be put to good use. First thing we need to know is how many NCOs have tactical experience. I want you to get with First Sergeant Tisher and find out. We'll use them for instructors."

"Yes Sir," Rodriguez replied. "I'll be glad to." Rod knew what he was volunteering for. Anything he could do to help train the soldiers in basic soldiering skills would have a positive impact on how the soldiers would perform in a tactical field environment.

Marshall added, "Along those same lines, we'll need to start having some tactical training sessions before we go to A.T.. Our soldiers should be prepared when we hit the ground at Mount Eden Base Camp."

"Yes Sir," replied Rodriguez. "I've got some lesson plans already prepared and can begin next drill." He knew of several NCOs he could rely on to help provide additional instruction. The wheels were turning and Rod was excited to be onboard.

"That's what I like to hear, Rod," replied Marshall. "You may choose whoever you need to assist you. Just get with Lieutenant Stiles so she can put the training classes on next month's unit training schedule."

First Lieutenant Rod Rodriguez was the unit's only infantry officer. Rod Rodriguez had two years of active duty experience, and had previously worked with Captain Marshall on several occasions when Marshall was serving as the battalion S-1. Marshall felt Rod Rodriguez was a squared away officer and was surprised when the battalion commander did not choose Rod as the 683rd commander.

Rod Rodriguez was born in San Juan, Puerto Rico in the old, historic section of town. His father was a member of the San Juan City Council and owned a hotel. His mother was originally from Havana, Cuba, and her family owned a large coffee plantation. Rod was a gifted student and entered the Virginia Military Institute in 1978. After he graduated, he was commissioned and stationed at Fort Benning, Georgia. He left active duty in 1981, got married, moved to Akron, Ohio, got a job with Goodrich Tire and Rubber Company, and started a family.

Marshall switched gears.

"All right, everyone. Let's talk about what's going on today," he said.

Marshall laid out the day's training schedule. It seemed like a lot of work for everyone, an attempt to make up for lost time. The mechanics would be turning wrenches. The clerks would be compiling and filing. The shop would be inventoried. The main shop heater would be repaired. And there would be no pinochle, dancing contests or naps. It was time for one more piece of motivation.

"We represent this nation as America's finest. That's why we volunteered for this service," Marshall told the officers. "Now, let's make sure that we all live up to that title. Starting today, we will. Dismissed!"

There were 10 minutes before the soldiers and officers had to be in formation. Enough time for a cigarette, a latrine pit-stop, and a hot cup of coffee. More than enough time to mull over what the new commander had said.

They filed out of the conference room, ready to start talking about Marshall's ambitious plans to mold the unit into shape – and make A.T. more than two boring weeks in the woods. Marshall watched them go, silently hoping all would go well.

A loud crash startled him from his thoughts.

"Oh, sorry to startle you, Sir," said Lieutenant Meglynn, picking herself up off the floor. She had somehow tripped over one of the metal folding chairs in the room. Her fall had ended up knocking three more chairs to the ground. She clumsily started to pick up the chairs. Marshall silently wondered if she had injured herself.

Marshall grabbed a chair from Meglynn.

"Lieutenant, that was a hard fall," he told her. "I'll take care of the chairs. You get some ice for that knee."

"Sorry, Sir, and thank you," Meglynn said, hastily running out of the room.

As Marshall put the chairs back up, he was thankful for his predecessor's wisdom in putting Meglynn in charge of clerical work in lieu of bomb disposal.

While Marshall was meeting with the officers, First Sergeant Tisher was holding court with the NCOs in the unit orderly room. All the sergeants – ranging from staff sergeants to sergeants first class were there, and the room was packed pretty tightly.

"Listen up," Tisher said. "The Old Man wants everyone to know his highest priority is to get this unit, personnel and equipment, ready for A.T.."

Tisher ignored what sounded like a low groan coming from some of the NCOs and concentrated on the ones who stared at him intently. He continued articulating Marshall's plan for the next five months.

"From now on, like the Old Man said, everyone here will use the chain-of-command if they've got a beef," Tisher said, looking squarely at Sergeant Schmoot. In response, Schmoot looked away and slumped down in his seat.

"You know I'm serious," Tisher said. "Nobody will bypass the chain of command. Understood?"

The group all nodded in agreement, with several muttering, "Yeah Top." Schmoot slumped down lower and pulled the bill of his Army issue baseball cap further down on his forehead. Tisher contemplated continuing the conversation about chain of command a little longer. If Schmoot slumped down any further, he'd slide out of the chair, Tisher thought.

Suppressing his desire to watch Schmoot make a fool out of himself, Tisher opened the floor to the sergeants for questions and comments.

Sergeant First Class John Lemasters, an ex-marine who fought in both Korea and Vietnam, raised his hand. Lemasters was the oldest, most decorated, most respected, and most experienced soldier in the unit. When Lemasters spoke, he was usually right on the money. Tisher called on him.

"Top, I've served under lots of commanders," Lemasters said slowly. "Looks like we finally got ourselves a good 'un."

"Yeah John," said Tisher, "I've got the same good feeling about this Old Man. He knows maintenance, he knows how to work with the NCOs and officers, and he's concerned about the welfare of the troops. We've got us a keeper this time."

First Sergeant Tisher looked at his watch and gasped in silence. There were only about five minutes until everyone had to be at morning formation, and it was already apparent to everyone that Marshall was exceedingly punctual. He raised his voice to get everyone's attention.

"All right everyone! We've got five minutes to formation. Let's all get there and show the Old Man how serious we are about getting into shape for A.T.," Tisher said.

"And don't be too anxious to rush home this evening. I want all of you to be back here after final formation to go over what needs to be done next drill," Tisher again ignored the groans.

"And one more thing. The Old Man wants all section and platoon sergeants to attend the training meeting on the Wednesday prior to the next drill." Tisher cut off the impending groans with a tantalizing promise. "We know your time is valuable, and you will get paid if there are funds available."

"Now get your butts outta here!" Tisher said, gesturing toward his office door.

The halls of the Reserve Center buzzed as the soldiers moved from their warm meeting rooms to the frigid outdoors for morning formation in the parking lot. Was their new commander crazy, or just over-ambitious? Were all of them really going to spend time concentrating on perfecting their soldiering? Did they see Schmoot almost fall out of his chair?

At precisely 0659 hours, Marshall walked onto the parking area where morning formation was beginning to assemble. Soldiers ran from all areas of the building to be in place on time. As everyone was lining up, Meglynn nearly tripped over an untied bootlace. She got behind the headquarters platoon, quickly tied her bootlace, and snapped to attention as First Sergeant Tisher blew his whistle at 0700 hours.

Marshall smiled. He was already making a difference.

Tisher presided over the formation, while Marshall stood at the rear of the assembled soldiers and listened.

"683rd! This unit has sat on its butt for too long!" Tisher said.

"Today we will get ourselves ready. More precisely, we need to get ready for A.T.."

The soldiers listened intently as Tisher focused their attention on motor stables.

"We are going to A.T. as a fully operational maintenance unit. Therefore, every truck, tractor and trailer will be convoyed to Fort Knox during A.T.," Tisher said. "I know what you're thinking. Our equipment ain't been maintained since before some of you were born. Well, fix it! We've got five months. Let's take advantage of our time and catch up on some badly needed maintenance – so we can get to Mount Eden in one piece."

Tisher noticed a frightful look on some of the soldiers' faces and asked Marshall if he had anything to add.

"No Top. Carry on," replied Marshall from the back of the formation.

"Fall out!" Tisher shouted with a grin.

With what sounded like a collective sigh, the entire 683rd did an about face and went to work.

Marshall asked First Sergeant Tisher to have Staff Sergeant Mooney report to this office immediately after the morning formation. Marshall walked to his office and helped himself to another cup of coffee. As he began to pour, Marshall heard a soft knock on his doorjamb.

"Sir, Sergeant Mooney reports," he said. He quietly entered Marshall's office and snapped to attention, rendering a precise salute three feet in front of the commander's desk.

Marshall grinned, returned the salute and asked Sergeant Mooney to have a seat.

Sergeant Mooney was a handsome, single and physically fit 29-year-old NCO with more than 10 years of active duty experience. He had been assigned to the 683rd as its full-time supply sergeant, and had the daily responsibility of running unit supply operations. The supply sergeant's job was to make sure a soldier was outfitted with clothing and equipment for all eventualities. If the soldier or section was supposed to have something, the unit supply sergeant was going to get it for them.

Marshall welcomed Mooney to his office.

"Sergeant Mooney, please sit down," Marshall said. Mooney sat. "It's a pleasure to finally meet with you," Marshall continued. "Chief James tells me you're the best."

Mooney seemed a little embarrassed by that statement.

"Well Sir, I try and do my best," he stammered.

Marshall got straight to the point.

"I'm also going to try and do my best, and I need your help," Marshall said. "With A.T. coming in less than six months, I've got to know the operational status on every piece of rolling stock we've got, and what we need to augment every section, and how many radios we're authorized by the MTO&E."

This document, known as the modified table of organization and equipment, record what the 683rd was supposed to have in equipment and personnel per the Army's written guidelines. It listed every section within the unit, the personnel needed –and their ranks and MOS—and what equipment each section was supposed to have on-hand. The MTO&E is different for every type of unit in the Army, and was continually modified and updated to incorporate the changes in equipment, personnel requirements and mission.

Mooney was the one person in the unit who needed to be able to rattle off the MTO&E specs at a moment's notice.

Sergeant Mooney did not disappoint.

"Sir, we'll need to borrow a radio. We're short one," Mooney said. "The other two are okay, but I'll have them checked tomorrow to make sure.

I don't know about what else every section needs, but I'll get with the platoon sergeants today and find out," Mooney said. His voice was confident and reassuring. Just what Marshall needed from his unit supply sergeant.

"One more thing," Marshall said. "The unit is going to do weapons qualification at Knox. We'll need to have firing ranges coordinated and reserved for every weapons system, and the ammunition ready when we get there. Can you handle that?"

"No problem Sir," replied Mooney, smiling at the new commander. "I've still got some friends at Fort Knox who can help us take care of that. I'll start making some calls and formal requests as soon as I leave your office."

Marshall was overjoyed.

"Full speed ahead," Marshall said. He was glad to have some real solid people to work with to balance out the work that would need to be done. Mooney saluted and started to walk out of the office. In a flash, Marshall remembered a hasty promise of advance planning.

"Sergeant, one more thing," Marshall called to Mooney. "Make sure you get with Lieutenant Stiles so she can plug in the weapons qualification dates and times into the A.T. training schedule."

Back in the motor park, Sergeant Schmoot and Chief McCarthy were looking over their section's vehicles and trailers.

"Man oh man Chief, the Old Man was right," Schmoot said, looking at the equipment with wide eyes. "This equipment does need some serious work on it before we can move it outta here."

Chief McCarthy looked at him with a raised eyebrow, like he had just said something idiotic.

"Dennis, I can't see us taking all this stuff to Knox. That'll be too much work," McCarthy said. "Who's going to do it all? I can't. I have a bad back, remember? Besides, how the hell can we take all four parts trailers with us? We only have one 5-ton tractor! I think we'll just take one trailer."

Sergeant Schmoot grinned.

"I don't think Captain Marshall has the same idea as you do, Chief," he said.

"Oh, probably not!" McCarthy replied. "Now let's play pinochle and forget this crap."

"Hey! Chief! Sergeant Schmoot! Taking a breather?" Both soldiers froze as Chief Robert James walked up to them.

"Uh huh," McCarthy replied hastily.

Chief James stated in a matter-of-fact manner, "Your deuces and 5-ton won't make the trip they way they're sittin' right now.

You better have some of your people stop by the motor pool for some assistance and parts."

McCarthy and Schmoot groaned affirmative responses and walked off to the maintenance shop.

Throughout the day, the shop hummed with activity. All the soldiers were busy working on the equipment. This would be the last time for six months that they would see another unit's vehicle in the 683rd shop. From then on, the 683rd Heavy Equipment Maintenance Company's vehicles would get some overdue attention.

FEBRUARY DRILL, SATURDAY

Although the ground was still frozen in February, Marshall could feel a change in the soldiers – and the mood – of the 683rd. Things were coming alive. Spring had sprung.

After morning formation, Marshall strolled among the soldiers in the motor park. People were working. He sighed. It was getting better.

His thoughts were interrupted by a scream from a male soldier inspecting a deuce-and-a-half.

"Holy Toledo!" the soldier yelled in a high-pitched voice. "There's a bees' nest! Run for it!"

Several other soldiers looked up from what they were doing. Some of them ducked behind their equipment to shield them from the bees. A couple of female soldiers giggled at the soldier's lack of machismo.

Marshall stepped into the path of the running soldier, who was still screaming about the bees.

"Soldier," Marshall said firmly.

The screaming stopped and the soldier halted, somewhat embarrassed.

"You seem to have a problem with bees in your vehicle?" Marshall continued. "Let's go check it out."

Marshall strode back to the deuce-and-a-half. The soldier who had made the scene shuffled behind the commander.

"Sir, there's a large nest in the wheel well," the soldier said in a much deeper tone of voice. "I just didn't want anyone to get stung.

Marshall smiled.

"I see," he said.

Marshall looked underneath the deuce-and-a-half's massive tire and saw a hornet's nest the size of a large football. Yikes, he thought. At least the soldier had seen something worth screaming about. If it weren't February, this nest might give them some trouble.

"Well, soldier, you do have one massive hornets' nest under this vehicle," Marshall said as he stood up. "However, they are dormant during winter. They won't be moving around and causing you any problems. Just carefully remove it and get rid of it."

The soldier saluted.

"Yes, Sir," he said.

"What is your name, soldier?" Marshall asked.

"Private Franklin, Sir," he replied.

"Well Franklin, you're going to have to toughen up when it comes to hornets," Marshall said. "The Army has adversaries that can do worse damage. Carry on."

Marshall continued on his walk. Five months remained before annual training and, despite the frozen hornets, things were starting to come together. There was a feeling of purpose that wasn't present before, Marshall thought. Morale was beginning to improve.

Everyone certainly looked busy. As the new commander, Marshall had insisted there would be no slack time, so everyone would have to have something to do. Some soldiers, like the ones toiling away at the vehicles, were working in their MOS, otherwise known as military occupational specialties.

Marshall stopped in front of some soldiers working on a 5-ton tractor. They immediately put their tools in their left hand and saluted the commander.

"Carry on," Marshall said with a smile as he returned their salute.

The soldiers relaxed and smiled back at Marshall.

"How's the repair work going?" Marshall asked them.

"Sir, it's going great," said a middle-aged soldier with a large streak of grease on his forehead. "This here tractor's only problem is it's been sitting here in the same spot since I was watching 'Howdy Doody,' if you know what I mean."

Marshall was pleased. "That's great, I hope you can get her to move," he said. "Now, which of you is the assigned operator of this vehicle?"

Marshall was answered only with silence as the soldiers looked at each other. He asked another question. "Which of you would like to be the operator?"

Again, there was no answer. Marshall asked a third question.

"Who among you is licensed to operate this fine piece of Army machinery?"

More silence. Marshall pulled his notepad out of his pocket and took down the soldiers' names. If they were going to get the equipment to Fort Knox, he thought, they were going to have to train some people to drive it there.

Marshall noticed Chief James helping out a soldier under the hood of a deuce-and-a-half.

"Chief, can I see you a minute?" Marshall asked.

James climbed down from the truck and gave a few bits of instruction to the soldier as he was leaving.

"Good morning Sir," James said. "It looks like things are beginning to change around here for the better. At least we've got soldiers from each platoon working on their equipment."

Marshall grinned.

"They're doing marvelous work, but they can't make the equipment move," Marshall said. "I've got the names of those who need to be licensed and trained on the equipment. It's pretty lengthy. I'll get with First Sergeant Tisher and have him schedule drivers' training classes for all the assigned operators and assistants."

James looked earnestly at Marshall. "Sir, if you don't mind, I'd like to handle that," he said. "I used to teach the course."

Marshall was pleasantly surprised.

"Chief, I was told your patience and good nature was legendary. Now I can see why," Marshall said. "That would be great. When can you start?"

"How about this afternoon?" James replied. "I have all the handout materials here and the lesson plan. It will take three drills to get them registered and licensed as operators."

"Wonderful," Marshall said. "How many assistant instructors are you going to need? We've got about eight different types of vehicles, not including power generation equipment, that require licensed operators."

"It's not so bad," said James. "The section NCOs are all licensed to operate their vehicles and generators. It's the young soldiers that need the training. I've got Sergeant Penny and Baxter to help with the instruction. We can start today and have them on the road driving by April drill."

"Great Chief," Marshall said. "I'll notify Top that you'll begin drivers' training right after noon chow down here in the motor pool office.

"Anything else you need to help with the class?" Marshall asked.

"Yes sir," James replied. "I'll need a larger coffee pot."

Both men grinned.

Getting soldiers trained to operate the equipment was only one of the big issues Marshall wanted to address.

"By the way, Chief," Marshall began, "did you and Sergeant Mooney get a chance to check out the commo equipment?"

The unit's radio equipment looked like it was salvaged from a garbage bin, Marshall thought. He was not about to assume that it could provide reliable communication.

Chief James had anticipated this question.

"Sir, we've checked out all three radios, and found all three need repair," he said seriously. "We loaned them out to the battalion headquarters last year and took 'em back without doing a close check."

Marshall furrowed his brow. Did HQ accidentally run over them with tanks? How could they be in such bad shape? James continued his answer before Marshall could ask more questions.

"I had Sergeant Mooney put 'em in on a job order to get 'em fixed, and for us to borrow some components to make an operational set," James said with a smile. "Matter of fact, we should get them back next week. I know that we could use some more radios, and we're working on getting some to borrow right now. I think battalion headquarters owes us a favor on that scorecard."

"Wonderful, Chief," Marshall said. "Um, do I need to know what happened to our radios when battalion headquarters was using them?"

James shook his head no in response.

Marshall changed the subject.

"Chief, what's the story on the tire situation?" Marshall asked.

"Sir, I can get one new tire per vehicle," said James. "That'll add up to about 24 tires, maybe more. We need to turn in that many to get new ones."

"Some are better than none," Marshall said. "We've got this drill period to have every section determine the worst tire on their trucks. They'll have to dismount that bad tire off the rim, install the spare, and move the best tires to the front axle. We don't want to have any front-end tire blowouts at convoy speed."

James nodded vigorously,

"Now, do we have the right equipment to switch around so many tires?" Marshall asked.

James stroked his chin, trying to recall if there was something available in the service section of the 683rd.

"We might have a portable tire de-mounter, Sir," James said. "Once we get them all off, Sergeant Penny and I'll haul the old tires down to Columbus for the swap-out with new rubber. That'll make me sleep a bit better at night."

"Me too," replied Marshall, who hoped that the new tires would end his nightmares of blowouts in the most inopportune places.

A chilly wind whipped through the yard, making Marshall huddle inside his warm jacket a little more. He glanced at the soldiers working despite the chill.

"Let's walk around and see how everyone's doing," he said to James. "The sooner they get the equipment all checked out, the sooner we all can go inside and thaw out."

Spurred on by the cold, Marshall found that several soldiers who were working on their vehicles quickly finished up their preventative maintenance checks. The clanking metal eruptions of long-cold engines being forced to start – and the whining of engine starters trying to turn their stubborn diesel engines over – filled the air. Plumes of black smoke belched from the exhaust stacks of those trucks that finally gave in and started, as soldiers lightly tapped on the throttle pedal, revving the engines to a higher idle speed.

"Well done, soldier!" Marshall said to a young-faced soldier in the driver's seat of a truck. The soldier looked relieved that his vehicle had started up correctly, especially since the commander was watching him.

"And this lovely vehicle does more than start," Marshall said. "Wait until Chief James shows you how well it actually moves across the ground."

Other soldiers, Private Franklin included, looked exasperated when their vehicles did not start up. Marshall put a hand on a frustrated Private Franklin's shoulder and offered condolences.

"Soldier, I hate to be the one to tell you this, but I think this deuce-and-a-half's battery has froze to death," Marshall said. Franklin tried to hide all the frustration from his face.

"Chief James and Sergeant Penny have a portable battery charger to help you resurrect this deuce-and-a-half," Marshall informed Franklin.

Franklin felt a bit embarrassed.

"Thank you Captain Marshall, Sir," he stammered.

"No problem, Soldier," Marshall replied. He hoped Franklin would start paying attention to the fact that it was winter. Things left outside tended to freeze up.

As the wind blew colder, Marshall decided it was time to walk over to the shop office and meet with Chief Farley.

When Marshall entered the shop office, the soothing smell of fresh hot coffee greeted him. He helped himself to a cup and casually walked over to the maintenance production board to see the status of the jobs in the shop.

Farley greeted the commander as he entered his office. He walked over to the coffee pot to refill his cup, making sure Marshall saw him drop a quarter into the coffee fund donation can.

Marshall smiled, reached into his pocket for a quarter, and did the same.

"An offering to the entity that gets us through wintertime drills," Marshall joked.

Farley laughed.

"I see you're checking out the production board," Farley said. "As you can see, we've only got our equipment in shop now, Sir. I thought it best to clear out the rest of the jobs that belonged to other units."

"Good thinking Chief," said Marshall. "I'm glad to see things are moving in the right direction. That is, attention moving in the direction of our own equipment. Now tell me, do you think our equipment will make it to Fort Knox?"

Chief Farley reflected on the question momentarily.

"Everything should be OK, except for the 20-ton crane," Farley said. "But we really don't need to take that monster to A.T.. I'm amazed the Army still wants to keep that beast in the inventory."

Sergeant First Class Robert Bradley, the shop NCO, chimed in with his experience on the 20-ton crane.

"We had 'em in Vietnam, Sir, and gave 'em all to the engineer units," Bradley said. "Nice piece of equipment as long as you ran them everyday. Other than me, Sergeant Bitsko is the only qualified operator we've got in the unit."

The 20-ton rough terrain crane was a beautiful and expensive piece of Army equipment developed for off-loading large amounts of heavy cargo from supply ships and railcars. It was engineered to go off-road in nearly every type of environment, from desert sand to Alaskan wilderness.

The problem everyone had with the 20-ton crane was during peacetime because they were never used. They were too big to bring indoors, so the cranes just sat outside and slowly deteriorated. When they were needed after sitting for years, they would not always work.

"The crane might not run so well and would definitely be difficult to haul," Marshall said thoughtfully. "I'll take that under consideration."

He turned to Farley to ask him about other matters.

"How are you coming along on coordination efforts with your old buddy at Boatwright?" Marshall asked.

"Captain, I've got great news," Farley said. "My buddy tells me they've got their hands full with jobs in-shop and they have to get them out in the shortest amount of time possible. He said if we process a formal written request, specifically asking that our soldiers work as assistants to his technicians, he would approve it."

Marshall knew any training, even watching others working on the equipment, was better than none.

"Chief, we'll just have to start talking with the right people and get the paperwork going," Marshall said. "It's time Major Breedlow got involved. If you can spare a moment, let's go pay him a visit."

Marshall and Farley climbed into the Marshall's tan 1980 Buick Electra to drive back to the 683rd Orderly Room.

"Sergeant Bradley seems to be somewhat quiet," Marshall said to Farley as they navigated the pot-holed access road. "How long have you been working with him?"

"I've known Bob for over eight years," Farley said. "He and I were in the same company in Vietnam. Bob's one of the best automotive repairmen I know. He just loves working on mechanical equipment. It helps to keep his mind off things."

"Keep his mind off things, Chief?" Marshall asked.

"Well, Captain, Bob has his good days and bad days. We lost some good soldiers over in Vietnam. Bob's brother was one of 'em. He's still missing in action."

The Electra pulled up at the 683rd orderly room, and Marshall and Farley got out of the car. They headed next door to the 694th Maintenance Battalion Headquarters to see Major Breedlow. Their first order of business was to ensure the 683rd track and tank turret sections would have permission to work in Boatwright during A.T..

Breedlow was sitting in his office when Marshall and Farley walked in and saluted.

"Gentlemen! To what do I owe this pleasure?" Breedlow called to greet them. "You look happy. Please don't tell me that some of your problem children have been transferred to my section."

Marshall grinned.

"Sir, problem children behave once you've shown them some tough love," Marshall said. "I'm not dropping anyone off at the battalion orphanage just yet."

"Well that's a relief," Breedlow said with a smile. "What can I do for you?"

"Remember that matter of needing more pertinent work and better training that I discussed with you last month." Marshall asked. Breedlow nodded. "Chief Farley has hit on a great solution for us, but we need your help."

Major Breedlow smiled as Chief Farley explained the plan to get some of the 683rd's soldiers into Boatwright during A.T.. He pledged his support, and vowed to work with Chief Farley and lend assistance in the coordination effort.

"Now, Chief, fire up those typing fingers," Breedlow said to Farley. "It's paperwork time!"

Farley chuckled. It was true. The Army had enough paperwork to overwhelm any enemy with bureaucracy as well as tactics.

After leaving Breedlow's office, Marshall went into his own. He glanced at paperwork on his desk when he heard a slight knock from Lieutenant Rodriguez.

"Captain Marshall, we've got a new unit armorer assigned," Rodriguez said. "She's in the first sergeant's office."

The unit armorer was responsible for maintaining, securing and accounting for all the unit's weapons. When that task was accomplished, and the arms room was locked up, the unit armorer would assist the unit supply sergeant with the daily operations in the unit supply room.

"That's excellent news," said Marshall. "How long has it been since we've had a unit armorer?"

"More than a year, Sir," Rodriguez said.

"Well, let's hope that year ends now," Marshall said. "When the first sergeant is done, have her report to me for her initial interview and welcome."

"Yes, Sir," Rodriguez said. "She's already finished in-processing. She's transferring in from active duty, and she looks like she'll be a real ass-set." Rodriguez was grinning the entire time he was talking about the new unit armorer.

Why was Lieutenant Rodriguez smiling so much, Marshall wondered. Had somebody already told him the good news? And why had he mispronounced "asset?"

"From the grin on your face, I'm guessing you expected this, but I wanted to tell you myself," Marshall said. "I've been tasked to be the overall convoy commander for all units going to A.T. That means the 683rd needs a convoy commander. You're the senior lieutenant, so you're it. Congratulations." Rodriguez was shocked. This news had nothing to do with his grin. He had no idea what to say or do.

"Yes, Sir," Rodriguez said, quickly saluting and dropping the grin. He left the office and walked toward the orderly room's reference library. Rodriguez thought it was probably a good time to start learning about how to command a convoy.

After Rodriguez left, Marshall heard a singsong voice outside his door.

"Oh Captain!" The voice called with an equal measure of sass and smiles. "It's paperwork time! Get your pen ready because I know that signing these orders today is going to become one of your fondest memories in the U.S. Army Reserve. Ummh...ummh, sheer poetry."

Marshall chuckled as the figure of Sergeant Vivian Tea appeared in his doorway. She carried a manila folder bursting with papers in one hand and two new ballpoint pens in the other.

"Bring it on, Sergeant Tea," Marshall replied. "My entire military career has been building up to this point."

She smiled and set the paperwork down on Marshall's desk. Staff Sergeant Vivian Tea was a full-time treasure with a clairvoyant ability. Rarely would Marshall have to dictate a letter or request something to be typed up or processed. She was the finest clerical assistant he'd ever had the pleasure of working with in the military. At age 28, she had risen quickly through the ranks after being recruited in the stripes-for-skills program. The short-lived program recruited talented civilian applicants for immediate promotions to sergeant after they finished their initial military training.

Vivian Tea had a rare gift. She was brilliant, had a rapier wit, a funny and sarcastic way of treating her peers, and an unshakeable sense of duty and professionalism. She was a soldiers' soldier and a sergeants' sergeant.

As Marshall scribbled his signature on document after document, he wondered who possibly took the time to read and scrutinize it all. He surmised that the job went to some high-ranking bureaucratic paper pusher who justified their duty position by creating all the administrative paperwork requirements.

He heard First Sergeant Tisher's voice outside his office door.

"Report to the commander." Tisher's voice instructed.

Suddenly, Marshall thought, it felt like a cool breeze started blowing and sultry jazz music started playing in the background. A tall blonde woman entered into his office with a sensual smile on her face. Marshall blinked his eyes several times. His mind could not comprehend what was standing in front of him. She could have been walking down a runway at a fashion show. And the only person who Marshall had seen that looked that good in fatigues was his wife. Marshall noticed out of the corner of his eye that several male soldiers stood outside his open office doorway, gawking at the woman.

She snapped to attention and saluted Marshall.

"Good morning, sir," she said in a husky voice. "Specialist Francine Peoples, reporting for duty." She gave a subtle smile at the commander.

Marshall was momentarily surprised. Specialist Peoples was striking. Her beauty could cause quite a distraction to the men in the unit. But then again, he thought, she could probably soldier with the best of them.

Marshall returned Peoples' salute.

"Welcome to the 683rd Specialist Peoples. Have a seat," Marshall said.

Peoples gracefully sat down. Marshall signaled with his hand for Tisher to come in to the office. He was well aware of what others might think or imply. In a flash, Tisher entered Marshall's office, almost tripping over a chair in the small office. Marshall sighed inwardly. His office door stayed open.

"Thank you, sir," said Peoples in a low, breathy voice. "I'm glad to find a unit who needed a unit armorer. That's my primary MOS, my secondary MOS is unit supply clerk."

The 683rd had been without unit supply clerks and a unit armorer for more than a year. With annual training coming, she couldn't have come at a better time. Marshall tried to ignore the gawking male soldiers that stood outside his office. They probably agreed with him that Peoples appeared at the right time.

"Your skills in both areas are definitely needed, and we're glad to have you," Marshall said with a friendly smile. Peoples smiled back.

He briefed her on the 683rd's mission. Peoples nodded sincerely.

"Captain, I may not look it, but I am a hard worker and will put everything into my duty position," Peoples said. "I will pull my weight in this unit, and I promise, I won't let this unit down." Peoples looked Marshall straight in the eyes, again smiling coyly as she spoke.

Marshall cleared his throat. He was getting a little uncomfortable. He decided to ignore Peoples' subtle come-ons.

"Like I said before, welcome aboard," Marshall said to Peoples. "We're looking forward to having you with us."

He trained his gaze on Tisher.

"Specialist Peoples, report to First Sergeant Tisher's office. He'll give your further instructions and an in-briefing. Dismissed."

Tisher and Peoples stood and saluted Marshall, and Tisher led the way back to his office. As he started walking out the door, Tisher banged his shoulder against the doorframe and bounced abruptly out of the office. Marshall stifled his laughter until Tisher and Peoples were out of earshot. He then quietly chuckled and shook his head in amazement.

In the first sergeant's office, Tisher looked over Peoples' paperwork from active duty. He was impressed. That pretty young girl had racked up more commendations than most soldiers did in 10 years of service.

Peoples smiled at him.

"Does my paperwork surprise you, Top?" she asked. "It surprises most people. I don't know why. I'm a soldier first."

Tisher's face colored with embarrassment. He looked up at Peoples' probing gaze, thinking he had a daughter her age. Avoiding looking directly at her, Tisher finally spoke.

"Welcome to the 683rd, Peoples," he stammered. His mind immediately went into overdrive. Man, this gal's looks just might create some problems.

"Thank you, First Sergeant," Peoples replied. She reached out to shake his hand. As she grabbed his hand and gave it a firm handshake, Tisher felt a rushing tingle. Wow, he thought. Her hands were soft.

He cleared his throat loudly. This was no way for the First Sergeant to behave. He decided to get tough toward the new specialist.

"You know about the FBI background check we've got to do on you because of the security regulations concerning the Arms Room," Tisher said. "Anything you wanna tell me now that the FBI will find out about you anyway?"

It was Peoples' turn to blush.

"Well Top, I got caught with a man in my tent in the field," she said slowly. "That incident created quite a stir."

Tisher grinned and chuckled at the thought.

"So who was the lucky guy?" Tisher asked.

Peoples smiled coyly.

"My last company commander," she said.

Tisher stifled a laugh. Again, he pondered if she might become a problem child for the 683rd.

Meanwhile, Lieutenant Stiles sat with Sergeant First Class Huddle in a corner of the unit orderly room. Stiles was trying to put together the A.T. training schedule, but could barely think straight after an all-night party the night before.

"Sergeant Huddle, I told the Old Man that I would get this training schedule done today," Stiles said with a hint of despair creeping into her voice. "I can't come up with any ideas!"

"Quit trying to re-invent the wheel, Ma'am!" Huddle said.

"Just copy an old A.T. schedule that the unit did a few years back," Huddle said. "I'll find something in the files we can use. We'll just retype with different dates and send it forward for approval."

Stiles looked up at Huddle.

"You think that'll work?" she asked hopefully.

"Sure thing, Ma'am," replied Huddle. "No one ever looks at the damn thing, much less uses it. Our last commander thought pre-planned training was a waste of time. Everything changes once you get in the field. We'll just submit an oldie but goodie and let the Old Man change it once we get to A.T."

"Sergeant Huddle, this could be the beginning of a beautiful friendship," Stiles said with a smile. "Let's find an old schedule, do some typing, and get outta here."

Huddle yanked open a creaky metal filing cabinet.

"Ma'am, by the time higher headquarters approves this schedule and returns it, we'll be loadin' up for A.T.," Huddle said.

"That's great because I got loaded last night and need to go back to bed," Stiles said. Both of them started pawing through the files looking for an old schedule.

As the day dragged on, Marshall alternated signing paperwork and having horrific visions of his soldiers bumbling their duties while gaping at Specialist Peoples.

While Marshall signed and sighed, Lieutenant Kate Kiley drove up to the unit orderly room to speak the commander. Her husband, Staff Sergeant Fred Kiley, was a section NCO in the service section. Lieutenant Kiley was the 1st automotive platoon leader. While Marshall was well versed in husbands and wives both serving in the Army, he never dealt with a husband and wife serving in the same unit before.

Lieutenant Kiley softly knocked on Marshall's office door, distracting him from a particularly ghastly vision of Private Franklin behind the wheel of a 20-ton crane and running into all of the unit's other vehicles because Franklin was staring at the new unit armorer.

"Sir, may I see you about a personal matter?" Lieutenant Kiley asked.

Marshall looked up and smiled.

"Sure, come on in. Have a seat," he said. "Glad to take a break from the paperwork. What's going on?"

Lieutenant Kiley quietly closed the door to the office before sitting on the gray steel folding chair.

"Sir, I've got a problem with one of my NCOs," Kiley mentioned in a soft voice, not wanting to be overheard.

Marshall had always known there was potential for officer and NCO personality conflicts. Overcoming difficult personalities and a willingness to work together were important abilities for junior officers to possess.

"How so?" questioned Marshall.

Kiley didn't hesitate.

"It's Sergeant Lufton, Sir," Marshall mentally flipped through the soldiers to determine who Lufton was. After a moment, Marshall recalled that he had the look of a 1970s rock star, with hair a little bit on the unruly side.

Lufton's hair obviously made an impression on Lieutenant Kiley as well.

"I've told him that if he didn't get a haircut, I'd send him home without pay for the weekend," she said. "He's been obstinate and won't listen to me. He doesn't show respect, and personally, Sir, I know he doesn't like me."

Marshall nodded.

"Relax, Lieutenant," he told Kiley. "Let's start off with the fact that you can't send him home without pay. Only I can. Secondly, the fact that Lufton's haircut isn't to your standards doesn't mean that it does not meet Army standards. Remember, Elvis Presley's haircut met Army standards."

Kiley nervously laughed. Marshall continued.

"Personality conflicts are a part of life as an officer," Marshall said. "You'll always have your detractors and those who won't like you, but they'll follow your orders."

"But don't worry about Sergeant Lufton. I'll have the First Sergeant talk to him," Marshall said.

Kiley seemed to be both surprised and relieved.

"Thank you, sir," she said, getting up to leave. She slowly walked toward the door, then quickly turned around and walked back to Marshall's desk. If she was going to ask, she reasoned, now was the time.

"There is one more thing," Lieutenant Kiley said. "You know Sergeant Kiley and I are married, right?"

Marshall wondered where this was going.

"Yes, so I've been told," he replied. "How long have you been married to each other?"

"Fred and I were married three years ago when I was a spec-4 and he was a sergeant," Kiley said. "I applied to go to OCS and was accepted. We both decided it would be a good career move. Fred has been so supportive and wants what is best for both of us."

Marshall's nepotism alarm started to go off. He began to suspect that Kiley may want to have her husband in her platoon. Time to nip that request in the bud.

"You know, Lieutenant, that a husband and wife cannot be in the same platoon," Marshall said. "That would cause a problem when it came to the NCO evaluation report being unbiased, and the other soldiers might not be comfortable with a husband and wife team together in the same platoon."

Kiley shook her head.

"Oh no Sir," she replied. "Fred is very happy in the platoon he's in already. I wouldn't want him to be in my platoon. That would cause problems."

So why was she still here, Marshall wondered.

"I'm glad you agree," Marshall said. "I've been very impressed by both of you so far, and I want you to know that I do not have a problem with a husband and wife team in the same unit. As long as you are not in a position to be his direct superior, there is no problem."

"I'm glad, sir." Kiley smiled at Marshall. Suddenly, her mode and mannerisms became very shy. She started avoiding looking him in the eye. "But, um, I was hoping that Fred and I would be allowed to sleep in the same tent in the field at annual training. Since I'm not his supervisor and all. Um, yeah."

Marshall was surprised that Lieutenant Kiley was even asking this question.

"Lieutenant Kiley, none of the married soldiers will be sleeping with their spouses in the field for two weeks, and neither should you," Marshall said. "That would set a bad example for the soldiers and bring a lot of criticism on you. Besides, you're going to be the OIC for those personnel working at Boatwright, so you'll be staying on main post."

Lieutenant Kiley was supremely embarrassed. Because she had the higher rank, her husband insisted that she ask Marshall for permission. Now the new commander might have the impression she was some kind of nymphomaniac, she thought. She was going to let Fred wait until after the drill was over before she would give him Marshall's views on the matter, along with a piece of her mind for having been put to the task. "You're right, sir, but I thought I'd ask," Lieutenant Kiley said awkwardly. She got up to leave.

Marshall, not wanting the conversation to end on a sour note, added the only slightly complimentary thing he could think of.

"I appreciate your candor, Lieutenant Kiley," he said.

"Thank you Sir. I'm a little embarrassed," she replied, looking at her feet.

Marshall smiled.

"It's no problem, Lieutenant. This is just between you, me and your husband." Marshall said confidently.

"With regards to Sergeant Lufton, I'll have the First Sergeant look into the matter," Marshall finished.

"Thank you, Sir," Kiley said, saluting smartly. She exited the commander's office.

Marshall decided to abandon his paperwork for a while to visit First Sergeant Tisher and ask him about this situation of Lieutenant Kiley and Sergeant Lufton. Marshall tapped on Tisher's door as he was hanging up his telephone. Tisher used his hands to beckon Marshall to come inside.

"Top, what's going on with Lieutenant Kiley and Sergeant Lufton?" Marshall asked.

Tisher rolled his eyes.

"Captain, that's Mr. McCarthy's influence at work," he said. "She doesn't know how good an NCO she's got."

Marshall trusted First Sergeant Tisher's judgment when it came to NCO business. However, he wanted to get to the bottom of the situation.

"Lieutenant Kiley said Sergeant Lufton's haircut isn't regulation and wants to send him home with no pay," Marshall said. "She also said he doesn't like her. Sounds to me like this might go a little deeper than Chief McCarthy's influence here."

Oh boy, Tisher thought. Another chance to see how Marshall handles the never-ending soap opera of the 683rd.

"Sir, I'll have Sergeant Lufton report to your office pronto," Tisher said.

As Marshall went back to his office, Tisher got on the phone and called the shop. While walking, Marshall could have sworn he heard Tisher yelling into the phone: "Jerry, get your butt up here to the Old Man's office now!"

Within 10 minutes, Sergeant First Class Jerry Lufton walked into Tisher's office. He raked a hand through his mop of hair.

"Hey Top, what's going on?" Lufton asked, brushing snow off his field jacket.

Tisher gave his young sergeant a hard look.

"Jerry, your lieutenant wants your butt in a sling," Tisher said.

Lufton groaned. He had been expecting this.

"Top, I didn't have a chance to get a haircut before drill," he said. "I was out of town on a job all week, and drove over 350 miles to get here." Lufton touched his hair again. "Besides, don't you think I look like George Harrison?"

Tisher had no time for shenanigans and ignored the question.

"Come on," he said to Lufton. "Let's you and me see the Old Man."

Tisher strolled over to the commander's office, which was located next to his, and lightly rapped on the open door. Marshall looked up, glad for another distraction from the mounds of paperwork.

"Beggin' your pardon, sir," Tisher said. "I've got Sergeant Lufton here to see you."

Marshall looked at his watch. It had taken Lufton only 14 minutes to get there. Marshall loved a punctual soldier.

"Come in," Marshall said.

Both walked in, Lufton saluted and reported. Marshall opened his mouth to speak, but Lufton interrupted him.

"Sir, I apologize for not having a haircut to Army standards," Lufton said. "I was out of town on a construction project and couldn't get to a barbershop before drill."

Marshall surveyed Lufton's appearance. He looked like an unkempt version of George Harrison, though nowhere near as handsome. Lufton's hair was getting long and his mustache needed trimming. His uniform looked like he slept in it and his boots needed a shine.

"Sergeant Lufton, I'll let you slide this time," Marshall said. "You know the standards, and one of my personal standards is that all NCOs and officers set a good example to the soldiers. I'm confident you'll meet those standards next drill. Otherwise I'll have no choice but to send you home – and to a barbershop — without pay."

Lufton, standing stock still in front of the commander's desk, barked a reply.

"Sir, there won't be a next time," he said. Marshall was pleased.

"Very good, Sergeant. I'll take your word on that," said Marshall. "I'd also like to see a pressed uniform, shined boots, and a trimmed mustache as well. I'm sure that's not asking too much?"

"No Sir!" Lufton immediately responded.

"Wonderful," Marshall said. "On a different note, how are you and your platoon leader getting along?"

Lufton squirmed a little.

"Permission to speak freely?" he asked. Marshall nodded.

"Well Sir, it's a difficult situation." Lufton replied. "You see, I was her platoon sergeant when she was a private. I think she's just giving me back the same grief I gave her. Truthfully, I've had it comin', I used to be pretty mean to her when she was one of my grunts. You know the saying sir, what goes around comes around."

Marshall was shocked. Not only were two married Kileys in the same unit, but one who was a newly commissioned second lieutenant was now her old sergeant's boss. Marshall looked at Tisher and shook his head.

"Top, on active duty this doesn't happen," said Marshall. "A newly commissioned officer is never assigned to the unit she came from."

Tisher chuckled with delight.

"Sir, this ain't active duty, and in case you haven't noticed, the rules don't necessarily apply here."

Marshall shook his head more. Time to make the rules apply.

"Sergeant Lufton, you have a situation that should be changed," Marshall said. "Are you willing to transfer to another platoon in the unit?"

Before Lufton could answer, Tisher interjected.

"Beggin' your pardon sir, but why not transfer Lieutenant Kiley instead?" Tisher asked. "Jerry here has signed the hand-receipt for all the property in the section. You know that means he is responsible and accountable for everything they've got, and switching him would create a lot more work. An inventory for both the first and second auto platoons would take us until A.T., and they wouldn't be able to get any other work done between now and then. Switching the officers will only take ten minutes, since they're not signed for anything."

Marshall liked the Tisher's plan.

"Good thinking, Top," he said. "I'll have Lieutenants Smith and Kiley switch platoons. That will cause the least amount of hassles and should resolve the problem." He looked at Lufton. "Is that OK with you?" Marshall asked.

Lufton loved what he heard. He respected Lieutenant Smith.

"Yes Sir!" he yelled. "Thank you! Thank you! Thank you! I owe you one."

Marshall felt good.

"You're welcome Sarge, and I'll remember that you owe me one," Marshall said. "Just promise me you'll set a good example from now on."

Lufton snapped a salute to his commander.

Marshall looked at his watch. It was about time to end the day's drill.

"Carry on, Sergeant!" he said as he returned the salute. "Now we'd all better get going to formation."

Precisely eight minutes later, the soldiers of the 683rd were standing at attention in formation in the parking lot behind the Reserve Center. Marshall noticed that Lieutenant Kiley seemed to be glowering at her husband, and several soldiers were ogling Specialist Peoples out of the corners of their eyes.

"At Ease!" Marshall shouted. "Soldiers, you've all been working hard these last few drills," Marshall said. "But I have one very important question for all of you. Who do you love?"

Quizzical looks came into the eyes of the soldiers. What kind of a question was this?

Someone in the back of the formations yelled back, "The new armorer!"

Everyone in the formation started laughing, and Marshall too found it hard to resist not laughing.

"And we are very glad to have Specialist Peoples as the new unit armorer." The soldiers began to applaud and whistle simultaneously.

Marshall quickly replied, "You didn't give me that warm a welcome." All the soldiers laughed at the comparison. Peoples was definitely better looking than Marshall.

Marshall nodded and smiled. "As you may know, tomorrow is Valentine's Day. There is no drill scheduled for tomorrow. Be with those dear to you. See you in March. Dismissed!"

MARCH DRILL - SATURDAY

After a relatively easy February, the personnel of the 683rd Maintenance Company arrived at Ravenna Army Ammunition Plant ready for business. Everyone was busily preparing for their big training event in July. Soldiers diligently worked in the shop, readying the equipment and themselves. Paperwork prepared by the unit's admin team was entering the military's large river of paper, and Sergeant Lonnie Adkins was a little cagey, having given up cigarettes two weeks ago. Lieutenant Meglynn spent 10 minutes at her desk before spilling coffee. Not a single red hat was worn with a uniform, though Tisher could have sworn he saw one of the mechanics use what used to be a proudly worn red ascot to wipe oil off of a deuce-and-a-half's dipstick.

In the month since he'd been in his office, Captain Marshall found that about a foot of paperwork had accumulated on his desk. Sighing, he delegated the morning formation to First Sergeant Tisher and got ready to get writer's cramp.

After spending 15 minutes listening to Tisher tell them what they had to do during the weekend drill, Second Lieutenant Sarah Burks had a lot of things on her mind. There was so much to do at drill, and having a commander who seemed to know what he was doing made her nervous. Burks only met Marshall at his initial introduction and briefing in January, but she could tell he knew exactly what her platoon – tech supply – would be required to do at A.T. Burks, on the other hand, had no idea what her platoon was supposed to do at A.T. Now, she reasoned, was the perfect time to find out.

Sarah Burks was a senior in college, and another early commissioning program recipient. Her major was in sociology, with a minor in human relations. She was single and had short black hair, a slender build and a desire to succeed. Serving in the Army Reserve before entering active duty was a good way to gain experience, she thought, and she felt she was ready to be tested and become a better officer. Well, as long as she had some clue about what she was supposed to do.

Burks softly tapped on Marshall's door.

"May I come in, sir?" she asked.

Marshall gladly looked up from the ominous stack of paperwork that did not seem to get smaller, despite the scores of pages he had already signed.

"Sure. What's on your mind?" Marshall asked, gesturing for Burks to take a seat.

Burks quietly entered the office and sat in one of the uncomfortable steel folding chairs that was pushed against the wall. She looked around the office for some token of personality. A photo, a knickknack, a weird coffee mug. Anything to start him off easily, since she was about to admit to him that she knew nothing about what she should know everything about.

Having no luck, she slowly let out a deep breath and got right to the point.

"I need to know what you want my section to take to annual training, Sir," Burks said.

Marshall shifted his weight in his chair and wondered if this was another test from his two favorite detractors in the tech supply platoon—Chief McCarthy and Sergeant Schmoot. Marshall wondered if Burks had been listening to him. One of the directives he had repeated on numerous occasions was to take every piece of equipment each platoon had.

Marshall focused on Burks' mannerisms and body language, as the young lieutenant began fidgeting in the steel chair. He could just envision McCarthy and Schmoot trying to intimidate her. In Marshall's head, he could hear McCarthy loudly asking Schmoot if he thought their young officer would get her act together by the time A.T. comes around. Burks shuddered, as if she could hear the voices echoing in her head too.

"What are your people doing during drill?" Marshall asked, breaking Burks' reverie.

Burks froze. Oh no! A direct question! Despair began trickling through her veins. The new commander will know instantly that what Chief McCarthy and Sergeant Schmoot said about her not knowing anything was true, she thought. She took her time in answering, not wanting to appear unable to handle the responsibilities of commanding her platoon, and not wanting her lack of confidence to show through.

"Right now I've got them doing maintenance on all our vehicles, but I don't know which ones to take to A.T.," she said slowly and evenly.

Aha, thought Marshall. McCarthy and Schmoot were using their relative experience in terms of age—and supreme laziness—to keep tight control of the tech supply platoon out of Lieutenant Burks' hands. Taking a couple pieces of equipment to A.T. would not require the tech supply section to work very hard to get things ready, meaning that McCarthy and Schmoot would be able to spend more of their drill time doing nothing and Burks would be the one left looking irresponsible.

"How much equipment does your platoon have?" asked Marshall, already knowing the answer.

"Three deuce-and-a-halves, and four 12-ton trailers with one 5-ton tractor," Burks said automatically. Marshall nodded his head. At least Burks knew something and wasn't as clueless as Marshall sensed she felt.

"Take 'em all," Marshall replied. "You'll need every piece of equipment in the field to perform your tech supply mission."

"But Sir, I've only got 16 people in my section," Burks said. "Only four have valid military driver's licenses. How will it all get there?"

Marshall restrained himself from wincing. Burks sounded like a teenage girl. A whining officer doesn't stand much of a chance in the military—or in the civilian world, for that matter.

Marshall decided to go over the facts and plans of the upcoming A.T. mission with Burks to better explain the situation.

"Listen, I know how important it is to have everything in the field to perform your mission," Marshall said. "When I was on active duty, my unit went into the field to discover we had left something behind, which came back to haunt us. It made us feel stupid. And Lieutenant, be it a ridge-pole on a GP medium tent or a hydraulic press, a maintenance company needs everything to do its job effectively." Burks nodded in understanding.

"If you look at the time remaining before A.T., we've got four months—or a total of eight days—to get all our people trained to be drivers and all our equipment operational and loaded for the trip," Marshall continued. "I've got Chief James and Farley working on borrowing some additional equipment for this A.T., including three additional 5-ton tractors to haul all of your platoon's trailers. Chief James is conducting driver's training classes in the motor pool office. I do hope you've already got some of your people attending those classes."

Burks' expression was still grim.

"I understand, sir, but I thought we'd only be taking what we had, which means we would need a total of four drivers."

Marshall smiled, knowing Burks had been lead astray. However, he knew something Burks didn't.

"Lieutenant Burks, I know you've got at least two more drivers: Mr. McCarthy and Sergeant Schmoot," Marshall said. "If your section can't get a few soldiers trained up before A.T., I'm sure those two will be glad to fill in and be drivers."

Burks finally broke into a smile.

"Yes Sir. I think I get the picture," she said. "I'll get with them and see what we can do."

"Sounds good, Lieutenant." Marshall said.

Burks did not immediately turn to leave. She had another question, but the little voice inside her head told her to run away. However, she reasoned, she would not know the answer if she didn't ask the question. She swallowed and ignored the inner voice.

"One more thing, sir," she began. "We've got repair parts in the trailers left over from another unit. They used to have the mission of repair parts for the entire command. When they were de-activated, the 683rd took it over and inherited their trailers with all the parts dumped in."

Marshall grinned. At least they had a more sizeable inventory. An Army tech supply section is like a mobile auto parts store. Its mission is to have an adequate stock of parts – especially the parts that wear out quickly – to maintain the equipment of the other military units the maintenance company is supporting.

Marshall had experience with tech supply and their parts trailers. The tech supply platoon worked well when everything was inventoried and stored in defined locations. In the well-ordered tech supply, the records of how many parts the platoon had – and where they might be found – were maintained manually, and the number of repair parts the platoon needed were adjusted and restocked accordingly. When a tech supply platoon was functioning properly, it was a lifesaver. A fully functional pipeline of quickly repaired equipment was one of several vital factors to winning on the battlefield.

Marshall knew it took a long time to set up parts trailers correctly and asked Burks the progress of her platoon's work. "Have the parts been inventoried and placed in bins?" Marshall asked.

"Not yet, sir. We were starting that last drill," Burks replied. Marshall smiled.

"Sounds like your section has a lot to do here and at annual training," he said.

Burks nodded in agreement.

"Yes Sir, and we have a lot more work to get ready for it," she said, standing up. "Thank you for your advice, Sir."

Burks saluted and turned to leave the office, amazed at how easy talking to Marshall was. She thought that he would have made her feel stupid for not already knowing what to do. But actually, Burks reflected, she felt empowered.

Marshall ended the meeting with some parting guidance. "Any time you have any questions, or any problems, don't hesitate to bring them to me," Marshall said. "That's using the chain of command. You've got my support, Lieutenant."

Burks smiled and exited the office, ready to take charge of her tech supply platoon and give it some needed direction. As she walked toward her section, she started thinking of appropriate ways to deal with the two rabble-rousers who had made her feel so unprepared.

Second Lieutenant Sean Smith and Lieutenant Kate Kiley were in the shop switching platoons as instructed by Captain

Marshall. In actuality, these two soldiers exchanging positions was just a minor paper shuffle. However, both officers needed to talk over the nitty-gritty of personnel and equipment issues. Smith was agreeable to the switch, but more than a little confused.

"Kate, I really don't know why the Old Man directed us to do this, but orders are orders," he said.

Sean Smith was a young, dedicated officer who wanted to learn as much as he could to become an effective leader. He too, was a senior in college, majoring in law enforcement. The early commissioning program was his opportunity to gain experience in the military and help earn some extra money to pay his college expenses. Sean was more than six feet tall and was in excellent physical condition with a slender and muscular build. He was articulate, handsome, intelligent and married. Like the other early commissioning program lieutenants in the 683rd, he too had not been to his training course.

Kiley laughed.

"There is a very good reason," she said. "You don't know this, Sean, but Sergeant Lufton was my supervisor when I was enlisted."

Smith was surprised.

"I didn't know you were a grunt, Kate," he said. "I'm impressed!"

"Thank you," she said quietly. She decided to tell him how she moved up the ranks to become a commissioned officer, something she never told anybody. Knowing that her husband would appreciate it, Kiley especially highlighted Fred's support for her to enter officer candidate school.

"Being a commissioned officer has its advantages, and I owe it all to Fred. He motivated me to go through OCS and get my commission," Kiley told Smith. "Now I'm trying to motivate him to become a warrant officer."

Smith smiled at Kate's comments. He liked working with her, and didn't mind having a fellow officer being a female. He thought the Army's policy of introducing female officers, NCOs and soldiers into the non-combat units was a very good idea. They brought a great deal of talent that was overlooked in the past. He briefly wondered if this meant he should be just as supportive with his wife's Avon sales.

Smith had a new level of respect for Kate, but didn't get the big picture.

"That's cool, but why the switch of platoons between you and me?" he asked.

Kiley thought Smith had already figured it out. She carefully selected her words to precisely explain the situation. "Captain Marshall doesn't like the situation of Sergeant Lufton, who was my section sergeant when I was enlisted, being in the same platoon with me. He says it's awkward."

Something in Smith's head clicked.

"I can see his point. It's an awkward position to be in."

Kiley chuckled and shrugged.

"I didn't think so," she said. "I was looking forward to getting even."

Chief James, Sergeant Lemasters, and Sergeant David Mulberry were talking with Sergeant Tea in the unit orderly room. Sergeant Tea was everyone's favorite NCO. Her sense of humor and professionalism made all 683rd personnel appreciate her being there – even Chief McCarthy.

Sergeant Tea's eyes sparkled as she looked at her favorite teasing target.

"Sergeant Lemasters," she began, "you gonna take care of me out in the field in my delicate condition?" She patted her abdomen gently.

The three men looked like they had just been jolted with a cattle prod.

"Vivian, are you pregnant?" Chief James asked in amazement.

"Uhm uhm uhm, Mr. James, you are so sharp this mornin'," Tea said, playfully tapping him on the arm. "Tyron and I just found out last night."

The men weren't quite sure what to say. Pregnancy was a woman thing, and not usually an Army thing.

Sergeant Mulberry quickly broke the awkward silence.

"That's fantastic Viv," he said, giving Tea the brightest smile he could produce under the circumstances. "I guess you'll want to be excused from A.T. I'll go ahead and process the paperwork."

Mulberry turned to leave the office, get away from the pregnant lady, and start the paperwork. Tea suddenly changed to a serious demeanor.

"Don't you dare!" she said. "If anyone is gonna process paperwork, it will come from me. I've been looking forward to some fresh air and being away from this stinky, smoke-filled place and my hubby for a while. Besides, I've got to take care of the rest of my Reservist children in the field." She smiled and rocked back and forth in her padded swivel chair, looking at the surprised faces to her immediate front.

Sergeant Lemasters smiled and treated Tea like one of the guys.

"Don't worry Vivian. You ain't gonna get any special treatment from me," he said.

Tea let out a small laugh as she smiled at her favorite NCO and fluttered her eyelashes.

"Oh Honey, I wasn't expectin' any from you. I wouldn't want you changin' on account of lil' ol' me." Tea giggled while acting out her southern belle charm.

The men all chuckled, feeling a little more at ease.

"Viv, how far along will you be at A.T.?" Mulberry asked. "Are you gonna be, um, you know…" Mulberry tripped over his words, but made motions with his hands indicating a big belly.

"I'll be in my fifth month," replied Tea. "If this baby is anything like my first, I won't be showing until my sixth month. But who knows, right now I feel like eating everything in sight."

She looked at Sergeant First Class Lemasters and sweetly smiled.

"John, could you get me some cantaloupe with a couple scoops of French vanilla ice cream in the middle?"

Lemasters rolled his eyes towards the ceiling, knowing she was playing with him again.

"That's jist what we need in the field: a hungry, crabby pregnant female in my section," he said, throwing up his hands. "Mercy sakes alive, you're a handful already."

Tea smiled.

"I bet you say that to all the pregnant soldiers, don't you hun?" she asked. The verbal sparring had begun.

Lemasters became serious.

"Honestly Vivian, I never had to deal with a pregnant soldier in the field," he said.

She smiled coyly. She had Lemasters right where she wanted him. She put her hand on his shoulder.

"Don't you worry none. I won't disappoint you, Sergeant Lemasters. This baby will be our little secret," Tea said.

Everyone in the orderly room laughed. Lemasters chuckled, turned bright red, and shook his head in disbelief.

"All right everyone! Back to work!" he said, hoping the scarlet hue was diminishing from his face.

Lemasters took his own advice and grabbed some binders from a bookshelf. He had been designated as the field first sergeant. It was not an official position, but a necessary one that First Sergeant Tisher felt compelled to assign. Lemasters' duties in this unofficial position were to assist the commander and first sergeant and look after the soldiers. There were times when more than one NCO was needed to fill the role as the first sergeant, especially in a field environment. Enter the field first sergeant. With a unit as large as the 683rd, it was a necessity. And with only a few months before A.T., he needed to start planning.

Sergeant First Class Terry Siler and Lieutenant Rodriguez were in the motor park, walking around and looking at the condition of vehicles. Sergeant Siler was a seasoned NCO who had seen it all. Well, at least he had seen all that a man in his mid-thirties could see. He was a Vietnam War veteran and enjoyed serving in the Army Reserve. With 17 years of service under his belt, he was counting the days until he'd reached 20 years of service and, more importantly, earned a retirement he could start collecting when he turned 60. He would be sad to leave the Army Reserves behind, but as a consolation could spend more time enjoying his family life and fishing on the weekends on the beautiful blue waters of Lake Erie.

Even though the weather was starting to be a bit milder, the ground was still snow covered and slushy, making walking a haphazard and messy chore. Lieutenant Rodriguez was worried about his responsibilities for the convoy.

"Sarge, we've got to get the drivers and assistant drivers list to the Old Man by the end of drill," Rodriguez said nervously. "Who's going to be the lead vehicle in the convoy? Who gets the radio? This is so much to handle! We've got to put this all together in less than two days."

Sergeant Siler chuckled softly at the lieutenant's nervousness.

"No sweat L.T.," Siler replied matter-of-factly. "I've done this before.

"We just change the names on the assigned vehicle roster with those drivers we've got and those that we're training. Those getting their military drivers licenses will be the assistant drivers. To determine the three groups of vehicles traveling in the convoy, we just divide the total amount of vehicles by three and stagger them at five-minute intervals."

Rodriguez stared at Siler, mouth agape. Siler obviously knew what he was taking about. Rodriguez began to feel a little more confident, but wondered why the Old Man hadn't put Siler in charge.

Siler continued his explaining.

"As for the vehicles with radios, the only one that needs a radio will be the convoy commander's jeep. That'll be you, Sir," Siler said.

Siler patted Rodriguez on the back and winked at him.

"Don't worry L.T.," Siler said. "I'll be ridin' with you. Nothing will go wrong."

Rodriguez smiled. He hoped Siler was right.

"I'm glad that you've got that all figured out," Rodriguez said. "How do we organize the serials, the groups that we go in for the convoy? What about the 5-ton wreckers? Where are they placed in the convoy?"

Siler knew that the lieutenant was far from confident about this job. But he knew from experience just where to place the 5-ton wreckers in a convoy road march.

"They go in the last serial, called the trail party, so they can pick up all the broken down vehicles along the way," Siler said.

He ignored Rodriguez shaking his head and muttering to himself that he should have figured that out himself.

"Judging by the shape of the tires on these vehicles, they'll be busy," Siler said. "We'll be the first vehicle in the second serial of the convoy. That way we can control all three."

Siler's confidence and experience still hadn't put Rodriguez's mind at ease.

"How do the 5-ton wreckers look?" Rodriguez asked. "Are the drivers experienced?"

Siler smiled at the worried lieutenant.

"The 5-ton wreckers are in great shape and we've got good people in the recovery section," Siler said. "They know what they're doin'. All you and I have to do is make sure that the assistant drivers have a good map and know where the hell they're goin'." He looked at Rodriguez. "Now, take a deep breath and calm down a bit."

As many frustrated motorists driving to their summer vacation destinations on the interstate highways know, a military convoy can stretch for miles and never go over the speed limit. Military convoys travel at convoy speed, which is 55 miles per hour. Accidents involving military convoys on the highways are rare due to the low speeds. Most accidents occur when military vehicles are doing training exercises on military posts. And, of course, in city traffic during rush hour.

Flat tires are a completely different subject. The active duty Army treated the Reserves like a little brother, sending them their hand-me-down equipment. The equipment was still in good condition, but, just like clothes passed down from one brother to another, the equipment was well-worn, faded, and kind of out of style. Active forces got the new equipment, and older equipment was sent back to the mechanic shop to be banged into "Code B" condition and given to the Reserves. Code B meant that the equipment would work, but had accumulated many years in service and many hours in the shop being worked on. The Code B vehicles were as close to new as possible, with new paint jobs, engines, transmissions, canvas, brakes and so on. But the tires were usually the originals. If they could hold air, Army mechanics would say, they were fair.

After taking his deep breath, Lieutenant Rodriguez did not feel much calmer. He kept asking Sergeant Siler questions, wanting to know as much as he could about the upcoming convoy.

"Now, Sergeant Nugot is the head of the recovery section," Rodriguez said. "I've heard he's got a peculiar nickname, Road Kill. How'd he get that name?"

Siler looked at Rodriguez with a surly smile.

"Sir, you don't want to be in a vehicle behind him. Trust me."

In the orderly room, Sergeant Mooney and Sergeant Lemasters were working on the list of equipment the headquarters platoon was taking to A.T. First Sergeant Tisher had delegated that task down to Lemasters, his field first sergeant. It was an exercise in aggravation. Looking over the checklist Tisher and Marshall had given him, Lemasters was visibly flustered at what the unit had to take.

"Dang it, Sergeant Mooney!" Lemasters yelled. "We're takin' all the weapons! Even them crew-served weapons, the M60 and M2 machine guns. That means you gotta update and submit your ammo forecast, or we'll be throwin' rocks at the targets on the ranges. The Old Man told me that everyone is going to qualify with his or her own weapon."

Mooney exhaled slowly. He told Marshall that getting everything together was a can-do situation, but now he was having some doubts about his abilities.

"Sarge, I know you don't want to hear this, but I don't know if we'll be able to get the ranges, much less the ammo."

Lemasters grunted under his breath. No, he didn't want to hear that. But he knew that Mooney had an ace in the hole.

"Jackie, you ain't gonna' let this company down," Lemasters said. "I know you can sweet talk any supply-type. Just make sure you bring some of yer extra tradin' materials with ya, OK?"

Mooney smiled conspiratorially. Every supply sergeant in the Army knew how to wheel-and-deal to get things done. Most of the time, they would trade some excess this for someone else's excess that. This was usually referred to as the underground supply pipeline. Even though everything that was traded stayed within the Army, this practice was frowned upon because it circumvented the supply system. It was also against regulations, and those who were caught could face criminal charges depending upon the severity of the infraction and the sensitivity of the goods being traded. Not that this stopped anyone from doing it.

One of the favorite items of trade was, and will always be…Army coffee.

Army coffee had a reputation for being the finest quality coffee in the world. It was highly prized for its rich, full-bodied flavor. In the mid 1970s, the Department of Defense decided to save a few million dollars a year by cheapening the coffee with less costly blend, which broke the hearts of thousands of coffee aficionados in the military. This single action may have contributed to the coffee shop boom in the Seattle area. But the military palate for superb coffee did not diminish with the cheaper blend.

Sergeant Mooney knew what Lemasters wanted him to do.

"OK!" replied Mooney. "But I'll need some extra time down at Fort Knox before the unit arrives to get things arranged, know what I mean?" Mooney winked at Lemasters. The two men were reading each other loud and clear.

"Jackie, I'll make sure the Old Man knows yer gonna need some extra time ta arrange the logistics," Lemasters said. "You jist better make sure thangs are gonna happen. Captain Marshall's in his office. Let's get with Top and let 'em know what needs to be done."

Both NCOs walked over to First Sergeant Tisher's office, past everyone in the orderly room, which was buzzing with work on the A.T. administrative paperwork requirements.

Tisher was in his office looking over rosters of personnel, determining which sections will have to be augmented by soldiers from other units who could not make their own annual training exercises due to scheduling conflicts. Army Reserve rules state that every soldier needs two weeks of A.T. each year.

Sergeant Lemasters and Mooney politely tapped on Tisher's door.

"Come on in," Tisher called, waving them inside.

Lemasters and Mooney entered the office, and quietly pulled the door closed behind them.

"Top, we've got a little plot that we want to let you in on," Mooney said.

Tisher turned to Mooney and Lemasters. "Tell me about your scheme," he said with a grin.

Tisher liked what he heard. Sending Sergeant Jackie Mooney to Fort Knox early was a great idea. He could do some advanced reconnoitering for the unit and get things started before the advanced party, which Tisher would be in charge of, arrived. Sergeant Mooney would be the 683rd's point man.

They went over what items needed to be requested and organized for the upcoming weapons qualification at annual training, and Tisher vigorously agreed that about 30 pounds of coffee was a necessity for the operation. Sergeant Lonnie Adkins would have to readjust his coffee requisition to handle the new requirement for Mooney's trading' material.

Before Lemasters and Mooney left Tisher's office, they had a solid plan. Mooney would leave for Fort Knox two weeks before the unit. With two additional weeks, he could sign for all the ranges, make sure the ammunition was ready to be drawn, and get the barracks buildings for the personnel working at Boatwright. He would make sure things went smoothly for the 683rd when they arrived in force at Fort Knox.

Mooney's second duffel bag would be extra bulky. Not just with clothes and gear for an additional fortnight, but with 15 two-pound cans of Army coffee. Those cans of coffee would be received with great welcome and appreciation.

"And don't worry," Tisher said as the two men turned to leave. "I'll make sure Lonnie brings our personal coffee supply."

As they laughed, Tisher heard a crinkle on his chair. He stood up, confused.

"What you sittin' on, Top?" Lemasters asked.

Tisher picked several pieces of paper up off the seat of his chair and started laughing.

"It's the maintenance augmentees!" he said with a laugh. "I asked one of the clerks to put the lists on my chair if I wasn't here. She did exactly what I asked her to do. I just wasn't looking before I sat down."

Lemasters grinned.

"Now if you gentlemen will excuse me, I have to be sure to thank Specialist Cork for a job well-done before drill finishes," Tisher said. He looked straight at Lemasters. "Sergeant Tea asked me to remind you about some cantaloupes with ice cream, by the way."

MARCH DRILL - SUNDAY MORNING

When First Sergeant Tisher entered the Reserve Center on Sunday morning, he was shocked. The center was actually humming. Yes, there were soldiers busy with maintenance, paperwork, planning, cleaning the center. But there was literally something humming!

He decided to concentrate on the busy soldiers and ignore the humming sound. But Tisher couldn't ignore it. It was driving him crazy! He watched the soldiers quickly come to morning formation, appearing excited for drill. Tisher would have been more impressed by this display, but ohhh, that infernal humming!

He sniffed the air. Someone had also been smoking a whole lot. He made a mental note to see who took the most smoke breaks. Whoever was smoking that much wouldn't be able to catch his breath at A.T.

Tisher handled the morning formation quickly.

"Soldiers, I'm not going to waste time with trivial information today," Tisher said loudly. "We've got a chain of command here, and I think you all know what you're supposed to be doing. Formal drivers training classes are going on down in the motor pool office. Sergeant Baxter would give instruction on the 5-ton tractor, while Chief James will be teachin' on the deuce-and-a-half."

The soldiers looked at each other wide-eyed. This was the shortest morning formation ever. And completely not Sergeant Tisher's style. Something must be wrong.

"OK, now I want you all to...." Tisher's concentration was shattered by the continued humming. He shook his head.

"Does anyone know what that humming noise is?" Tisher asked the assembled personnel softly.

"Top, the mess unit was trying to surprise us with breakfast," replied Private Franklin.

Of course! The smoke detector! Tisher rolled his eyes.

"I thought they were taking classes on food preparation," he said.

"They are, Top," said Lieutenant Meglynn. "The problem is someone stored a box in the oven in the break room. They turned it on to preheat it, and, well, it was pretty smoky this morning.

"But it's OK, sir," Meglynn smiled. "There's no damage to anything, except for whatever was in that box. And I already ate breakfast before coming to drill."

Tisher chuckled.

The formation was finally over and soldiers scattered. Moments later, the humming stopped. Tisher did a little dance of joy. His stomach responded with a rumble. A little more breakfast probably would have been good this morning.

Sensing more impending danger, he walked to the break room kitchen to see what else might be hiding there.

In the company commander's office, Captain Dave Marshall was opening the windows, and looking over the operations order that came down from divisional headquarters. Commonly referred to as an op order, it gave detailed instruction on the: who, what, when, where and how an Army mission was to be accomplished. It rarely ever said why the mission needed to be done. Marshall smiled wryly. The reason why was usually the Army's stock answer for everything: For the good of the country.

Marshall was cautious as he read over the four-page op order. Not wanting to miss any details, he made it a practice to read important paperwork three times. The first time was to get the gist of the information. The second time was to determine what areas pertained to the 683rd and how it would affect their current plans. The third time was to study it in detail, writing down all the information to be copied into the soon to be developed 683rd op order. This information would be passed down to the platoon leaders, NCOs and soldiers. Any information of importance to the unit must be provided to all the 683rd soldiers, Marshall thought.

Marshall asked the first sergeant to come into his office. Tisher closed the door behind him when he entered.

"What's up, Boss?" Tisher was smoking a corncob pipe and holding a cup of coffee in the same hand. In the other was clutched a glazed doughnut. The sight proved the first sergeant was multi-task talented.

"Top, I can see you're a man of many talents." Tisher smiled and shrugged as Marshall spoke to him. "I'm glad to see you switched to a pipe instead of the cigarettes. It's healthier. But what is that crazy tobacco you're smoking? It smells like you've shredded the newspaper and put it in your pipe!"

"You didn't hear?" Tisher asked. "The mess section showed up early to surprise us with breakfast. Unfortunately, someone thought the oven was a file cabinet."

Marshall shook his head.

"At least someone sprang for doughnuts," Marshall said. "Is there any other paperwork on its way to being part of our sustenance?"

Tisher shook his head no.

"I looked and found nothing except for Sergeant Adkins chewing the hell out of some sunflower seeds and apologizing," Tisher said.

"His heart was in the right place," Marshall said. "But who put paperwork in the oven?" As he spoke, an image of Chief McCarthy and Sergeant Schmoot trying to get rid of papers by shoving them in the oven instead of putting them away appeared him his brain. Marshall shuddered and changed the subject.

"By the way, Top, Colonel Finder was right in his warning about me being the overall convoy commander," Marshall said. "I've just been formally tasked."

Tisher smiled at him.

"And they couldn't have picked a better one," he said.

Marshall smiled back at him.

"Brown nosin' kinda early this morning, aren't we?" Marshall asked.

Tisher couldn't hold back his glee as he took a bite of his doughnut and a swig of coffee. He then took a puff on the pipe to finish things off.

"Yes Sir!" Tisher said enthusiastically. Marshall laughed to himself as he looked at Tisher. His vigorous bite of the doughnut actually left behind a small streak of brown frosting on his nose. Marshall wondered how he should tell his first sergeant.

Tisher broke Marshall's thoughts.

"And Lieutenant Rodriguez will do just fine."

Shaking his head in amusement as he chuckled along with the First Sergeant, Marshall couldn't help but concur.

"I think you're right, Top," Marshall said. "I'm sure you know by now you're going on the advanced party to get things set up three days before we arrive for A.T. Besides Sergeant Tea, who else do you want to take with you?"

Tisher's smile became a broad grin, realizing he would receive an extra three days pay for his troubles.

"Well, thank you, Sir," Tisher said. "And have I ever told you what a great commander you are?"

Marshall grinned like the Cheshire cat. Tisher had set himself up perfectly.

"Excuse me, Top, but you've got something brown on your nose," Marshall said.

Tisher mockingly touched his nose with his thumb. He almost dropped his pipe in alarm when he saw the streak of chocolate brown frosting on his thumb print. Marshall laughed. "From now on, only glazed doughnuts when I'm around you, Sir," Tisher said with a chuckle.

Tisher and Marshall stopped laughing and began a serious discussion of who and what should make up the advance party. Tents, generators, food, vehicles, personnel and the field site area assigned to the unit dropped into the discussion.

Marshall called Sergeant Lemasters, Sergeant Mooney and Sergeant Tea to come into his office. Tisher playfully added another caveat.

"Tell them to finish their doughnuts first!" he shouted.

As Lemasters, Mooney and Tea entered the office, they were bewildered at the laughter.

"Did we miss something?" Mooney asked.

"No," said Tisher. "The Old Man has just had enough brown nosing for the day." Tisher and Marshall continued to laugh. Tea shrugged her shoulders at Lemasters and Mooney. "Shall I start taking notes now so you can savor this moment again when we're in the field?" Tea asked.

The laughter was quickly replaced by discussion, and a well-defined plan began to take shape. Tea carefully recorded the discussion on her steno notepad so it could be written up as an internal action plan and later adopted into the 683rd op order for all to read and follow.

As they left the office an hour later, Lemasters turned to Tisher.

"Really, what was that all about?" he asked.

Tisher smiled.

"I found out the hard way that drinking, smoking, eating a chocolate doughnut without a napkin, and kissing up to the Old Man doesn't really pay." Tisher rubbed his nose for emphasis.

Lemasters chuckled.

"Better you than me," he said. "I grabbed a doughnut with pink frostin' and sprinkles this mornin'!"

In the motor pool office, Sergeant First Class Joe Baxter was helping Chief James with the 5-ton tractor portion of Army driver's training classes. Sergeant Baxter was a dairy farmer in his civilian life. He was an average height with a very powerful build. He had sandy blond hair and was beginning to go bald. Most people thought his hair loss might be due to him pulling his hair out. Just by looking at Baxter's hands, most people could tell he worked on a farm. But when his hands weren't tugging on cow udders, they seemed to be tugging at his rapidly receding hairline.

Baxter was another seasoned NCO who served in Vietnam. Being a self-employed farmer, Baxter needed some extra money every month and a retirement to look forward to. Every time he had some money saved up, something on the farm would break down and need serious fixing or replacement. With all the hard luck that was constantly confronting him, his parents should have named him Job, not Joe.

Sergeant Baxter was trying to emphasize some important points to soldiers who were tasked to drive the 5-ton tractors. "You're gonna be drivin' the 5-ton tractors we're borrowin' from the 646th in Youngstown," he said. The soldiers all looked like they were daydreaming. Baxter ignored them and pushed up his sleeves. It was March already, he thought. Why was the heater still running at full blast?

"These trucks are the older models with dual fuel tanks," Baxter continued. Not a single soldier was looking at him. He raised his voice. "These ole gals run on MoGas. Gasoline to you rookies. Do not mix diesel with gas, hear me!"

In the overly warm classroom, the eight students were doodling on notepads, staring out windows, and stifling yawns. For a brief moment, Baxter sympathized with his high school algebra teacher. And then he continued teaching.

"You also gotta manually switch the fuel tank lever under the seat when you hear the engine start to sputter, and flip the switch on the fuel gage that's mounted on the dashboard of the truck," Baxter said. "This is important. You hear me?"

One soldier yawned wide enough to catch a fly in response. "If you only can remember one thing from this lesson, make it be this: the fuel tank lever is under the driver's seat," Baxter said. Nobody was looking at him. He was frustrated beyond belief. Time to get the soldiers' attention.

"Sex!" Baxter said in his normal tone of voice.

The eight male soldiers in the room sat bolt upright in their seats. Baxter chuckled. Now they were listening to him. He cleared his throat to continue, but was interrupted by soft footsteps.

"I'm sorry I'm late," said Specialist Pam Williams, taking a seat in the back of the classroom. The male soldiers turned around and looked at her hungrily. Baxter hoped that she hadn't heard what he just said.

"This is a driving class, right?" Williams asked. Baxter nodded. "So why are you talking about sex?"

Baxter flushed bright red. He ignored the question and continued with his driver's orientation, bulldozing through the topics and ignoring the soldiers who were not paying attention. Meanwhile, the soldiers sat through another hour of instruction, catching quick glimpses of Williams and thinking about other fantasies as the day wore on.

In the motor park, Sergeant Nugot was showing another new driver the 5-ton wrecker. Nugot had been driving 5-ton wreckers his entire military career, both active duty and Reserve. In his civilian occupation, he was a wrecker operator for a towing service his father-in-law owned. He was 25 and a country boy at heart. Lanky, tall with long black hair he had to grease up and comb back to meet the Army's haircut regulations, Nugot was an amiable young man. There wasn't much Nugot didn't know about what the military termed as recovery operations. He once towed a broken down deuce-and-a-half nearly twenty miles with a ¼-ton jeep.

"Drivin' the 5-ton wrecker is the best job in the whole convoy, Tony," commented Nugot to his new assistant driver, Specialist Tony Cutnoff.

"How so, Sarge?" asked Cutnoff.

Nugot motioned Cutnoff to follow him to the front of the wrecker. He wanted to impart some of his institutional knowledge to his newly assigned assistant.

"You're normally in the trail party, which means you just cruise along in the back, waitin' for someone to breakdown," Nugot said, eyes shining. "Then we get to criticize them about their lousy operator's maintenance, ask them for some smokes, maybe get some of their pogey bait, grab a few sodas as payment, put'em on the hook or tow-bar and have 'em sit on each others' lap for 100 miles before we meet up with the rest of the convoy."

Specialist Tony Cutnoff took all the information in. He had been in the Reserves for two years and attended the nearby university. As a college junior majoring in mathematics, he was extremely intelligent, handsome, and single. He wasn't looking for a serious relationship just yet. But like any young, single soldier, he was always on the prowl for love.

"Sounds cool to me," Cutnoff said with a shrug. "Hey Sarge, what's pogey bait?"

Sergeant Nugot chuckled to himself.

"Didn't they teach you anything in basic training?" Nugot asked. "It's junk food."

Cutnoff responded with another shrug and asked another question that had been on his mind.

"How come they call you Road Kill, Sarge?" Cutnoff asked. Nugot grinned. Little did Cutnoff realize that Nugot had a rather morbid sense of humor when it came to dead skunks on the highway.

At the shop office, Chief Farley called a meeting with all the platoon sergeants and a few of the lieutenants. The topic of discussion was new tires.

Chief James opened the meeting with good news. Well, relatively good news.

"I've got a trailer full of new deuce-and-a-half tires, one for each vehicle to have a good spare," James said.

"Only a spare?" Lieutenant Rodriguez asked, suddenly having visions of a broken-down convoy clogging up the highway.

"The tires that are on all of the vehicles function now, even if they just barely function," James explained. "You won't be able to replace any tires with the spare until you have a tire failure, which means you better put your best tires on the front two wheels and the worst ones one the outer of the duals. You don't want to have to replace an inner flat when you're in the convoy, so look over what you've got and start tire swappin' now."

Several of the soldiers had a worrisome look on their face. Rodriguez felt a sense of dread was in the air. He tested tires for a living and knew what could happen with a fully loaded truck after a tire blew.

"I'm having a class in one hour for all drivers and assistant drivers on actions to take when they get a flat and how to change it," James said. "Every driver from each platoon that's gonna be in the convoy better be there for the class, no excuses." Rodriguez stood up and mouthed "Everybody will attend!" to the soldiers.

All those in attendance said "Yes Sir" in unison.

"One more thing," James continued. "The extra 5-ton tractors we're picking up are in pretty good shape, but our trailers they're gonna be pullin' aren't."

He looked directly at Schmoot and McCarthy.

"Those sections with trailers better make sure all brake-hoses and fittings are perfect before we roll," James said, staring directly at the two men.

Schmoot and McCarthy shrugged off the verbal warnings. "He just wants us to do more busywork," McCarthy said. Schmoot nodded.

"Yeah," Schmoot said. "We're only taking one parts trailer, not all four."

As they cackled, Lieutenant Sarah Burks hung up the phone in an office in the tech supply warehouse.

"All right!" she said. "We've got the extra 5-ton tractors from the 646th ready for pick-up next drill!"

The 683rd personnel were geared up and in full stride to get ready for annual training. Every unit vehicle was scheduled to enter the 683rd shop for a good going-over, as directed from the commander on down. No one wanted a mechanical breakdown on the way to Fort Knox. The technical inspectors of the shop office were lending their assistance making sure any overdue maintenance was being done on everything that entered a maintenance bay.

Chief James was happy to see the change for the good as the soldiers realized the seriousness of the situation. Their vehicles and trailers would have to make it to Fort Knox, Kentucky, a distance of 400 miles. All the sections were busy checking and rotating tires. The worst tires were removed and sent to the motor pool for demounting and replacement with a new tire. Chief James vowed he would not let the 683rd down. James saw Lieutenant Rodriguez moving about the shop area like a cat being chased by a stray dog. If I don't intervene, James thought, this lieutenant will have a nervous breakdown before the convoy even starts its engines!

"Lieutenant Rodriguez," James said with a bright smile. "I can understand that you're worried about these old vehicles." Rodriguez nodded vigorously.

James continued in a confident voice, "Let's you and I look at these vehicles and find out for ourselves what is roadworthy and what isn't."

Rodriguez's heart rate slowed a little and he walked slowly through the motor pool with Chief James.

APRIL DRILL, SATURDAY

The Northern Ohio weather was beginning to warm up. The occasional rain showers and moderate temperatures removed that last vestige of snow. Trees and shrubs were beginning to bud and the grasses began to slowly turn from their dormant brown into a lush carpet of bluish green. Everyone who had suffered through the winter weather had a renewed sense of hope. They felt as though they made it through another one. All the soldiers were looking forward to spending more time outdoors enjoying the mild weather after being cooped up indoors for four months of brutal winter weather.

Marshall assembled the officers and platoon sergeants in the conference room for an in-progress review (IPR). It was time well spent to determine what still needed to be done for A.T.

The 683rd's annual training maintenance mission was forecasted to not be very demanding during the first week. Using known criteria from past experience, all those assembled knew the majority of mission work would come during the second week of A.T., when mechanical equipment would have to make the return trip back to Ohio in good working condition. During the first week of A.T., Marshall wanted his officers and NCOs to conduct as much soldier training as possible. To make sure there was no second-guessing going on, everyone at the meetings would have input. Tactical training during the first week of A.T. was planned out in detail.

"All right everyone, we've got two months before A.T.," Marshall said, opening the meeting. "Does anyone have any concerns or problems that need to be dealt with now?"

The silence that met Marshall's question led him to volunteer the different groups. "I'll start with the headquarters section and work my way through each one separately," he said.

Each section brought its concerns to the table, and all

concerns and problems were dealt with. Some issues could be easily fixed, while others would take some action from the higher headquarters.

The tech supply section was the last one to be asked about the concerns and problems. Chief McCarthy became the spokesperson, since Lieutenant Burks was conducting a training class at the shop.

"Captain Marshall, I don't think we need to take all our trailers to annual training," McCarthy said with a slight patronizing whine to his voice. "They'll just be in the way."

Sergeant Schmoot quickly nodded his head in agreement.

Marshall looked at McCarthy with his eyebrows raised. He had he made his thoughts clear to Lieutenant Burks during their last meeting in Marshall's office.

"Are all the repair parts inventoried and properly stored in the trailers?" Marshall asked.

"No Sir, not yet," McCarthy replied.

Marshall raised his eyebrows.

"Will the repair parts be properly inventoried and stored before we leave for A.T.?" he asked.

McCarthy looked smugly at the commander.

"No Sir, I don't think so," he responded.

Marshall looked McCarthy straight in the eyes.

"Without the trailers, what are your soldiers going to do in the field for two weeks?" Marshall asked him.

McCarthy and Schmoot were silent for several seconds. Both knew what Marshall was getting at.

"It would seem to me that this A.T. period would be an excellent opportunity for our tech supply section to become fully operational, and to get those parts trailers ready," Marshall said. "Mr. McCarthy, all those trailers with borrowed 5-ton tractors and your newly trained 5-ton drivers will be going to A.T."

Both McCarthy and Schmoot nodded their heads and muttered, "Yes Sir."

Marshall moved on to the unit training officer.

"Lieutenant Stiles, how are you coming along with the unit

training schedule?"

Stiles smiled.

"Sir, it's been forwarded to higher headquarters," she said. "We should get an approved copy back by next drill."

"I'd like to see a copy of what was submitted," Marshall said.

Stiles squirmed. She and Sergeant First Class Huddle had a copy, but much of it was badly retyped to change the dates.

"No problem, Sir." said Stiles, "I'll bring you a copy after the meeting is over."

Sergeant Huddle interjected.

"Sir, in the past we've always had to change the training schedule on a daily basis because of the conditions and opportunities that come up."

Marshall agreed. He knew what the training NCO was implying.

"I realize that things change and the training schedule has to be flexible to accommodate those changes," Marshall said. "I'm sure there are going to be plenty of changes once we get there. Like I said before, be flexible, adapt and overcome. It will save us all a lot of grief."

All in the room took Marshall's advice seriously. The only thing that remained constant in the Army was change.

At the motor park, the newly trained drivers were ready for their first road test. Sergeant Baxter had a total of eight soldiers ready to be given their final exam—the road test.

The Army road test was like any civilian driver's license road test. The student driver would have to demonstrate his or her skills to a qualified instructor. The instructor would sit in the passenger seat and grade the driver's abilities as they drove through a road course that had been set up previously.

The milder weather had turned the dirt and gravel area of the motor park into a soft muddy mess. The soldiers were wearing their field jackets with insulated liners, scarves and gloves. The olive drab (OD) ball caps were worn year-round as part of the standard uniform.

Sergeant Baxter had allowed the soldiers several minutes

to enjoy a smoke break while Baxter unlocked the padlock and chain from the steering wheel. There were no locks on the doors of the deuce-and-a-half, no key to start up the engine. Just a starter button and a lever on the dashboard to engage the electrical current from the batteries. Baxter's clipboard had a one-page score sheet to evaluate each driver. He knew all the soldiers would pass the test. It was just a standard formality, another rite of passage for the soldier to accomplish.

Specialist Peoples volunteered to be the first one behind the wheel of the deuce-and-a-half. She was both scared and excited.

As part of the driver's test, each student had to do the pre-operational checks prior to engine start. Peoples had the operator's manual out and went over each item on the checklist page. Baxter was impressed. To check the oil, Peoples stood on the fender of the truck, which was about three feet off the ground. When she bent over to grab the oil dipstick, the eyes of the remaining seven soldiers were on Peoples' assets. Nobody complained about Peoples taking her time while checking the oil level. They all just stared and enjoyed the view.

When she was done checking all the fluids and tire pressure, and finished a walk-around visual inspection of the vehicle, Peoples climbed into the cab of the truck. Baxter climbed into the other side of the cab with his clipboard. He was ready, and also a little nervous.

"Okay Peoples, get this truck started," Baxter instructed, waiting to see what Peoples learned from the driver's training classes.

Specialist Peoples checked the handbrake to make sure it was on before she started the engine, put the gearshift in neutral, flipped the ignition selector switch to ON, depressed the clutch, and pushed the starter button. After the engine turned over for several seconds, it roared to life. The rumble of the engine and the air pressure warning-buzzer in the truck cab added to the confusion.

Baxter shouted to Specialist Peoples in a loud voice.

"Let it idle for a while. It needs to warm up," Baxter said. "Keep the engine RPMs around 1,000." The whine of the turbocharger was distinct as it whistled up and down with the engine RPMs.

This beast has come to life and I am its master, Peoples thought.

Black smoke was belching from the exhaust stack while the engine began to warm up. The smell of diesel was in the air.

"Put this truck in gear and drive down to the stop sign," Baxter told Peoples.

Peoples depressed the clutch, put the gearshift into second gear instead of first, quickly released the clutch, the large truck lurched forward and abruptly stalled. The only thing Peoples could say was, "Ooops, sorry."

Baxter was thinking, boy, this is going to be a long day.

Inside the shop, just outside the motor pool office, Private First Class Jessie Dweedle was hammering on a rim split-ring assembly. The split ring had to be removed before a tire could be de-mounted from the large steel rim. He had become fairly proficient at de-mounting and mounting truck tires after Chief James brought in a hydraulic tire de-mounter.

Private Dweedle was another country boy that grew up tall and skinny. He was strong and good-natured, but barely made it through high school. His ambitions were to own his own service garage someday, and marry his high school sweetheart after he saved up enough money.

Jessie's uniform was always stained with oil and grease, even though he wore coveralls. He did not mind getting dirty, nor doing what he was told to do. Chief James liked Dweedle, and recommended him for a promotion.

Chief James had returned from the staff meeting and saw Dweedle hammering away. He finally got Jessie's attention.

"Jessie," Chief James asked, "how many did you get done today?"

Dweedle grinned a smile with a front tooth missing.

"This'll make nine, Sir," he said.

Chief James was visibly pleased.

"Good work Jessie," James said. "You keep this up and

you'll be a sergeant before you know it."

Private Dweedle smiled.

"I gotta make spec-four first, Chief," he replied.

Little did Dweedle know he was going to be promoted later that afternoon at final formation.

"Nine down," said James, "twenty more to go."

In the orderly room, Lieutenant Stiles carried in a copy of the A.T. training schedule for the commander to review. Earlier in the day, she had taken the original to the copy machine and made another copy to hide the newly typed entries and tape that was all over the original.

Marshall looked over the A.T. training schedule and noticed the telltale signs of new typing.

"I see that you and Sergeant Huddle used an old training schedule and changed the dates," Marshall said as he looked up from the training schedule at Stiles.

"How could you tell, Sir?" Stiles asked, knowing she was caught red-handed.

Marshall signaled with his hand to come a little closer to his desk.

"You see here, you forgot to change the signature block on the corner," he said, pointing to the form. "It still shows Captain Breedlow as the commanding officer."

"My apologies, Sir," said Stiles, racking her brain for a believable excuse. "Sergeant Huddle and I found this old one that fits what we are going to be doing at Fort Knox. Do you want me to re-submit a new one, Sir?"

Marshall looked at Stiles.

"No, that won't be necessary," he said. "This will do just fine, except that Major Breedlow won't be there with us. There'll be lots of changes once we get to the field site. Just be prepared to make plenty of addendums to it once we're on the ground. Then I want to look it over before you send it forward, OK?"

"Yes Sir, I will," responded Stiles.

In the late afternoon, Sergeant Jackie Mooney was checking

one of the jeep-mounted radios. As he placed it on a desk, he noticed a large black ant crawling out of the back of the radio by the internal cooling fan.

Private Huck Hudson was standing next to Mooney.

"What the heck is that?" Hudson asked.

Mooney shook his head in disgust.

"Huck, looks like we just lost the engineer," he said in a deadpan serious voice.

1700 hours, and the 683rd was ready for final formation. First Sergeant Tisher called the soldiers to the position of attention. He quickly turned the formation of 683rd soldiers over to Marshall.

Standing in front of the entire unit as they stood at attention, Marshall called out in his commander's voice.

"Private Dweedle, front and center...Post!"

Private Dweedle quickly left the formation and marched up to Marshall and saluted.

Sergeant Lemasters read the promotion order.

"Private First Class Jessie L. Dweedle is hereby promoted to the rank of specialist fourth class, effective this date, April 10, 1982. Signed, Captain Reginald Van Skeeguy, adjutant, 694th Maintenance Battalion."

Marshall removed Dweedle's old rank from his oil-stained lapels, and pinned the specialist rank on.

"Specialist Dweedle, I want to see to you in a clean uniform from now on," Marshall said. "I also want to congratulate you on your promotion and the outstanding work you're doing in the motor pool. Keep it up."

Specialist Dweedle saluted the commander, then did an about-face movement and returned to his position in the formation.

"At ease," Marshall commanded. In unison, everyone moved to a more relaxed position. "Let's give Specialist Dweedle a hand," Marshall continued. The entire 683rd clapped for several seconds.

Marshall decided it was time to congratulate everyone.

"You all deserve congratulations as well for the outstanding work you've been doing getting ready for A.T.," he said. "By next drill, everyone should have their vehicle load plans ready. Load up will be conducted during the June drill, which is only a couple of months away."

Marshall went on to inform the 683rd of what was unfolding for annual training, who would be supported, what units they would be located with, and what personnel and equipment will be augmented.

When the soldiers heard Marshall say the mess section of the 646th S&S Company was going to be co-located with the 683rd, many soldiers and NCOs cheered. One of the loudest shouts of approval was heard from Sergeant Adkins, who wore a very big smile.

Marshall grinned as he continued to go over the scheduled training events and mentioned the upcoming round robin training exercise. This exercise was set up to have multiple stations each soldier would go to and successfully complete. All training stations in the round robin training exercise were to focus on the tactical skills he determined were needed before the unit arrived at Mount Eden Base Camp.

The soldiers of the 683rd were called to attention after all the announcements were made and then dismissed. Tomorrow would be another eventful day.

APRIL DRILL - SUNDAY

Morning formation had been completed. Everyone was present and accounted for. Marshall assembled the 683rd primary staff in the conference room for a follow-up IPR meeting. The agenda was to plan the remaining drills before A.T.

All those in attendance rapidly drained the coffee pot, and the two-dozen doughnuts evaporated from the large box that Marshall brought. Marshall didn't want the IPRs to become redundant, with the same information discussed over and over again. Progress had to be measurable and ongoing. An officer's job was to manage all the details, and there were a lot of details for Marshall to oversee.

"Now that I've fed you, it's time for feedback on your progress for A.T.," Marshall said. "Let's begin with driver's training and the overall equipment status. Mr. James, how are we doing there?"

Chief James quickly looked at his notepad.

"Sir, we'll have 22 new drivers qualified after today's drill if everyone passes the road test," he said. "As for the vehicles, 85 percent of them are operational. The remainder will be up and running before July drill."

Marshall was pleased to hear of the great strides Chief James had been able to accomplish in such a short amount of time. The possible need for additional equipment came to his mind.

"What about the vehicles we need to borrow?" Marshall asked.

"This afternoon the 646th will be bringing the additional vehicles we need to pull our trailers, and another two quarter-tons for the convoy," replied Chief James.

Marshall took his U.S. government black ink pen and checked those items off his checklist, thanking Chief James for a job well done.

Marshall's attention turned next to the radios. Would they work? "Sergeant Mooney, are all the radios operational?" Marshall asked.

Sergeant Mooney was ready for that question. He had sat through countless IPRs and knew how important his responsibilities were. He made it a point to follow-up on all the unit commander's taskings and requests before the meeting.

"The Chief and I are going to do the operational checks later this week," Mooney said. "We still have some time to get them repaired or replaced if need be." He smiled, remembering what he had said to Hudson the day before.

Marshall checked off another item on his list.

"How about the ammo forecast and firing ranges at Knox?" Marshall asked.

"Sir, the ammo forecast has been updated and resubmitted to higher headquarters," Mooney said. "I'll check to make sure it's processed and arrives at Fort Knox in time."

"And the firing ranges?" asked Marshall.

"Sir, the ranges have been requested, but I'll have to drive down to Fort Knox sometime next week and make sure we've got 'em reserved," Mooney responded.

Marshall was pleased with what his full timers were telling him. "How are we doing on new truck tires?" he asked.

"Sir, we've got nearly all of the new tires mounted and issued back to the sections," James said.

"Any possibility of getting more?" Marshall asked.

"No Sir," James said, shaking his head. "I had to stretch a few rules to get the 29 new ones. I've kinda used up all my favors with my buddies down in Columbus."

The new tires would come in very handy on the way to Fort Knox.

The meeting went on for another 45 minutes with all platoons involved in the discussion. Marshall made sure every staff member was aware of the Army's most quoted training motto, the six Ps: *Prior Planning Prevents Piss-Poor Performance.*

Marshall was visibly pleased with the progress and attitude

of the officers and NCOs. Everyone was working together for a common goal. Even tech supply was busy the entire drill period. Chief McCarthy and Sergeant Schmoot seemed to be planning to get everything prepared for the trip to Fort Knox.

Chief Murphy was helping himself to another quarter pounder with cheese as he sat in his warehouse office near the 683rd main shop. Although his doctor had warned him to lose weight and go on a diet, McCarthy couldn't resist his favorite fast food chain. Any time he was driving in his car, he would find himself pulling into the drive-thru window for a quick cheeseburger and a milkshake.

"You get enough to eat, Chief?" asked Sergeant Schmoot as he finished his fish sandwich.

Still chewing on a rather large mouthful of food, McCarthy nodded his head.

"Well Chief, what are we going to do about these trailers?" Schmoot asked.

"Nuthin'!" McCarthy replied. "We've got some serious inventorying before we load 'em onto the trailers. That'll keep the troops busy for a couple of drills."

As McCarthy stopped talking, Lieutenant Burks walked into the warehouse from outside and headed straight for Chief McCarthy's office.

Seeing McCarthy had finished his lunch, she addressed both men directly.

"As you know, we are taking all four parts trailers with us to A.T. That is a certainty," Burks said. "I just signed for the additional 5-ton tractors we needed from the 646th Supply Company. I want both of you to supervise the load up of all the parts from the warehouse into these trailers. The parts need to be loaded as soon as possible. Can that be accomplished before the end of drill?"

Chief McCarthy slowly got up from his desk. He was not in a pleasant mood, being told what to do from a woman younger than his youngest daughter.

"We're preparing an inventory list of the parts and cross-checking the corresponding stock numbers, Ma'am," McCarthy said. "That's in the works. We should have all the trailers loaded by June drill."

Casting a glance over to Schmoot, McCarthy grinned.

"Dennis, time to go to work," McCarthy said with mock sternness.

Later that afternoon, Specialist Jessie Dweedle was hard at work, taking off the old tires from the deuce-and-a-half truck rims and putting the new tires on. The platoons would take back their new one and mount them on the trucks. It was the least they could do.

Several soldiers were assigned to help Dweedle, who enjoyed their company while he worked. Once Dweedle started telling jokes and stories, he wouldn't stop talking until he took a smoke break. Jessie had a reputation as the motor pool clown. He took it upon himself to make sure everyone was in a good mood.

In the 683rd orderly room, Sergeant Vivian Tea got a phone call from her husband.

"Tyron, I can't come home right now. I've still got work to do," Tea said. She paused as he responded.

"Well, you'll just have to wait until I get home," she said. A muffled exclamation could be heard out of the phone.

"Uh huh, that's right," Tea said. She broke into a laugh.

"No, I won't wear that while I'm cookin' dinner," she said. "Listen, you just get that large roast out of the freezer."

The telephone squawked again and Tea's eyes grew wide.

"What?" she asked. "Tyron, you better not let the children hear you say that."

She paused again.

"Okay, I love you too. Bye," Tea said, hanging up the phone.

Tea looked up and saw every eye in the room was staring at her. She smiled and shrugged.

"Men. They're always hungry," Tea said.

The soldiers all knew what she was implying and went back to work.

Marshall was sitting in his office going over the operations order he had drafted for A.T. Everything seemed to be falling into place, and unit morale was getting better every drill. His primary concern was focused on the trucks they would be taking. Safety was foremost in his mind. His other concern was to make annual training challenging and rewarding.

Second Lieutenant Meglynn was settling into her position as headquarters platoon leader very quickly. She had gained some confidence and started taking ballet classes at a local school of dance to overcome her clumsiness and have better control of her body coordination. It was also a great boost for her physical endurance, since she had two hours of class every other day to condition her body and mind.

"Sergeant Tea, do you have an updated A.T. roster that I can look at?" Meglynn asked.

"Yes Ma'am, sure do. Here you go. I just retyped it," replied Tea as she gently handed the paperwork over to her.

"Thanks Sergeant Tea," Meglynn said. "Hey, can I ask a personal favor of you?" she asked, moving closer to Tea's desk.

"Sure Ma'am, what is it?" Tea asked.

Meglynn lowered her voice.

"You know, I've been quite the klutz around here since I joined the unit, and I'm trying to get over that image," Meglynn said. "I'd like to ask if you could give me some advice on being a better officer."

Sergeant Tea was a bit surprised and flattered at the lieutenant's request.

"Sure thing Ma'am," Tea said with a nod. "You're on the right track. Being a second lieutenant ain't easy 'cause everyone expects you to have most of the answers and be a leader when you pin on the gold bars. Don't worry Ma'am, I'll be glad to keep you straight."

Meglynn was pleased to have Sergeant Vivian Tea as her personal mentor.

"Thanks Sergeant Tea," she said. "I really appreciate this."

"You know," Tea said, "we got ourselves a good commander. I'm sure you can learn a heap of leadership skills just watchin' him do his job. But I'll help too."

Meglynn was delighted. She felt as though the stigma of being the laughing stock of the Army Officer Corps had been lifted off her shoulders. She sat down at her desk and began to look over the A.T. roster, focusing on the number of personnel each platoon was taking.

As she finished taking a sip of coffee and set her cup down on the desk, she inadvertently placed the foam cup on the edge of an eraser, which immediately tipped the cup over. Meglynn immediately grabbed the A.T. roster up from the desk and prevented any coffee from getting on the paperwork.

"Whew, that was close," she said to herself. When she looked up, she noticed Sergeant Tea was smiling, giving her the thumbs-up.

The remainder of the day went by without incident. The 683rd was busily getting ready for A.T. When July drill came, the 683rd would be ready, willing and able.

MAY DRILL - SATURDAY

Everything and everyone continued to improve, including the weather. Trees were beginning to leaf, and green was the predominant color that painted the landscape as far as the eye could see. The colorful flowering trees and shrubs added to the natural beauty that enveloped the woods, fields and residential neighborhoods. Field jackets and gloves were left in closets as soldiers enjoyed wearing their summer uniforms. Cabin fever was gone. The soldiers in the 683rd had a renewed sense of optimism as they enjoyed the delightful weather.

The many platoons and sections were busy loading up their trucks, vans, and trailers for the trip to Fort Knox. Many were using vehicle load plans—hand-drawn sketches of the cargo space in the trucks with all the equipment that was being loaded into them—for the first time. Copies of each load plan were given to the drivers, platoon leaders, and the convoy commander to provide an accurate accounting of what every vehicle was carrying.

Every platoon had vehicles and trailers lined up to be brought in the main shop for loading. Large items like generators and air compressors that could not be loaded by hand were lifted by overhead crane onto flatbed trailers. Once they got to the field site, they would be off-loaded by the 5-ton wreckers. The portable tire demounter was also loaded for the trip.

The main shop was alive with activity as the sections made sure all their tools, equipment and reference manuals were inventoried and loaded carefully. Marshall had put the word out they every platoon and section must be able to perform their mission in a field environment. It would serve them well at Fort Knox.

Removing an individual from his or her comfort zone and

subjecting them to intense and physically demanding situations was the essence of good realistic training. When a soldier could hack it, he or she quickly developed a sense of pride and confidence. It was always good to realize one's personal strengths and weakness. Excellence was, and will always be the norm. If one did not know their strengths and weaknesses, it was the NCO's job to enlighten them.

In the company orderly room, Sergeant Tea and First Sergeant Tisher were working on the manning roster, a complete list of all assigned and attached personnel in the 683rd who would require unit orders for the two-week annual training period.

Nothing could be done without the administrative paperwork being properly prepared and submitted. Once the unit orders were received by higher headquarters, the 683rd Heavy Equipment Maintenance Company would be allowed to move to Fort Knox and enjoy two glorious weeks on active duty in the fresh air and sunshine in the deep woods of Kentucky.

"Viv, what's the total number of troops we'll have in the field?" asked First Sergeant Tisher.

"Top, I count 214 going to Fort Knox, 28 going to basic training, 14 going to the NCO academy, and 22 scheduled for deferred basic training later this year," replied Tea.

"How many are attached, Viv?" Tisher asked.

"We're getting 23 personnel from the 646th Supply Company. Eight cooks including Sergeant Emery, and 15 supply types," replied Tea.

Tisher knew Sergeant Emery's mess section would be a definite morale booster.

He pondered over the 15 supply types and felt they would be put to good use working in the parts trailers Chief McCarthy and Sergeant Schmoot would have in the field.

Tisher looked at the paperwork thinking two months before A.T. How quickly time flies when you're busy. With luck, the same thing will happen at Mount Eden.

Sergeant Lemasters walked into the orderly room and entered Tisher's office.

"Hello Top, Vivian. How are thangs goin'?" asked Lemasters in his heavy West Virginian accent.

"Well John," replied Tisher, "looks like we're gonna have 214 in the field."

Lemasters grinned.

"Shoot, looks like we got ourselves a good time in the field, even with Vivian," Lemasters said.

Tea smiled at Lemasters and shook her head slowly. She was not showing any outward signs of being pregnant. Healthwise, all was going well.

"John, you're gonna be my right-hand man out in the field," mentioned Tisher, "We're gonna have troops on main post and in the field. The Old Man wants to make sure that everyone is accounted for daily and properly supervised."

"No sweat, Top," replied Lemasters, "As long as you keep Vivian outta my hair, thangs'll work out fine."

"Sergeant Lemasters, it's not me you gotta worry about being in your hair," Tea replied slowly. "From what I hear, it's those bugs you gotta worry about."

Both NCOs laughed at Tea's comment. They had been out in the field before and were not worried about any bugs at Mount Eden Base Camp. In a couple of months, the fire ants and chiggers that inhabit Mount Eden Base Camp would hungrily respond to the 683rd arrival. All three read over the unit manning roster one more time, making sure every platoon's assigned personnel were accounted for.

Lieutenant Rodriguez was in Marshall's office, being briefed on his duties as the unit's convoy commander.

"Do you have the strip maps prepared for your drivers?" asked Marshall.

"Yes Sir," replied Rodriguez. "Sergeant Siler and I drew up the maps and we're putting copies in all the driver's log books."

The driver's log book, which had all the maintenance

records and other important data, was always in the vehicle when the vehicle was dispatched from the motor pool.

"Have you checked with the state highway departments of Ohio and Kentucky about any road construction sites along our route of travel?" Marshall asked.

The question took Rodriguez totally by surprise.

"No sir, I haven't," Rodriguez said. "Do you have their phone numbers?"

Marshall knew being tasked as convoy commander was new to Rodriguez.

"I'm sure the unit mobilization officer has that in his mobilization plans," Marshall said. "Just get with him and he'll give you that information."

"Sir," asked Rodriguez, "who's the mobilization officer?"

Marshall pulled out the additional duty roster that Sergeant Tea prepared for him earlier in the week and looked it over. Marshall looked at Rodriguez and smiled.

"You are," Marshall said.

Rodriguez had that sinking feeling of helplessness in the pit of his stomach.

"I see here that Mr. Farley was the mobilization officer before you," Marshall said. "Why don't you get with him?"

A sigh of relief came over Rodriguez and he quickly excused himself to meet with Chief Farley and go over his newly assigned duties.

Marshall chuckled to himself after Rodriguez left his office. His officers were beginning to understand they had to be totally prepared for anything that life—or the Army—could throw at them.

At the main shop, most of the platoons had successfully loaded half their equipment onto their vehicles. The remainder would be loaded the following month.

Individualized soldier training was taking place after lunch. Topics were the fundamental soldiering skills that many had already forgotten since they had successfully completed Army basic training.

Marshall had made training mandatory for all soldiers, NCOs and officers. The training classes were conducted in lieu of working on the equipment, which was received as a welcomed break.

Marshall arrived at the shop area and observed how the training was being conducted. The round robin concept of training kept the soldiers intensely focused on specific areas of soldiering skills for about 15 minutes each. After each particular training topic was done, it would be time to rotate to another training area within the shop with a new instructor and another soldiering skill to be learned.

The troops were enjoying the change of pace and learning as they made their way through the various instructional stations. Even the officer and NCO instructors were enjoying themselves. The instructors were sharing their great depth of knowledge, which they were pleased to pass on. Marshall liked what he saw.

Over at the service and recovery platoon area in the main shop, Sergeant Jim Nugot was working on his 5-ton wrecker with Specialist Tony Cutnoff. They had been excused from the round robin training to fix the many faults on their wrecker.

Nugot had found he had a flat tire on the rear inside hub. Lucky for him, he had a clean, dry shop to work in instead of the damp and soggy ground in the motor park.

Nugot was trying to break loose a well-tightened lug nut from the axle. He couldn't use the air ratchet because training was being conducted simultaneously in the shop. He had to break the lug nut loose the old fashioned way, by hand.

The three feet long breaker bar wasn't long enough to apply the needed amount of force to break the lug nut free. Both Nugot and Cutnoff tried with all their might, but the lug nut wouldn't budge.

Sergeant Baxter saw what was happening and decided to come over and watch, especially to make sure they didn't get injured in the process. Baxter knew sooner or later they would ask him how to handle it.

After several minutes, Baxter decided to bring himself into

the conversation.

"You boys doin' OK?" he asked, knowing both men were near the point of exhaustion.

"This damn lug nut just won't come off, Sarge," Nugot said.

"Got any ideas?"

Baxter smiled.

"Maybe," he said. "Did you try using all your weight on the breaker bar?"

Cutnoff looked rather puzzled.

"You mean do a handstand on the bar?" Cutnoff asked.

"Not exactly," replied Baxter. "Try putting your foot on it instead, and grab hold of the wrecker so when it gives, you won't bust your butt on the concrete floor."

Cutnoff took Sergeant Baxter's advice. He put one foot on the breaker bar and held onto the wrecker. He slowly lifted his weight onto the bar. The breaker bar didn't move.

"Just bounce up a little," Baxter said.

As soon as Cutnoff did, the lug nut gave a loud pop and a squeal as it broke free. Cutnoff wasn't expecting lug nut to let loose so quickly and almost lost his grip on the wrecker. As he eased himself down onto the floor, he took the lug wrench and spun the difficult lug nut off the wheel stud.

"The rest'll all be just like that," Baxter said. "Just be careful and make sure you loosen them lugs, not tighten 'em by mistake."

Baxter walked off as Nugot and Cutnoff found a new way to have fun. Taking off the lug nuts and creating a horribly loud, irritating noise made their day.

"Tony, you get a chance to talk to our new unit armorer?" asked Nugot.

"Nope, but she's sure a cutie," Cutnoff said. "You think she's got a steady? Someone to cuddle up to on a cold Ohio winter's night?"

"Peoples," Nugot said slowly in a low voice, "Francine Peoples. Judging by the way she carries herself, and that drop-dead gorgeous face and chassis, I don't think she's worried about finding a man in her life. She's probably got 'em standing in line outside her door just for a chance to ask her out on a date," he mused. "She's got a pretty sharp mind too, from what I've heard."

"She's smart too?" asked Cutnoff. "That's a dangerous combination in a woman, Sarge. A guy like me doesn't stand a chance," he lamented, thinking Peoples would never give him a second look.

"Don't worry, Tony, the right one will come along for you," Nugot said. "Maybe she won't be waggin' a tail either."

"Funny Sarge, very funny," replied Cutnoff as he went back to work on the wrecker.

"You know, her mom is the arts and culture critic for the local paper in Akron," replied Nugot. "She's earned the nickname Poison-Pen Peoples. I'm sure some of her mother has rubbed off on her."

"Great," replied Cutnoff is a sarcastic tone. "I'm sure that's an endearing quality that will serve her well. Sounds like she's officer material to me."

Both men got a good chuckle from Cutnoff's analogy as they refocused their efforts to remove the tire from the wrecker.

"Williams! Peoples!" yelled Sergeant Lemasters as the round robin training ended at the main shop area.

Both Peoples and Williams walked up to Lemasters. Williams was first to speak.

"What's up Sarge?" she asked.

"You and Peoples got yerselves a fine job fer tomorrow," he said with slight grin.

"Oh?" pondered Peoples out loud, "And what would that be Sergeant Lemasters?"

"You'ins are gonna be mountin' the weapons racks in the empty 12-ton trailer we picked up from the 646th today," Lemasters said. "That'll have to be done before the end of drill tomorrow. If'n you need extra help, jest let me know. I got faith you kin do it."

"You can count on us, Sarge," smiled Peoples as she wanted to let him know they wouldn't let him down.

As Lemasters walked away, Williams looked at Peoples with a puzzled look.

"Hey girlfriend, we could have asked for some help," Williams said. "Now we're stuck on a nasty detail."

"Honey," replied Peoples coyly, "We can get all the help we need anytime we want it. You just got to know how to ask for it. Besides, I've mounted weapons racks before. It's not that hard once you get a rhythm going."

Chief Farley was in the shop office going over some paperwork as Lieutenant Rodriguez walked in.

"Chief, can I ask you a question?"

"Sure L.T., what can I do for you?" replied Farley, not wanting to be impolite or disrespectful.

"The Old Man tasked me as the convoy commander and I just found out I'm the new mobilization officer," Rodriguez said. "Can you give me a clue as to what's going on since you were the mobe officer before me?"

"Sure thing," Farley said. "Let me get this paperwork out of the way and I'll get the mobilization notebook out and go over it with you. It's fairly well laid out and up to date. Lucky break for you!"

"I'll just help myself to some coffee," said Rodriguez as he walked over to the coffee pot and grabbed a cup from the stack next to it.

Farley grinned and said nothing. He had tried a cup a few minutes earlier that tasted like tar. Maybe the L.T. likes his coffee strong, pondered Farley.

Rodriguez's reaction to the old coffee was pretty straight forward, as he spit it back into the cup with a single comment of "Yuck!"

Sergeant Lonnie Adkins was setting up the folding tables with his two cook helpers, preparing to serve afternoon chow. He had picked up the prepared meal from the local caterer in Ravenna. The luncheon menu consisted of green beans, boiled pirogues with butter and sautéed onions, tossed salad, rolls, broiled chicken, Polish sausage, coleslaw, applesauce, fruit punch, coffee, and peach or apple pie.

"You know, fellas, we're gonna have ta start cookin' this stuff instead of just servin' it when we get to A.T.," sighed Adkins.

"Can't wait, Sarge," replied one of his cook helpers. "At least we can take credit for the food, whether it's good or bad."

"Yep, it's about time too," replied Adkins as he looked up at the noonday sky. "Better get the food set up inside the shop. Looks like it's gonna rain, boys."

Within several minutes, the sky opened up and the rains came down just as the last table loaded with the catered food was brought into the shop. Lonnie had excellent timing when it came to predicting when it would rain. He could smell it coming.

Everyone inside the shop was glad to take a break and dive into lunch. Within 15 minutes, Sergeant Adkins and his helpers served over 200 683rd soldiers, with more coming from the headquarters building by the main gate. They found out through the 683rd grapevine what was for lunch. The Polish sausage was not your regular mass produced store-bought variety. It was the authentic homemade kind.

The lunch break at the shop ended as quickly as the rain shower, and the 683rd went back to work, preparing for A.T.. In the 683rd Orderly Room, Sergeant Vivian Tea was patiently waiting for her lunch to arrive. Sergeant Lonnie Adkins promised to bring her whatever lunchtime chow was left over, since her appetite was steadily growing.

"Sergeant Adkins, 'bout time you got your skinny little behind up here! I'm starvin'!" Tea called as she saw Adkins' shadow approach the orderly room. "You wouldn't want to see your favorite Admin NCO lyin' flat on her face with hunger, now would you hun?" Adkins walked into the orderly room with two plates piled high with the luncheon leftovers.

Adkins had a big grin on his face as he set the two plates down on Tea's desk.

"Nah Viv, I'd really hate to see that. 'Specially now that

you're eatin' for two," Adkins said. "Might as well enjoy puttin' on the feedbag while you can. Gettin' the extra pounds off ain't no fun after the baby's born. My wife is still tryin' to lose the last 15 pounds after Zack was born."

"Maybe you ought to cook for her," quipped Tea as she made herself a sausage sandwich.

"That's the problem, Viv, I do," replied Adkins. "Matter of fact, ever since we got married, I've been doin' all the cookin'. She does the dishes and the other household chores."

"Sounds like a marriage made in heaven to me," Tea said. "Well, almost. The only thing better would be you doin' the dishes too."

Adkins smiled and shook his head. He didn't want to try and match wits with Vivian. He knew he'd lose.

First Sergeant Tisher walked out of his office and spotted Adkins.

"Hey Cookie, how's it goin'?" Tisher asked. "How'd the troops like the chow today?"

"Well Top, we fed 221 today. With Vivian, that'll make 223," replied Adkins.

"I heard that, Sergeant Adkins," said Tea as she was in between bites of food.

Both men smiled, enjoying the opportunity to needle Sergeant Tea whenever they had a chance.

"Lonnie, you ever meet Sergeant Ralph Emery, the Mess Sergeant of the 646th?" asked Tisher.

"Sure did, Top," Adkins said. "I met him at a mess operations class in Canton last year. He seems like a very knowledgeable NCO. Matter of fact, he taught some of the class."

Tisher's face was serious, although he was hiding back a rather large smile. His eyes did give him away.

"Well, Lonnie, Ralph is very happy to be doin' an A.T. with the 683rd," Tisher said. "Matter of fact, he'll be sending three of his cooks with the advanced party to get the field mess operations going before the main convoy arrives. And by the way, when the entire unit is in the field, I want three squares a day, no C-rations, comprende'?"

Before Adkins could answer, Sergeant Tea was standing next to him, endorsing Tisher's order.

"You heard the man! No C-rations!" Tea seconded in a direct tone of voice. "Three hot meals a day and a night time snack for yours truly."

"Anything for you Viv, anything," replied Adkins.

"Okay, and don't forget the ice cream. I gotta have my ice cream, or I'll get real crabby," warned Tea.

Sergeant Adkins nodded his head in agreement and smiled, "You got it."

MAY DRILL - SUNDAY

At 9 a.m., Specialist Peoples and Specialist Williams were working together in the 683rd shop, fastening empty weapons racks inside the newly designated weapons trailer. The interior walls of the trailer had universal mounting brackets that were installed vertically every three feet. This would allow the users to safely secure any equipment against the trailer walls so it wouldn't move while traveling.

Peoples would be driving the 5-ton tractor to A.T. with the weapons trailer attached. The security and accountability of the 683rd weapons was an awesome responsibility, which she gladly accepted as part of her job as unit armorer.

Inside, the trailer was very spacious and roomy, painted pale green with recessed lights in the ceiling and small lockable windows with screens for ventilation. The double doors on the back end of the trailer were the heavy-duty variety and lockable from inside and out. Trailers were ideal for hauling items that need to be kept safe and out of the weather. On the inside, they were spacious enough to mount workbenches, shop machinery, and storage shelves. Army maintenance units normally had six or more trailers on their MTO&E.

Williams was working on the inside the trailer, laboriously bolting weapon racks to the trailer wall mounting brackets. Each weapons rack was designed to hold 10 M16 rifles, and came with a locking bar and a security chain. The weapons racks had to be double-stacked due to the large number of M16s being taken to A.T. Peoples was working outside of the trailer, lifting weapon racks to Williams as needed.

"Okay Fran, I'm ready for another one," shouted Williams from inside the trailer.

The weapons rack Peoples was trying to move seemed heavier.

"Now's a good time to turn on the charm and get some help," Peoples grunted to herself as she pulled the empty weapon rack along the shop floor.

"Could someone please give me a hand with this?" she called out.

Four soldiers instantly appeared and lifted it onto the trailer.

Inside the trailer, Williams stood in amazement as she thanked them and shook her head in disbelief. She knew that Fran Peoples could get almost anything she wanted by using her good looks and charm. She thought to herself, Better stick close to that gal during A.T., I might just catch a couple of good looking strays that Fran won't bother with.

Chief McCarthy and Sergeant Schmoot were inside one of the four tech supply section's parts trailers. Parts were scattered about everywhere on the floor, benches and shelving. The repair parts were hermetically sealed in a heavy-duty white aluminum foil pouch. Parts packaging was standardized on all parts and components that civilian manufacturers sold to the military. The label included a barcode, a national stock number identifying the item, and a description of the part printed in large letters. There was other information as well, such as lot number, manufacturer, and date codes. The packaging not only protected the parts from all types of weather conditions, but also careless handling. If a part was manufactured incorrectly, it could be easily recalled using the lot number on the label. If the part had a limited shelf life, the date code would help determine if it had expired.

The interior of the tech supply's parts trailer looked like it had traveled over thousands of miles of bad road. It was a mess. On the other hand, a well-organized repair parts trailer had all parts stored in a proper bin location and easily found through a standardized numbering system. It would take time to set up, but once it was organized, a tech supply section could find any repair part in a matter of seconds. If a part were no longer in inventory, an organized tech supply section would know when the replacement would arrive. They would also adjust their stockage level requirement of that particular part so they wouldn't run out the next time.

"Denny, are all the parts loaded onto the rest of the trailers?" Chief McCarthy asked.

Schmoot looked at McCarthy.

"Yes, Chief," he said. "I had all the parts taken out of the warehouse and placed in the trailers. I did just what Lieutenant Burks told me to do."

McCarthy grinned to himself.

"Maybe the Old Man was right, although I hate to admit it," he said. "Looks like we've got a good two weeks of work straightening out these trailers at A.T. if the rest of them look like this one."

"Yes, Sir, it sure will. And yes, Sir, they sure do," Schmoot responded.

Both men exited the rear of the trailer and walked down the metal steps attached to the rear bumper. McCarthy and Schmoot started a slow walk-around inspection of the trailer. As they got near the front of the trailer, McCarthy saw one of the pneumatic airbrake hose fittings not attached to the holding bracket. He picked up the end of the airbrake line hose and looked at the cast metal fitting.

"Looks like we'll need to get this fixed before A.T.," mentioned McCarthy.

"What do you see Chief?" asked Schmoot.

"There's a bug nest in this one and the rubber gasket is cracked."

Both men checked the remainder of the trailers and found several more that needed fixing.

Chief James and Sergeant Penny were walking through the motor park, looking at the vehicles to determine what was needed to get them up to road-worthy condition. The trucks and tractors that previously had ripped and missing canvas now sported new canvas. The pungent smell of the new canvas filled the air as both men went over their checklists. Any vehicles that did not meet their inspection standards had to be worked on by the section that owned it. Marshall had made it his policy that everything, except the 20-ton crane, would go to

A.T. Equipment had to be in good operating condition, inside and out.

As James and Penny continued through their checklist, they came to the tech supply trailers and spotted McCarthy and Schmoot inspecting the brake line hoses.

"I see you've found some bad hoses. I was wonderin' how long it was going to take you," quipped Chief James.

"You got the hose and fittings?" asked McCarthy.

"No, but I know for a fact your tech supply section does," James said. "They're probably in one of your trailers."

Both McCarthy and Schmoot looked at each other. They would be working the rest of the day trying to find the parts that were buried deep in the back of one of the trailers.

Marshall, First Sergeant Tisher, and Sergeant Lemasters were in the First Sergeant's office looking over the Fort Knox topographical training map. The only information they had received from higher headquarters regarding the location of the 683rd field site was a set of map grid coordinates. The scale of the topographical map was 1:50,000, which meant one inch on the map represented 50,000 inches on the ground, or the equivalent of 4,167 feet. Not much detail, but one could visualize what the surrounding terrain looked like.

"Top, it looks like we're going to be located on a downward slope of the mountain," Marshall said. "You get the same read as me?"

The First Sergeant and Lemasters were both wearing their reading glasses. Both looked at the grid coordinates and the map carefully.

"Yes, Sir, that's the downward slope of hill 532," replied Tisher. "Looks like we'll be in hillbilly country, John." He gave Lemasters a quick jab on the shoulder.

"Yeah Top, I'm gonna feel right at home," replied Lemasters with a broad grin.

Marshall enjoyed the brief humor, and asked a more serious question to both sergeants.

"Does this unit have a field layout drawing?" Marshall asked.

Neither NCO understood what Marshall was asking.

"It's a drawing that shows each section, their tents, the road network, the location of their equipment, vehicles, and fighting positions," Marshall explained.

"No, Sir, we've never done one before," Tisher said. "Never had to."

Marshall nodded.

"That's what I figured," he said. "I'll have Lieutenant Rodriguez prepare one for the unit. It'll be good training for him.

"Sergeant Tea?" Marshall leaned out of the office. "Could you call the shop and have Lieutenant Rodriguez report to my office in the next hour, please?"

"Yes, Sir," replied Tea.

The shop office received the phone call from the orderly room. Sergeant Bradford answered the call, and was delighted to hear that Sergeant Vivian Tea was on the other end of the telephone line.

"Vivian, are they treating you well up there?" asked Bradford. "Just remember, if you ever feel you need a change of scenery, we got a cushy job waiting for you here at the shop office."

"And what'll you have me doin', Sergeant Bradford?" asked Tea.

"Well, I won't have you fetchin' my coffee," said Bradford.

"Honey, I don't do that now," Tea said. "Besides, it's too cold down there in the shop office. Dirty, too. I like a place that's clean and warm."

"Oh well. At least I tried," Bradford said. "Now, what can I do for you Viv?"

Tea explained Captain Marshall wanted to see Rodriguez.

"Hey L.T.! The Old Man wants to see ya," bellowed Bradford across the shop office.

Rodriguez nodded his head in acknowledgment, got up from his desk and walked out the exit.

"He's on his way, Viv," said Bradford, "By the way, Viv, you got any sisters in the Army?"

Tea laughed. "Thousands of 'em," she said.

Lieutenant Rodriguez arrived at the unit orderly room. Marshall spotted him walking in and showed him the map of where the 683rd was supposed to be during A.T.

"I've been meaning to ask you, Rod, why did your parents name you Rodriguez Rodriguez?" Marshall asked.

A broad smile came across Rodriguez's face.

"Well, Sir, I was named after my great grandfather on my mother's side," he said. "His name was Rodriguez Jose Raoul Simone Suarez, but everyone just called him Pedro."

Both men smiled at the subtle humor as Marshall began to discuss the need for a field layout drawing.

"The unit has never done one from what I gather, but it's not very difficult if you know where to look for some help and directions," Marshall said, handing Rodriguez two Army field manuals. "Just use these field manuals and follow the directions. It's pretty easy once you get the hang of it.

"Oh yeah, one more thing to remember," Marshall said. "Once we get to the field site, you'll need to get sector drawings from each section so you can incorporate them into your field layout drawing. Start drawing up a typical one now. You'll have to constantly update it while we're there. Any questions?"

Rodriguez just smiled and shook his head. He knew what to do next.

Back at the 683rd shop, Peoples and Williams were finishing up the weapons trailer.

"Well, this is the last rack to be mounted. Looks like we got 'em all, Fran," said Williams.

Peoples was physically exhausted. Her four helpers quickly vanished after helping a few minutes.

"It's a good thing takin' these things out is easier than puttin' them in," said Peoples as she slowly eased herself down to the floor the trailer and relaxed her weary back.

Williams looked at her with one eyebrow raised.

"Fran, I've been doin' all the work," Williams said. "You've just been complaining about how heavy everything is for the past four hours."

Peoples looked at her and realized her moans and groans had not fallen on deaf ears.

"I'm sorry, Pam. You're right," Peoples said. "I've been putting on an act for so long, I'm starting to believe it. I'll make it up to you at A.T."

"How so?" inquired Williams.

Both women began discussing their personal plans for A.T. while the rest of the shop was busily fixing their equipment. The noise levels within the shop were high, but distinct female laughter was heard amidst all the noise.

"You done?" asked Sergeant Lemasters as he walked up to the newly outfitted weapons trailer that Peoples and Williams had just finished.

"Aye aye, Sarge," replied Peoples, eyeing his 1st Marine Division patch that was sewn on his fatigue shirtsleeve.

Lemasters grinned at the response Peoples gave. He quickly realized this young unit armorer had a fairly good knowledge of military units.

"You an ex-leatherneck, Peoples?" asked Lemasters.

"No, Sarge. But I used to date one," replied Peoples as she maintained her composure while speaking.

"Well, let's just take a look see at what you and Williams got done," said Lemasters as he walked up to the rear of the weapons trailer and peered inside.

"Hummmh, looks like everythin's mounted right," he said, walking up the steel steps and pulling hard on the racks to see if he could work one loose.

Finally, after going through the entire trailer, he exited down the steel steps.

"Good job," Lemasters said. "Carry on."

Peoples and Williams breathed a sigh of relief and began to put their tools away. It had taken them nearly the entire day to complete their task.

"Not bad," they both mentioned to each other as they walked back to the toolboxes.

"Top, we've got just one more drill to go before it's goodbye Ravenna, hello Mount Eden Base Camp," mentioned Captain Marshall as he was looking over the A.T. personnel roster with First Sergeant Tisher.

"Yep, I'm really lookin' forward to this A.T., Sir. This unit is firin' on all cylinders, if you know what I mean," replied Tisher.

"I think everyone's going to be surprised at what the troops can do once you get them out of a garrison environment and into the field."

First Sergeant Tisher was implying that he felt the unit would perform well in the field once they were away from the weekend drill routine. The weekend drills could never truly bring a dysfunctional unit together, due to the break in the evening when everyone would go their separate ways and resume a civilian life style. It would take a common hardship to forge a bond among the soldiers, and Tisher knew it.

Marshall had the feeling Tisher was speaking from experience.

"This is going to be a true test of leadership for all of us," Marshall chimed in. "Anything you want to throw out before we call it a day and get on with final formation?"

Tisher looked at Marshall.

"Yes. So should I reserve a hotel room on Post for the A.T. period?" Tisher asked.

"For who?" asked Marshall, with an inquisitive look.

"For you, Sir," Tisher said. "All our past commanders never stayed in the field with the troops."

Marshall had a shocked expression that Tisher was surprised to see. He heard something he just couldn't fathom. It was contrary to everything he learned. To be a good officer, one had to lead by example.

"Top, I've never heard of a commander staying on Post while his soldiers were in the field. That's absolutely absurd and downright despicable," stated Marshall.

Tisher didn't take but a moment to respond.

"Well Sir, some of our past commanders insisted on sleeping in clean sheets and a hot shower every morning," Tisher said.

"That's why they're past commanders, Top," Marshall replied. "I'll sleep in the field with the troops. We'll setup a GP small tent as the CP and our sleeping quarters. Sound good to you?"

"You bet, Sir. Anything you want to say at final formation?" asked Tisher.

"No Top. Just give them the two-minute warning that A.T. will be here after next month's drill is over," Marshall said. "Time to load up everything we're taking. Let's get this show on the road, shall we?"

They made their way to the door as the 683rd soldiers were waiting for them in formation in the parking lot.

JUNE DRILL - SATURDAY

Morning formation was over, and the platoon sergeants and officers were in the conference room for the last in-progress review.

"All right everyone, let's get this IPR rolling," Marshall said, his voice lowered an octave so everyone could hear him clearly over the din of chatter.

Each platoon and section leader reported on progress and what needed to be accomplished before the end of the drill weekend. They accounted for all their personnel, had their unit orders, and knew what vehicles they would be taking and who the drivers and assistant drivers were.

The advanced party of 17 personnel, headed by First Sergeant Tisher, would leave three days earlier than the main convoy. Their job would be to prepare the field site and make initial coordination with Fort Knox.

Everything appeared to be in order, which made Marshall feel a little more confident about the massive undertaking they were about to encounter. Every detail of the movement from Ravenna to Fort Knox—including maps of the route of travel, refueling stops, repairs of broken down vehicles, time tables, rest stops, and emergency plans—was covered. Marshall was one who liked to be prepared for the unexpected.

Marshall made his last comment before closing the meeting.

"Make sure all your vehicles are loaded and ready by the end of drill," Marshall said. "If you're not going to take something to A.T., put it down on a list and make sure I get a copy before noon tomorrow."

The meeting was adjourned and everyone left for the respective sections. Tisher walked over to Marshall. He noticed his commander had become more serious as the A.T. date was quickly approaching.

"Sir, I noticed you look kinda worried," Tisher said.

"Yeah Top, I'm concerned that things are going too well," Marshall replied. "You know. Murphy's Law. If anything can go wrong, it will."

Tisher smiled.

"Don't worry, Sir," Tisher said. "Me and John will keep an eye out for old Murph for you."

Back at the motor pool office, Sergeant Penny was holding a preliminary safety briefing for all the convoy drivers. They would receive one more safety briefing before the convoy headed out the main gate.

"If ya get a flat tire or mechanical problems, pull over to the side of the road and start your repairs," Penny said. "You other drivers that are followin', don't pull over to help, just pass'em by. The 5-ton wrecker will be by eventually. If the convoy leader has to pull off the road for repairs, the next one in line becomes the leader.

"That means everyone here better be readin' their maps and knowin' where the hell you are. One wrong turn can add hours to the trip and waste lots of fuel."

Most of the soldiers were paying attention to the briefing, except for a few that seemed to be more focused on Fran Peoples and Pam Williams.

One of the personnel attending the safety briefing was Sergeant Johnny Burkette. Burkette was assigned to drive the fuel truck, which was a 2½ ton truck with the cargo bows and canvas removed and loaded with two 400-gallon fuel pods.

Burkette worked as a bartender in the evenings. He wore prescription sunglasses and took catnaps whenever he could. It was rumored that he once fell asleep while riding his motorcycle and woke up lying in a ditch. Some thought he had a touch of narcolepsy, which he quickly dismissed.

Burkette was in the front row of the briefing, remaining motionless as the others quietly left.

"Johnny, you awake?" yelled Sergeant Penny, knowing Burkette was sound asleep.

Burkette flinched slightly and slowly got to his feet.

"I am now," he said

"You gonna stay awake drivin' that fuel truck, or will you be makin' the lead story on the 6 o'clock news?" quipped Penny jokingly.

Burkette just grinned and shuffled his feet out the door.

First Sergeant Tisher and Sergeant Lemasters were having a heated debate in Tisher's office.

"Top, I ain't gonna ride on no damn bus to A.T.!" Lemasters shouted. "Why don't you get someone like Mr. McCarthy, who needs a soft, wide seat to sit on fer 400 miles? I wanna be part of the convoy! The Old Man is gonna need me!"

"Settle down, John," Tisher said. "Mr. McCarthy is the OIC of the bus. You're the NCOIC. It's too late to be changin' unit orders anyway."

First Sergeant Tisher's voice dropped to a whisper.

"Besides, the Old Man wanted you to keep an eye on McCarthy and make sure the troops are in good hands," he said.

Lemasters suddenly changed his tune.

"Well, that's diff'rent," Lemasters said. "If the good commander wants me on the bus, then by God, I'll do it."

Tisher was now wearing a broad grin.

"I thought you'd be the best choice, John," Tisher said. "McCarthy won't be able to buffalo you around."

"He better not, if he knows what's good fer 'em," mused Lemasters. He had little respect for McCarthy and made sure his opinion was known. Anyone that would treat others callously and act like a know-it-all was on Sergeant First Class John Lemasters' personal moron list. He resigned himself to the fact he was going to have to ride the bus to Fort Knox with Chief McCarthy and would show as much military courtesy as he could muster.

"It's gonna be a long day," Lemasters admitted to the First Sergeant. "Who else is gonna' be on that bus?"

They went over the bus passenger list, discussed meal tickets for their stopovers, and discussed whether the bathroom onboard the bus was big enough to accommodate McCarthy's over-sized backside.

Marshall and Chief Farley were in the shop office discussing the layout of the field site at Mount Eden Base Camp. "Chief, I'd like to have both automotive platoons set up maintenance tents with at least six sections. They can decide how many to bring," stated Marshall, drawing on his past experience in the field.

"Sir, we've got maintenance tents, but they're still in depot packaging," Farley said. "They've never been used."

Marshall was surprised to hear that.

"Chief, just make sure they bring enough pieces to make up a medium-sized maintenance tent with doors and lights," Marshall said. "They'll appreciate working in a sheltered environment in the field."

"Sir, I'll see to it that everything is packed and ready," Chief Farley said. He knew the work involved with setting up a maintenance tent.

The maintenance tent resembled a canvas-covered quonset hut, with metal ribs and bows forming the framework of the tent. Each end had a massive canvas door that could be opened to allow trucks to exit at either end. It could be fitted with a heater for winter, and overhead electrical lighting to work during darkness. It just took a while to put it together.

"Chief, there's one more thing," added Marshall. "Make sure all the sections bring enough tentage, with tent poles, tent pegs, ridge poles, engineer tape, sand bags, generators, light sets, and the appropriate field manuals. They can't come back to get something they forgot once we're in the field."

Farley smiled.

"We've got it covered, Sir," he said. "The sections have loaded all of what you mentioned this morning. I went over that with 'em. The only thing left is to load up the maintenance tents. They'll groan a bit, but they'll get over it. Don't worry, Sir, we got you covered."

Marshall realized he was startling to rattle off his laundry list without asking if things had already been done. Marshall started to feel confident in Farley's abilities and more comfortable about the upcoming A.T.

In the unit supply room, Sergeant Mooney was going over his list of things to get ready. As the commo chief, he was in charge of making sure all the radios, field phones, switchboard, and other pieces and components were available and in working order. He was also entrusted with the CEOI (communications equipment operating instructions), a booklet that had all the frequencies, call signs, and encryption codes and decodes for the radios.

Sergeant Russell Bierce was Mooney's assistant commo NCO, as well as the NBC (nuclear, biological and chemical) NCO. Bierce was a quiet, highly decorated Vietnam veteran. It was rumored he saved his entire infantry platoon while under enemy fire. He was a modest man, and never did talk much about his past. He enjoyed soldiering, but had no great ambition to move up through the ranks.

"Sergeant Bierce, did you check out all the radios yet?" asked Mooney.

"Sure did, Sergeant Mooney," Bierce replied. "I got all the radio vehicle mounts installed and wired up, and the antenna masts mounted and secured."

"Outstanding, Sergeant Bierce!" shouted Jackie Mooney. There was nothing he enjoyed better than someone who could soldier as well as he could.

"I've got copies of the CEOIs made for each radio operator and all the radios are ready to be installed the morning we pull outta here," Bierce replied with a sense of confidence.

"Sweet Georgia Brown," Mooney mused when he heard Bierce's reply.

Back at the main shop, Specialist Jessie Dweedle was replacing the last truck tire in the demounter tire machine. He had spent nearly all his time during the past several drills changing tires for the entire unit.

Sergeant Johnny Burkette was picking up his newly mounted tire from Dweedle.

"Hey Jessie, you done a hell of a job of the tires. I appreciate it," said Burkette.

"Thanks, Sarge," Dweedle said. "You need any help puttin' that one on your deuce? I got some spare time on my hands now I'm all finished."

Burkette smiled at the offer. He wasn't buddy-buddy with Dweedle, although they were both assigned to the motor pool. "Sure thing Jessie. Could always use a little help from my friends," replied Burkette, borrowing a line from a Beatles song.

As Dweedle and Burkette rolled the newly mounted tire up to the deuce-and-a-half in the shop bay, Dweedle noticed that Sergeant Burkette had some electronic test equipment hooked up to the engine. He had an injector pump meter, oxygen sensor, exhaust gas meter, and other special tools on work benches next to the truck.

"What's up with all the testing gear?" asked Dweedle as they positioned the new tire onto the empty truck axle.

Burkette's eyes were still hidden by his sunglasses, but his big smile revealed his gold tooth as he repositioned the toothpick in his mouth with his tongue. Time to let Dweedle in on his secret.

"Jessie, I'm fine tuning this baby to be the boss deuce in this unit," Burkette said confidently. "This baby will be haulin' 800 gallons of fuel, and I'm not gonna be laggin' behind anyone on the convoy. Matter of fact, I'll be blastin' by you all to get to the next fuel stop, so this baby better be the pick of the litter, if you know what I mean."

Dweedle took it all in. His curiosity was in high gear.

"Sarge, could you give me a rundown on what the electronic stuff does?" Dweedle asked.

"Sure, Jessie," Burkette replied. "Let's get this tire bolted on and then I'll give you the guided tour of how all these gizmos work."

Dweedle was excited. Someone besides Chief James was giving him some good instruction on some high tech gear the unit had recently acquired. This was going to make his day.

Sergeant Lufton and Lieutenant Sean Smith were going over their detailed load plans when Chief Farley walked over to give them the news about the maintenance tents that Captain Marshall wanted the automotive platoons to take with them to A.T.

"Hey Jerry, L.T., just got the word from the Old Man. Each auto platoon will be taking at least one maintenance tent with six sections. Roger that?" asked Farley.

Both Lufton and Smith looked at each other.

"We got enough room, Sarge?" Smith asked.

Lufton grinned.

"I was wondering what we'd be hauling on the flatbed trailer. Now I know," Lufton said.

"Well L.T., let's get the troops up to speed and get it loaded while we've still got some time. The metal frames and anchors are ready to go, and the canvas is still in the burlap cover. Everything's brand new."

His voice had a touch of excitement. He was starting to realize that his new commander knew quite a bit about maintenance operations in the field. A maintenance tent would make their efforts much easier. It was just the initial hassle of loading and then erecting a large tent.

"We'll need to bring the five kilowatt generator, another light set and the portable air compressor too," remarked Lufton, realizing what was going to be needed when they set up their operations inside the maintenance tent.

Lieutenant Smith nodded his head in agreement and directed his gaze to Chief Farley.

"Did you tell the other auto platoon yet?" Smith asked.

Farley shook his head.

"No, I thought I'd tell you guys and see what kind of reaction I got," he replied.

Smith smiled, "I'll tell Lieutenant Kiley," he said. "I'd like to see her face when I give her the news."

All three parted company. Sergeant Lufton began shouting at some of his soldiers that were gainfully employed to form up as a detail. Chief Farley headed back to the shop office to take care of more planning and paperwork, while Lieutenant Smith briskly walked over to Kate Kiley's platoon area to give her the news.

As he informed her of Marshall's decision to take a maintenance tent, a loud, high pitched "What?" was heard over the noise in the shop. Apparently Lieutenant Kiley thought they were all done loading up their vehicles for A.T. Then she remembered what Marshall had been advising them from his first day as commander: Be flexible, adapt and overcome. It was time to put those words into practice.

Lieutenant Debbie Stiles was in her platoon's work area with her NCOIC Sergeant Huddle. Going over their load plans, they were in a debate about what and what not to bring to A.T. The list they had comprised several months earlier had gone through numerous revisions, and it was now time to make sure everything they were taking was identified and loaded.

"Ma'am, as much as I'd like to, we can't take the M88 to A.T.," Huddle said with a touch of exasperation coming through his voice. "It belongs to the recovery section, it's nearly impossible to haul, and Fort Knox won't allow it on Mount Eden either."

The M88 was the Army's premier tank recovery vehicle. It weighed in at more than 60 tons and had an enormous boom to lift tank turrets, massive cables and winches to pull tanks out of muck and mire. It also had large tracks that could plow up patches of ground into bare dirt. It was an awesome machine that required special hauling permits, a special trailer with massive tires and brakes to haul it, and a perfectly maintained 10-ton tractor to pull the massive load on the trailer.

"But Sarge, it'll be good training," replied Stiles as Captain Marshall walked over to speak with his training officer.

"Am I interrupting something?" asked Marshall as approached Stiles and Huddle.

"Sir, I'd like to see us take the M88 to A.T.," Stiles said. "It'll be great training for our people."

Marshall saw the frown on Huddle face as Stiles was talking. He was not in favor of taking the M88, nor having any part of the discussion that might embarrass his young and inexperienced boss. Marshall decided it was an excellent opportunity to reason things out with his young lieutenant.

"Well, let's weigh the pros and cons of taking the M88," he began. "Let's start with the cons. First, the M88 belongs to the recovery section, so they would have to make that primary decision to take it.

"Second, the M88 requires a special hauling permit to be allowed on the interstate highways," Marshall continued.

"Third, the trailer has to be in tip-top working order to haul the 60-ton vehicle. That means good tires, good brakes, good brake lines and air hoses. It would travel up and down some very steep inclines along the way to Fort Knox. The 10-ton tractor also has to be in perfect working order.

"And finally, Fort Knox will not allow us to bring a tracked vehicle to their wooded training area," Marshall finished.

Stiles was taking it all in. It was the same thing Huddle had told her. Finally she mustered up the courage and responded.

"And the pros, Sir?" she asked.

Marshall just grinned and nodded his head.

"The troops in the recovery section would have a ball driving it around," Marshall said. "But I'm afraid it would be like a bull in a china shop. There would be a lot of mess to clean up afterwards."

Huddle smiled and nodded his head in agreement as Stiles looked a bit disappointed. The realization of what was required meant there wouldn't be a M88 going with them to Mount Eden Base Camp. For the 683rd, it meant they didn't have to concern themselves with a possible nightmarish scenario.

In the arms room, Specialist Fran Peoples was unlocking the weapons racks and inspecting the condition of the 250 M16 rifles stockpiled inside. Private Hudson was tasked to assist her as she would check each one for cleanliness and insert the bolt assembly that matched each weapon by serial number. She would pull the bolt to the rear using the charging handle, then slowly let the bolt go forward to the locking position, making sure each bolt was seated properly.

"This is the second one I've found that doesn't match, Hudson," Peoples said matter-of-factly. "Make a note of the serial number and put a yellow tag on the carrying handle. We don't want to take it to A.T."

Private Huck Hudson enjoyed being stuck in the arms room with one of the most beautiful women he'd ever worked with. His admiration for her beauty began to diminish when she started barking orders to him. He soon realized his chances of wooing her were slim to none.

"You got it," replied Hudson as he copied down the serial number of the M16 and the number tag on the bolt. Both the weapon and bolt would have to been turned in for repair or replacement. He took out a yellow tag and placed it on the carrying handle of the M16 and placed it back into the weapons rack.

"What's next after we're done with the '16s?" he asked.

Peoples looked at her watch, then looked at the number of weapons left to check.

"If we get these next two racks done in 20 minutes, we'll check the M60 machine guns. We'll do the 50-cals next drill."

Hudson smiled. This was new territory for him and he enjoyed working with someone who knew how to work with weapon systems. Especially a good-looking someone.

The remainder of the drill went by quickly for the soldiers of the 683rd. The following morning promised to be the start of another very busy day.

JUNE DRILL - SUNDAY

It was one of those rare precious sunny days in northern Ohio. The sun was shinning brightly, no clouds in the sky, the temperature was near 74 degrees and the relative humidity was low. The old rumor mill had it that Ravenna was picked as the site of the Army ammunition plant during World War II because of the ever-present cloud cover. The only redeeming quality of the northern climate was a short but lovely spring, a mild summer, and a brief, colorful fall. Five months of snow, cold, and damp winter was a test of will for all those over the age of 12.

Preparation for annual training was nearing completion. It was the last day in June to get things in order. The upcoming July drill would give the 683rd a day and a half to get all final preparations in order before the start of A.T. The 683rd's Annual Training would officially commence on Sunday. The advanced party was scheduled to leave three days earlier. The chartered bus would leave on Sunday at 10 a.m., and the convoy would leave at 8 a.m.

Captain Marshall and Chief James were in the motor park, looking at the vehicles. It had been decided earlier that the trucks loaded with expensive equipment would be parked in the shop for added security. There was always the possibility of midnight prowlers looking for an easy target of opportunity to steal military hardware.

"Chief, is everything mechanically ready?" Marshall's voice was in search-mode, looking for a positive response.

"Sir, these trucks will make it to Fort Knox, and every truck has a good spare tire to handle any flats along they way," James replied.

"How about the drivers and assistant drivers? Have they had enough road time?" Marshall asked. Marshall knew that drivers could not get enough windshield time in the Army Reserves because of the limited driving opportunities.

"Well, Sir, we've got most of the NCOs driving," James said. "They're all good drivers with lots of experience. The new ones will get their chance behind the wheel on the way down to Knox and back."

Marshall's face began to show a slight smile.

"Chief, I got a feeling this is going to be an adventure."

Marshall left Chief James to oversee the 683rd personnel doing their motor stables. With A.T. looming in the forefront of everyone's thoughts, everyone was more focused getting the trucks ready for the long drive.

Walking through the shop, Marshall saw most of the equipment had been loaded onto trucks. Each maintenance bay had at least one truck being loaded or worked on. The shop's center aisle had a row of loaded trucks lined up, two abreast. Marshall was satisfied with what he saw and departed for the orderly room to discuss other pressing issues with First Sergeant Tisher.

"Top, what have we got left to do before A.T.?" Marshall asked, not wanting to beat around the bush.

"Sir, the only thing left to do next drill is get the vehicles lined up outside the orderly room on Saturday morning, load the weapons in the weapons trailer, give each soldier his A.T. orders, issue out the field gear and M17 gas masks, then kiss good old Ravenna Army Ammunition Plant and Reserve Center goodbye for two weeks," Tisher said.

Marshall was relieved to hear that Tisher had a good feel for what remained to be done.

"Top, if I'm reading you right, we can sit back the rest of the drill, drink coffee and catch up on some paperwork," Marshall said.

Tisher wore his broad grin.

"Sounds like a winner to me, Sir," he replied.

Chief McCarthy and Sergeant Schmoot were going over their to-do list with Lieutenant Burks at the near-empty warehouse building. Except for the old desks and chairs, one fairly new coffee maker and a couple of beat-up field tables, the warehouse was empty.

"Mr. McCarthy, are all the parts inventoried and loaded on the trailers?" Burks asked

"Yes Ma'am," replied McCarthy as he was snacking on a candy bar. "We'll have to redo the sorting and inventory of the repair parts when we get to A.T. With the extra fifteen personnel coming from the 646th Supply Company in the way of attached warehouse personnel, that should help with the set-up of the trailers. If all goes well, we should be completely operational within a week."

"That's fine, Chief," Burks said. "Just keep me posted on the progress daily when we're there."

At the motor pool office, Sergeant Baxter was having a meeting with Specialist Jessie Dweedle and Pam Williams. The maintenance tent requirement was about to be tasked down to the working level.

"I want both of you to head up the loading of one maintenance tent we're gonna take to A.T.," ordered Sergeant Joe Baxter in his normal monotone voice.

Both Williams and Dweedle looked at each other a bit bewildered.

"Load everything up on the deuce with the headquarters-6 bumper number. It's empty right now. I want it done before the end of drill. Any questions?" Baxter asked.

"Oh, I almost forgot," he added. "Make sure the tire mounting machine is loaded onto the empty 1½-ton trailer."

"How many sections you want loaded, Sarge?" asked Dweedle.

"Six sections with all the framing and both door sections," Baxter said. "Grab as many motor pool personnel as you can to help. You're both in charge, so get goin'."

Dweedle and Williams walked out onto the shop floor, looking for some volunteers. Williams spotted Fran Peoples carrying on a conversation with a couple soldiers.

Williams walked over to Peoples.

"Hey, girlfriend," Williams said. "How about you and your buddies givin' us a hand?"

"What's up Pam?" asked Peoples.

"Oh, just some help loading a few pieces of canvas for the maintenance tent and one tire mounting machine, and I don't mean Jessie."

Peoples grinned at Williams and looked at her male following.

"I just love a contest of male strength," Peoples said in a sultry voice. "Now, who's the strongest amongst you hunks of manpower?"

In short order, Peoples had eight volunteers that loaded the deuce and trailer within 15 minutes. Williams thought to herself, that's what I call girl power.

Sergeant Bob Bitsko was in the motor park working on his beloved 20-ton rough terrain crane. He made it his personal goal to keep the machine operating. Parts were becoming scarce, and numerous times he would have to order common items like air cleaner filters and oil and fuel filters months in advance.

The Army supply system finally came through and his shipment of parts arrived the week before drill. Bitsko was excited to get to work on his favorite piece of Army equipment.

Wondering where he should start first, Bitsko looked over the operator's manual for the 20-ton crane.

"Hmmmmh, looks like the fuel filters should be changed first," Bitsko said as he double-checked the logbook. "Yep, hasn't been changed in two years."

As he opened the drain plug on the fuel filter housing, he held an old foam cup under it to catch a fuel sample. Looks like we got some water contamination here, he thought to himself as he could see more water than fuel in the drained sample.

He tossed the sample on the gravel road and checked the next fuel filter.

"Yep, you got water too," he grumbled to himself.

This meant only one thing. The fuel in the 20-ton crane fuel tank had not been emptied in over two years. The fuel tank would have to be completely emptied and sent to the civilian maintenance shops for repair or replacement. Bitsko did not like the idea of having to drain the tank and remove it all by himself. It was a two-man job that took several hours to do.

Chief James was in the motor park and Sergeant Bitsko walked over to him and explained what he had found.

"Is that so?" replied Chief James as Bitsko gave him the lowdown on the 20-ton crane. "Well, looks like we got something to do when we get back from A.T."

Bitsko looked a bit bewildered.

"You know, Chief," he said, "I was all set to pull maintenance on her when I found out her fuel system was full of water. Dang."

"Glad to have you lookin' after it," James replied as they walked toward the crane. "Accordin' to the logbook, the last time that thing's had any work done was when it was serviced by the recovery section six months ago. Looks like it was too cold to do any kind of a thorough job. That water was probably frozen and didn't show up when they checked the fuel filters. Good thing you caught it, Sarge. Good job."

"Thanks, Chief," Bitsko said. "It's a nice piece of equipment, but it's got to be maintained. I used to love to operate one when I was back in Vietnam. I was pretty good and loading and off-loading with this baby." Bitsko started to smile, remembering his carefree days as a young private first class.

"You might get a chance to use it here, but I kinda doubt it," replied Chief James.

"Yeah, I have to agree with you on that," Bitsko said. "Not much of a need for one around here, unless we get called up because the Russkies are invadin' Europe."

Chief James nodded with a slight grin.

"Yep, but I kinda doubt that'll happen," James said. "Those Russkies are too busy just tryin' to keep things on the inside in order. They got more problems to deal with on their plate already. Startin' World War III ain't one of their priorities at the moment. Besides, there so bogged down in Afghanistan right now, they can't mount any kind of new offensive."

Bitsko looked at James in amazement.

"How do you know all this stuff, Chief?" he asked.

James looked him in the eye.

"I keep up with current events and used to be an intelligence officer back during the days when people were busy buildin' bomb shelters and Nikita Krushchev was poundin' his shoe on the desk at the UN," James said seriously.

Bitsko was becoming more curious about Chief James' past.

"How long you been in the Army, Chief?" he asked.

James closed one eye and raised the eyebrow of the other and looked up at the top of the nearby trees.

"This year will make 41 years of service," he said. "Next year, they're forcin' me to retire. Just as well. I'm looking forward to spendin' more time with the family and my grandkids. I wanna take 'em fishin' and huntin'. That'll be great. Maybe spend more time with the Mrs. and plant a bigger garden. Who knows?"

Bitsko was a bit amused at Chief James.

"You get to meet any famous people?" Bitsko said.

"Well, my good friend Joe DiMaggio sends me a new coffee maker every Christmas," James said with a twinkle in his eyes. "Most of the young officers I met along the way have retired or went on to get their stars. I served with three Army chiefs of staffs and knew a whole bunch of others. It's really a small Army when you think about it. Kinda like a family. The reunions happen all the time."

Sergeant First Class Fred Kiley was working in his direct exchange section making certain all the equipment and exchangeable DX parts were loaded onto their 2 1/2 –ton M109 van and deuces. Sergeant Kiley's section was a part of the tech supply platoon. Their job was to rebuild brake linings, motor starters, alternators, and other small components.

The DX Section was staffed with 12 personnel. Its mission was to take in a bad component that needed repair and exchange it with a newly rebuilt one. During the spring and summer months, brake linings were a particularly popular item that kept the section busy.

"Don't forget to load up extra brake linings for our trucks and trailers!" Kiley shouted over the noise in his section as his people were busily moving and loading their equipment.

"Gotcha covered, Sarge," yelled one of his personnel from inside the trailer portion of the M109 van.

Kiley was concerned about how many different units they would be supporting at Mount Eden Base Camp, as well as their own needs for replacement components. He was a cautious and caring NCO that didn't like to let anyone down. Especially when it came to doing his job. It was a matter of personal pride.

His wife and fellow member of the 683rd, Second Lieutenant Kathy Kiley, was his first love and soul mate. They were a perfect couple that enjoyed their civilian and military life working together. Whenever they could, they would eat their meals together, and often work late together. It didn't matter as long as they were with each other.

"Fred, is your section going to be working after drill?" Kathy Kiley asked her husband as she walked over to see him.

"Well, hello there, stranger," replied Fred Kiley with a broad smile across his face. He was always happy to see his lovely wife.

"No, Honey. We should be all done before the end of drill today," he continued. "Do you want to got out and catch a dinner and a movie tonight?"

Kathy was always amazed at how much he could eat and not gain a pound. He once ate 10 cheeseburgers and three plates of fries in one sitting at a favorite bistro. Fred said he wasn't full, but his jaws were tired from all the chewing.

"Sounds good to me. I just don't feel like cooking tonight," she replied.

Sergeant Fred Kiley smiled.

"Well, I sure feel like eating and relaxing," he said. "It's a date!"

He then turned his attention back to those section personnel working and loading the trucks.

"All right everyone, take five!" he commanded.

His section personnel respected him and the way he treated them. He was the first to roll up his shirtsleeves and get involved with the work they were doing. Kiley believed in leading by example, and having been an enlisted man that came up through the ranks, he knew how he liked to be treated and how to interact effectively with others.

Sergeant First Class Wilbur Heinz and First Lieutenant Rod Rodriguez were working on the convoy operations plan in the 683rd orderly room. Rodriguez had checked with the Ohio and Kentucky departments of transportation to determine if there would be any road construction in their route of travel to Fort Knox.

"Sarge, I checked this morning with our friends from the transportation offices of both states. No major road construction on any of the roads we're taking to A.T.," said Rodriguez.

"L.T., this will be a first," Heinz said. "We normally take a couple of back roads when we go anywhere." He was very pleased to hear there would be no deviations from their route of travel.

"We just got to make sure all the drivers have a strip map, just in case one of 'em gets left behind because of a flat tire," mentioned Rodriguez as he continued with his reviewing of the convoy plan.

"Don't worry, Sir," Heinz replied. "All these guys know how to get to Fort Knox. They won't get lost."

One hour later, First Sergeant Tisher was holding final formation in the parking lot. He then turned the formation over to Captain Marshall, who had a few words to say to the assembled personnel of the 683rd.

"Stand at ease!" commanded Marshall, as everyone in the formation relaxed.

"Everyone has done an excellent job getting things ready for A.T.!" Marshall said.

"Make sure your loved ones know what's going on and who to contact in the orderly room in case of emergency. Sergeant Mulberry and Specialist Cork will be here while we're gone. At Mount Eden Base Camp, we may not have telephonic communications with the outside world, but our group headquarters will. In any event, they will be able to get word to us in the field." Soldiers nodded at the commander's advice.

"The next drill will be Friday evening, July the ninth. Drill will be from 1900 hours until 2300 hours, so come prepared to load up anything that hasn't been accomplished this drill. Have a safe and enjoyable 4th of July. See you next month! 683rd...Ten hut! Dismissed!"

JULY DRILL - FRIDAY EVENING

The advanced party had phoned in to report their arrival at Mount Eden Base Camp. So far, all was going well. First Sergeant Tisher reported they had forgotten a few items for their tents and generators, and requested the main convoy bring the missing items along.

Sergeant Mulberry was the full-time civilian administrator of the 683rd during the week and assumed all the responsibilities of the company commander when Captain Marshall was not present. One of his daily functions was to make sure all incoming and outgoing correspondence was properly received, reviewed, and processed. He wouldn't be going with the 683rd to annual training due to the enormous amount of never-ending paperwork the 683rd received on a daily basis. Mulberry would spend the next two weeks with his administrative assistant, Specialist Charlie Cork, handling the paper load.

"Charlie, where is our file copy of the unit A.T. orders?" Mulberry asked, looking all over his desktop and inside numerous desk drawers.

"I've filed them away already, Sarge," Cork said. "If you need to find something, just ask me."

Mulberry had the same problem at home as he did in the office. He just couldn't seem to find things when he needed them. Sometimes he wondered if it was due to all the artillery and mortar fire he had to endure in Vietnam.

In reality, Sergeant Mulberry was a bit disorganized and needed the help of his clerks (and wife) to keep pace with the daily requirements of his job and family life.

"Found 'em!" exclaimed Mulberry as he walked over to the commander's office to go over the A.T. roster and account for all the 683rd and attached personnel. "Sir, I've got the A.T. roster and unit orders."

Mulberry lumbered into Marshall's office and spread out the paperwork on the desk.

"Sir, you're not going to believe this," Mulberry said. "We've got 100 percent of our personnel that are able to go to annual training, going."

"Is that unusual for this unit, Sarge?" Marshall inquired, wondering why that would be so significant.

"Sir, as long as I can remember, we've always had a few that couldn't go for various reasons," Mulberry said.

Marshall took it as a compliment. Unit morale was improving as underscored by the number of personnel the 683rd was going to have in the field at annual training. Marshall looked at Mulberry, who still had a look of amazement on his face.

"Well, Sarge, looks like we're doing something right," Marshall said.

As soon as Marshall finished uttering those words, Lieutenant Meglynn entered the room on crutches. She had a plaster cast from her left toe to above her knee.

"Sir, sorry to be the bearer of bad news," she said with her cheeks pink. "I broke my ankle yesterday after ballet class."

Marshall had a look of concern on his face.

"What happened?" he asked.

Meglynn looked down at her left foot and shrugged her shoulders, as if she was ashamed.

"I didn't watch were I was going and took a bad step off the sidewalk and broke my ankle."

"Ouch!" Marshall said with a twinge. "How long are you going to be in the cast?"

"Oh, about eight weeks," replied Meglynn. "The doctor told me not to put any weight on it for a month. He told me to stay off my feet for the first week or so."

Marshall stroked his chin, contemplating what needed to be done with Meglynn since her present physical condition required light duty, which precluded her from going to Mount Eden for A.T.

Sergeant Mulberry interjected, knowing that the situation could be easily remedied.

"Sir, we'll have the lieutenant do a home station A.T. with us," Mulberry said. "I'll just amend the A.T. orders to reflect that. Battalion will sign off on the change and she can do a home station A.T. with us in the orderly room."

Marshall liked what he heard and looked at Meglynn.

"Sound good to you?" Marshall asked.

"Yes Sir, it sure does," she replied with a smile of relief on her face.

Marshall concurred.

"Then it's settled," he said. "You'll pull your two-week A.T. here in the orderly room. You can go home after the duty day is done and report back in the morning."

Mulberry, Meglynn and Cork left Marshall's office to begin preparing the amendment to the annual training orders. Marshall felt relieved that the situation was resolved easily.

Shortly after Marshall went back to looking over the paperwork on his desk, Major Breedlow knocked on the door for an unexpected visit. Marshall was glad to see him. Breedlow had been one of the previous company commanders of the 683rd, and took the unit to Mount Eden Base Camp four years earlier.

"Greetings Dave," said Breedlow. "I just wanted to drop by and get an update on what's goin' on. You need any additional help?"

Marshall appreciated his interest and felt there were a few questions he could answer.

"Sir, I've been concerned about the area itself, as far as the terrain and the location we've been given," Marshall said.

"Dave, we were located on the same patch of ground years ago," Breedlow responded. "The slope of the hill isn't too bad, and there's plenty of tree cover to hide the tents and vehicles under. The only problem we had was the chiggers, fire ants, wood ticks and deer ticks."

"How did you handle those?" Marshall was concerned about the unforeseen enemy.

"The best way to protect yourself is to take a flea collar and put it between your boot laces," Breedlow replied. "The Army insect repellant doesn't work well on those varmints, but flea collars do."

"Flea collars?" Marshall was rather surprised at the recommendation.

Breedlow grinned.

"The chiggers are the worst," he said. "You'll see what I mean. They can make you miserable."

"Anything else I should know?" Marshall inquired.

"Nah, just have a good time in the field," Breedlow said. "You've got some great soldiers in the unit and you've done a super job getting everyone to work together. Just keep a watchful eye on your problem children."

The rest of the 683rd was down in the shop area loading what they needed to complete their loading plans. Every item determined to be vital to the maintenance support mission was double-checked and re-inventoried to make sure it would be available for A.T. Whatever challenge would come their way, each platoon and section was going to be ready. Marshall had insisted from his first day as the commander that he wanted everyone to be able to perform their job in any situation. Marshall's words did not go unheeded.

The shop office had the Cleveland Indians baseball game blasting loudly on the radio, informing everyone who was an Indians fan of the progress of the game against the Seattle Mariners. The Tribe was winning, to the delight of all those fans in the shop. The All-Star Game was going to be played on the 13th. Several Indians players made the All-Star Team for the American League. It was a very good year for baseball. The Indians represented the underdog team of baseball. Every year at the start of the professional baseball season, true Indians fans always believed they had a chance to go all the way to the World Series. Indians fans were true optimists. Their glass was always half full. Unfortunately, the 683rd was going to be at Mount Eden for the All-Star Game.

Sergeant Bradford was busy packing up the necessary reference manuals to take to Mount Eden Base Camp. The shop office had three tech inspectors, including Sergeant Bradford, who were experts in diagnostics and repair. Their job was to inspect a broken down piece of Army equipment, determine what needed to be fixed, write down all the repair parts by name and stock number, determine the man-hours required to fix the equipment, and fill out the parts requisitions for the repair parts and submit the requisitions.

Bradford and Chief Farley would determine the workload of each platoon and their skill levels before assigning the job order to get the equipment fixed. Normally the only delay would be getting the repair parts.

Later that evening at final formation, Marshall addressed the assembled 683rd soldiers.

"I've been informed that besides the advanced party, there are other occupants located at our field site at Mount Eden Base Camp. In particular, some six and eight legged insect critters," he said. "Make sure you have plenty of insect repellent, either Uncle Sam's or the store-bought kind, and use it. I've been told that pet flea collars laced between your bootlaces work well. The Army doesn't issue flea collars unless you walk on all fours and can wag your tail."

Several soldiers made a barking sound, while a few others meowed. Marshall ignored them.

"You'll have to get the flea collars on your own," he said. "The critters I'm talking about are fire ants, chiggers, deer ticks and wood ticks. All wonderful creatures found together in one location, so be advised and be prepared."

"You've all been doing an outstanding job getting ready for A.T.," he continued. "Keep up the good work. I'll see you all bright and early tomorrow morning. Dismissed!"

After the personnel had departed the formation, Marshall drove directly to the nearest late-night pharmacy and bought two black flea collars. They wouldn't be too noticeable when placed between his boot laces, he thought.

JULY DRILL - SATURDAY

Shortly after morning formation, the 683rd Orderly Room was buzzing like a beehive. Just outside, the 683rd convoy vehicles were lined up into three groups, also known as serials. The 5-ton tractor, attached to the weapons trailer, was parked close to the orderly room exit door.

Sergeant Bierce was busy installing radios and Specialist Peoples was in the arms vault signing for all the weapons and unlocking the padlocks securing the M16s to the weapons racks.

Sergeant Lemasters had already organized a weapons loading detail. Thirty soldiers were standing in a line from the arms vault to the weapons van.

Inside the weapons trailer, Specialist Williams was placing the M16s in the racks as they were being passed to her from the line of soldiers in a process resembling a bucket brigade. Everyone was helping one another to get things loaded and secured for the convoy the next morning.

In the conference room, Marshall held his officers' meeting to go over the day's upcoming priorities.

"Today is our last day to make sure everything is ready to hit the road for A.T.," he began. "Anyone have any concerns, questions or comments?"

The group remained silent for several seconds.

"OK, let's cover areas that need to be discussed," Marshall said, breaking the silence. "Does every assistant driver have a map of the route the convoy is going to travel?"

All heads nodded in agreement.

"All vehicles fueled up? Operator's checks done? Everyone know what serial they're in? Sign placards on the last vehicle in each serial? Sign placards on the first vehicle?"

All heads were nodding and smiling in the group, including Chief James, whom Marshall was focusing on.

"Looks like we're all set then," he said, satisfied.

Marshall decided to direct a question to Chief McCarthy.

"Bus commander, are all your people taken care of? Meal tickets and C-rations?"

"Yes Sir, the troops are all taken care of and accounted for," McCarthy said.

"Very good!" replied Marshall. There were still a few more issues to broach.

"With the weapons trailer being fully loaded, we're going to need a posted guard around it starting after final formation and continuing until tomorrow morning," he said. "Mr. McCarthy, I want the people traveling by bus to perform the guard duty. They'll be able to catch up on their sleep on the way down to Fort Knox. Guards will pull two-hour shifts and Sergeant Lemasters will be the NCOIC."

Chief McCarthy was visibly upset with the commander's directive.

"Sir, those soldiers should be with their families for the evening," McCarthy said.

Marshall was ready for McCarthy.

"I agree, Mr. McCarthy," he said. "I want only the unmarried soldiers pulling guard duty tonight. Married soldiers are exempt."

Chief McCarthy was visibly flustered. Marshall was faster on the draw than McCarthy had given him credit for.

Sergeant Lemasters was busy supervising the load up of the weapons trailer.

"All right you sad sacks, look alive!" he shouted. He looked inside. "Williams, how's it goin' in there?"

"Just about done with the last row, Sarge," she replied.

"All right!" Lemasters replied. "After we git the crew-served weapons loaded, you stay in the trailer until we git the padlocks on each rack and chains attached to the crew-served. Got it?"

"Yes Field First Sergeant!" shot back the reply from Specialist Williams. She respected and liked Sergeant Lemasters. She felt anyone staying in the military that long deserved respect.

Seven male helpers accompanied Specialist Peoples as they approached the weapons trailer. They were carrying six machine guns with chains and padlocks. The chains and padlocks Peoples carried were so heavy that she needed help getting up the steps of the weapons trailer. Several soldiers rushed up and gently assisted her up the steps by placing their hands on her backside and gently and firmly giving her a boost.

"Thanks boys, I enjoyed that," replied Specialist Peoples in her Mae West voice.

Twenty minutes later, the weapons and the weapons trailer were properly secured.

Chalk numbers were written of the back bumper or fender of each vehicle so the driver in the following vehicle would know if they were in the correct position within the convoy. Each driver in the convoy was given a detailed map of the route the convoy was supposed to take. The detailed map consisted of four pages along with an itemized list of phone numbers for emergency repairs by area Army Reserve maintenance facilities. The drivers were instructed to let their assistant driver be the navigator.

Radios were checked and Sergeant Bierce provided instructions on proper radio procedures, including the most important instructions of all: Turn the radio off before starting the vehicle engine. This would prevent the radio from being damaged by a sudden rush of electrical current from the alternator.

Communications and electronic operating instructions, commonly referred to by its acronym CEOI, would be given out in the morning after they had been issued to the person using the radio. The CEOI was treated like a secret document, and control of its use was restricted to only those who had a need and a proper security clearance. Before the convoy left the next day, Sergeant Bierce would make sure every radio would be on the correct frequency.

After the weapons were loaded and secured in the trailer, Specialist Peoples was busy issuing the 683rd soldiers their field gear, which was stored in the unit supply room. Only the officers and NCOs were allowed to keep their field gear at their homes. There wasn't much of a problem with NCOs and officers suddenly leaving the unit without notification. The same did not hold true for the enlisted personnel below the rank of E-5 (Sergeant). Younger soldiers were quite mobile and would often find new employment wherever they could. Many times they would leave town and not inform the Reserve unit of their whereabouts.

Field gear, normally called TA50, was valued at more than $500. Pawn shops would welcome the items like sleeping bags, blankets, cold weather gear and entrenching tools. Marshall did not want to tempt the younger soldiers, nor did he want to incur investigations and waste government time and money. He made it his policy to store the TA50 in the unit supply room the first day he took over as commander. This policy was adopted throughout the United States Army Reserve.

Sergeant Lemasters walked over to Marshall's office and saw him reviewing more paperwork that Sergeant Mulberry had prepared for him.

"Got a minute, Sir?" Lemasters asked.

"Sure Sarge," Marshall said. "What's on your mind?"

Lemasters walked in and closed the door behind him. He didn't want their conversation to be overheard by some of the nosy clerks working in the orderly room.

"Sir, I jest wanna say I think you're doin' a great job as commander," he said.

Marshall wasn't expecting any compliments and was a bit surprised.

"Why thank you, Sergeant Lemasters. I certainly appreciate that comment, and think all the NCOs are doing a fantastic job," Marshall said. "It's a big job getting everyone to move in the same direction. I couldn't do it with out all of your support."

Lemasters grinned.

"Well Sir, you sure got mine. I'll keep a close eye on the troops fer ya, and one on McCarthy too."

Marshall was grinning as the old Sarge was talking. Marshall had great respect for Lemasters and the other old soldiers of the 683rd.

"Sarge, there is one thing you can do for me while we're in the field," Marshal replied.

"What's that, Sir?" Lemasters quickly replied.

Marshall carefully chose his words.

"I'd like to make sure that every soldier that does well in the field gets some kind of recognition," he said. "My first group commander on active duty had a motto: Reward good performance, record poor performance, make recommendations and check-check-check!"

Lemasters grinned.

"Sounds like that man knew what he was talkin' about," he said.

"Yeah, he made his way from enlisted man to lieutenant general," Marshall replied. "He's one of those leaders you come across that you'd like to emulate."

Lemasters had a puzzled look on his face.

"You'd like to what?" he asked.

Marshall chuckled.

"Be like," he replied.

"Ohhhh. I got 'cha," Lemasters said. "Well, Sir, I best be back to overseein' our troops. I speak fer all the NCOs: we appreciate your efforts, Sir."

Marshall looked as Sergeant Lemasters stood up and snapped to a salute.

"Carry on good Sergeant!" said Marshall as he returned the salute and watched Lemasters exit his office.

That was a nice visit, thought Marshall as he continued with the review and signing of paperwork on his desk.

Chief McCarthy and Sergeant Schmoot were supervising their tech supply personnel as the tech supply parts trailers with borrowed 5-ton tractors were being positioned into the convoy serials.

"Wow, Chief. I never thought I'd see the day when we'd have all our trailers hooked-up and ready to go," Schmoot said, scratching his head. "They're quite a sight."

Chief McCarthy was looking over the long line of tech supply vehicles. He knew his section's work was just beginning.

"Yeah, Dennis," McCarthy replied. "I was hoping we wouldn't have to bring it all along with us, but the Old Man is persistent."

"We don't have enough camouflage nets to cover up all the tractors and trailers, but we do have enough for the tents," Schmoot observed.

McCarthy had to smirk when he heard what Schmoot said. "I don't think we'll need to worry about camouflaging anything, Dennis," he said. "Once we get to the field and Captain Marshall sees all the equipment that's been brought, he'll wish he hadn't. Then he'll realize I was right. Besides, how the hell can you hide all this equipment we're bringing? Can you tell me that?"

Schmoot looked rather puzzled.

"What do ya mean, Chief?" he asked.

McCarthy became serious and raised his voice when he spoke to Sergeant Schmoot.

"We've got over 30 vehicles, not counting trailers, going to the field," McCarthy said. "This unit has only 18 camouflage nets for the tents. There's no way you can conceal a maintenance company this size unless you've got a perfect spot to hide them in the woods. You ever been to Mount Eden, Dennis?"

Schmoot was going along with Chief McCarthy. He wanted to hear him lay it all out.

"No, Chief, I haven't," he replied.

"Well, Dennis, let me tell you," McCarthy began. "That area has maybe three or four acres of flat ground. The rest is all sloped. The woods are thick with brush and small trees. The last time I was there, about eight years ago, you couldn't even drive a ¼-ton through the area."

Schmoot decided it was time to pose a question for the Chief.

"What if they've had the engineers come in and clean up the area?" he asked. "I've been with the engineers before, and they can turn an area like that into a perfect spot to bivouac an entire brigade."

Chief McCarthy chuckled.

"In your dreams, Dennis," he responded. "In your dreams."

Little did Chief McCarthy know that the engineers had done precisely that over the past several years. Mount Eden Base Camp was beautifully prepared for the 683rd and numerous other Army units to occupy and conduct field training.

The chiggers and fire ants, however, still remained and were eagerly awaiting the next occupants.

Lieutenant Rodriguez and Sergeant Heinz were in charge of lining up the 683rd vehicles for the convoy. Each serial was parked in a separate grouping and lined up according to platoon and type of vehicle. The lead vehicle in each serial was a ¼-ton jeep with radio for command and control. Rodriguez felt confident that everything was going according to plan, and all drivers and their assistants were well briefed and prepared for the long road trip the following morning.

"Hey Sarge, when do you want to have Sergeant Burkette top-off the fuel tanks?" Rodriguez asked.

"Well, Sir, I told Sergeant Johnny this morning to top off every one and get refueled before the end of drill," Sergeant Heinz replied. "He should be just about done by now."

Lieutenant Rodriguez walked over to the second row of parked trucks and saw Sergeant Burkette and his assistant filling up the last truck. He walked over to get his attention and find out how far he had gotten.

"Sergeant Burkette, how many more trucks do you have to fuel?" Rodriguez asked.

Sergeant Johnny Burkette was wearing his signature pair of sunglasses and smiled, showing his gold-filled front teeth.

"Sir, we're all done," Burkette said. "I've even filled all the five-gallon jerry cans on all the trucks and ¼-tons. I just gotta refill my fuel pods, and we're greased and ready to glide."

"So very fine, Sergeant!" Rodriguez and Burkette gave each other a high five. "Let's get ready to glide."

"Right on, Sir!"

A.T. - DAY 1 (SUNDAY)

It was a gorgeous July morning. The assembled members of the 683rd stood in formation getting their last bit of instruction and safety briefings by several NCOs. All the 683rd troops were present and accounted for. Captain Marshall took the formation from Sergeant Lemasters.

"Good morning, 683rd!" shouted Marshall.

"Good morning, Sir!" echoed loudly from the troops.

"Looks like we have a beautiful day to travel," Marshall said, surveying the blue skies and sunshine. "I want all of you to drive safely and arrive in one piece at Fort Knox. If you have any road emergency, pull over and let the rest of the convoy pass. You will become part of the trail party after you've been fixed up.

"I've asked the chaplain to give us a word of prayer before we leave for Fort Knox."

Chaplain Dillon asked everyone to remove their hats, and began his prayer of traveling mercies for the 683rd.

With the prayer finished, Captain Marshall took charge of the formation.

"Thank you Chaplain," he said. "All right 683rd, the first serial will depart at 0800 hours. The second serial will depart at 0810 hours and the third at 0820 hours. I will meet you at the first refueling stop, which is the Union 76 truck stop on Interstate 71. Fall out!"

The entire unit did an about-face movement and shouted "683rd!" much to the amazement and delight of Marshall.

Marshall looked at his watch. It was 0730 hours. Time to leave and get to the first refueling point and wait for the other units in the overall convoy. Chief James volunteered to be Marshall's driver. Marshall was glad to be riding with the most knowledgeable driver in the 683rd to Fort Knox.

"Sir, we're ready to roll," James said. "I checked out the radio, and we are all set."

Marshall smiled knowing he was in good hands.

"OK, Chief," he said. "Let's head out to the first check point and refueling stop."

Neither man knew that the jeep mounted radio was still on. Chief James started the jeep's engine and unknowingly damaged one of the internal components of the radio. They could no longer send radio messages, only receive them.

"By the way, Chief, who's driving the refueling truck?" asked Marshall.

Chief James thought for a second.

"Oh, that'll be Sergeant Johnny Burkette," he replied.

Marshall seemed to be a little puzzled at the choice of driver for the refueling truck.

"Isn't he the one who fell asleep while riding his motorcycle?" Marshall said.

Chief James chuckled at hearing what Marshall just said.

"Shoot Sir, I didn't hear about that one, but he sure nods off a lot during drill," James said. "That's why he always wears those wrap-around sunglasses. I hear he's a bartender by trade. Tends bar in the Flats up in Cleveland."

Marshall shook his head slightly.

"I sure hope he's had a good night's sleep," he said. "I hate to think of what can happen if he didn't."

"Don't worry, Sir. You've got Specialist Dweedle in the truck with him," James said. "He'll probably do most of the driving if Burkette starts droppin' off."

The ¼ –ton Army jeep was now about a mile away from the Reserve center. The Ohio convoy commander was ready to make contact with the other unit convoys, even though the range of the radio was 20 miles.

"Time for a radio check with the other convoy commanders," said Marshall as he glanced over his shoulder to get the handset and turn the radio on. He saw the power switch was already set in the "On" position and groaned.

"Chief, the radio power switch was on when you started the jeep," Marshall said.

Chief James had that bad sinking feeling in the pit of his stomach. He was hoping and praying the radio was still functional.

Marshall attempted to contact the 683rd since they were only a few miles away.

"River Edge 2, this is River Edge 1, over."

Nothing, just a background hiss, was heard on the radio as Marshall released the push-to-talk-button on the radio's handset. Marshall tried several more times, but no response was heard.

Marshall looked calmly over to his driver.

"Chief, looks like we're not starting out too well," Marshall said. "Can we get another radio?"

Chief James shrugged his shoulders and gave a reluctant look at his commander.

"No, Sir, That was the last one in the battalion that worked," he said. "We'll have to get it fixed at Knox."

"Looks like we better start using smoke signals to communicate with the convoy. The radio's worthless," replied Marshall.

Marshall and James continued down the road and onto the interstate, toward the refueling stop. Marshall wondered how long the good weather would last, and how he was going to control all the convoys without a working radio.

The ride in the ¼-ton jeep was quite pleasant that Sunday morning. Traffic was light and the warm weather and sunny sky made the start of their journey enjoyable.

Arriving at the refueling point, located at the interstate junction on I-71, Marshall and James awaited the first convoy from the 646th Supply and Service Company. The 646th personnel would be attached to the 683rd for the entire annual training period to supplement the 683rd Mess Section and Tech Supply Section.

Marshall spotted a column of military vehicles turning into the truck refueling area.

"Chief, looks like the 646th is right on time," he said.

Marshall looked at his watch. 0915 hours, just as planned. As the 646th vehicles were getting refueled, Marshall and Chief

James walked over to meet with the drivers and discuss the next refueling stop.

Marshall met Sergeant First Class Ralph Emery.

"Sergeant Emery, glad to meet you, and I'm very glad you and your people are joining us for the A.T.," greeted Marshall.

Sergeant Emery was a tall and muscular man in his mid-40s with a big smile.

"Sir, the pleasure is all mine," Emery said.

Marshall was quite pleased to finally meet Sergeant Emery, the owner and head chef of Ralph's Taj Mahal Restaurant.

"I've been told by my First Sergeant you're going to fatten us up while we're out in the field," mentioned Marshall, injecting a small portion of humor.

"Yes, Sir, I'm gonna do my best to make everyone forget about momma's cookin', and look forward to Ralph's cookin'," he replied.

Marshall grinned.

"Sarge, I'm sure you'll do just that," he said. "I'm glad to have you with us. My mess section is really excited to be working with you."

"Thank you, Sir. I'm glad to be workin' with ya'll."

Both men continued their pleasantries while Chief James checked with each driver to make sure they knew where to go and their map was correct. The 646th convoy departed the refueling stop at 0930 hours.

Marshall looked at the convoy schedule.

"The 403rd MPs are supposed to arrive now," he said, glancing at his watch.

Just as Marshall finished talking, the first MP ¼-ton jeep pulled into the 76 Station. A young sergeant stepped out of the vehicle.

"Good morning, Sir," called out the handsome young NCO, rendering a salute.

Salutes were returned from Chief James and Marshall.

"Good morning, Sergeant Pearlman," Marshall replied. "Glad to see your convoy is right on time."

Sergeant David Pearlman and his driver, Specialist Sarah Megs, were both out of their ¼-ton jeep.

"Yes, Sir. We're here to provide road security for the convoy," Pearlman said. "I've got eight vehicles and 20 MPs. Sir, if you like, I'll divide them up with each convoy that comes through."

Marshall liked the young Sergeant's proposal.

"That sounds like a great idea," Marshall said. "The first group left just a few minutes ago."

"Sir, I'll send a couple of vehicles after them once we've refueled. I'll have the rest divided into the next two convoys," Pearlman replied.

"Sergeant Pearlman, it's apparent to me you know what you're doing. Carry on!" Marshall said. He was visibly pleased. At least the MPs have got it together for the convoy, thought Marshall, forgetting to mention their radio dilemma.

Chief James remembered.

"Sarge, our radio's out and we're not able to communicate," James said. "Hang close to us so we can use your radio when the time comes."

"No problem, Chief," Pearlman responded.

At the same time on the highway, Specialist John Kayrule was driving the 683rd's lead vehicle. The pace was slower than expected due to newer drivers who couldn't figure out how to get their vehicles into proper gear. His assistant driver, Private Harold (Huck) Hudson was napping due to a late night send-off party.

"Hey Huck, get the map out," Kayrule called, shaking Hudson by the shouder. "We're gonna have to make a turn soon."

Hudson began to stir and wake up. He started looking for the map, but couldn't find it.

"Come on Huck, there's a turn-off just ahead," Kayrule said impatiently. "I don't remember which one we're supposed to take."

Hudson had no idea where to look, and began frantically searching, but it was too late. Kayrule stayed on the interstate and didn't exit. The convoy followed, not realizing they had missed their turn. The first serial of the 683rd convoy was now headed in the wrong direction.

Sergeant Siler switched with Sergeant Heinz at the last minute to ride with Lieutenant Rodriguez. Siler had more convoy experience and convinced Heinz to ride in the last convoy element. Siler's ¼ -ton jeep was the lead vehicle in the second serial of the convoy, approximately a mile behind the last vehicle of the first serial. He noticed the vehicles were still in the wrong lane up ahead, and began to realize that something had gone wrong.

"Damn! They've missed the turn!" Siler shouted.

Lieutenant Rodriguez was in the back seat reading a book when he overheard Siler's remarks.

"What's going on Sarge?" Rodriguez asked.

"Sir, the lead vehicle in the first convoy element missed the turn off," Siler said. "Looks like they're heading to Cleveland."

Siler turned to the frightened-looking young soldier behind the wheel of the jeep.

"All right Private Franklin, step on it!" Siler yelled. "We've got to catch-up to the lead vehicle and get 'em back on the right road."

Franklin, who was driving Sergeant Siler's jeep, and Rodriguez simultaneously made the sign of the cross. Then Franklin stepped on the gas pedal, weaving in and out of the civilian traffic on the interstate.

After 15 minutes, the ¼-ton jeep finally caught up to the first serial of the 683rd convoy. They were 13 miles south of Cleveland.

As the jeep passed the lead vehicle of the first serial, Sergeant Siler yelled out to Kayrule.

"Hey, you moron! Follow me! You're goin' the wrong way!"

Sergeant Siler's jeep took the lead, and got off the interstate at the next exit. The remaining vehicles in the first serial followed. Siler had a spare map and walked over to Kayrule's truck, which was stopped on the exit siding.

"You idiots realize you just added over 40 miles to the trip? Not to mention another hour of driving!" Siler said. "What happened to your sense of direction?"

"We couldn't find the map, Sarge," Kayrule sheepishly replied.

"Here, take mine!" Siler yelled in disgust. He pointed out the exit and route they would need to follow to get back on track.

Kayrule and the first serial of the 683rd convoy began their road march to the refueling point more than an hour behind schedule.

The second element of the convoy was making good progress toward the refueling point, and the lead vehicle driver was aware of the correct turns to be made on the interstate. Sergeant Tony Sartino had driven trucks while on active duty and was an over-the-road driver in his civilian occupation. There was nothing more enjoyable to him than to be behind the wheel.

"Nothing like a gorgeous day for a drive, right Ricky?" He looked over to his assistant driver, Private Rick Vance, who was studying the map. "Don't worry Ricky, I've been down this road hundreds of times. I know it like the back of my hand."

A loud bang let Sartino know his pleasant drive had just been interrupted by the convoy's first flat tire. Sartino pulled his lead vehicle over to the side of the road and got out of the truck to see which tire was flat. The convoy vehicles behind him began passing and honking their horns.

"Thanks, guys!" Sartino yelled at the passing traffic. "Don't laugh too loud! You'll probably get yours."

No sooner had he said those words than another bang was heard. Flat tire number two. The trail vehicle of the second element pulled over on the side of the road about 50 yards ahead of Sartino's truck.

"OK, Private, time to break out the spare," said Sartino in a disgusted voice.

Back at the refueling point, Marshall and Chief James had greeted the other unit convoys and made sure they were fueled up and heading in the right direction with their MP escorts. No problems had been observed so far, except that the 683rd was now overdue.

"Chief, see if you can raise the convoy on the radio."

Chief James walked over to the MP ¼-ton and asked Specialist Megs to contact the 683rd convoy. No reply was received over the radio, just a static hiss was heard on the assigned frequency.

Chief James walked back to Marshall.

"Sir, let's go see if we can find our lost convoy," James said.

They jumped into the ¼-ton jeep and headed onto the interstate in the direction they had come from. After traveling several miles on the interstate, Marshall spotted a large group of military trucks on the opposite side of the road about a quarter mile away.

"Chief, would you look at that?" said Marshall in a subdued voice.

The convoy was pulled over on the side of the road and completely occupied the interstate rest stop. Chief James pulled the jeep into the crossover median and headed to the stranded convoy. At the rest stop, three trucks were having their tires changed.

Lieutenant Rodriguez reported to Marshall.

"Sir, our lead vehicle missed the first exit and was headed to Cleveland," he began. "We finally caught up to them just about 15 miles south of city and traffic was bumper to bumper."

Marshall took the news well.

"How many flats so far?" he asked.

"This makes five so far," Rodriguez said, pointing to the nearest truck. "We've passed two others that are about four miles down the road. They should be here any moment."

Sergeant Sartino's truck passed by the rest stop and he honked his horn. The deuce-and-a-half horn was deafening as it passed by.

Marshall grinned.

"Looks like they'll be the first ones to refuel," Marshall said. "All right, convoy commander, let's get 'em back on the road and to the refueling point. These stragglers will become part of the trail party."

Rodriguez informed Sergeant Siler of what had to be done. Siler nodded attentively and began to shout orders to his convoy drivers.

"OK everyone! Let's crank 'em up and head 'em out to the refueling point!" Siler shouted.

All the convoy drivers and their assistants climbed back into their trucks and started their engines. One by one, the convoy vehicles began to exit the rest stop, relieving the congestion that prevented motorists from entering.

The convoy was now grouped together and slowly moving down the interstate well below the 55 mph speed limit. Cars were zooming past the convoy, many honking their horns in protest of the sluggish speed the convoy was making.

It took longer than an hour to completely refuel all 30 vehicles, which now comprised one massive 683rd convoy. The 683rd was ready to continue their journey south to Fort Knox, Kentucky. The only problem was the unit was now two hours and 15 minutes behind schedule. As they separated back into three separate elements, the interval between serials was five minutes apart and closing.

Second Lieutenant Stiles was trying to read her map while the ¼-ton jeep driver was trying to keep a good speed for the convoy. Their ¼-ton was the lead vehicle of the third serial and Stiles wanted everything to go as planned with no problems.

"Just follow this interstate until we get to Columbus, then we've got to watch for a fast exit to the left," directed Stiles. She knew her driver, Staff Sergeant Bradford, needed little direction.

"Ma'am, make sure you warn me before that exit comes up," Bradford said. "I'd hate to make a mistake like those knuckle heads did in the first serial a couple hours ago."

Bradford spotted a dead skunk on the road ahead. He slowly moved to the left side of his lane to avoid it. He knew what was about to happen next.

Sergeant "Road Kill" Nugot was merrily driving his 5-ton wrecker in the rear of the convoy. No trucks were on his 5-ton wrecker hook yet, but he was confident someone's vehicle would be there before long. Nugot noticed all the trucks and vehicles in the convoy in front of him were slowly moving to the left side of the lane.

Nugot was starting to get excited.

"I think we've got some action here!" he shouted. He let out a loud howl as the wrecker's rear tire ran over the dead skunk. "All right! Peeh yewwhy! We got us a stinky convoy now!"

The skunk smell was overpowering and all the civilian traffic behind the 5-ton wrecker sped up to get past the stench.

Specialist Tony Cutnoff was the assistant driver, and immediately noticed the stench himself.

"Sarge, please don't do that again," Cutnoff said.

Nugot just smiled at Cutnoff and asked him for a cold soda pop from the cooler.

As the convoy proceeded south on the interstate, many people were honking their horns and waving to the soldiers. Some were shaking their fists because the convoy was going slow and taking up the entire right lane. By now, all three serials were within one mile of each other. Columbus was the next big town the convoy passed through. Fifty-five miles south of Columbus was the location of the next refueling stop.

Sergeant Johnny Burkette was waiting at a closed truck scale station for the 683rd to top off their gas tanks. Chief James had carefully planned all fuel stops for the convoy. Vehicle range when fully loaded had been calculated so no one would run out of fuel. As the 683rd entered the truck scale station, Burkette was catching up on his sleep with a half-eaten can of beans and franks in his hand.

A couple more vehicles rolled into the truck scale station with several flat tires, including Nugot's wrecker with a flat right rear inner tire—the same tire that hit the dead skunk. Nugot made sure that Cutnoff helped him do most of the heavy lifting. Everyone in the convoy stayed upwind of the wrecker.

Lieutenant Stiles saw Burkette motionless and went over to investigate.

"Sergeant Burkette, are you all right?" Stiles asked.

He woke up from his nap suddenly, and dropped his can of beans and franks on Lieutenant Stiles boots.

"Sorry Ma'am," he said. "You surprised me."

Stiles wasn't happy to have her shined boots covered in beans.

"Stay awake, Sergeant!" she scolded. "You've got a dangerous commodity you're hauling! No more sleeping on the job."

"Yes Ma'am," was Burkette's only reply.

Topped off and ready to go, the 683rd headed towards the Queen City of Cincinnati. Sergeant Burkette passed the entire convoy for the next refueling point. He had to refill his fuel pods and wait for the 683rd to meet him in Kentucky about another 200 miles down the road.

All was going well until the mess section deuce-and-a-half blew a driver-side front tire. Luckily, Sergeant Lonnie Adkins had it under control on the side of the road. He waved to the unit as it passed by. No one wanted to be hauled by Nugot's wrecker, and Sergeant Adkins and his assistant were replacing the flat tire as quickly as possible.

The highway through Cincinnati was jammed with traffic. A billboard on the on the roadside was promoting the Johnny Cash concert, which started in less than an hour at the Civic Center. The billboard had a banner pasted diagonally on the front stating the concert was sold-out. I-71 South was filled with concertgoers trying to pass the 683rd convoy, which was now approximately a mile long. The exit for Kentucky consisted of several merges and turns, which slowed the convoy down. A roar of unhappy motorist car horns could be heard as the convoy slowed down to take the traffic merges.

Crossing into Kentucky, the 683rd convoy faced its next daunting challenge: a hill climb over two miles long. A car would have no problem maintaining speed going up the hill, but the heavily loaded deuce-and-a-half trucks with rookie drivers was another story. Marshall and Chief James were in front of the convoy, and reached the top of the hill where they pulled off onto the shoulder and waited for the convoy to pass. After waiting ten minutes on the shoulder of the interstate, the convoy had not appeared.

"Chief, I think we've got a problem here," Marshall said. "Let's go back down the hill partway and see what's going on."

Chief James slowly backed the ¼-ton jeep on the side of the road until they could see about a half mile down the hill. Off in the distance, a large line of military vehicles could be seen slowly inching its way up the hill. Motorists were passing the convoy in the far left lane and honking their horns in displeasure as they crested the hill and spotted Captain Marshall's ¼-ton jeep. A few choice words were shouted from some of them. One shouted to go back to using mules, which made Marshall grin.

Another two minutes went by before the first truck crested the hill. The truck was only going about 9 mph and the RPMs on the engines were screaming.

"Chief, why are these trucks going so slow?" Marshall asked.

"Well, Sir," Chief James began, "We've got some rookie drivers at the wheel that couldn't find the right gear. They had to downshift into first in order to make it up this hill. If they had shifted properly, they would have all been in second gear and made it up here a lot faster."

The safety rule of not passing each other during a convoy meant that they could only go as fast the vehicle in front of them. Once every vehicle had reached the top, the convoy began to pick up speed. The steep hill would always be fondly remembered as the Killer Hill whenever they spoke about A.T. '82.

The convoy was doing well with regards to speed and maintaining proper interval between vehicles. They were more than three hours behind schedule. Chief James knew that it was better to have everyone arrive safely than to try and speed up. As Marshall and James were leading the way, the chartered bus carrying the other 683rd members passed by and honked its horn. Marshall and James waved as the bus disappeared down the interstate.

"Looks like some of our people will get there on time," said Marshall.

"Well, Sir, at least they'll be rested to help offload all this equipment when we get there," replied Chief James.

Several hundred yards ahead, a 683rd 5-ton tractor was pulled over on the side of the road.

"I bet ya a dollar to a doughnut I know what the problem is," Chief James yelled out to Marshall as he pulled the ¼-ton over and parked in front of the stranded vehicle.

Chief James walked over to the 5-ton tractor cab and climbed up on the driver's side step and started talking with the soldiers inside the cab. A moment later, the engine turned over and the tractor came to life.

Chief James hurried back to the jeep.

"I kinda figured they weren't paying attention in class," James said. "They heard the engine sputter and flipped the switch on the dashboard for the second fuel tank. When they did, the fuel gage read full. They forgot to rotate the lever under the driver's seat to actually switch to the other fuel tank."

Marshall understood the driver's error.

"Do all the gas tractors have the same setup?" he asked.

"Yes, Sir," James said. "We'll probably find a few more down the road here. They've all got about the same range."

As soon as Chief James was finished speaking, another 5-ton tractor from the convoy was pulled over on the roadside.

"Chief, I think we've found another one who wasn't paying attention in class," Marshall said.

"Sir, I think you're right."

Chief James pulled in front of the stranded 5-ton and informed the crew how to remedy their situation. Again, Chief James worked his magic and the vehicle came to life.

As Chief James and Marshall proceeded down the road, the other two remaining 5-ton tractors were sitting on the roadside with the same problem.

Marshall and Chief James got back on the road and saw Sergeant Nugot's wrecker ahead on the side of the road. Nugot had one deuce–and-a-half on a tow bar, and he and Specialist Cutnoff were placing another tow bar the rear of the crippled deuce to hook-up the other deuce-and-a-half. Chief James pulled the ¼-ton jeep over to see if they needed further assistance. The smell of skunk was still quite strong on the wrecker.

Nugot spotted Chief James and greeted him warmly.

"Hello, Chief," Nugot said. "Looks like business is booming."

Chief James smiled.

"What's the problem with the vehicles?" he asked.

Nugot scratched his head from under his hat.

"Losing power on the engine on this one. Most likely a dirty fuel filter or air cleaner. The other one has three flat tires. Unsafe to drive."

Chief James nodded in agreement.

"OK, the next fuel stop will be about 40 miles down the road," he said. "The contact maintenance team with the motor pool supply truck will be there for repairs and some fresh tires."

Chief James looked at the drivers of the stranded vehicles.

"Welcome to the trail party," he said. "The commander and I can take two of you in our ¼-ton."

Two soldiers quickly volunteered to ride with the Marshall and Chief James. Anything to get away from the stench emanating from Nugot's 5-ton wrecker. As Chief James walked by the wrecker, he noticed there were two skunks drawn in chalk on the rear mud flaps of the wrecker. On the driver's door, Nugot had drawn a good likeness of Flower, the skunk in the movie Bambi. Below the picture was written "Li'l Stinker".

Chief James shook his head and climbed back into the ¼-ton.

"Well Chief, at least Sergeant Road Kill is living up to his reputation," said Marshall with a grin.

"I'm gonna' have to have a long talk with that young Sergeant," Chief James said, rather unhappy with what he had observed. "That's not a good way to take care of Army equipment," Chief James had mumbled to himself.

Chief James was going to make sure the wrecker would be washed from top to bottom, and then repeated until the smell was gone once they reached Mount Eden Base Camp. Marshall was thinking the same thing. He didn't have to tell Chief James what needed to be done. It would be taken care of, according to the Book of Chief James, Chapter 1, verse 1 – "Thou shalt not abuse nor misuse government equipment. Amen."

Chief James pulled the ¼-ton jeep into the refueling point and found numerous vehicles parked and being worked on. Several were having flat tires removed and two are being fixed by motor pool mechanics. The Chief got apprised of what was going on while Marshall instructed his two passengers to dismount, and wait for their truck being towed in by Sergeant Nugot. While they were waiting, Marshall encouraged them assist the other drivers repairing flat tires.

For a sleepy little truck stop in the hills of Kentucky, it became very busy over the next several hours. Marshall looked at the sky, which started clouding over.

"Mr. James, looks like we better have the drivers button-up their vehicles," Marshall said. "I smell rain."

Marshall's warning was well taken. Within 20 minutes the rain began to pour and would not let up until the next day.

By the time the trail party was ready to go, the convoy was now over five hours behind schedule. The convoy trail party departed for Mount Eden Base Camp, which was another three hours driving time away.

As the convoy continued down the road, the rains became heavier, and the speed of the convoy was reduced to 35 mph due to poor visibility. The convoy crawled on. Marshall looked at his watch. It was 1:30 a.m., and still 20 miles to go before they entered Fort Knox.

Chief James took a side road before the main entrance to Fort Knox.

"Chief, is this the right way?" Marshall asked.

"Don't worry, Sir, I've been here hundreds of times," James said. "Just be thankful it's raining."

"Why's that?" inquired Marshall.

"You can't smell the pig farm, and man is it a big one that stinks to high heaven. I guarantee ya, Sir, the troops will not have to be told to wear their gas masks when they pass by. It'll be automatic."

The Chief grinned when made that remark. Nugot's wrecker would be greatly outclassed in stench power by the pig farm.

Chief James made a slow left turn onto a dirt road as the heavy rain continued. On the side of the road was a sign that read "Military Training Area—Government Property – No Trespassing." The convoy trail party drove up the dirt road two miles until a clearing was seen on the right hand side. A soldier wearing a rain poncho with a flashlight from the 683rd directed the convoy to pull over and park.

"Well Chief, we've made it. Great job," said Marshall in a weary voice, as they both put on their rain ponchos.

They climbed out of the ¼-ton jeep and watched the 683rd vehicles come in one by one.

"Chief, I'm going to see First Sergeant Tisher," Marshall said. "Let me know the count of vehicles."

"You got it, Sir!" was Chief James reply.

Marshall walked down a muddy path into the wood line and spotted a GP medium (general purpose) tent with the flaps partially open. He walked in and found First Sergeant Tisher and several others huddled around a field desk, sitting in folding chairs playing cards.

"Welcome to wonderful Mount Eden Base Camp, Sir!" First Sergeant Tisher stood up, smiled and held a salute for his commander, as did the others in the tent.

"Glad to finally be here, Top," Marshall replied as he returned the salute. "We've had our share of flats and breakdowns along the way. Seventeen flat tires so far, and probably more that I haven't heard about."

Tisher shook his head in amazement.

"Top, I'd like to have full accountability of all personnel and vehicles before I hit the hay tonight," Marshall said.

Tisher readily nodded in agreement and looked over to Sergeant Lemasters.

"John, get me a rundown on accountability for the commander," Tisher said.

"No problem, Top." Lemasters replied.

"I get to use my field first sergeant," said Tisher as he smiled and watched Lemasters leave the tent while the rain was pouring down.

"By the way, Sir, you were right about those chiggers out here." Tisher unbuckled his belt and lowered his pants to his ankles. On his thighs and legs were welts and sores.

"Good God, Top, that looks horrible!" Marshall said.

Tisher pulled his trousers back up and buckled his belt,

"Well, Sir, they look worse than they feel," he said. "I'll be all right. They just itch like crazy. Kinda like a poison ivy rash."

Marshall wasted no time in giving out his first order in the field.

"Top, anyone who has chigger bites is going on sick call tomorrow morning after formation. You included. I also want you to put the word out to the troops. Let 'em know about the chigger situation."

"Will do, Sir," Tisher replied. "You've got a commanders' meeting with Colonel Biggs tomorrow at 0730 hours at his CP. Vivian will give you some paperwork to take to the meeting."

Marshall was having difficulty staying focused. It had been a very long day and fatigue was starting to take hold.

"Top, is our tent ready?" he asked Tisher

Tisher looked at his commander, knowing he was ready to fall asleep standing up.

"You bet, Sir," Tisher said. "I've got some soldiers setting up your cot and sleeping bag for you."

"That's fantastic Top," Marshall said, stifling a yawn. "I'm really looking forward to putting in some quality rack time. I hardly slept last night."

Sergeant Lemasters walked back into the tent with his rain poncho completely soaked.

"Sir, all troops and vehicles are present and accounted for."

"That's very good news, Field First Sergeant," Marshall said. "Thank you."

"You're welcome, Sir," Lemasters replied.

Marshall looked around at everyone in the tent. Tisher realized that he hadn't given his commander much of an initial status briefing.

"Sir, I've got Sergeant Lemasters here taking charge of the first guard mount," Tisher told Marshall. "I'll have a duty roster ready tomorrow for your signature."

"Excellent, Top," Marshall said. "Make sure I get up at 0600 tomorrow. I don't want to miss my first meeting with Colonel Biggs. Good night all."

Marshall followed Tisher to the GP small tent, which also doubled as the headquarters (CP) tent. Home sweet home for the next two weeks.

A.T. – DAY 2 (MONDAY)

Captain Marshall awoke to the Tisher's alarm clock. He quickly shut it off. The alarm noise was very irritating to his overly sensitive ears.

Dawn was slowly lighting up the inside of the tent as he unzipped his sleeping bag and gazed around the tent to find his boots. As he sat up on the edge of his cot and took in his new surroundings, Marshall noticed there were two occupied cots at the opposite sides of the tent with people inside their sleeping bags. He knew one of them was First Sergeant Tisher by the large volume that filled the sleeping bag, but he wasn't too sure about the other. Marshall decided it was not important at that moment.

As he spotted his boots and began to put them on, he observed a large trail of fire ants crawling about on the tent floor. The ants were going to and from a wastebasket filled with trash and half-eaten C-rations. Another housekeeping item to have the first sergeant inform the troops about during formation, thought Marshall.

Marshall got fully dressed in his field uniform, consisting of fatigues, helmet, holster with .45-caliber pistol (model M-1911A), his ammo belt with first aid kit, magazine pouch for the .45 magazines, and his canteen with canteen cup. The commander of the 683rd was combat loaded and ready, almost. Nature called.

Marshall stepped out of the tent and began to survey the 683rd field site. He heard a generator humming at the bottom of the hill as his eyes focused in the morning light. As he looked around, he began to see the entire 683rd had pitched their sleeping tents within shouting distance around the CP tent. The 683rd was now camped inside the woodline of the forest. Some of the larger tents had been hastily put up in the rain the night before and were partially collapsed. The smaller two-man half-shelter tents were in similar condition. He knew from past experience that pitching a tent in the rain and the dark was a hasty endeavor. As long as the tent repelled water, it was temporarily good enough.

The distinctive sweet smell of breakfast being prepared filled his nostrils as Marshall spotted the mess tent about forty meters below his CP tent. A visit to the mess area was second on his priority list. As he walked around his new surroundings, he could make out the half-shelter tents that were scattered about to his left and right below him. Several soldiers were already up and beginning their morning routine of washing and shaving as they greeted him with a cheerful good morning. The rains from the past evening had left the ground damp and covered in dew as an early morning mist hung in the air. The air temperature felt cool and pleasant as his aching bladder reminded him of his first priority he had to take care of that morning.

Marshall spotted the old wooden clad latrine near the crest of the hill about 70 meters above his present position, and began a brisk climb toward his first objective. The structure was the Army's atypical fixed field site latrine. A walled partition divided the structure with separate entrances for men and women. He noticed the latrine had wire screen windows about seven feet above the ground for ventilation and privacy.

Marshall was pleased to see Uncle Sam had built a nice outhouse for the soldiers at Mount Eden Base Camp, and walked in to inspect the facility. As he lifted up the first toilet seat lid, which was one of six in a row atop a wooden box, he found a spider's nest complete with spider. Marshall gently lowered the toilet seat back down, and went to the next and lifted the seat. Another large spider web with spider was found. He thought to himself, I've got a mission for the decontamination team.

Marshall opted to take care of nature's first call and wait a while for call number two. He made his way back to the 683rd CP tent to inform Tisher of what he discovered.

"Top, we've got a bit of a problem with the latrine up on the hill," he said as he poked his head back in the CP tent.

Sergeant Vivian Tea sat up in her sleeping bag.

"What kinda problem is that, Sir?" she asked.

"Sergeant Tea, so good to see you this morning," Marshall replied trying not to act too surprised. "I hope my snoring didn't keep you awake last night."

"Oh no Sir. I'm so used to Tyron snoring, I can shut it out," she replied.

First Sergeant Tisher joined in the conversation.

"Sir, you were saying?" Tisher said.

Marshall motioned Tisher to follow him out of the tent. The First Sergeant walked out of the tent in his trousers and boots.

"What's up, Sir?"

"Top, I've got a mission for the decon team," Marshall said. "Spiders have nested in the latrine on the ceilings and under the toilet seats. I want them to use their truck-mounted tank and pump unit and blast that place clean with their high-pressure water hoses until there is no dirt on the floor, spiders on the ceiling or under the toilet seats. I want them to use their disinfectant and brushes and give it a good going over right after morning chow."

"Sir, I can see you're a commander who knows what he wants," Tisher replied. "I'll have the decon team get on it right away."

The unit's decon team, was a special section within the 683rd with six personnel assigned, and one large tanker truck complete with a high-pressure washer system. The section's mission was to spray clean any equipment that had become contaminated with nuclear, biological or chemical agents before the equipment could sent to the maintenance shops for repair.

Marshall still had one more item for his first sergeant.

"Top, what is Sergeant Tea doing sleeping in our tent?" he asked.

"Sir, I meant to tell you last night," Tisher said. "In her condition, she can't sleep on the ground in a half-shelter like the other troops. She's starting to have backaches and needs a cot to sleep on."

Marshall pondered the information for a moment.

"OK, I can sympathize with that. But is there any other tent she can stay in?"

"No, Sir, the headquarters section didn't make any provisions for that," Tisher said. "She'll be fine with us, Sir. Besides, I'd like to have her stay close just in case she might have any complications."

Marshall realized he couldn't argue with the First Sergeant's logic.

"All right Top, but if she has any problems or complications she's going to the Army Hospital on Main Post."

Tisher grinned at his commander.

"Thanks Sir," he said. "I'll let Viv know, and I'll inform the decon team they've got a top priority mission this morning."

"One more thing Top,' replied Marshall, "We've brought a vestibule for this tent. Why not attach it to the opposite side so Sergeant Tea can have some privacy?"

First Sergeant Tisher smiled.

"I'll have it installed after morning formation," he said.

Marshall began his early morning walk over to where the mess section had set up. They had picked a good location on partially flat ground below the 683rd sleeping areas. The cooks were busy preparing the morning breakfast meal as the aroma of hickory-smoked bacon filled the crisp morning air. Two large coffee urns were filled with hot freshly brewed coffee.

Marshall helped himself to a cup as Sergeant Adkins walked over to greet him.

"Good mornin' Sir!" Adkins held a salute and gave his commander a smile. "Hope you're hungry for breakfast."

Marshall returned the salute.

"You bet, Sarge," he replied, walking over to the serving line where the food was covered and ready to be served.

Sergeant First Class Ralph Emery walked over to meet his new commander in the field, snapped to attention and saluted.

"Good mornin' Sir," he said.

Marshall returned the salute.

"Good morning to you, Sergeant Emery."

Sergeant Emery smiled.

"Sir, how you doin' this fine mornin'?" he asked.

"Sarge, I'm doing very well," Marshall replied. "I just needed a cup of joe to get me goin'."

"How you like that coffee, Sir?" Emery asked.

Marshall had noticed the flavor was perfect.

"Sarge, this is the best coffee I've had since the Army did away with their premium blend back in '76," he replied.

"Why thank you, Sir," Emery said. "That's the chicory I've added. It gives it a southern flavor."

"Sergeant Emery," Marshall replied, "I see that we're in excellent hands. Please pass on as much knowledge as you can to Sergeant Adkins. I'm sure he'll want to learn as much as you can teach him."

"Sir, I'm glad to be here with you all," Emery replied. "I'll do my best."

Marshall enjoyed Sergeant Emery's special coffee and began his informal reconnoiter of the 683rd field site. He walked up to a soldier who was sitting on the ground wearing a poncho, sound asleep with his M16 lying across his lap. It was apparent Marshall had caught one of the 683rd guards asleep while on duty, a very serious breach of security.

"What's your name soldier?" Marshall asked in his command voice.

The soldier awoke from his sleep realizing he was in big trouble.

"Private Cries, Sir." He quickly rose to his feet.

"How long have you been on guard duty, Private Cries?" asked Marshall.

"Sir, I've been on guard duty since 0200," he replied. "My relief never showed up."

Marshall sympathized with the soldier, but gave him a warning.

"You know, Private Cries, sleeping on guard duty is a serious offence."

"Yes Sir, I know it is," Cries said. "I'm sorry. I just started nodding off when I saw people getting up for breakfast."

Marshall decided to give Private Cries an opportunity to become a better soldier.

"Private Cries, what should I do with you?" Marshall asked.

"Sir, let me pull guard the whole week," Cries said apologetically.

Marshall felt he was sincere.

"All right, Private. Inform the Sergeant Lemasters you'd like to volunteer for more guard duty," Marshall said. "You don't have to tell 'em I caught sleeping on duty. That'll be between you and I, got it?"

Private Cries was visibly relieved.

"Yes, Sir. Thank you, Sir!" he said.

Marshall continued his recon of the area, as Field First Sergeant Lemasters went around to each platoon area shouting at the sleeping soldiers to rise and shine. The ground was gently sloped with good tree cover overhead. No need for camouflage nets, he thought to himself. The old burlap camouflage nets were heavy, bulky, and would get caught on every little uneven surface.

The 683rd platoon sergeants had designated sleeping areas for the soldiers to pitch their half-shelters. Each soldier was issued one-half of a tent, hence the term half-shelter. Included were a three-sectioned tent pole, a small length of tent rope, and five tent pegs. That way, two soldiers had to share a tent by mating their half-shelters, tent pegs, poles and rope together to form a two-man tent. The only problem was, in the Army inventory there were two types of half-shelters: one type had buttons; the other type had snaps. Both were incompatible with each other, which made buddying-up in the field difficult. Marshall noticed there were some abandoned half-shelters on the ground. Tent-mates would have to be determined later that day.

The 683rd soldiers were now awake, shaving, washing and brushing their teeth before chow. Marshall looked at his watch. 0630 hours, time to oversee the feeding of his troops.

Marshall walked back down to the field mess area to refill his cup with another good blast of Sergeant Emery's coffee. The 683rd soldiers were forming a long and well-spaced single file line for chow.

First Sergeant Tisher walked over to the commander to give him an update on the present situation.

"Sir, I put the word out to the decon team," Tisher said. "That clean-up chore is being done now."

Marshall looked up the hill and noticed the decon section was moving towards the latrine, with rubber overalls and gloves at the ready.

"Excellent news, Top," Marshall replied. "I'm sure the troops will appreciate their efforts."

Marshall spotted Chief McCarthy in the chow line and walked over to talk with him.

"Mr. McCarthy, could I see you for a second?" he asked.

McCarthy left his spot in the chow line and walked with the commander.

"Chief, all officers eat last. Soldiers eat first," Marshall said. "That's my policy, and as long as I can remember, that's always been an Army tradition."

"Can I get a cup of coffee, Sir?" Chief McCarthy asked with a hint of sarcasm in his voice.

Marshall grinned and nodded his head towards the coffee pot.

"Help yourself, Chief," he said.

Several other officers were in line and Marshall went over to each one and enlightened them about tradition. From that moment on, officers of the 683rd Maintenance Company would be the last ones to eat. If the food ran out, at least the soldiers were fed.

The combined 683rd and 646th Mess Section was serving a fantastic cornucopia of breakfast. Eggs to order, bacon, sausage, ham, biscuits, toast, French toast, jam, jelly, hot syrup, waffles, fresh fruit, cereals, pancakes, S.O.S. (slop on a shingle, a.k.a. ground beef in gravy), coffee, orange juice, stewed prunes, fresh fruit, milk, chocolate milk, and hot water for tea. The 683rd was well taken care of in the mess operations department.

At 0700 hours the first sergeant blew his whistle and held morning formation. The 683rd soldiers were wearing their tactical field gear. First Sergeant Tisher quickly turned the formation over to Marshall.

"Good morning 683rd!" Marshall shouted.

"Good morning, Sir!" was the formation's response.

"Welcome to Mount Eden Base Camp, our home sweet home for the next two weeks," Marshall said. "This week we're going to put our soldiering skills to work. Week number one will be the tactical phase of our training. Don't expect much maintenance mission work during week one. This is a time to learn what tactical operations are supposed to be like for a maintenance company in the field. We will have weapons qualification later in the week, and everyone will take and pass the Army PT Test that will be conducted on Saturday morning. Everyone will train hard, and become a better soldier.

"Now here's a heads up. I want all vehicles off the road and parked inside the woodline. All tentage will be erected inside the woodline. There will be no visible sign of the 683rd from the road, other than a camouflaged sign directing them to our gate guard," Marshall noticed some soldiers nodding in agreement. "683rd, ten-hut!"

First Sergeant Tisher came to the front of the formation.

"Top, take over the formation, I've got a commanders' call meeting with Colonel Biggs. Let the troops know about the fire ants and chiggers. Anyone with bites goes on sick call including you."

"Yes Sir," Tisher said. "I'll be on the first deuce to Main Post for sick call."

Marshall began his walk to Colonel Biggs' CP tent, which was about a quarter-mile away from the 683rd area. He decided to jog the distance and make up some time. Marshall spotted the group headquarters CP tent near the tree line.

As he walked in the tent, Colonel Biggs was already conducting his meeting. Marshall excused himself and sat down in a vacant seat in the front row that was intentionally left for him.

"Well, it's the late Captain Marshall," Biggs said. "Good morning."

Marshall was somewhat surprised by the group commander's salutation.

"Good morning, Colonel," Marshall replied. "Sorry I'm late. I was told the meeting started at 0730 hours."

"The meeting was changed to 0715 hours," Biggs calmly replied. "Your people apparently didn't get the word, or forgot to inform you.

"I also understand that your convoy was rather late arriving yesterday. Why is that?"

"Sir, so far we've had 17 flat tires on the way down, and several breakdowns as well," Marshall replied, keeping his composure. "All personnel and equipment have arrived safely, Sir."

"Seventeen flat tires? That's incredible," replied Biggs. "Why weren't the bad tires replaced before the convoy started?"

"Sir, command policy states no tire can be replaced until it becomes unserviceable," Marshall said. "I had my personnel put the best tires on the front axles and each vehicle carried a new tire as a spare. We still had seventeen flats and probably a dozen more will need to be replaced."

Colonel Biggs was awestruck and turned to one of the other men in the tent.

"Major Brown, I want you to look into this policy for me," Biggs said. "Seems apparent it needs modification."

The meeting went on for another 20 minutes. During the meeting, units with missing reports were identified, and the 683rd was already late with all the required reports.

"Well commander," Biggs said, interrupting the meeting and directing his eyes to Marshall, "looks like the 683rd is not starting out very well."

"I apologize for that, Sir," Marshall replied. "I assure you it will not happen again."

The remaining three other unit commanders were all relieved that the 683rd was taking the brunt of the hits the first day. Marshall made a promise to himself that this would be the last day the 683rd was delinquent or late on any requirements from higher headquarters.

Biggs informed the company commanders of their scheduled appointments with Reserve Affairs OIC, Major Brask. Each unit commander would meet the assigned A.T. evaluators that Major Brask had arranged for them.

Biggs then asked the commanders for anything they'd like to bring up before he adjourned the meeting. Captain Eldon Healy, Commander of the 928th Service & Support Company, advised everyone the laundry and shower sections should be up and running by noon the following day, and the bakery section would have bread and rolls as well.

It was Marshall's turn to speak.

"Anyone who needs repair of vehicles, canvas, glass, body work, or instruction on preventative maintenance can call our shop office," Marshall said. "It may not seem important now, but by next week, we'll be very busy fixing the engineer unit's equipment, as well as everyone else's. We've also got an MP detachment attached to us, and we'll be instituting roadside spot checks so the MPs will have something to do while they're out here. Any vehicles or drivers that don't pass the safety inspections will have the vehicles impounded at our shops.

"Sir, there is one more thing. My soldiers are starting to get chigger bites, and there are a multitude of fire ant mounds in our area. That's all I've got, Sir."

Biggs raised an eyebrow and thanked all the commanders and let everyone know that he expected everyone to have good training accomplished while out in the field.

After Colonel Biggs had dismissed all those present at the meeting, he asked Marshall to stay.

"Tell me, Captain Marshall, about the chigger and fire ant problem you have," Biggs said. "I have never been aware of these insects inhabiting the Mount Eden Base Camp area."

"Sir, my first sergeant showed me his chigger bites on his legs and thighs last light when I arrived," Marshall said. "He is covered in bites. Sir, and the bites are getting infected. I've got him reporting to sick call this morning."

Biggs showed a look of alarm on his face. His lips were pressed together as he pondered this news.

"Tell me of the fire ants," Biggs asked in an inquisitive voice.

"Colonel, there are mounds every 100 feet or so in my area," Marshall said. "There's a large mound outside of my CP tent. From what I understand, if you don't disturb them, they'll leave you alone. But if you leave food in waste cans, they find it and help themselves."

Biggs was again in deep thought.

"What about these chiggers? I haven't encountered them before."

"Sir, neither have I, but they are disgusting," Marshall said. "Apparently they are so small you can hardly see them. They crawl up your boot and make their way to a warm and damp part of your skin. Like a mosquito, they help themselves to a fresh blood supply. Apparently you can't feel them doing it. A welt appears and becomes infected almost immediately. I've been told the Army's insect repellent works, but doesn't last long enough if it's hot and humid. Flea collars seem to work." Marshall pointed down to his boots and showed Colonel Biggs his black flea collars that were under his boot lacings.

"Sir, I know it's not regulation, but the old soldiers say this is the best way to prevent chiggers from bivouacking on your body."

Biggs suddenly displayed a smile on his face. He seemed to enjoy Marshall's sense of humor.

"Thank you, Captain Marshall, for this information," Biggs said. "I'll let my staff people know of your situation. Perhaps we can get some assistance from Main Post if this problem becomes overwhelming."

"You're welcome, Sir," Marshall replied. "I'll let you know what the doctors prescribe when my soldiers come back from sick call.

"Sir, there is just one more thing." Marshall felt he needed to push this point. "The officers' call at 0715 hours doesn't allow any of the unit commanders to hold formation with their units. 0730 hours would be much better for all of us."

Biggs pondered the point that his young commander made, and concurred.

"All right, Captain Marshall, your point is well taken," he said. "I'll adjust the time to 0730 hours."

"Thank you, Sir." Marshall saluted Biggs, who promptly returned the salute.

Marshall returned to his CP tent, and met with Sergeant Tea and First Sergeant Tisher. "Top, I really got embarrassed this morning," Marshall said. "The meeting was changed from 0730 to 0715 hours, and we didn't have the reports they wanted."

Tisher looked over to Sergeant Tea, who shrugged her shoulders and finally spoke up.

"Sir, I'll have those reports done for you before you report to that meeting from now on," she said.

"That'll be fine, Sergeant Tea," replied Marshall, knowing that she would never allow her commander to be placed in that kind of position again.

Marshall quickly realized that Tisher had somewhere else to be.

"Top, I thought you were going on sick call," he said.

"I am, Sir. The truck is leaving in 10 minutes," Tisher said. "The first one was filled up and left five minutes ago."

Marshall looked at Sergeant Tea.

"How many did we have report for sick call, Sergeant Tea?"

Sergeant Tea looked through her sick call roster.

"Eighteen this morning," she replied. "All of 'em with chigger bites."

"Top," Marshall said, "this does not sound very good. Did you put the word out about using insect repellent and flea collars?"

"Yes Sir, I did," Tisher replied. "Looks like a lot of our troops weren't prepared for the chiggers." He pointed to his trousers.

Marshall grinned.

"Top, get your butt on that deuce, pronto," Marshall said. "I need to see the field first sergeant about our defensive positions and perimeter."

"Yes Sir," replied Tisher.

Sergeant Lemasters was walking toward the CP tent as the first sergeant was leaving to get on the deuce-and-a-half headed for sick call.

"John, I want you to take charge while I'm gone," Tisher said. "The Old Man has some things he wants done."

"Right, Top," Lemasters replied as he walked into the CP tent. "Sir, Field First Sergeant Lemasters reporting as ordered!"

Marshall was grinning at Lemasters.

"Sergeant Lemasters, we've got some things to discuss about the field layout and perimeter defense," Marshall said. "Have a seat on the cot."

Lemasters sat down as Marshall went over what he wanted to see with regards to the field layout of the 683rd.

"The defensive fighting positions need to be emplaced immediately so the sections can move their equipment and tentage into the woodline," Marshall explained, as they both went over a sector map that had been hastily sketched by Lieutenant Rodriguez.

"You know," Marshall thought out loud, "I think it would be an excellent idea if Lieutenant Rodriguez was here. Sergeant Tea, can you ring up the switch board and have them get a hold of Lieutenant Rodriguez and have him report immediately to the CP."

"Not a problem, Sir," Tea replied.

Both men went over the sector sketch while waiting for Rodriguez, who showed up about two minutes later.

"Sir, you wanted to see me?" he asked.

"Yes, Rod. Come on in and have a seat on Top's cot. Just be careful not to get any of his chiggers on you," Marshall said.

"No thanks, Sir," replied Rodriguez. "I think I'll stand."

Marshall chuckled.

"I don't blame you," he said. "Those chigger bites look pretty nasty.

"OK, let's get back to the defensive plans and sector sketch. The defensive positions are supposed to be improved on a daily basis, and the sector sketch needs to be updated constantly to reflect new positions, fields of fire, booby traps, trip wires, heavy weapons emplacements, and the road network, showing route of travel and all 683rd section areas and tentage," Marshall looked at Rodriguez. "Looks like you've got some work to do today, Rod."

"Yes, Sir, that it does," he replied.

Marshall continued.

"Sergeant Lemasters, I would like you to oversee all sections moving their vehicles and tentage into the woodline today. All vehicles must be combat oriented, which means if they have to driven out of the woodline, they won't have to back-up. All vehicles can't be locked up. No chains locked on the steering wheels, and all windshields must have foliage or a tarp over them to reduce reflection."

"Sir, I'll put the word out at the noon formation," Lemasters said. "It'll be done before dark, Sir."

"Good," Marshall said. "Let's go over to the mess area and get another cup of that excellent coffee. I'm buying."

The commander led the way. Lemasters and Rodriguez felt their commander knew what had to be done, no matter how difficult the task. Lemasters excused himself to attend his duties as the field first sergeant.

Sipping on some of the excellent coffee that Sergeant Emery had left for the soldiers while the mess section was busily getting the noon meal ready, Second Lieutenant Stiles walked over to see Marshall.

"Good morning, Sir. Don't you just love this coffee?" asked Stiles.

"It is excellent," Marshall responded. "I'd like to go over the training schedule with you if you haven't got any pressing issues to deal with," Marshall said to Stiles.

"Yes, Sir. I was just coming over to the CP tent to go over some changes with you," she said. "There are a few things that need to be amended already."

Marshall grinned.

"Yes, there's a few things to be changed today, tomorrow, the next day, and all of next week," he said. "Let's adjourn to the CP tent, shall we?"

Marshall and Stiles walked over to the CP tent, where Sergeant Tea was typing up reports. The unit training schedule was on the field table located in the middle of the tent. He picked it up and began to go over the day's scheduled training events with Stiles.

"There are lots of gaps in the schedule that are labeled Commander's Time. I'd like to do away with Commander's Time anywhere it appears and plug in some good tactical training," Marshall said. "Let's make every minute worthwhile for the troops, no slack time."

The young lieutenant understood the commander's requirements, and thought it best to ask exactly what he'd like to see inserted into the unit training schedule.

"Sir, what training would you like to see added to the schedule?" she asked.

Marshall reflected briefly.

"The decon team just had a mission which I hope they completed. They should get credit for it so plug that in. A class on preparation of fighting positions would be ideal for today. You could also have a class on use of the challenge and password.

"For the rest of the schedule this week, let's get the first sergeant's input as well. I'm sure Top has some good ideas about what the soldiers need."

After Marshall's conversation with Stiles had concluded, he realized that nature's call remained unanswered. Time to inspect the decon team's work. As he entered the latrine, the interior was wet. The walls, ceiling and floors were clean. All toilet seats were raised and soaking wet, along with the toiler paper next to it. The smell of chlorine bleach was evident as Marshall inspected the decon team's handiwork. The spiders were gone.

Time to relax and catch-up on some reading of Colonel Biggs' field directives and standard operating procedures (SOP) for the field. Nature's call was finally answered.

Sergeant First Class Lufton was supervising the erection of the automotive platoon's maintenance tent. He realized Marshall was right about requiring them to bring a maintenance tent. His mechanics could do excellent work in the Army's ingenious canvas shelter. The troops were busy putting the aluminum frame together and the sound of hammering and shouts for tools and parts to assemble the framework was heard throughout the wooded field site. The smell of new canvas was strong in the air. Lufton was giving instructions while the troops were arguing what parts went here and there.

Marshall spotted the Army field manual on assembling the tent lying on the ground and picked it up.

"Sarge, I do believe this belongs to you," Marshall said as he smiled while the troops continued to work on the structure.

Sergeant Lufton nodded in appreciation.

"I was waitin' for 'em to realize they had to get the manual to find the answers," Lufton said. "I guess I'll save 'em some time."

"All right everyone! Look what the good commander found," Lufton said to the soldiers, holding up the field manual for everyone to see. "I reckon you'll find your answers inside."

The maintenance tent went up quickly after they began to look over the manual and correct a few minor errors they made assembling the frame. Lesson learned: read the manual first.

Over at the recovery section, Sergeant Nugot's 5-ton wrecker was parked. On the mud flaps, skunks, possums, and squirrels were neatly drawn in chalk with Xs through them, reflecting Sergeant Nugot's road tally.

Sergeant First Class Baxter was not impressed with Nugot's morbid sense of humor, nor the stench emanating from Uncle Sam's expensive piece of equipment.

"Nugot! Get yer butt over here!" Baxter shouted.

Nugot walked over to the section sergeant.

"What's up Sarge?" he asked.

"Get a bucket of water and some soap and clean the stench off this wrecker NOW!" Baxter said.

Nugot knew it was going to happen sooner or later.

"Right away," he replied. He got a bucket with some soap and water and began the chore of washing the rear wheel wells. Man, does that stink, he thought to himself. Better put on my gas mask.

While Nugot was scrubbing his wrecker, a few skunks in the area had been alerted by the smell of one of their kin from Ohio. They wandered closer to the wrecker to see who had shown up for a visit. The skunks stayed hidden from view. They would investigate the smell close up after nightfall.

First Sergeant Tisher arrived back at the field site from sick call. He spotted Marshall and walked over to see him and report on what the doctors at the medical center on Post had found.

"Sir, it was an interesting trip to Main Post," Tisher said. "We took the long way around because the floating bridge is out. Remember that pig farm you passed on the way in? Bring your gas mask. It stinks to high heaven."

"Thanks, Top. That sounds like good advice," replied Marshall. "So what did the doctors prescribe for your chigger bites?"

Tisher grinned and pulled a bottle of calamine lotion out of his breast pocket.

"They gave use three cases of this."

Marshall's expression turned to disgust.

"We're not having an outbreak of poison ivy rashes," Marshall said.

Tisher agreed with his commander.

"Sir, these young doctors have never seen chigger bites before," he said. "They didn't know what to do. I told 'em if they don't have anything else, give use some calamine lotion to help dry up the sores and relieve the itching."

"Top, you and I are going to stop at the PX after chow and get some proper chigger bite medicine," Marshall said.

Both men walked down the hill to the mess area. Noon chow was being served, another feast for the soldiers of the 683rd. The troops had choices of fried chicken, sliced ham, hush puppies, corn on the cob, mashed potatoes and gravy, beans, biscuits, fruit, apple and peach cobbler, fruit punch, sweet tea, coffee and milk. Again Sergeant Emery had worked his magic. The soldiers just couldn't believe their eyes. Most of the soldiers were eating better at Mount Eden Base Camp than they did at home.

As Marshall and First Sergeant Tisher were standing watching the troops get served, Sergeant Pearlman and Specialist Megs walked up.

"Sir, would you mind if my MPs dined at your mess facility?" asked Pearlman.

"Not at all, Sarge," Marshall responded. "You are welcome to dine with the 683rd for every meal. I'll make sure Sergeant Emery knows so he can add your people to the headcount."

Pearlman and Megs appeared to be overjoyed at Marshall's willingness to allow them to eat at Sergeant Emery's field kitchen.

"Sir, I don't know how to thank you," Pearlman said. "We tried the 928th's mess and it was horrible this morning."

Both Pearlman and Megs walked to the end of the line as the remainder of the MP Detachment appeared and joined the chow line.

"Top, I'm sure there won't be any problem having the MPs dine with us," Marshall said.

"Sir, I think you've made a very wise decision for all of us. I'll let Ralph know they'll be attached for ration support," Tisher replied as he started walking towards the end of the chow line, "I better get in line so our hungry officers can eat."

Marshall decided to walk around the back of the mess tent and see how the food storage area was set up. He spotted two soldiers peeling potatoes, looking rather disgusted.

"Afternoon, men," Marshall greeted the soldiers. "Don't get up. I just wanted to take a look around."

"Sir, did you ever peel any potatoes while you were on KP?" asked one of the soldiers in a wise-guy manner.

Marshall walked over to the field table and picked up a spud peeler.

"Let's see," he said. "First one to peel six potatoes gets the rest of the day off. Ready, set, GO!"

Both soldiers started peeling furiously, as their commander slowly and methodically stroked the spud peeler over the potato. The skilled hands of the master potato peeler showed-up his younger apprentices as he finished his last spud. The other two soldiers were still working on their third and fourth respectively.

"To answer your question, I've peeled quite a few potatoes in my Army career," Marshall said. "I'm the spud peeler in my house. My wife always gives me that chore."

Marshall sat down with the soldiers and gave them a hand for a while as the chow line got shorter. He and the soldiers discussed the field training and asked them what they expected to get out of it. Both men mentioned no more KP duty—in a respectful manner.

Sergeant Emery wandered in the area and spotted the commander peeling spuds with the troops.

"Captain Marshall, what are you doin' on KP, Sir?" Emery asked.

"Sarge, I'm just earning my keep around here," added Marshall. "Men, I'm sure the good sergeant won't have you peeling potatoes all day."

"Oh no, Sir," responded Emery. "They're gonna be fetchin' water from the water trailer next, Now hurry up with them spuds!"

Marshall's turn in the chow line finally came. He was the last man to eat, and there was still enough food left over.

Specialist Fran Peoples was sitting on the side of the hill leaning against a large tree eating her lunch, watching all the soldiers. She had attracted a large following of male admirers that just couldn't seem to stop staring at her. She knew the affect she had on young healthy males, and used it to her advantage.

Specialist Pam Williams was nearby, watching some of the soldiers acting foolishly. Men, she thought to herself. What children they can be when a pretty girl is around.

The stillness of the afternoon was cut short as the Field First Sergeant's whistle was blown.

"FORMATION!" yelled Sergeant Lemasters. Lunchtime was officially over.

As all the 683rd assembled for formation, Sergeant Lemasters called for an accountability report of personnel. After receiving each section's report, he turned the formation over to Marshall.

"At ease!" Marshall said.

"So what do you think of the chow?" Everyone gave a grunt of approval. "Next time you're in the chow line, let the cooks know how much you appreciate the good work they're doing, and to keep it coming," Marshall said.

"Starting this afternoon, the 683rd is tactical. Weapons, including crew-served, will be drawn. Fighting positions will be prepared and manned. Guard mount will be conducted 24 hours a day until the tactical phase is over on Saturday."

A rumble of grunts could be heard among the formation.

Marshall continued after a pause.

"Weapons will be inventoried by serial number by every platoon, once in the morning and once in the evening," he said. "Anyone who loses a weapon will immediately report it through the chain of command. All work stops until the missing weapon is found.

"Weapons will be carried or worn. Weapon stacks will be guarded if you're in a work detail, and you will sleep with your weapon. Everyone understand this?"

A resounding, "Yes Sir!" was the 683rd's reply.

"There is no saluting in the field during the tactical phase unless it's a visiting V.I.P., so let's get that out of the way," Marshall said. "Present arms!"

All the soldiers came to attention and held a salute.

Marshall returned the salute and yelled, "Order arms!" Everyone in the formation dropped his or her salute.

"OK, that's taken care of," Marshall said. "From now on, no more salutes while we are in the tactical phase."

"In case of you haven't noticed, we've got company. The chiggers and fire ants are thick out here and prevention is the key word. Use plenty of the Army insect repellant on your neck, arms and legs, and re-apply it at least twice a day. Don't leave any food or food wrappers in your tent, because the fire ants will find it. If you've got flea collars, use 'em by lacing them into your boots. If you've got chigger bites, Sergeant Lemasters will issue you some calamine lotion. He'll give you a class on the proper first aid to treat the bites."

"Starting tomorrow, the armament and track sections will be on main post working at Boatwright. There will be a staff meeting at the shop tent at 1500 hours. Ten-hut!"

The 683rd snapped to attention as First Sergeant Tisher reported to Marshall at the front and center of the formation.

"Top, take charge of the unit," Marshall instructed in a soft voice for only Tisher to hear.

Formations were vital to get important information to all soldiers from one source, whether it was the First Sergeant, the unit commander, or their respective platoon leader or NCO. Formations were a common occurrence and held three times a day: morning, afternoon and evening. Keeping soldiers informed was vital to good unit cohesion and morale. The soldiers wanted and needed to know what was going on.

Several minutes later, First Sergeant Tisher turned the formation over to the sections. Tisher, Lieutenant Stiles and Second Lieutenant Smith were aware they were to accompany Marshall to Main Post to meet with the Reserve Affairs Coordinator, Major Josh Brask. Both Lieutenants got into the back of the ¼-ton as Tisher cranked the jeep's engine over.

"Okay Top, let's check out the floating bridge and see what's going on there," said Marshall as he attached the safety strap across the passenger entrance well of the ¼-ton jeep.

"Yes, Sir. Sure beats the hell out of going past the pig farm," Tisher replied.

The road through the training areas was a wooded, winding dirt road through the hills. After 10 minutes the road turned into a concreted steep grade that ended at the river's edge. The river was approximately 120 feet wide at the bottom of the gorge, with two deuces parked on either side. The floating pontoon bridge was attached to a series of steel cables and separate towing cables were attached to the back of each deuce. It was a fairly simple setup, and the ¼-ton jeep proceeded down the slope until they saw a sign written in chalk: Floating Bridge Out.

Marshall decided to investigate the situation and walked down to the soldier manning the floating bridge. The soldier was sitting on the bridge, fishing.

"How's the fishing, soldier?" Marshall asked.

The soldier reached down and pulled up a good-sized stringer of fish that he'd caught for the day.

"Not bad," Marshall said. "Tell me, what's wrong with the bridge?"

The soldier looked up at Marshall and slowly got to his feet.

"Our truck won't start," he said, pointing to the deuce-and-a-half next to Marshall's ¼-ton jeep.

Marshall got the feeling the soldiers were in no hurry to have the floating bridge operational.

"I'll have some of my technicians come over and have a look," Marshall said.

"OK, Sir," the soldier fisherman replied.

As Marshall got back into the ¼-ton jeep, he gave Tisher some bad news.

"Top, we've got to take the pig farm route," Marshall said. "Let's stop at our shop office tent first. I've got a mission for our automotive contact team."

They departed the area and retraced their path, winding back up at the 683rd field site. Marshall walked into the shop office tent and informed Chief Farley of the new mission for the contact team, which was now priority number 1.

Driving down the paved road towards Fort Knox's main entrance, the pig farm stench hit the passengers like a brick wall nearly a quarter of a mile before the pig farm appeared. Everyone except for the first sergeant put on their gas masks.

"Boy, that's nice. You guys are gonna make me suffer," Tisher said as he laughed and coughed at the same time. It took a minute before they passed the pig farm. "All clear!" Tisher yelled.

Everyone removed his or her M17 gas mask. The stench was still present.

"Gotcha!" laughed Tisher.

They all have a good laugh and suffered the stench for another minute as Marshall signaled to the first sergeant to speed up. They passed some nice residential homes off the side of the road that had to abide with the smell when the wind was in the wrong direction.

The main entrance loomed in the distance on the right with a large painted placard: "Welcome To Fort Knox, Home of the United States Army Armor School."

The Reserve Affairs Office was near the Post Headquarters building. The streets and buildings were old and well kept. Tisher drove through the Post, past the gold vault.

"Sir, would you like to make a small withdrawal?" asked Tisher jokingly.

"No Top, I brought enough for the next couple of weeks", Marshall replied.

Marshall pointed to his watch and the first sergeant acknowledged him. It was time to meet with their Reserve Affairs Coordinator.

The meeting with Major Brask began on time. Marshall introduced Lieutenant Stiles, Smith and First Sergeant Tisher to Major Brask. The first item on the agenda was the 683rd armament and tank automotive platoon training with Boatwright Maintenance Facility, the drawing of billets and other housekeeping requirements.

After all the procedures and guidelines were discussed in detail, Major Brask changed the subject.

"Your evaluator is Lieutenant Humphrey of the 509th Maintenance Company here on post," Brask said. "He's been in on active duty for approximately three months now. I've briefed him on your unit and he'll be out to visit your field site location soon."

Marshall looked a bit bewildered.

"Is he ordnance branch?" Marshall asked.

"As a matter of fact, he is," Major Brask replied.

Both knew that ordnance officers were few in numbers. The lieutenant's lack of experience was troubling Marshall. The 683rd would be given an evaluation by an officer with little or no experience about maintenance companies. That was bad news.

They continued the conversation about other training requirements including weapons qualification.

"Your Sergeant Mooney has been a very busy soldier these past few weeks," Brask said. "He's accomplished a great deal of coordination and it appears everything is in order for your unit to do weapons qual."

"Not many Reserve units do enough prior planning to squeeze in that kind of training while they're out in the field," Major Brask added. "My congratulations to you and your staff." Brask knew he was dealing with a seasoned company commander.

"Thank you, Sir," replied Marshall. "I wanted to make sure that everyone gets a chance to fire a weapon this year during A.T. The ranges here on Post are some of the best in the Army. It would be a shame not to use them."

A few other items were discussed and Brask and Marshall were satisfied with what had been covered.

"One more thing, Sir." Marshall added. "We're supporting an engineering company that has a training area and road improvement mission. Our maintenance funding isn't adequate enough to cover any major repairs, like transmissions or engines. When the time comes—and it will—we'll need some extra funds to handle those repairs."

Major Brask looked at Marshall with a confident smile.

"Good Commander," Brask said. "When that happens, we'll be ready to work with you and get the funding that is needed."

Sounds good to me, Sir," replied Marshall as he and his staff stood up and saluted Major Brask.

Before departing, Marshall wanted to have a private word with Brask.

"Sir, do you mind if you and I discuss something in private?" Marshall asked.

Brask smiled.

"Sure, no problem," he replied.

First Sergeant Tisher, Lieutenant Stiles and Second Lieutenant Smith left the room.

Marshall quickly spoke his mind to Major Brask.

"Sir, I've got serious concerns about this rookie evaluator," Marshall said. "He doesn't have the background or experience to give our unit a fair evaluation."

Brask listened to Marshall's concerns.

"Look, Captain, we've been tasked to provide the Reserve units with evaluators," Brask replied. "Unfortunately, the only other branch-qualified evaluator left on Fort Knox is a company commander who doesn't have the time. Lieutenant Humphrey is the only officer that's ordnance branch qualified. Don't worry. I'll give him some coaching."

Marshall didn't like what he had heard.

"When do we get a chance to meet this rookie?" he asked.

Brask looked up and smiled, waving his hand at someone he spotted outside his office door.

"Rookie Lieutenant Humphrey reporting for duty, Sir," said Second Lieutenant Humphrey as he entered the room and saluted Major Brask.

Marshall felt his heart sink in his chest. He knew Lieutenant Humphrey had been listening in on their private conversation. Things were starting off badly as Brask introduced Humphrey to Marshall.

Marshall stood and shook Humphrey's hand.

"No offense, Lieutenant, but I've got a large heavy equipment maintenance company with a tremendously complicated mission and over 200 personnel in the field," Marshall said. "Not too many people in ordnance branch would want to tackle a company command as difficult and demanding as this one, much less try to evaluate it."

"Sir, your unit is no different than any other," Humphrey replied. "It shouldn't pose a problem."

Marshall looked at Brask with one eyebrow raised.

Brask decided it was his turn to jump into the conversation.

"Well, looks like the good lieutenant here will have no problems then. Captain, if you'll excuse me, I've got to brief Lieutenant Humphrey on several things."

Marshall stood up and saluted Brask.

"Sir, I appreciate your time," Marshall said. "Lieutenant, I'll look forward to seeing you at Mount Eden. Good day."

Marshall walked out of the office and exited the building, shaking his head in disbelief.

"Top, we're in trouble," Marshall told Tisher. "This rookie evaluator is a smart-ass that'll want to get even. Better batten down the hatches."

"Oh, I almost forgot! Let's hit the PX," he said.

At the Main PX, the 683rd party walked in. The PX was setup like a large department store. Marshall headed straight for the section that had all the first aid supplies. What he was looking for was all gone. Someone had already bought all the chigger relief medication. Marshall found out from a clerk that it was on back-order and would arrive in a couple of weeks.

Time for plan B. Marshall walked over to the cosmetics counter.

"How many bottles of clear nail polish do you have?" he asked.

The clerk behind the counter was a bit amused at the question, and counted 15 bottles.

"I'll take'em all," replied Marshall.

He spotted Tisher and informed him of his purchase.

"Are you going into town tonight, Sir?" Tisher asked.

Marshall got a chuckle out of his first sergeant's question.

"No, Top, these are to cover up the chigger bites," Marshall said. "It'll heal the bite without using a bandage. Best thing to do is cover a bite as soon as it appears."

"Sir, I'm sure the troops will appreciate that," Tisher replied. "I'll issue these to the section sergeants so they can disburse 'em out to those who need them."

"I bought all the clear nail polish they had, so it's got to last the entire A.T.," Marshall said.

"Sir, I'll make sure the NCOs are aware," Tisher responded. "Who would have ever thought that we'd be giving clear nail polish to our soldiers?" Tisher reflected as they both walked out of the PX.

"It's the new Army, Top," Marshall replied.

Returning to the field site at Mount Eden Base Camp, Marshall and Tisher prepared for the upcoming staff meeting at the shop office tent. As they were preparing for the meeting, trucks were being pulled into the woodline. The sound of trees broken in half and brush being crushed echoed through the field site as drivers slowly backed their trucks and trailers into the wood line. The thundering roar of the big diesel engines was heard over the noise of the electrical generators as the drivers backed their vehicles over ditches and stumps. Occasionally, a "Whoa!" or, "Turn right! No, your other right!" was overheard from the ground guides as the trucks were being moved. An occasional boom or thud was heard when a truck's bumper hit a large tree. It was quite an orchestration of noise as the 683rd's vehicles disappeared into the woods. Marshall and Tisher looked at each other and smiled when they overheard one of the NCOs yelling at his driver.

"Top, looks like some folks are going to need help from the service section," said Marshall.

Just as he finished talking, a loud ripping of canvas was heard as one of the trucks nearby was backing up in the woods.

"I think you're right, Sir," Tisher mused.

All 683rd section leaders were assembled in the shop office tent for the afternoon staff meeting. Trucks and trailers were still being backed into the woods as the meeting was about to take place. Shouts from the soldiers could be heard guiding the large vehicles.

As the first sergeant and Marshall walked into the tent, Sergeant Lemasters shouted "Ten-hut!"

All within the tent rose.

"Please be seated," Marshall promptly said. "I'll try and keep this as brief as possible. First Sergeant Tisher will distribute clear nail polish to each section. This is to be used to cover the chigger bites. Use it sparingly."

"I can see—and hear—that everyone is pulling their vehicles into the woodline. Make sure they're partially camouflaged when parked. All tentage has to be inside the woodline as well. Those on the edge of the woods will have to either camouflage their tent, or move it if it can be seen with the naked eye from the road."

"We've had our initial meeting with the Reserve Affairs Office and have set up the track and armament sections to be working on main post at the Boatwright Facility. Those soldiers will stay on Main Post until weapons qualification, which is scheduled for Thursday of this week."

"Sergeant Mooney has secured all the ranges and we will shortly be tasking each section for safety NCOs and officers for each range. Safety personnel must attend a safety briefing at Range Control prior to weapons qual. Ammo will be drawn the day of firing. Sergeant Mooney will coordinate all ammunition handling and accountability. Lieutenant Stiles will have a roster drawn up for all range safety personnel by tomorrow morning."

"For those sections that will be working at Boatwright, please see me and Lieutenant Kiley after the meeting.

"One more thing. The 683rd will be setting up roadside spot checks starting tomorrow, and our friendly MP detachment will be the enforcement. Chief Farley and Chief James will set up the teams. I don't want to see any of our vehicles or drivers failing our own roadside spot check. Any who do will report to me personally."

"Any questions or comments?" Marshall drank from his canteen. His speech had left him parched.

One hand was raised in the back, and Sergeant Pearlman stood to make a comment.

"Sir, just to let you know, the group headquarters had to move their CP tent this afternoon. They were trenching around their tent and found an unexploded dud. This whole training site used to be an impact area about 70 years ago."

"Thank you, Sarge," Marshall said, looking rather surprised. "Did anyone here find any duds in your area?"

The assembled NCOs and officers all shook their heads.

"Well, if you do, the action to take is leave it alone, report it immediately, and do not disturb the area," Marshall said. "We'll notify the Main Post explosive ordnance disposal team to take care of it. It'll most likely wind up in the Post museum."

All the personnel had a chuckle as the rain began to fall heavily.

"I hope everyone has dug a drainage ditch around your tents," Marshall said.

The assembled group looked at each other hoping to catch an affirmative nod from their section sergeants.

As the rain came down harder, a small stream of water entered the tent. Marshall saw multiple streams of water coming through the tent. The streams were all getting bigger.

Chief Farley noticed this as well, exited the tent, and yelled at some section soldiers to start trenching around the tent immediately. Too late, the streams were getting bigger and deeper.

"That's why you need to trench around your tent," Marshall added, using the present example as a teaching point. "Top, I turn the meeting over to you."

Marshall walked to the back of the tent and let First Sergeant Tisher take over the meeting as the stream of rain water grew deeper as it ran through the tent.

"Thank you, Sir," Tisher said. "As you can see by the flood we're experiencing, the Old Man is absolutely right. Trench the area around all your tents. This includes the half-shelters as well. There's nothing worse than a wet sleeping bag or wet clothes. I want every section to check and make sure this is done now."

One member from each section and platoon got up and left the tent to check on their areas. As Tisher resumed his discussion, shouts were heard from the Section NCOs telling people to get busy trenching around the tents. Moments later the sound of digging was heard above the din of rain.

Tisher went on to inform the sections about the wearing of the tactical uniform, and the weather forecast, which was hot and humid.

He concluded his talk with a safety advisory.

"Every soldier should be drinking at least three to four canteens of water per day," Tisher said. "Heat exhaustion is preventable, and I will not tolerate a lack of close supervision of our soldiers. You all know the signs of heat exhaustion and heatstroke. Let's make sure there are no casualties out here in the field. Any comments or questions?"

Tisher opened the meeting and heard from each section. Some of the questions he answered on the spot. Some others were turned over to Marshall, who handled them or took note to see if it could be taken care of through higher headquarters.

Chief McCarthy brought up a point.

"Top, I've got concerns that the command out here in the field hasn't taken the necessary steps to rid the area of biting insects." McCarthy said. "I can't prevent my soldiers from making formal complaints or writing their congressmen."

Marshall fielded the comment with tact.

"Chief, I appreciate your comment on that subject, and will definitely bring that up in tomorrow's meeting with Colonel Biggs," he replied. "It's a situation that needs to be taken care of. Thank you Chief."

It was a response that seemed to please everyone in the meeting, including Chief McCarthy and Sergeant Schmoot.

"Okay everyone, except for those sections that'll be at Boatwright, meeting adjourned," Marshall said.

The track and armament section leaders met with Marshall and Lieutenant Kiley after the meeting and went over the details of having their personnel on Main Post. Information was provided on who they were to see in the morning, what buildings they would have for sleeping quarters, and where they were to report to at the Boatwright Maintenance Facility.

Marshall placed the entire Main Post section under the control of Lieutenant Kate Kiley. Her NCOIC (Non-

Commissioned Officer In Charge) was Sergeant First Class Huddle.

The meeting adjourned and all exited the tent. The rain was beginning to let up, and the dirt road network had become sloppy with thick mud.

Marshall made his way to the CP tent and found Lieutenant Rodriguez waiting for him inside.

"Sir, I've got the field layout map started with the preliminary sections drawn in," Rodriguez said.

"Good," replied Marshall. "I'd like to see it."

The area the 683rd occupied at Mount Eden Base Camp was drawn in black. The roads and terrain were all drawn in properly, using the correct military symbols.

As Rodriguez began to flip over a sheet of clear acetate with colored markings that represented boundaries and defensive positions, fire ants clustered on the red markings.

"Rod, what did you use for the red color?" asked Marshall.

"Sir, I didn't have any red markers, so I used some ketchup," replied Rodriguez.

"Hmmm, I see. Looks like the ants like your work," Marshall mused. "Go ahead and show me the rest of the layout."

Rodriguez continued with his presentation of the field layout to Marshall.

Sergeant Lemasters walked into the CP tent and sat down to observe the presentation of the field layout map by Rodriguez. He also spotted the fire ants on the clear acetate, and the commander whispered "ketchup" to his field first sergeant.

"Sir, I've got some red markers in my map case," Lemasters remarked. "Let me git you one. You kin save that ketchup fer chow."

Rodriguez thanked Lemasters and continued with his presentation of his field layout map.

"Rod, that is very good," Marshall said. "When we get some VIPs in the area, I want you to show them the 683rd's field layout with a formal presentation. Keep it updated daily, and get rid of that ketchup."

"Yes, Sir," replied Rodriguez, as he was bitten on his finger by a red fire ant. "I'll get rid of these little pests as well."

"All the vehicles and tentage have been moved into the wood line, Sir," Sergeant Lemasters reported. "Most of the vehicles got some scratches, and a couple rookie drivers broke some mirrors, and a few tore up some canvas. Other 'n that, it went purty good."

Marshall reflected on the information

"Anyone get stuck?" he asked.

"If'n they did, Sir, It weren't fer long," Lemasters replied. "They're all combat-oriented, and the chains and locks ain't bein' used."

Marshall took the information well.

"That's good news, Sarge," he said. "Let's go take a look-see, shall we?"

Both Lemasters and Marshall exited the CP tent while Rodriguez made ketchup-less corrections to the field layout drawing.

The 683rd field site was busy with soldiers trenching around their tents and relocating their platoon headquarters tents. Vehicles were parked nearby and dispersion of equipment was excellent.

As Marshall and Lemasters continued on their walk, soldiers were filling sandbags and stacking them around the generator emplacements for protection as well as noise reduction. Fuel cans for the generators were stored in a separate area nearby. White engineer tape, which was a white cloth fabric tape about two inches across, was being used to show walkways in the dark.

"Very good. Looks like those training classes paid off, Sarge," remarked Marshall. "Let's check the vehicle over there."

Both walked over and found Sergeant Burkette in the cab, unmoving. Marshall stood on the running board and looked inside to see the steering wheel was chained and locked.

Marshall nodded at Sergeant Lemasters.

"Sergeant, just what the Sam Hill are you doin'?" Lemasters yelled.

Burkette was startled out of his slumber.

"I was just unlocking the padlock from the steering wheel, Sarge," Burkette replied.

Sergeant Lemasters began to get into Burkette's face.

"I don't wanna see you wearin' them sunglasses no more out in the field!" Lemasters yelled.

"Sarge, these are prescription glasses," Burkette calmly replied. "I can't see past my nose without 'em. I've gotta wear 'em. I broke my other pair before we got here."

Lemasters couldn't argue with that. Burkette would be allowed to wear his sunglasses in the field, both day and night. He did have another pair of glasses just in case, another pair of sunglasses.

As Lemasters and Marshall continued their walk through the area, they saw some soldiers draping their wet sleeping bags over tree limbs.

"Sarge, have the section sergeants see Sergeant Mooney for some blankets," Marshall said. "Looks like a few soldiers will need 'em tonight. They learned a valuable lesson today."

Sergeant Lemasters decided to check on all the soldiers and the condition of their gear.

Marshall saw Lieutenant Stiles and walked over to see how the unit training schedule changes were going.

"So Lieutenant Stiles, are you ready to discuss the unit training schedule?" Marshall asked.

"Sir, I'm ready. Just let me get my briefcase," replied Stiles.

Marshall noticed that the troops are forming a line for chow.

"How about you, Sergeant Huddle and Sergeant Lemasters meet with me at the shop office tent after chow?" Marshall asked.

Stiles concurred and quickly left to do more work on the training schedule. Marshall spotted Tisher and walked over and discussed the impromptu meeting.

"Yes Sir, I'll be there," Tisher said. "I'll get John and Huddle. Be there at 1845 hours?"

Marshall nodded.

"That'll be fine, Top."

Marshall was greeted by smiling soldiers as they walked to the chow line.

After numerous greetings from the soldiers, Marshall turned to Tisher.

"Top, why are these troops so happy?" Marshall asked.

"Must be the chow, Sir. It definitely isn't the weather or the chiggers," replied Tisher.

"Yeah Top, I have to agree with you on that."

Soldiers were being served their evening meal. Sergeant Emery and his talented staff of cooks had prepared another masterpiece of culinary excellence. The main course for the evening meal was roast beef with mashed potatoes and gravy. The meal was fit for a king, and the soldiers of the 683rd knew it.

As Marshall was overseeing the chow line, several new individuals from other units started to appear in the line.

"Top, looks like we've got some guests for dinner," Marshall said.

First Sergeant Tisher also noticed them and walked over to investigate. Tisher began talking to the soldiers and let out a loud laugh. He walked back to his commander smiling and shaking his head.

"Sir, these guys are from the 928th. They heard about Sergeant Emery's chow and decided to investigate," Tisher said. "One of 'em said he lost a couple of pounds eatin' from his field mess. I told 'em they could eat here tonight, but this was their last meal here, and to tell anyone else coming from the 928th that they'd be turned away next time."

Marshall quickly realized that the word about good food from the 683rd Field Mess was getting around quickly.

"Top, we'll have more visitors showing up at our door. Good food is hard to pass up when you're out in the field," Marshall said.

As the chow line finally diminished and all the 683rd officers had been served, Marshall walked over to the head count table.

"How many did we feed tonight?" he asked.

The soldier looked at the last signature and counted up all the officer signatures.

"Two hundred and twenty-six, Sir."

Marshall looked over at Sergeant Emery who was standing behind the soldier.

"Sarge, how many people did you draw rations for?"

Sergeant Emery smiled.

"Two hundred, Sir, but I always try and serve as many as we can," Emery said. "Don't want to turn away a hungry soldier."

"We've got people from other units in our chow line," Marshall confided in Emery. "Unless they're VIPs or have a very good reason to be here, you'll have to start turning them away. Otherwise, you'll be feeding all the personnel at Mount Eden Base Camp in a few days. That'll run your headcount over 600."

Sergeant Emery had a kind heart, and loved making people happy by filling their stomachs with good food.

"Yes, Sir. I'll make sure the head count is made aware of that," replied Emery.

Emery knew the Old Man was right. The number of soldiers could snowball well over 300 if nothing was done to prevent other units from infiltrating the 683rd chow line.

Marshall had his meal and enjoyed the fine chow that Sergeant Emery and his people had made. Afterwards, he complimented them on an excellent job. The soldiers appreciated the commander's words of encouragement.

Walking to the shop office tent, Marshall realized he was late to his own meeting. As he entered the tent, all were present and awaiting his arrival.

"Sorry I'm a little late," Marshall said. "Let's go over the unit training schedule day by day and see what training is plugged in, and what needs to be added."

The group came alive as copies of the changes to the training schedule were passed out. Each day was gone over and details of the training were written up and re-typed as the meeting continued on into the evening. After several hours, Sergeant Huddle and Sergeant Tea left to type up the changes.

Marshall decided to close the meeting with a short speech on his training philosophy.

"Everyone here should know by now that the first week is going to be very busy with mandatory tactical training," he said. "There should be no Commander's Time or free time at all. If there isn't anything going on, something's wrong. A soldier with nothing to do in the field will find something to do. That is not good training and reflects poorly on us. It's our job to make sure every soldier is well trained and prepared for any eventuality.

"That's all, meeting adjourned."

Sergeant Lemasters looked at his watch. 2105 hours. Time to check on the 683rd guards before retiring for the evening. He met with the sergeant of the guard, Sergeant Nugot, and told him that he'd be around to spot-check on the guards.

"Sergeant Nugot, if'n I find any of yer guards asleep, you'n yer sleepin' guard will be pullin' guard duty the entire time we're out 'n the field, understand?" Lemasters said sternly.

Nugot got the message.

"Yeah, Sarge. Read ya loud 'n clear," he replied.

The evening faded into darkness of night. Another busy day for the 683rd was coming up. Marshall finally got to lie down on his cot on top of his extreme cold weather mountain sleeping bag, good for temperatures down to 30 degrees below zero. The temperature outside was in the mid-seventies, and sleeping inside a zipped up bag was not a good idea.

Marshall laid on top and used a bed sheet he brought with him to cover up. The morning would come quickly.

A.T.- DAY 3 (TUESDAY)

First Sergeant Tisher's alarm clock went off at 0545 hours. Slipping out of the warm and comfortable sheets on his canvas cot, Captain Marshall noticed that the sun had not yet come up. As Marshall dressed and put on his field gear and helmet, he woke up First Sergeant Tisher. Tisher looked at his watch, got up from his cot, and turned on the coffee maker on the field desk next to him. The generator outside became noticeably louder as it began to labor to meet the increased demand for electricity.

Marshall was already outside the tent, heading for his first cup of coffee at the field mess. Everyone he met was in good spirits and happily going about their morning routine of shaving and washing. All seemed to be very content to be in the field.

Field First Sergeant Lemasters was making sure everyone was up for morning chow, occasionally yelling at a couple of sleeping soldiers that were comfortably snoozing in their Army down-filled sleeping bags.

Sergeant Emery had another breakfast feast prepared, and the 683rd soldiers lined up ready for another treat. As the morning meal progressed, Marshall took the time to look over the changes to the training schedule Lieutenant Stiles had made for the day. It looked like a full day of training, which Marshall had insisted on.

After everyone was done with the morning meal, Lemasters blew his whistle for morning formation.

As the sections reported their personnel status to the first sergeant, all were present, except one: Specialist Peoples. This concerned Marshall and Tisher. Peoples was the unit armorer and the only individual with keys to the arms trailer and weapons racks.

The first sergeant acted without hesitation and looked directly at Sergeant Bradford.

"Sergeant Bradford!" shouted Tisher. "Go find our missing unit armorer!"

"Right away, Top!" Bradford replied.

Sergeant Bradford headed toward the weapons trailer, thinking Peoples had to be nearby. As he looked inside the cab of the 5-ton tractor attached to the weapons trailer, he found the missing soldier. Specialist Peoples was sound asleep, snoring away. He opened the door to the 5-ton tractor and tried shaking her, but she remained asleep.

Undeterred, Bradford got out his canteen, removed the cap, and poured the contents onto Peoples. Peoples awoke instantly and began swearing a blue streak.

"Get your butt out of there and get in formation!" Bradford yelled. "The whole unit is waiting on you, Peoples!"

Peoples was soaking wet in her white T-shirt and did not care. She ran to formation as is, soaking wet in a T-shirt, no bra, no boots, no field gear, and mad at the world for disturbing her slumber. Finding her spot, she slipped into formation trying not to be too obvious.

Tisher welcomed Peoples to the formation and warned everyone about the consequences of missing formation in the future.

The daily laundry list of information was given out to the soldiers, including the day's activities and information for the personnel scheduled to train at Boatwright.

After the formation was dismissed by the first sergeant, the soldiers made their way back to their sections. Many just couldn't take their eyes off of Peoples and her wet T-shirt.

"All right boys, show's over," Peoples said in disgust.

"Fran, up late last night?" asked Specialist Williams as she walked over to see her friend.

"I didn't get to sleep until three this morning," replied Peoples. "The boys were, how can I say, excited to see me."

Williams shook her head in disbelief.

"Fran, you better not get caught," she said.

"Don't worry about me, Pamela," Peoples said with a wave of her hand as she put her field gear on. "I'm just having a little fun out in the field, among other things."

Lieutenant Stiles walked over to the two women soldiers to provide them with some guidance.

"Ladies, for your information, the uniform out in the field also includes the proper undergarments, which includes a bra," Stiles said. "No more feeling 'au natural,' understand?"

"Yes Ma'am," replied Peoples and Williams.

Stiles departed, leaving both women by the weapons trailer. Williams looked at her friend as she continued to put on her field gear.

"Fran, you're big trouble. You know that?"

"Honey, you ain't seen nothing yet!" laughed Peoples as she winked at Williams.

At the commanders' meeting, Colonel Biggs was pleased to announce that everyone's paperwork was on time and appeared to be accurate. The discussion by Biggs turned to unit dispersion and he looked at Marshall with an inquisitive look.

"We looked for the 683rd last evening, but couldn't find your unit," Biggs said. "Did you move a large portion of the 683rd to Main Post, Captain Marshall?"

"No Sir, we've just sent our track and armament section to Boatwright this morning," Marshall replied. "The rest of the 683rd is in the wood line, except for the shop office tent, which is well camouflaged."

"Well, you've done a very good job," Biggs said. "As for the rest of you here, if your equipment is in plain sight, it must be camouflaged. Otherwise, like Captain Marshall here, you'll need to place your equipment inside the wood line.

"Now are there any comments or questions for the commanders to bring up to my staff?" asked Biggs.

Many of the company commanders in the meeting took their turn informing Biggs and the staff of what operations they have going on.

Marshall's turn came last, but Biggs knew that he would have a lot to say.

"Sir, first of all, I'd like to let everyone here know that we are beginning the roadside spot checks today," Marshall said. "We have a MP section attached to enforce it. Vehicles will be impounded if found to be unsafe or improperly dispatched. Secondly, we will be sending out maintenance assistance teams to every unit, including the engineer outfit.

"And finally, Sir, my soldiers are getting chigger bites on a regular basis. I don't know how the infestation is in this area, but in our location they are everywhere. Sir, if we don't do something soon to try and get rid of these chiggers, I'm afraid our soldiers may file a congressional complaint."

"Yes, I see," replied Biggs. "Perhaps we should contact the post engineers to help in this matter.

"Major Brown, please contact the Post engineers and inform them of our chigger situation."

Major Brown replied in the affirmative as Biggs asked if there was anything else that needed to be addressed.

"Yes, Sir, there is," responded Marshall. "My soldiers are starting to get a bit gamey. Is the field shower point operational yet?"

The 928th Commander quickly responded.

"Not yet, we're missing a part to our boiler," he said. "I'm having the part procured on Main Post through the Reserve Affairs Office. It should be here soon."

"Sir, I hope you don't mind, but I'd like to have your permission to allow the 683rd to take a shower run to our barracks on Main Post every evening," Marshall interjected.

"That's fine, Captain Marshall," Biggs replied. "And that goes for all units as well."

"One more thing, Sir, "interjected Marshall again. "My automotive contact team fixed the deuce for the floating bridge. The bridge is now back in operation."

"That's a relief," replied Biggs. "That pig farm is a major annoyance."

As the commanders' call meeting began to wind down, Biggs put out a warning.

"Be aware, gentlemen, we will soon be having VIPs in the area, so make sure your people display the proper military courtesy to all visitors," he said. "Meeting adjourned."

Marshall left the CP tent and noticed some of the group headquarters soldiers were digging a trench around the tent next to it. A metallic clank was heard when one of the soldiers hit a hard object using his entrenching tool.

"Oh crap, another dud. Better call EOD!" the soldier yelled to his buddy.

Making his way to the 683rd Shop Office tent, Marshall asked Chief Farley about any automotive mission work the 683rd had received in the past 24 hours.

"Sir, the only job my people have had so far is fixing the deuce at the floating bridge," Farley said. "The rest of the sections have been busy fixing their flat tires."

"How many new flats have they found, Chief?" Marshall asked.

"Oh, about 15 more since we've arrived," Farley said. "Most of 'em are the inner tires on the deuces. The drivers knew they had flats on the inner tires and decided they'd fix 'em once we got here."

"Do we have enough new tires to go around?" asked Marshall.

"Not a problem, Sir. Chief James has picked up all the new tires we need plus some more in case we get any new flats on the way back home," Farley said.

"Sounds good, Chief!" Marshall replied. "By the way, have you made contact with the engineer unit yet?"

"I've been in contact with their head of maintenance," replied Chief Farley. "I'm going to make a personal visit later on today and start making coordination. From what I understand, their mission is going to be 24 hours around the clock. We'll probably see lots of 5-ton dump trucks coming our way soon."

"Chief, you can count on it," replied Marshall.

Sergeant Lemasters was screening personnel going to sick call at the CP tent. Sergeant Tea was busy preparing the paperwork for each soldier.

"What's wrong with you, soldier?" Lemasters asked a tired-looking young male soldier.

"I've got sores on my legs and crotch. You wanna see?" he responded.

"Hell no! Keep yer pants on, Troop, and git on the deuce. Next man!"

Another 15 soldiers walked up to Tea and reported for sick call. All had chigger bites.

Marshall walked up to Lemasters.

"What's the count today, Sarge?" he asked.

"Got 22 of 'em, Sir," Lemasters said. "Most, I suspect, just want some extra time in the mornin'."

"Anyone reporting for sick call has that right, Sarge," replied Marshall. "We can't turn them away or deny them from seeing a doctor, even if they don't know what to do about chigger bites other than prescribe calamine lotion. Besides, that lotion may come in handy if we start getting attacked by poison ivy."

Lemasters grinned and turned his head to spit some chewing tobacco on the ground.

The roadside spot checks began, and violators were being held at the roadside waiting for the vehicles to be towed to the designated impound area. Sergeant Nugot got the call to fire up his 5-ton wrecker and start bringing the impound vehicles into the 683rd Shop area. As Nugot climbed into the 5-ton wrecker cab, he noticed a family of skunks ran out from under the wrecker.

The roadside spot check quickly found its first violator. Colonel Biggs' driver did not have his ¼-ton jeep properly dispatched. Specialist Megs politely informed Biggs that they would give him a lift to where he had to go, but his ¼-ton jeep would have to stay. The MPs took Biggs to his headquarters in time for the EOD Team to give him an update on what they had found.

"Colonel, we've found another artillery shell next to one of your tents," the team leader said with a salute. "We've removed it and thought you'd like to know it's probably going to be in the Post Museum. We haven't seen shells like these in such good condition.

"I hope you don't mind, Sir, but there appears to be more duds in that one area," he continued. "We've found 'em using a metal detector. You'll have to have your people move that tent again."

In the motor pool trailer, Specialist Dweedle was rolling new spare tires out the back of the trailer. As he got near the end of the open doors, he turned to his left and his boot caught the edge of an old nail on the wooden floor of the trailer.

Dweedle fell to the ground as he let go of the tire and landed on his back. As he looked up from his new position on the ground, the spare tire he was handling fell off the trailer and landed squarely on his chest. He groaned loudly.

Marshall and First Sergeant Tisher were returning from measuring the four-mile physical training test course in the ¼-ton jeep. Both saw an Army MedEvac helicopter take-off from the 683rd area.

"Top, we better see what that was all about," said Marshall.

As they pull into the shop office area, Marshall walked over to Chief Farley.

"Who just got evacuated by chopper?" Marshall asked.

"We had an accident over in the motor pool area," Chief Farley replied. "Apparently Dweedle fell off the back of a trailer and got hurt. He's complaining he hurt his back and he can't take a deep breath. He might have cracked some ribs."

Marshall looked at Tisher.

"Let's get over to the motor pool," Marshall said.

As both men arrived at the motor pool area, Chief James was there to greet them and fill them in on what happened.

"Sir, Dweedle fell off the back of the trailer, and a spare tire fell on his chest while he was on the ground. He couldn't move, so I called in MedEvac."

Marshall looked at Tisher.

"We better get to the emergency room," Marshall said.

They both got back into the ¼-ton and headed toward Main Post. Fortunately, the floating bridge was still operational.

As they headed toward Ireland Army Hospital, a modern eight-story hospital on Main Post, Marshall turned to Tisher.

"Top, Dweedle is going to have to go through the emergency room and then be admitted," Marshall said. "We won't be able to see him for at least another hour. Let's stop at the PX and do some shopping for the troops. Maybe they've got a new supply of chigger medicine."

"Great idea, Sir!" Tisher replied. "We can see Dweedle right after we're done. The PX is close to the hospital."

After pulling into a parking space at the PX, both men walked into the entrance—just as Specialist Dweedle was coming out of the PX with two cartons of cigarettes under his arm.

"Jessie, what the hell are you doing in the PX? We were going to visit you in the hospital," exclaimed Tisher.

"Oh I'm okay, Top. I just got the wind knocked outta me," replied Dweedle.

"Need a lift back to the field?" Tisher asked, knowing full well Dweedle was not going to walk back to Mount Eden Base Camp. Dweedle nodded his head.

"Get yer butt in the ¼-ton while me and the Old Man use the PX," Tisher said.

"Yes Sir, Top," Dweedle replied as he trotted off to the parked ¼-ton.

Both the first sergeant and Marshall had a good laugh about Dweedle's miraculous recovery.

After Marshall and Tisher had returned to the 683rd field site, Field First Sergeant Lemasters was holding afternoon formation. The noonday meal had just ended. All 683rd personnel were accounted for by their platoon sergeants.

Lemasters went over the day's schedule and had a tasking from higher headquarters that needed attending to.

"I need four volunteers fer trash detail," Lemasters said.

Before he could get the last words out of his mouth he saw six hands go up, waving frantically.

"OK. See me after formation," Lemasters shouted. He was momentarily amazed. Why would anyone want to volunteer for one of the more unpleasant jobs?

What Lemasters didn't know was all aluminum cans and glass bottles had a five cents deposit. The rumor of hundreds of dollars to be made hauling trash had spread throughout the lower ranks of the 683rd. Trash detail had taken on a new meaning.

Later that day, Colonel Biggs entered the 683rd area with his ¼-ton driver not knowing where to go. The 683rd area was empty, except for a camouflaged sign with the unit's designation painted on it.

As he exited the vehicle and began to walk around, Biggs spotted a path and headed in the direction of the wood line. A young 683rd soldier halted the group commander and gave the challenge. Biggs gave him the correct password, and the guard called the switchboard on his field phone to notify the sergeant of the guard of their high-ranking visitor.

"Good afternoon, Sir!" Captain Marshall came up to greet overall field commander. "Sir, we've dispensed with salutes in the field while we're tactical. My apologies if my people haven't shown the proper courtesy."

Biggs gave an understanding nod and complimented the 683rd field layout.

"Captain Marshall, your unit is so well positioned inside the wood line that my people are having difficulty finding the 683rd."

"Thank you, Sir," replied Marshall. "I'll let our people know that. Would you like to inspect our position, Sir?"

"By all means, Commander, please lead on," replied Biggs.

Both commanders walked through the area. Biggs was very pleased with the fighting positions and defensive perimeter that had been set up.

"Colonel Biggs, my soldiers would like to start patrolling and perform some night reconnaissance operations," Marshall said. "With your permission, this evening would be a probing mission to check on the other units' defenses. The other units could be warned at tomorrow's commanders' meeting that aggressor action may be possible, if that's all right with you."

Biggs paused and thought for a while.

"If your soldiers would like to do this, I have no objections, other than safety concerns. No physical contact or hand-to-hand fighting."

"Yes, Sir," replied Marshall. "I'll make sure everyone is well briefed before they start."

The two continued their walk through the 683rd area. The 683rd field site was functioning perfectly, and every soldier was either working or attending a training class.

"Sir, we've scheduled weapons qualification for the .45 caliber pistol on Friday," Marshall said. "I believe we have extra ammo for your personnel if they need to qualify at the pistol range."

Again, Marshall caught Colonel Biggs off guard.

"Thank you, Captain Marshall," he said. "We weren't planning on having our personnel qualify this A.T., but I'm sure there are many within the headquarters that need to. I'll have Major Brown provide you a list of those who'll participate."

Curious about all the other logistical and safety requirements, Biggs asked more questions.

"Do you have the necessary safety personnel, medics and ambulances?"

"All taken care of, Sir," Marshall replied assuredly. "My full-time staff made all the arrangements months ago. We're all set."

"Are you going to have all your personnel qualify on Thursday and Friday?" Biggs asked.

"I've got all the ranges reserved for M16, pistol, M60 machine gun, M203 grenade launcher, and the M2 .50-caliber machine gun. All ammo, ranges, safety personnel and medics are ready to go, Sir," replied Marshall confidently. "I'll rotate personnel from the field site to the ranges so all personnel will have an opportunity to fire and still maintain a presence in the field."

Biggs was impressed with Marshall's planning.

"Sounds like you've got everything planned," Biggs said. "I hope everything goes according to plan for you."

"Me too, Sir," replied Marshall cautiously.

One hour later, Field First Sergeant Lemasters and Sergeant Mooney were going over range fire operations and requirements with the selected safety NCOs and officers.

Chief McCarthy raised his voice for a question.

"Who's in charge of all the ranges?" he asked.

"I am," replied Lieutenant Smith. "Captain Marshall has delegated that job to me."

Marshall walked in the tent and told everyone to remain seated and carry on.

"OK, Sarge, where are we at?" asked Marshall, regarding the range fire planning as he took a seat next to Lieutenant Smith.

"Sir, I'm jist bout ready to assign ranges," replied Sergeant Lemasters.

"Please go ahead," Marshall instructed.

"OK, Mr. McCarthy, you've got the zero range and the M2 range," Lemasters began. "All you NCOs here are safety NCOs on every range. Here's the weapons range assignments."

Lemasters pulled back a large piece of paper from an easel. All the ranges, times, safety officers, safety NCOs, equipment required, number of firing orders, number of firers, number of loaders, names of the medics and times and location of the range control safety briefings for each range were neatly printed on the easel.

Sergeant Mooney added some pointed comments.

"Everything will run as smooth as a Swiss watch as long as everyone here knows the what, when and where," he said. "I've got maps of the firing ranges and times each range is supposed to be open. Fort Knox has a dedicated Range NCOIC assigned to each range to assist us. We've got to be there on time with ammo, weapons, firers, and safety personnel. They'll operate the range tower, issue all commands, and do all the scoring electronically."

"Then what do they need us for?" Chief McCarthy piped in.

"Chief, Range Control won't operate the zero range. We'll have to do that, and we've got to provide all the safety personnel for all ranges," Sergeant Mooney replied.

Chief McCarthy was beginning to get the picture.

Sergeant Lemasters jumped in.

"If'n any of yer soldiers don't qualify, I'll march 'em back to the field site, which is over seven miles," he said. "You make sure you tell yer troops that, 'cause I ain't puttin' up with no 'bolo' firers."

Marshall decided to address the meeting.

"I'd like to add a few comments if I may," the commander began. "First of all, Colonel Biggs was very pleased with the layout of the 683rd's field site. He was impressed with all of you. Keep up the good work."

"Secondly, this will be our only week of tactical operations in the field. Everyone knows that we'll be busy fixing equipment next week. Finally, Sergeant Mooney is correct. Range fire will go smoothly as long as everyone knows and does their job and works together. Be flexible, use teamwork and anticipate the unexpected, overcome and adapt. Everyone will do fine."

"Sarge, please continue," Marshall concluded, looking over to Sergeant Lemasters.

"Thank you, Sir," Lemasters acknowledged.

"Now each range'll need ammo loaders. They'll be one of the more important groups on the range." Lemasters continued on with the meeting, and covered all the necessary items for range fire.

After the meeting, evening chow was being served. The smell of fried fish floated though the air as the 683rd lined up once more for an evening feast. Marshall and everyone in the 683rd couldn't believe their good fortune to have Sergeant Emery cooking for them. Life in the field wasn't so bad when the chow was good. It made the chigger and fire ant problem a minor distraction that everyone could live with.

Field First Sergeant Lemasters was holding a training class on land navigation. He was teaching how to use the sun's shadow to tell direction.

"Now when ya put a stick in the ground, you kin tell by the direction the shadda moves which is north an' which is south."

All the soldiers looked at each other.

"Shadda?" several asked out loud.

"SHADDA!" replied Lemasters.

"Ohhh…shadow," replied one of the NCOs in the back.

"That's what I said! Shadda!" snorted Sergeant Lemasters.

Everyone at the class began to howl with laughter. A couple of soldiers in the back began to sing "Me and My Shadda" and the laughter became unstoppable. Lemasters wasn't amused, and just shrugged it off until the class finally settled down.

"All right, ya had yer fun. Now listen up!" Lemasters spoke in a loud and clear voice. "The Army's lensatic compass is used to give y'all precise directions. If yer wristwatch has a battery in it, ya gotta take it off, or it'll throw yer compass off by ten ta twenty degrees."

Everyone was still chuckling about the previous incident, and paid little attention to what Lemasters had just said.

"Now tomorrow, you'll have plenty of time ta laugh when yer on the land navigation course," Lemasters said. "If'n ya git lost, try'n back-track to yer last point and try again."

As the daylight began to fade, Marshall asked Lieutenant Rodriguez to get some volunteers for the night patrolling mission. Rodriguez returned shortly with a dozen soldiers.

"Sir, I had so many that volunteered, I've had to make up a roster," reported Rodriguez to Marshall as the group assembled outside the 683rd CP tent.

"That's great, Rod. I'm glad to see that we've got some soldiers who enjoy the night-life," mused Marshall.

Several soldiers grunted as they settled down on the ground for their initial briefing from the commander.

"Tonight is going to be a recon of Mount Eden and the other Reserve units' defensive positions," Marshall said. "There will be no physical contact, no hand-to-hand."

Several soldiers looked disappointed at their instructions.

"This evening, all I want you to do is gather intel on the other units," Marshall continued. "Tomorrow night, we attack!"

That seemed to please all the assembled soldiers. Sergeant Bierce was the NCOIC of the group and showed the rest how to put on camouflage on their faces and equipment. The assembled group began to gather brush and dead grass to compliment their camouflaged faces. Within 10 minutes the soldiers were covered with brush and dead grass, like an Army sniper's gilly suit. The 683rd night warriors were ready for a little action. They headed out silently for their recon in-force.

As the evening settled in on Mount Eden Base Camp, Specialist Fran Peoples was feeling a little lonely, and decided to go on a nightly prowl to the male soldiers' sleeping area.

She poked her head into Specialist Kayrule's pup tent.

"Time for weapons inspection," she said, smiling coyly. "Kayrule, looks like you're concealing a rather large caliber weapon there, soldier."

Kayrule grinned, hoping that Peoples was interested in a weapon that the Army hadn't issued him.

Peoples shot a glare at Kayrule's tent mate.

"Hudson!" she called. "Why don't you go get yourself a bowl of soup from the mess section? And honey, take your time eating it."

Private Hudson got out of his shared tent and made his way to the mess area to have a late night snack while Peoples and Kayrule had some private time alone.

Later, the night recon patrol returned and briefed Captain Marshall on all the weak spots they had found in the other units' defensive positions. Marshall thanked them all for doing an excellent job, and not being detected. They would have an opportunity to exploit the weakness the following evening.

For the moment, it was time to hit the sack. The 683rd slumbered off to sleep, getting ready for another busy day.

A.T. - DAY 4 (WEDNESDAY)

Captain Marshall was enjoying his first cup of coffee in the morning while the soldiers were standing in line for morning breakfast chow. As all the soldiers passed by, they greeted him cheerfully with smiles on their faces. Marshall didn't quite know why the troops were so satisfied to be out in very austere and difficult environment. They must love to soldier, he thought to himself as he looked at the growing line of hungry soldiers. Maybe it's the chow? It sure smelled good. Good enough to wake up all the inhabitants in the forest of Mount Eden Base Camp.

Marshall spotted Specialist Peoples passing by and walking toward the chow line.

"Good to see you up early this morning, Peoples," remarked Marshall, knowing the she had a habit of skipping morning chow to get some extra sack time.

"Good morning, Sir," replied Peoples. "I really worked up an appetite this morning." She walked to the back of the line, smiling at the soldiers. Marshall had no clue about what was going on with Peoples and her nocturnal adventures.

Sergeant Lemasters came over to Marshall.

"Good mornin' Sir!" said a cheerful Lemasters.

"Can I buy you a cup of joe, Sarge?" asked Marshall.

"Hell yes, Sir!" he replied enthusiastically.

Both walked down the hill to the mess section to fill their cups with the Army's best-kept secret: Sergeant Emery's great coffee.

Sergeant Adkins greeted them as they filled their coffee cups.

"Mornin' gents!" he said. "Hope you're hungry." Looking over the serving area, the assortment and quantities of breakfast food was astounding. "We've got enough assorted breakfast chow to feed about 250 this morning."

Marshall was surprised to hear how many personnel they were prepared to feed. He excused himself from Adkins to speak with Sergeant Emery. The unit could run out of rations due to an overdraw on their rations account.

As Marshall walked over to see Sergeant Emery, he noticed personnel from the group HQ were lining up in the chow line, and Colonel Biggs was walking over to see him.

Captain Marshall always made sure his VIPs were formally welcomed. He walked up to the boss in the field.

"Good morning, Colonel," Marshall said, shaking Biggs' hand.

Biggs began his explanation of his early morning visit.

"Two of my cooks were placed on bed rest yesterday after they reported to sick call. One of them had a bad reaction to some fire ant bites and the other has a fever," Biggs said. "We'll be dining with the 683rd until the cooks are back on their feet. I hope you can accommodate us."

"Not a problem, Sir," replied Marshall, knowing full well that the unfortunate circumstances of the group's cooks happened to be a blessing in disguise for the personnel of the group headquarters.

"Sir, I am afraid to tell you this," Marshall went on, trying to get Colonel Biggs to bite.

"What is it, Commander?"

"Well Sir, I'm afraid that once your personnel start eating at our field mess, they'll never want to go back to their field mess again," grinned Marshall.

Biggs smiled and got the message as he proceeded to the end of the chow line with his staff in tow.

Colonel Biggs and his people would soon realize that the 683rd Field Mess had the best food service operations at Fort Knox. The 683rd was firing on all cylinders and Biggs and his staff took notice. No matter what Mother Nature or the Army would throw in the 683rd's path, the 683rd was more than ready to handle the challenge and handle it well.

At the morning commanders' call, Colonel Biggs was raving about the morning meal.

"Captain Marshall, I would like to congratulate your mess section on such an extraordinary and wonderful breakfast," Biggs said.

"Thank you, Sir. I'll pass on those kind words," Marshall replied as his fellow commanders looked on with envy.

"Dave," Captain Eldon Healy, commander of the 928th, whispered. "Mind if I eat chow with your unit this afternoon?" Marshall grinned and winked.

Biggs informed the assembled commanders that there would be VIPs in the area at any time, and that the 683rd roadside spot check was impounding a large percentage of vehicles.

"Captain Marshall, even my vehicle was impounded," Biggs remarked. "My driver had apparently forgotten to have it properly dispatched. Again, kudos to your people, Commander."

Marshall nodded in thanks.

"Before I open the meeting for discussion, the post engineers will be spraying the field site to rid us of the biting pests we've come to know and love so well," Biggs said. "Please let your soldiers take proper precautions when the spray truck appears sometime this Saturday.

"Oh yes," Biggs added, "expect aggressor action from the 683rd night warriors. OK, any comments or questions?"

The other company commanders in the tent shot a nasty look at Marshall, who just shrugged.

"Hey, my people get bored easily," Marshall said.

Second Lieutenant Humphrey arrived at the 683rd field site and began his search for the well-camouflaged unit. Assigned as the 683rd evaluator, Humphrey felt he had more pressing obligations, but like a good soldier, he followed Major Brask's orders and was ready to evaluate the 683rd Heavy Equipment Maintenance Company. This was his initial visit, to meet the 683rd commander and gather information.

He spotted the camouflaged 683rd unit designation sign, pulled into a clearing and parked his ¼-ton jeep. A camouflaged direction arrow pointed Humphrey in the direction of the main guard post, where he was given the challenge, but didn't know the correct password.

"Sir, I'll get someone to escort you to the CP tent," the guard said.

Humphrey didn't like to be told what to do by an enlisted man.

"Get out of my way, Private!" he shouted. "I'll find the CP!"

Captain Marshall was contacted by field phone from the guard with regards to what had just happened. Marshall quickly walked out and saw Lieutenant Humphrey being held prisoner at the guard post.

Marshall walked up to the captured evaluator.

"Lieutenant Humphrey, welcome to the 683rd field site," he said. "What do you think of our guards?"

Humphrey had a look of frustration and anger.

"I'm not impressed!" he replied.

Marshall looked at the three guards that were detaining Humphrey.

"You can release him. He's our evaluator," Marshall said. "Did he know the password?"

"No, Sir, and he tried to run off toward the CP," the entrance guard replied. "I didn't know if he was a good guy or a bad guy, so I had to detain him."

Marshall smiled at the young soldier.

"You did the right thing. Carry on," Marshall said.

As Marshall and Humphrey walked away from the entrance area, Marshall told the evaluator he would get him a list of the challenges and passwords for the rest of the week.

"Sir, I've already got a list," Humphrey replied. "I was just testing your guard's reactions. He did well."

Marshall chuckled to himself, knowing that was a fairly good lie the young lieutenant was telling in order to save face.

"Would you like to me to give you a rundown of our operation in the field while we take a tour of the site?" Marshall asked him.

Humphrey was glad to hear Marshall offer some vital information about the 683rd's mission and what their goals and objectives were during annual training.

"Glad to. Lead the way," Humphrey said.

Marshall took the lead as the two men walked the sloped ground. Marshall pointed out several areas to Humphrey as they made their walk through of the area, visiting each section's area of operations.

Humphrey was mildly impressed with what he saw and took notes.

"I understand you've got some personnel working at Boatwright," Humphrey commented. "How'd you ever arrange that?"

Marshall was happy to provide some detailed information.

"We've made some coordination earlier this year to get our turret and track mechanics working on the new equipment. Our wartime mission is to provide maintenance support to the corps, which includes supporting combat units with mechanized track and artillery equipment as well."

Humphrey was mildly satisfied with his first visit to the 683rd field site, noting how the unit had set up and laid out their internal road network, pathways, sleeping areas, work areas, power generation, field mess, and defensive fighting positions. It was all there, and Humphrey tried not to show any emotion, which would give Marshall any clue as to what was going on in his head.

"Well, Captain Marshall, I've got to get back to Main Post and begin preparing some paperwork," Humphrey said. "Thanks for the tour. Everything looks satisfactory, except…. I'll be back later in the week to go over some things they want me to evaluate on the 1-R."

Marshall felt that whatever evaluation Humphrey would give the 683rd, Marshall wasn't going to like it, much less agree with it.

"If you need any particular information for your evaluation, just let me know," Marshall said. "I'll have my admin sergeant, Sergeant Tea, get that for you."

"Thanks, Commander. I will. Have a good day."

Both men shook hands as Humphrey abruptly left. At least he won't be in our hair too often, Marshall thought.

Sergeant Lemasters and Lieutenant Rodriguez returned from setting up the land navigation course a bit tired and winded from the warm temperatures and humidity that were ever present in mid-Kentucky during the month of July. The land nav course had eight different waypoints. Each waypoint had a large numbered sign, visible within fifty meters. Each four-man group would have to find as many waypoints as possible. A different colored marker was attached to each waypoint sign, so no one could cheat. One had to find the waypoint located on the map and mark the score sheet with the appropriate colored marker. The course was approximately five miles in length, and would take two hours to complete if done correctly.

The training schedule had land navigation set up for 1000 hours. All personnel that were available were required to participate. At 1000 hrs all available soldiers headed to the assembly area for the class. Lemasters was patiently waiting along with Rodriguez as they finally arrived.

"Listen up everyone!" shouted Rodriguez. "I'll need everyone to be broken down into teams of four, with at least one NCO per team."

The assembled soldiers began to select their teams and lined up in order. Rodriguez was impressed with the speed that everyone got ready.

In his best command voice, Rodriguez began his instructions to the assembled personnel.

"OK, here's how the land navigation course is set up," he began. "Each group gets a compass and a map. The map is marked with the location of each waypoint. There are eight total waypoints. You'll need to find at least six to pass. Each waypoint has a special marker attached which you must imprint your card. No two waypoints have the same colored marker."

Some grumbling could be heard from the group as the information was being given out.

Rodriguez continued.

"Now, you can use your compass to shoot a directional azimuth, or you can use the terrain features to identify your location. If you get lost, you've got a map and compass to get you back here.

"This course should take you about two hours to complete, but it's not a timed event. Try and be back before 1400 hours. I've made arrangements with the mess section to extend the afternoon meal to 1400 hours. Any questions?"

No one wanted to prolong the inevitable. They just wanted to get going.

"OK, I'm releasing groups in three-minute intervals," Lemasters said. "First group, head for waypoint number one. Second group, head for waypoint number eight. Go!"

Both four-man groups took off in the opposite direction at a brisk walk, compasses and maps at the ready.

Lemasters walked over to Rodriguez and took him aside.

"Sir, ya didn't tell 'em about takin' off their watches," Lemasters said.

Rodriguez looked at Lemasters and smiled.

"Yeah, I know," he replied.

As the groups began to enter the land navigation course, most made it to their first waypoint. Then one group began to go astray. A couple of groups remembered to have the compass man remove his battery-powered watch.

At the same time, Chief Farley was meeting with the engineer unit maintenance NCO that the 683rd was supporting for A.T. At the engineers' field site, Farley saw 5-ton dump trucks being driven by young soldiers. He spotted two drivers climbing into their trucks without doing preventative maintenance checks before starting the engines. We'll be seeing this equipment soon, Farley thought to himself.

"Sarge, I'd like to have my automotive techs come over and give your drivers a short class on preventative maintenance," Farley said to the NCO.

"Chief, with all due respect, my people have already had that training and they know what they're doing," replied the NCO.

"Is that so, Sarge?" asked Farley. "Then how come your drivers aren't starting out in the creeper gear when they've got their trucks loaded?"

The NCO was silent. Farley continued.

"Sarge, when these trucks start breaking down, which I suspect will be pretty soon, since you'll want to have them fixed so you can drive them back to your Reserve Center instead of leaving them here at Fort Knox, make sure you get them to us before Tuesday next week. Otherwise, we won't be able to help you."

"What makes you think they'll be broken down by then, Chief?" the NCO asked.

"Sarge, I've been in the Army for 22 years," Farley replied. "Five-ton dump trucks are like any other truck. The clutch won't last if you don't operate it right. When they start breaking down, give us a call or drop 'em off at our location at Mount Eden Base Camp."

"Anything else, Sir?" The NCO asked politely.

"Yeah, one more thing," Farley said. "When the truck breaks down, I want the assigned driver to help my people fix it. Maybe they'll take better care of their equipment in the future."

Later that day, three 5-ton dump trucks came into the 683rd Shop for clutch replacement, along with their assigned drivers.

At the land navigation course, the soldiers of the 683rd were wandering throughout the surrounding area of Mount Eden Base Camp. One four-man group had become completely disoriented due to the compass man wearing a battery-powered watch. The other groups were progressing nicely through the waypoints as they whooped it up and celebrated after finding each waypoint.

Sergeant First Class Wilbur Heinz was in the four-group that was badly disoriented. There is an old saying in the Army about a situation such as this: soldiers are never lost, they are only momentarily disoriented.

"Are you sure this is supposed to be the spot?" Heinz asked his compass man, Private Hamad.

"Yeah, Sarge," he replied. "It's supposed to be right around here, but I don't see it."

"Well, so far, we've only hit two of the waypoints, and we should have found the others by now," Heinz said in a disgusted voice. "Let's shoot a back azimuth to the waypoint we were just at and relocate waypoint number 3."

Little did he realize the direction they were headed in would place all of them in extreme danger.

Marshall and Tisher decided to drop in and visit the 683rd personnel training at the Boatwright Maintenance Facility and see how things were coming along. Fortunately, the floating bridge was still in operation, which helped shorten the trip to Main Post.

The Boatwright facility was a large gray building covering 10 acres in the middle of Fort Knox. It was a very large and modern shop that housed a large force of civilian technicians.

Outside, Tisher spotted several of the 683rd personnel working on an M109 self-propelled howitzer and drove over to see them.

"Well, how's the chow here on Main Post?" Tisher asked

Sergeant Huddle, who was supervising his people, responded honestly.

"Lousy, Top. We all wish we were back in the field with you guys."

Tisher was surprised to hear Huddle's remark.

"So what's wrong with chow on Post?" he asked.

"Not enough, bland and cold. I think I've already lost a few pounds," replied Huddle. "But the barracks are nice and we can't complain about the workload."

Marshall was sitting next to Tisher in the jeep, and was interested in what was going on.

"Where is Lieutenant Kiley?" he asked.

"Sir, she's in the facility with the track section," Huddle replied.

Captain Marshall walked into the facility still wearing his field gear, complete with side arm. The concrete driveways and parking areas were new. Except for the telltale signs of tank tread marks that were ever present, the entire area was neat as a pin.

The main entrance guard at the facility asked for Marshall's identification. After satisfying the guard's requirements, Marshall proceeded to the M1 Abrams area where the 683rd Track Section was working along side the civilian technicians.

"Well, good morning, Lieutenant," Marshall greeted Kiley.

She was not expecting him.

"Oh! Good morning, Sir," she replied. "This has been a wonderful opportunity for the soldiers."

"Looks like they're pretty busy."

Marshall observed the soldiers as they assisted the civilian technicians, and decided to speak to one of them.

"So, how's it going?" Marshall asked.

"Not bad, Sir," the soldier replied. "We're doing a bunch of go-fer work right now, but we'll be doing an engine change-out this afternoon."

Marshall acknowledged the comments made by the soldier and thanked him.

"Lieutenant Kiley, why don't you and I take a stroll and discuss training," mentioned Marshall.

As they walked through the middle of Boatwright, Marshall wanted to know how focused the training both 683rd sections were receiving was.

"Tell me, Kathy, how do you feel about the training both sections are getting?" Marshall asked.

"Well, Sir, both sections are getting the training we wanted, but to what extent remains to be seen," she replied.

"I see," said Marshall. "Do you feel it is challenging enough?"

Kiley answered quickly.

"I think so," she said. "The M1 Abrams is a complicated tank and the civilians are not letting the turret section work on the firing and laser optical components yet. They're telling me not even the active duty people are allowed to work on those parts. They've got some gizmos that require a top secret security clearance."

"I wonder if these civilian techs will follow these M1s into battle?" mused Marshall.

At the land navigation course, Sergeant Heinz and his group had become completely disoriented and had walked several miles in the wrong direction.

Spotting an unexploded artillery round on the ground, Heinz realized they had walked into some very serious trouble.

"Everyone, stop where you are!" he yelled. "DON'T MOVE!"

"What's wrong, Sarge?" Hamad asked.

"We've just walked into an impact area," replied Heinz. "See that unexploded artillery shell over there? That's a 155-mm howitzer round with an effective blast radius of 60 meters. Now everyone, slowly turn around and let's carefully tip-toe outta here, the same way we came in!"

The lost group of 683rd land navigation soldiers decided it was time to forget about trying to find waypoints and start finding a way out of their predicament. After a tense 10 minutes, the group retraced their steps and found a navigational benchmark. At last they knew where they were on the map—five long miles from Mount Eden Base Camp.

"Give me that compass," demanded Heinz. "I can't see how you've gotten us so far off course."

Heinz referred to the map and plotted a course to get them back to Mount Eden Base Camp. Using the compass, he plotted a directional azimuth that took them onto a straight path back to the field site. Sighting a radio tower in the distance, he decided to check his azimuth calculations with the compass man. 124 degrees, Heinz thought to himself.

"OK, Hamad, shoot an azimuth to that tower over there and tell me what the angle is."

Private Hamad shot his azimuth and looked down through the glass peep sight.

"146 degrees, Sarge," he said.

"WHAT???" shouted Heinz. "Give me that!" he yelled, grabbing the compass and shooting the azimuth a second time.

"What does that say?" he asked, showing Hamad his reading.

"Looks like 124 degrees, Sarge," was the sheepish reply.

One of the soldiers in the group chimed in.

"Try taking off your watch!"

Hamad complied, removed his battery-powered watch, and shot another azimuth that concurred with Heinz's 124-degree reading.

At the tech supply section CP tent at the 683rd field site, Second Lieutenant Sarah Burks had received a call from the shop office for three 5-ton clutch repair kits.

"Sergeant Schmoot, we've got our first parts requisition," said Burks. "This is a high priority request from the shop office, so let's get these parts down to them as soon as possible."

"Ma'am, I don't know if we've got these in stock," replied Schmoot. "We're still getting the trailers organized. We're finishing up on the last two."

"Sergeant Schmoot, you've got 15 minutes to come up with a definite answer for me," Burks said. "Either we've got them in stock or not!"

"Yes, Ma'am, I'll look for them right now," Schmoot replied, leaving the tent and walking over to McCarthy.

"Chief, the lieutenant wants to know if we've got these in stock," Schmoot said, handing the requisition over to McCarthy.

"Hmmm. This is an old stock number," McCarthy replied. "Tell her we'll have to place a requisition through Main Post to get these."

"No, Chief, you tell her," replied Schmoot.

Burks heard the bad news from McCarthy as Schmoot stood silently by his side. She called the shop office and told Chief Farley it was time to hit the panic button. Farley walked over to the tech supply section. He was fuming.

"Ken, you mean to tell me you don't have any 5-ton clutch repair kits?" yelled Farley.

"Nah. I looked high and low for 'em," replied McCarthy.

"I bet!" Farley said in disgust as he headed for the tech supply parts trailers. He walked into the first trailer, saw a pile of boxes in the front of the trailer and began to dig through them.

As he exited the trailer several minutes later, Farley spotted McCarthy smoking and joking with several other soldiers. Carrying several 5-ton clutch repair kits, he walked over to Burks.

"Ma'am, I found what we need," Farley said. "There's four more of these in the trailer. I think you better have those two report to sick call and have their eyes checked." Chief Farley walked off shaking his head in disgust as he mumbled some obscenities to himself.

Burks walked over to see her two subordinates, knowing she had been let down.

"Gentlemen, I'd like to see both of you in the tent, please," Burks said. "We've got some things to discuss."

In the tent, Burks was ready to drop the bomb on Chief McCarthy and Sergeant Schmoot.

"That's the last time I'm ever going to be embarrassed by the two of you," Burks said sternly. "Do I have to prepare an official counseling statement on what just happened? This will not happen again! Do I make myself clear?"

Both Schmoot and McCarthy were caught and had nowhere to hide.

"Yes, Ma'am," was their mumbled response. McCarthy muttered something about needing to clean up other soldiers' poor organization efforts and shuffled off to the parts trailer.

After Chief McCarthy left, Sergeant Schmoot confided in Burks that he'd like to work on Main Post with the Boatwright personnel if it were possible.

Burks laid down the law.

"Sergeant Schmoot, I need you here to oversee the organization of these remaining parts trailers," she said. "I also need you to oversee the enlisted soldiers in the platoon. Request denied."

Somewhere between the impact area and Mount Eden Base Camp, Sergeant Heinz and his group were in an open field, heading toward what they hoped was Mount Eden Base Camp. All in the group were getting tired and disgruntled over their misfortune and the close call in the impact area.

A Huey UH-1 Army helicopter was flying overhead, coming straight for them. Heinz knew what to do, having served two tours in Vietnam. He immediately raised his arms up over his head like he scored a touchdown.

"You are now under my control!" Heinz yelled.

The pilot of the chopper saw Heinz down below and nudged his co-pilot.

"Looks like we've got a pick-up." The pilot pressed his intercom button to talk with air traffic control and their backseat passenger. "Sir, mind if we set this bird down and pick up some stranded troops?"

"Go ahead," was the response.

The pilot and co-pilot gently brought the large helicopter down and landed in front of Heinz, who turned around and grinned to his group.

"We've just got a ride, people!" Heinz shouted.

Heinz went up to the front of the UH-1 and yelled his dilemma to co-pilot. The pilot gave him the thumbs up.

"OK people, let's go!" shouted Sergeant Heinz. Their luck just dramatically improved.

As the Huey took off, Heinz yelled to the crew chief that he would buy lunch for the crew. Another thumbs up came from the entire crew. Everyone aboard was hungry, including the 1st Army Commanding General who was also a passenger aboard the Huey.

As Marshall and Chief Farley were discussing the maintenance mission concerning the engineer dump truck jobs beginning to enter the shop, the faint sound of an approaching Huey was heard. It got louder as it came in for a landing near the shop office tent.

"Chief, I do believe that Huey is going to land in our area," Marshall said, wondering if another MedEvac mission was called in.

As he exited the tent, he spotted the Huey with a red placard and three white stars.

"Chief, call Group HQ!" Marshall said. "We got a three-star VIP that just landed in our area!"

Marshall walked out to the 683rd landing zone to greet the VIP.

Sergeant Heinz and his group were the first to exit the Huey as the helicopter's engine was shut down.

"Sir, we got a ride with the general," smiled Heinz.

"I'm sure you'll fill me in later, Sarge," replied Marshall, as he awaited the 1st Army Commander to exit the Huey.

Directly behind Marshall, Colonel Biggs and his staff pulled up in their ¼-ton jeeps. As the 1st Army Commander finally exited the Huey, Biggs was the first to greet the general.

Lieutenant General David Stone and his aide de camp Lieutenant Colonel John Zarkian exchanged formal introductions with Biggs and his staff. Marshall was finally introduced, and he asked the general if he'd like to inspect the training area and have some good Army chow.

"Lead on, Commander," Stone replied.

As Marshall was giving the general a tour of the area, he told Lemasters to alert the mess section that they would have a special guest for the afternoon meal.

Stone was impressed with the field layout of the 683rd and spotted his helicopter crew being served in the chow line.

"Commander, do you have enough food left over for us?" Stone asked,

"Sir, we've got people out on the land navigation course, so I've asked the mess section to hold the noon meal over a while," Marshall replied. "There should be plenty of chow for all, Sir."

Stone was impressed with the coordination, and walked to the end of the chow line. The noon meal consisted of roast beef, garlic mashed potatoes, mushroom gravy, garden salad, green beans, rolls, macaroni and cheese, and assorted pies for desert.

"Captain Marshall, did you know I was coming?" asked Stone.

"No, Sir," Marshall said with a smile. "This is a typical meal we've been having in the field."

The general and his entourage were seated at a large table assembled for visiting VIPs. Regular flatware, a linen tablecloth and folding chairs were placed in a clearing away from the mess tent for the VIPs to enjoy their meal.

Sergeant Emery came over to greet the general.

"Sir, this is Sergeant Emery, one of the finest mess sergeants in the Army Reserve," Marshall said with pride.

"Sir, it's an honor to meet you," Emery said. "I hope you enjoy your meal."

General Stone was seated and had already started eating.

"Sergeant Emery, this is quite a meal in the field," Stone said. "I am impressed."

"Thank you, Sir," Emery said. "I try to always do my best for the soldiers."

"It shows, Sarge. Well done!" Stone said.

The general and his entourage enjoyed the meal and surroundings. As they finished with apple pie and coffee, Stone bid Marshall and Biggs farewell. He was going to inspect the other training areas.

Marshall walked over to Emery after the VIP party left the area.

"Sarge, did you know the general was coming?"

"Sir, I've got my sources, but they didn't know about the general," Emery said. "I guess we just lucked out."

"Well, in any case, my compliments, Sarge," Marshall said.

The remainder of the 683rd completed the land navigation course and was catching up on their noon meal. Emery and his staff were happy to see the soldiers in the chow line and the food began to disappear.

Heinz informed Marshall what happened, including their compass man's battery-powered watch, which steered them into the artillery impact area. Marshall had a good laugh at the misadventures of the wayward group and told Heinz it was something they all would remember.

"It's something I'm sure you'll enjoy telling your grandchildren," Marshall mused as Heinz kept a serious face.

"Sir, I'm just thankful my guardian angel was watching over us," replied Heinz.

As evening approached, Lieutenant Smith was closely working with Sergeant Lemasters and Sergeant Mooney on the upcoming range fire scheduled for Thursday and Friday. Crew-served weapons qualification was scheduled for Thursday.

Lemasters and Mooney looked over the roster of firers and safety personnel listed in the range fire operations order that Smith developed. It was time for Mooney to bring Lieutenant Smith up to date.

"Sir, the M60 crews have to be at Range 14 on or before 0900 hours tomorrow, ready to rock and roll," Mooney said. "Range 3 is the M203 range, reserved at 1100 hours, and Range 18 is the M2 range, which we've got reserved for 1300 hours. Friday, we've got zero range 6 at 0800 hours, M16 qualification range 5 at 1100 hours, and .45-caliber pistol range 7 at 1400 hours.

"The M16 range and .45 range are run by the Fort Knox Range Committee, so we won't need our people in the range tower. Just safety NCOs and loaders."

Lieutenant Smith was deep in thought, going over the list of safety personnel that needed to attend the range control safety course.

"Sergeant Lemasters, how many NCOs and officers on this roster still need to go through the safety course?" Smith asked.

Lemasters knew how nervous Smith was regarding the conduct of range fire.

"Sir, all of 'em 'cept fer you 'n me and Sergeant Mooney need to attend the safety course at 0800 tomorrow at Range Control," Lemasters said. "You and I can handle the M203 range, since we already got the course under our belt. The rest'll be ready to go and handle all them other ranges after 0900."

"Sarge, I just wanna make sure we've got everything covered, from ammo to firers," replied Smith nervously. "I don't want to let the unit down!"

"Don't worry, Lieutenant," Lemasters replied. "Jackie and I ain't gonna let anythang bad happen, you kin count on it! Everythang'll run smooth, you'll see."

As evening approached, Sergeant Bierce was making some final touches to his operations order for his night warriors. Having been in the infantry in Vietnam, he was keenly aware of how to prepare for a night mission. As his group gathered in the shop office tent, Marshall walked in.

"Sir, we're just about ready," Bierce said. "I'm waitin' on a couple more soldiers from the service section."

"OK Sarge," Marshall replied. "I'm here to make sure everyone knows how to conduct themselves tonight, just in case things get a little out of hand."

The two remaining soldiers entered the tent already camouflaged and wearing enough dead grass and weeds to make gilly suits for everyone present.

Marshall turned the night patrol meeting over to Bierce, who quickly went over the operations order and their intended objectives for the evening.

"The group headquarters is barely guarded, which is our first target," Bierce glanced over to Marshall and saw his commander break into a wide grin. "I've got flour bombs that Sergeant Emery made up for us. Try to hit the CP tent with it and the staff tent, which is located right here." Bierce drew a layout of the group headquarters area and identified the targets. "They won't be expectin' us tonight. Don't fire your weapons unless fired upon first. We'll just give group a flour dustin' and go over to the 928th and open up on them."

Bierce drew another layout on the 928th position, and showed the targets he wanted to hit.

After several minutes Bierce was asking if anyone had any questions. Everyone was ready to go, and Marshall took the opportunity to add a few last words.

"Before you go on your search and destroy mission, let me advise you once again. No physical contact! No hand-to-hand! Period! I know these things can easily get out of control if you're not careful," Marshall said.

"Sergeant Bierce, I'd like a report from you when you return from your mission. Fill me in on everything that happens. What time are you going to start your patrol?"

"Sir, I was planning on crossing the line of departure around 2300 hours," replied Bierce. "The mission will take about an hour or more to sneak up on group and then hit the 928th."

"Are you taking the M60?" asked Marshall.

"Oh yes, Sir," Bierce said. "Sergeant Mooney got us the blank ammo and the blank adapter!"

Captain Marshall couldn't help visualize everyone being ruddily awakened by a very loud barking M60 machine gun.

As Marshall sat on his cot reading Lieutenant Stiles' latest changes to the training schedule, he glanced at his watch. It was nearly 2330 hours when he heard the unmistakable sound of the M60. The sound was close to the 683rd perimeter. Walking up to the main entrance area, he heard blanks being fired from his perimeter guards. The 683rd night warriors captured a small group of aggressors that tried to attack the 683rd position.

Marshall halted the action, yelling cease fire, and turned on his flashlight to survey the results.

"Sergeant Bierce, sounds like you and your patrol were successful," Marshall said. "I think you woke up every living soul within a couple of miles."

"Yes Sir," replied Bierce. "We've even got some prisoners from the 928th."

Marshall looked over and saw three soldiers being guarded by the patrol members.

"OK, night warriors, time to turn in," Marshall said. "You men from the 928th, you're released to go back to your unit."

"Awww, come on Captain!" said one of the prisoners. "We were promised a hot meal from your field mess. That's why we surrendered! We're starving out here in the field."

Marshall couldn't help himself, and gave out a laugh.

"Okay, you can come to the breakfast meal tomorrow," Marshall said. "Just don't tell Captain Healy."

A.T.- DAY 5 (THURSDAY)

The crisp dawn revealed a surreal dissipating fog over Mount Eden Base Camp as the soldiers of the 683rd were enjoying their breakfast. It was a peaceful time to relax and take in one of life's little pleasures: A beautiful morning and Sergeant Emery's fine cooking.

In the minds of all the soldiers on Mount Eden Base Camp, the day was starting off right. There was no rain and the weather forecast for the remainder of the day was sunny and clear, with a high of 88 degrees. The humidity level was projected to be low. Another perfect day was in store for the soldiers of the 683rd.

"Top, the safety NCOs and officers have to be at Range Control's range safety class before 0800 hours," Sergeant Mooney mentioned to First Sergeant Tisher while eating his breakfast.

"Jackie, I'll have 'em loaded up on three deuces after formation," Tisher replied. "I'm sure the Old Man will want to talk to them first. You ready to draw the ammo?"

"Yeah, I'm all set," Mooney replied. "I just wanna make sure everything goes as planned."

"Well, it looks like another great day for weapons qual," Tisher said, looking at the sky. "We've been really lucky this A.T. Lots of sunshine and the heat ain't so bad."

Field First Sergeant Lemasters walked over with breakfast piled onto his mess kit.

"Mornin' Top. Mornin' Jackie. We ready to have us some fun today?" Lemasters asked, setting down his brimming full plates.

"Jackie and I were just talkin' about that, John." Tisher said. "I think this is going to be an excellent day for the 683rd. We haven't had this much good training out in the field since I can ever remember."

The 683rd soldiers were visibly excited this morning. Many were going to fire crew-served weapons for the very first time since they joined the unit. During peacetime, weapons qualification was considered an exciting experience to look forward to. It was very safe as long as the Army's safety measures were strictly adhered to. Also, there was no enemy shooting back.

Marshall was giving some last-minute information to the assembled 683rd personnel.

"I want everyone firing today to have an enjoyable and safe time on the range," he said.

"One more thing. Specialist Peoples will reject any weapon that is not cleaned properly. If it does not meet her standards, you'll clean it again until it does."

All the faces in the formation became serious, except for Peoples, who smiled. Marshall continued.

"For all those attending the range safety class this morning, you will be allowed to participate in weapons qualification as well."

Marshall nodded to Tisher, who came to the front of the formation and took charge while Marshall went to his commanders' call meeting at the group HQ.

Walking up to Colonel Biggs CP tent, Marshall noticed the tell-tale signs of flour spots on most of the group's tentage from the 683rd night warrior attack. Oh boy, thought Marshall. I'm going to hear about this for sure.

Colonel Biggs greeted Marshall outside the tent.

"Captain Marshall, I see your people are very adept at tactical night operations," Biggs said. "We didn't hear a thing last night until the M60 stirred us out of our cots."

"Sir, I'll have my people over here to clean up the mess they've made," Marshall said.

"No, no, Commander. I'll have my people take care of that," replied Biggs. "Our guard was down. Our personnel should have seen this coming."

Both commanders walked into the tent. Marshall sat next to Captain Healy of the 928th who smiled.

"Thanks for letting my people go last night," Healy said. "You know, one of 'em was me."

Marshall looked rather surprised at him and held back a grin.

"Really?" Marshall quipped as he tried to keep from laughing out loud. "Was it you that surrendered for a meal with us?"

"Damn straight. I'm getting tired of that lousy chow my cooks are serving up in the field," Healy responded.

"Good morning, Commanders." Biggs began his meeting as the assembled unit commanders replied in kind.

"Did everyone notice the recent winter camouflage pattern on our tentage?" Biggs asked, as Marshall felt a small sense of pride. "Well, that is a result of no guards being posted after 2100 hours. Apparently the night warriors found our defenses vulnerable."

Biggs continued his discussion regarding the upcoming mandatory administrative requirements.

"Well, I believe I've covered just about everything. Does my staff have anything to add?" Biggs glanced over to his assembled staff officers who all shook their heads or said no.

"All right Commanders," Biggs said. "You have the floor."

Each unit commander took his turn in order according to size of unit. The 683rd was always last, being the largest unit in the field.

"Sir, the 683rd will have personnel at the crew-served weapons ranges today, and at the M16 and .45-caliber pistol range tomorrow," Marshall said. "If anyone needs to qualify with the .45 tomorrow, we can fit you in at Range 7 at 1400 hours. We've drawn enough ammo for additional firers."

After several moments, Marshall found several more firers for the .45 pistol range.

Colonel Biggs added one last statement before adjourning the meeting.

"Gentlemen, please remind your soldiers and food service personnel that the post engineers will be spraying the area to rid us of our pests some time on Saturday," Biggs said. "As far as I am concerned, if your training is done by noon Saturday, you can give your personnel the afternoon off to go onto Main

Post. No one is allowed to leave Fort Knox under any circumstances. The tactical phase will cease at 2400 hours Friday evening.

"Oh yes, one more thing," Biggs added. "General Markel will be visiting next week, so be prepared for his arrival. He will visit every unit at Mount Eden.

"Meeting adjourned."

Following customary military protocol, all the unit commanders rose in unison and held a salute for Colonel Biggs.

Walking back to the 683rd field site, Marshall spotted the roadside spot check team with three deuce-and-a-halves pulled over. As Marshall walked past, he spotted Specialist Megs.

"What did you find?" he asked her.

"All three are improperly dispatched, Sir," replied Megs.

Nugot and Cutnoff were busy placing tow bars on the vehicles. The skunk odor was still present on the 5-ton wrecker.

"Sergeant Nugot, I thought you got rid of that stench," said Marshall.

"I did, Sir," Nugot said. "That's new stink that some local skunk left. Sir, I didn't run 'em over."

"Well, Sarge, looks like you've made new friends out here in Mount Eden Base Camp," replied Marshall, walking away to find some better smelling air.

At the 683rd CP tent, Sergeant Tea was busily preparing more paperwork for the unit personnel going on sick call.

"How many today, Vivian?" asked Field First Sergeant Lemasters.

"Just five today Sarge," replied Tea. "Looks like our people have taken Captain Marshall's advice, or they just don't taste too good."

Many of the 683rd soldiers were putting flea collars in their boots to fend off the pests. Others were covering their socks in the Army's insect repellent. Whichever they were doing, it was having an effect on lowering the number of personnel going on sick call for insect bites.

Even the fire ants were beginning to leave the soldiers alone. The field site was policed every day by Field First Sergeant Lemasters and his hand-picked volunteers. Every piece of trash was picked up and bagged for proper disposal. No food, no fire ants.

The soldiers on trash run would diligently come by and remove the picked up trash everyday at 1000 hours. They would make sure every can and bottle was separated and turned in for cash at the local drive-thru in Elizabethtown, affectionately known as E-Town. Their efforts would net them a profit of more than $300, as well as numerous fire ant bites.

The 683rd field site had become a well-groomed area with excellent pathways and work areas. Platoons and sections were starting to take pride in their areas and began making groomed walkways. The engineer unit brought in wood chips from their tree clearing mission and the internal road network and pathways were covered with freshly dumped wood chip mulch. Mud and dust would no longer be an issue as the field site improved every day.

The 683rd soldiers were having an internal competition to determine who had the best foxhole. Individual defensive fighting positions became well equipped with overhead cover to shed rain and steps to enter and exit. There were some with areas big enough for one man to sleep in while another could keep watch. All were well camouflaged and blended in with the background. The field site had become their home away from home.

A Post Exchange snack truck pulled into the 683rd field site. Soldiers instantly migrated to what the old-timers called the roach coach as the snack truck driver honked his horn. The scene was reminiscent of the rats and mice being mesmerized by the Pied Piper of Hamlin. The soldiers had gone without candy bars, chips and soda pop for nearly a week, and couldn't wait to get their junk food craving satisfied.

After 20 minutes and hundreds of dollars in sales, the snack truck finally departed the area. Chief McCarthy bought himself several cans of soda pop and filled his canteen cup with ice the snack truck driver used to keep the soda pop cold. McCarthy did not notice the small note card above the ice bins that read "DO NOT USE ICE FOR DRINKING." He hoarded his newfound wealth of ice while Sergeant Schmoot drank his soda pop out of the can.

"That sure felt good going down," said Schmoot. Lieutenant Burks finished her candy bar. "Did you see the small sign above the bin of soda pop?" she asked. McCarthy shook his head. "The sign said don't use the ice for drinking, which means it just might be contaminated." The chief looked at her with raised eyebrows.

"Well, maybe it was placed there so he wouldn't run out of ice," replied McCarthy.

"I sure hope so for your sake," Burks snapped back. "All I need now is a sick section chief."

McCarthy chuckled and told her not to worry about it.

Later that afternoon, McCarthy was a constant visitor to the field latrine. He would not feel like eating for a while.

Lieutenant Smith, Sergeant Lemasters, and Sergeant Mooney were at the M60 machine gun range, waiting for their group of 683rd firers to arrive.

"Sarge, do you have the roster of firers with you?" asked Smith.

"Sure do, Sir," replied Lemasters. "Wouldn't leave home without 'em,"

"Hummm. Looks like we've got 12 people firing," Smith said. "How many rounds of ammo did you get, Sergeant Mooney?"

Mooney looked at his feet and brushed the gravel back and forth with the edge of his boot.

"Three thousand rounds, Sir."

"So let's see," remarked Smith as he stroked his chin. "At 100 rounds per man, that means we'll have 1,800 rounds left over."

"Well Sir, it's better to have too much than too little when it comes to weapons qual," remarked Mooney.

"Sir, I hafta agree with Jackie," replied Lemasters. "We ain't gonna turn it back in neither. Them men at the ammo point don't ever wanna see that ammo comin' back. We'll fire it up here at the range, Sir. Did ya ever fire the M60 before, Lieutenant? If ya hadn't, yer gonna."

At Mount Eden Base Camp, one of the young drivers from the engineer company was driving his newly repaired 5-ton dump truck back to his unit, wearing a set of headphones and listening to music on his portable cassette tape player. He was driving a little too fast for the narrow mountain road and misjudged a sharp turn. The truck went off the road and headed down the steep embankment to the bottom of a large and narrow gorge. Luckily for the driver, there were only a few small trees that were knocked over and no damage was done to the truck. Just a few minor dents on the front bumper. Driver and truck finally came to a stop at the bottom of gorge.

"Nugot, you and Cutnoff, I've got a recovery mission for you!" yelled Sergeant Bradford over the field telephone. "Get your butts over to the shop office tent with your wrecker ASAP!"

Within three minutes, they reported to the shop office ready to go on their first mission.

"Whatchya got, Sarge?" asked Nugot.

"I just got a call from group headquarters. The MPs found one of those hot-shot engineers just drove his newly repaired 5-ton dumper into a ravine about two miles from here. Here's the location on the map." Bradford showed the men where to look for the soldier and vehicle.

"You got all your snatch blocks and cable?" asked Bradford.

"No sweat, Sarge," Nugot said. "We're ready."

"All right. I want Sergeant Baxter to go along and supervise you two clowns," Bradford said. "Where is he?"

"He's at that Range Control safety course, Sarge," Cutnoff quickly replied.

"Great," replied Bradford. "That means I've got to ride with you two clowns in your stinking wrecker."

"Hey come on, Sarge," Nugot said. "When it comes to doin' my job, I'm the best. You'll see. Besides, I just washed that baby again this morning. She smells as sweet as lilac in May."

All three piled into the 5-ton wrecker and headed toward the stranded truck.

After they arrived at the scene, Nugot and Cutnoff quickly sized up the situation. The 5-ton dump truck driver was glad to see them and asked if he can lend a hand.

"You better stay back from this area," replied Nugot. "If the winch cable snaps, it can cut ya in half if it hits ya."

The driver walked down the road away from the wrecker about 50 meters. Cutnoff carefully made his way to the bottom of the gorge carrying the pulleys, snatch block and towing cable. He carefully attached a cabled clevis to the towing pintal, which was part of the frame of the dump truck. He signaled Nugot to begin reeling in their big catch of the day.

Within five minutes, the 5-ton dump truck was back on the road, unhooked and ready to haul dirt and gravel once more.

"You dirty birds did alright," remarked Bradford.

"Shoot, Sarge, I do this for a living every day. That was easy," replied Nugot.

"Yeah, maybe for you," remarked Cutnoff. "I did all the heavy work."

At Range 14, the M60 machine gun crews had arrived, received their safety briefing, and were firing away at their targets down range. Everything was going smoothly. Sergeant Mooney was the official safety NCO and Lieutenant Smith was the safety officer.

"Cease fire! Cease fire!" the range tower operator shouted into the intercom.

All the crews stopped their firing when they heard the command.

Mooney wondered what was gong on and shouted up to the tower.

"Why the cease fire?" he asked.

The tower operator pointed his hand out the window toward the far side of the range. A herd of deer was running across the boundary marker about 500 yards away.

"Why'd ya make us stop firin'?" yelled Monney.

"It ain't deer season yet, Sarge!" replied the tower operator over the range loud-speakers.

"It is in my backyard!" Mooney shouted back at the tower.

The tech supply section personnel had finished their inventory and rearranging of all four repair parts trailers. Lieutenant Burks was pleased with the efforts the soldiers had shown during the first week of annual training. The section was finally operational and ready to do their mission whenever called upon.

Looking over the stock records, Burks and McCarthy were discussing the stockage levels needed for the remainder of the year.

"Chief, we've got parts listed here that are a bit obsolete," Burks said.

"Which ones, Ma'am?" replied McCarthy.

"Like this one: alternator, Mark IV track vehicle. If I'm not mistaken, that's for a Sherman tank that's been out of the Army inventory for over 30 years," replied Burks with a bit of amazement in her voice.

Looking further through the pages of parts the section had carefully inventoried, there were a large percentage of parts that were no longer required or outdated.

"Chief, I want you to get with Sergeant Schmoot and go over this parts list and build an obsolete parts list," Burks said. "We can turn them in while we're here."

McCarthy did not want to hear he had just been given another week's worth of work to do, but he reluctantly acknowledged his new task.

"Yes Ma'am," he grumbled.

"Chief, looks like you're losing some weight since you've been here," Burks remarked as McCarthy stood up from the field desk.

"I didn't notice, Ma'am," McCarthy said. "But now that you mention it, my clothes are fitting looser. If you'll excuse me." He stood up and left the tent. McCarthy made a hasty trot to the field latrine. The contaminated ice had given him a mild dose of dysentery and was actively giving him lower abdominal distress.

It was 1100 hours at the M203 range. The assembled firers were getting their initial instructions in the bleachers from the Range NCOIC. Several of the newly instructed 683rd safety personnel had returned from the Range Control safety class. They were ready to watch over their soldiers and make sure everything went smoothly.

"You'll be firing 40mm HE (high explosive) rounds at targets from 100 meters to 200 meters from the firing line!" shouted the Range NCOIC. "If I witness any unsafe acts while on my range, I will give the cease fire command, at which time all weapon firing will cease. You will then be commanded to unload any live rounds and place them on the sandbag in front of your firing position. You will then place your weapon on the firing stake next to your firing position and the safety NCO will check your weapon. Is that clear?" shouted the NCOIC.

"Yes, Sergeant!" shouted the assembled 683rd firers.

"How many of you here have fired the M203?" asked the Range NCOIC. Several soldiers raised their hands.

The NCOIC then discussed using the M203 rear site mechanism and judging distances.

"After you've determined how far away your target is, adjust your rear site to the correct distance, load your 40mm HE round, and close the slide-breech. Aim through the front site post. Hold the butt of the weapon tightly against your shoulder, and after you hear my command to commence firing, remove the weapon from safe and start," he yelled.

"Each firer will have three targets in your respective firing lane which you must determine the distances and make adjustments accordingly. You'll have three minutes to load and fire three rounds of 40mm HE. Any questions?"

The soldiers in the bleachers were silent.

"All right, listen to my commands from the tower and follow them precisely!" the Range NCOIC shouted as he left to climb the range tower and open the firing range.

Specialist Williams was excited to finally get her chance to fire the M203.

The command finally came from the range tower after six minutes of waiting in the bleachers.

"Firers to the firing line!" the command voice boomed over the loudspeaker system.

Williams took her M203 from the weapons rack and walked down the gravel path to her firing position, designated by a numbered stake on the ground.

The Range NCOIC clearly spoke his well-orchestrated commands over the loudspeaker system.

"Firers, place your weapon on the stake next to your firing position, barrel pointed down-range!"

Williams placed her weapon on the stake and awaited the range tower's next command.

"Firers, assume a kneeling position!" The Range NCOIC then went into the Army's standard preparation phase to make sure there was no one was hiding in the impact area immediately to the front of the firers.

"Is there anyone downrange?" he boomed. "Is there anyone downrange? Is there anyone downrange?"

There was no response.

"Firers, the firing line is now secured!" the NCOIC shouted.

"Firers, take your weapon from the firing stake and secure one round 40mm high explosive. Lock and load!"

Weapons and ammunition clicked as soldiers loaded the M203 grenade launcher.

"You will have three minutes to engage three targets as they appear in your lane," the voice from the tower said. "Watch your lane! Commence firing!"

Williams was ready. Her M203 was loaded, and she watched for targets to pop up from the three ridges of earth in front of her firing position.

She spotted her first group of targets, a cluster of pop-up silhouettes in the last row. Williams calculated the distance to be 200 meters. She quickly adjusted the rear site and pulled the M203 tightly to her shoulder, ready to place the target on the front site post.

As she squeezed the trigger, nothing happened. Release the safety, she thought to herself, and did so with one quick flip of her finger.

Quickly aligning the group of silhouettes to her front site post, she thought the targets are probably farther than 200 meters. I better add some distance to this shot, she thought. She lifted the sight above the target and squeezed the trigger.

The M203 kicked like a shotgun and made a strange blooping noise she heard through her earplugs as the 40mm HE round went sailing into the air toward the target. Watching in amazement, she spotted her 40mm round arcing to the target.

A small cloud of dirt kicked up as the round hit the silhouettes. A muffled bang from the explosion finally met her ears.

Williams reloaded and spotted her next target about one hundred meters away. She took careful aim, added a little elevation to target distance, and pulled the trigger. The M203 recoiled back against her shoulder. This time, the kick was much harder. She forgot to pull the M203 tightly against her shoulder before firing, so the recoil had more momentum. Ouch! That's gonna leave a bruise, she thought to herself.

The second shot hit the target perfectly and a louder bang and cloud of dust was made. She glanced over to her left and noticed that the other firers were not as accurate. Their shots were falling short or long of their intended targets. Williams was beginning to gloat.

"Those guys couldn't hit the broad side of a barn," she said to herself as she placed her final round into the chamber. The last target was barely visible 160 meters away. She would not make the same mistake twice, as she pulled the stock of the M203 firmly against her shoulder. One-sixty, she said to herself and sited over the target and pulled the trigger.

Bloop! The 40mm HE sailed into the air and landed dead on target. The resulting small explosion, followed by a cloud of dust, confirmed that Williams was an expert shot with the M203.

"Cease fire! Cease fire! Cease fire!" boomed the Range NCOIC's voice over the loudspeaker system. "Well done, Firer number four."

Williams was pleased with the results. Except for a sore shoulder, it was a very good day.

At Range 18, the M2 .50-caliber firers were relaxing, eating their C-rations in the bleachers. The noonday sun felt warm with a gentle breeze blowing off the range.

The panoramic view of the firing range was spectacular. The firing range was over one mile in depth, without any trees or shrubs to block the view. The landscape was filled with beautiful green grass and old rusting hulks of Army tanks and trucks over one thousand meters away.

Specialist Dweedle was anxiously awaiting his turn to fire the M2 .50-caliber machine gun, or "Ma Deuce," as it was more commonly referred to in the Army.

The M2s were already placed on their respective tripod bases in front of their firing positions. All three M2s had been checked by Specialist Peoples for correct timing and headspace. M2s were extremely reliable, designed and built many years earlier.

Peoples had been selected as the alternate firer for the headquarters platoon. Dweedle was the primary firer. The Range NCOIC had already given the required briefing to the group, and the safety NCOs and OIC were making their way to the firing positions.

Over the loudspeaker, the Range NCOIC took charge.

"First firing order, proceed to the ammunition point," he yelled. "Secure one box of .50- caliber ammunition, 100 rounds linked!"

The first group of three firers marched over to the ammo point in step and picked up their respective boxes of ammunition.

"First firing order, proceed to your firing positions," boomed the voice over the loudspeaker.

The Range NCOIC then repeated the required phrase to warn anybody in front of the firing line.

"Is there anyone downrange? Is there anyone downrange? Is there anyone downrange?"

The questions were answered with a moment of silence.

"The firing line is now secure!" the NCOIC yelled. "Firers, you may now load your weapons."

All three firers opened the top of the M2's feeder tray and placed the belt of .50 caliber ammunition on the groove, sunny side down. They lowered the top and latched it securely into place.

"Charge your weapon!" came the command from the tower.

Each firer pulled back on the large charging handle on the right side of the M2 and then slid the charging handle forward until it locked in place.

"Firers, this is for familiarization only. Do not fire all rounds in one continuous burst. Short bursts only. You may commence firing!"

Range 18 roared to life as all three firers pushed the butterfly trigger on the back of their respective Ma Deuces. As the .50 caliber ammunition flew down range, an occasional tracer round was observed. The ground around the distant targets erupted as the .50 caliber ammunition found its way into the earth.

The silhouettes in each of the firing lanes were hit by dirt and rocks as the firers walked their rounds to the targets. Piles of spent cartridge casings under each M2 began to grow as the firers were enjoying every second of their awesome display of firepower.

"Cease fire! Cease fire! Cease fire!" boomed the NCOIC's voice over the loudspeaker.

"Are then any alibis?" asked the Range NCOIC. There was no response. All the firers had fired every round.

"Safety NCOs, clear all weapons," came the next command over the loudspeaker.

Each M2 had to be rodded with a cleaning rod by the safety NCOs to make sure there were no live rounds left in the chamber before the firers could be cleared to move away from the firing line. It also gave some time for the M2s to cool down. The barrels of the M2 .50-caliber machine gun could get white hot if too many rounds were fired in succession.

Peoples greeted Dweedle as he moved off the firing line.

"Good job, Jessie," Peoples said. "Just remember, as the primary firer, you've got to clean that Ma Deuce and pass my inspection."

Dweedle just grinned.

"Yeah, and you gotta show me how to do it right," he said.

"No, Hun," replied Peoples. "You gotta learn on your own."

Weapons qualification for crew-served weapons of the 683rd had been completed successfully. The soldiers returned from the ranges and enjoyed their evening meal. Marshall and Lemasters were going over the rosters of personnel that participated at the ranges and of safety NCOs and officers.

"Sergeant Penny, did you have any problems at the ranges today?" asked Marshall as he looked over the roster of personnel that participated at all three ranges.

"Nah, Sir. Everythin' went like off like it had oughta," replied Sergeant Penny in a whimsical fashion.

"There was one incident when Williams was given another shot with the M203," Penny recalled. "That gal can shoot, Sir. The Range NCOIC told her to try 'n hit the crossbar of the 200-meter target. By God she did. Blew it to pieces."

Marshall grinned as he heard the news. He was glad to hear the soldiers were living up to the challenges of annual training.

Specialist Peoples was inspecting the crew-served weapons the firing crews were attempting to turn in. She knew what she wanted to see and let her expertise take over.

"Clean it again, soldier," she said, handing back a sooty M60. "Try using a brush and some oil to get the carbon out of the feeder tray. NEXT!"

Another M60 firer brought his weapon to Specialist Fran Peoples for inspection and possible turn in.

"You gotta be kiddin' me!" she exclaimed. "Try again, and this time wipe the oil off!"

The 683rd belle had turned into a monster. No dirty weapon would be allowed to enter her weapons trailer. Some crews would have to bring their weapon back four and five times before she finally allowed the weapon to pass.

Peoples enjoyed rejecting dirty weapons. It finally gave her an opportunity to apply her training and expertise.

Sergeant Schmoot was concerned about Chief McCarthy's condition as he went to see him in the tech supply tent. The tent served two purposes. The first was for tech supply operations, and the second was as sleeping quarters for the NCOs and Chief McCarthy.

"Hey Chief, how you feelin'?" asked Schmoot.

"Denny, I feel like crap," McCarthy replied. "How's the inventory going?"

"Well Chief, we got it done about an hour ago," Schmoot said. "Looks like we've got lots to turn in that's obsolete."

McCarthy looked over at Schmoot as he stretched in his cot. "Just how much?" he asked.

Schmoot smiled.

"Oh, enough to fill up probably two deuce-and-a-halves," he replied.

Major Brown was walking past the 683rd area trying not to be noticed. The 683rd soldiers on guard mount saw him hiding behind a thicket of brush just outside the company area. As one of the 683rd guards approached him, Brown pulled the pin on a CS-tear gas grenade and threw it toward the 683rd perimeter.

The guard saw the grenade ignite and smoke began to stream out of the top in a loud hiss.

"Gas! Gas! Gas!" shouted the guard.

The warning was quickly echoed throughout the 683rd area. Everyone within the 683rd put on their M17 protective gas masks and made sure everyone else knew they had been gassed.

As the CS grenade slowly fizzled out and stopped, the wind shifted and began to blow the cloud of CS gas toward the group headquarters.

Marshall called Colonel Biggs on the field phone and warned him.

"Sir, this is Captain Marshall. We've just been gassed by an unknown chemical agent."

"Thank you, Captain Marshall," Biggs said, scanning the tent for his own mask. "I appreciate your report. Has your unit responded quickly enough?"

"Oh yes, Sir," replied Marshall. "The cloud has moved off and is headed your way. Thought you'd like to know that, Sir."

Marshall heard the phone being dropped onto a table and some rustling as shouts of "Gas! Gas! Gas!" were heard in the background on the other end of the phone.

Biggs picked the phone back up and resumed the conversation.

"Thank you, Captain Marshall," he said. "My people are just now starting to notice the effects of the gas."

"You're welcome, Sir," Marshall said. "See you in the morning."

The great cloud of CS gas continued to slowly dissipate as it floated through the Mount Eden Base Camp Training Area and into a civilian housing allotment about two miles away. The effects of the CS gas did not go unnoticed as many of the people in the housing area were outside trying to enjoy the evening. The Post Commander's office of Fort Knox would be getting several angry calls that evening from some area residents.

"All clear!" shouted Sergeant Bierce as he tested the air with his protective mask removed. The soldiers of the 683rd had survived the chemical attack to fight another day.

At the shop office tent, Tisher and Marshall had started their meeting on the upcoming weapons qualification scheduled for the following day. The safety NCOs and officers were present at the meeting to go over the details of both the M16 and .45-caliber pistol range requirements.

All aspects of the day's crew-served weapons qualification were gone over and analyzed. Various points were brought out that would be used to make the following day's weapons qualification go a bit smoother.

Sergeant Nugot was relaxing by his 5-ton wrecker getting ready to retire for the evening when he spotted a skunk next to his wrecker. He decided not to scare it away, and opened up a packet of crackers from his pocket.

"Here you go, little buddy," Nugot called out quietly to the skunk, wagging the cracker back and forth.

The skunk ran in the opposite direction without leaving a stink.

"Hmmm," thought Nugot. "Maybe I can make a friend of that little stinker."

He left the crackers next to the wrecker and crawled back into his tent. The skunk returned a few moments later and began to enjoy the gift that Nugot left behind. The skunk would return the following evening for another anticipated snack.

A.T.- DAY 6 (FRIDAY)

Dawn came to Mount Eden Base Camp peacefully. The murmuring of the power generators had a lulling effect soldiers got used to while they slept.

Suddenly, one of the generators sputtered and stopped as it ran out of gas. The silence was deafening. The din of its familiar hum had abruptly vanished. Everyone who was asleep awoke. All had come to realize something had suddenly changed in their tranquil environment.

Moments later, the loud voice of Field First Sergeant Lemasters was beckoning them to join him into the conscious world for breakfast.

The soldiers unzipped their sleeping bags, tried to stretch their arms and legs inside their small half-shelter tents, and lit up the first cigarettes of the day.

Getting dressed outside the half-shelter was the best way to get things done quickly, as long as the weather was pleasant. Most soldiers slept in their trousers, so putting on their boots was the first order of business. Next came the shirts—or blouses, as they were called in the military.

Personal hygiene was the first chore of the day. Undergarments were normally changed in the evening. Many found out the hard way that if they slept in sweat-soaked skivvies, they could wake up with an unpleasant rash. Night time was the best time to take a field bath using a washcloth, the outer portion of the steel pot (helmet) filled with water, and a bar of soap. The old soldiers referred to it as a whore's bath, but all would agree it really felt good to be clean.

After finishing up their personal hygiene, it was time to don the field gear. Putting on the web gear, or LBE (load-bearing equipment), was the first thing to do. The adjustable canvas web belt had grommet holes to hang all kinds of equipment on.

A canteen cover, complete with internal canteen cup and water-filled canteen was on the right hip side of the belt.

Next to the canteen and closer to the web belt's release buckle was an ammo pouch. Soldiers were issued two ammo pouches and located them on either side of the release buckle.

The officers would have a black leather holster with an M-1911 A-2 .45-caliber pistol, complete with a lanyard attached to the pistol belt and the butt of the pistol. It was easy for the pistol to slip out of the holster when crawling on the ground or rushing through the brush.

The entrenching tool, the Army's folding shovel, was on the other hip in a plastic carrying case. It could also be used as a mattock or pick, a hatchet, and a weapon.

The field suspenders were attached to four points on the web belt, and helped in transferring the weight of the LBE onto the shoulders. A first aid pouch and flashlight were attached on the front of the suspender straps.

A field pack, or rucksack, was issued to each soldier. Soldiers used it to keep their rations, mess kits, clothes and personal items with them.

The M17 protective mask, or gas mask as most called it, was strapped to right thigh, using two straps to secure it.

The steel helmet, commonly referred to as the pot, was the next item to be worn. The helmet consisted of an inner liner with adjustable headband. It had a reversible camouflage cover with summer and fall camouflage colors, an elastic camouflage band, and a chin strap which soldiers rarely used. The weight of the helmet was around two pounds. After wearing it for a week, the neck muscles got stronger and the burden of wearing it all the time didn't seem so bad. The headaches went away as well.

The M16 rifle was the last item worn. Ever wary of where their rifles were, soldiers would keep them at arms' length. Losing sight of their weapons for an instant would make soldiers seek them out instinctively. The weapon was the soldier's best friend and protector. Soldiers slept with them, ate with them, wore them, took them into the latrine, and if and when it became necessary, used them.

It took less than two minutes for a soldier to strap all his or her field gear on.

"Top, looks like we're in for another great day!" Marshall exclaimed as he rose from his cot. Sergeant Tea was snoring away in the vestibule portion of the CP tent.

"What a great day to be in the United States Army Reserve," replied First Sergeant Tisher as he sat up and began to put his boots on.

"Don't no one start singin' 'The Star Bangle Banner' now," moaned Tea as she began to stir. "What time is it?" she asked, rubbing her face with her hands.

"Zero Six Fifteen, good Sergeant," replied Marshall.

"Viv, I want you to stay here and hold down the fort while the rest of the unit goes to weapons qual," Tisher said. He was concerned about Tea's state of health and pregnancy.

"Thanks, Top," Tea replied. "I wasn't plannin' on being so close to any loud noises. This baby would kick me to death if I did."

Tisher grinned.

Captain Marshall was busy pondering the upcoming events of the day.

"Top, we've got some personnel that'll be left back as guards. They need to be rotated to the firing range after the first firing order is done," Marshall said. "We'll just have the first order take over the guard duty."

"That's a workable plan, Sir," replied Tisher. "How about it Viv? Can you honcho these people?"

Sergeant Tea was happy to know she didn't need to qualify.

"I'll make sure they're ready when the truck comes back to pick them up," she said confidently. "Sergeant Emery and I have a runnin' chess game. I've already beat him five times. I'll keep myself busy with the other paperwork that needs to be typed up, too."

"By the way Top, could you bring me my breakfast?" Tea asked, batting her eyelashes. "Two eggs over easy, please and four strips of crisp bacon. Wheat toast and orange juice."

"Anything else, your highness?" Tisher asked.

"No, that'll do for now," replied Tea. "Just tell all them soldiers to keep quiet while I get some more beauty sleep."

Both Marshall and Tisher laughed. Breakfast in bed for Sergeant Tea was something the First Sergeant was happy to do for the admin wizard of Mount Eden Base Camp.

After morning formation, the soldiers were loading themselves onto several large troop transport trailers pulled by the 5-ton tractors. The trailers had been borrowed from Main Post to haul 40 or more soldiers at a time to the weapon ranges. The trailers were commonly referred to as cattle cars.

As the 683rd soldiers boarded the troop trailers, cattle mooing was emanating from the troops as they moved onto the trailers to find a seat. Marshall remembered his days as a cadet going through basic training when they did the same thing.

The remainder of the unit boarded the deuces as they headed to the ranges. The trucks had to take the long way around and pass the pig farm since the floating bridge could not handle 5-ton tractors and trailers with troops on board. Everyone would be wearing his or her M17 protective mask shortly.

At the zero range, Chief McCarthy and his assembled safety personnel were going over their operational plans on how to efficiently conduct all the M16 firers through the range in the least amount of time.

"We've got 40 firing points all set with targets. One safety NCO per four firing points. Everyone got a paddle?" McCarthy asked the assembled group of NCOs and officers in the bleachers.

They all raised their paddles and waved them back and forth in unison.

"OK, let's go over this one more time," McCarthy said. "Here's how it's supposed to go. Each firer gets three magazines with one round in each magazine, right?"

"Right!" everyone answered.

"OK!" continued McCarthy. "After each round is fired, I call a cease fire. Safety NCOs check the weapons to make sure they're clear and then have the firers move from the firing line, look at their targets and make the necessary changes to their front and rear sites, right?"

"Chief," Lieutenant Smith piped in. "You definitely want to have the safety officers on the right and left sides give you the all clear before you let any firers leave the firing line."

"Yeah, that's right," replied McCarthy. "After I give the all clear when I see both safety officers giving me a white paddle, then you can allow the firers to move forward and look at their targets.

"If I see a red paddle, I won't let anyone move down range, right?"

"Right!" shouted everyone in the bleachers.

Sergeant Mooney walked over to McCarthy.

"Chief, we've got a slight problem," Mooney said.

"What's that?" replied McCarthy.

"The loudspeaker system is not working. Looks like you'll have to use the bullhorn," said Mooney. "I'll let Range Control know about the loudspeaker problem when I open the range."

McCarthy looked at Mooney.

"When will that be?" McCarthy asked.

Mooney strolled over to the range tower and looked at the 683rd trucks pulling into the zero range parking area.

"Right about now, Chief," Mooney said.

Field First Sergeant Lemasters was standing in the parking area, and barking out orders for the troops to move to the bleachers as soon as they dismounted from their vehicles. The sound of discontented cattle mooing could be heard over the grumbling as the 683rd soldiers moved to the bleachers.

As the soldiers were filing into the bleachers, Sergeant Heinz, the zero range NCOIC was making a head count. One hundred forty-eight firers was the magic number as the 683rd settled down for some instruction on the zero range operations. Lemasters handed Heinz the roster of 683rd personnel that were remaining at Mount Eden Base Camp field site.

"How are we gonna handle these people?" asked Heinz as he reviewed the roster of personnel at Mount Eden.

"Sarge, the Old Man already figured that out for ya," replied Lemasters. "After the first firin' order is done at the qualification range, we're supposed to load 'em up and take 'em back to Mount Eden. We then bring them folks on that roster back to the qualification course as the last firin' order. Got that?"

"That's fine, but how are they gonna zero their weapons?" asked Heinz.

"They ain't," replied Lemasters. "They're gonna use someone else's weapon that's already been zeroed and fired."

Heinz looked at Lemasters for a brief moment than shook his head.

"That's not how I'd want to qualify, without even zeroing my own weapon," Heinz said. "What if they bolo?"

Lemasters grinned at Heinz. He knew that Heinz liked to split hairs when it came to Army doctrine.

"Sarge, I guess sometimes ya just gotta relax and go with the flow. Know what I mean?" Lemasters said.

"Sergeant Heinz!" Chief McCarthy shouted to get the attention of his Range NCOIC.

"Sir!" replied Heinz as he walked over to McCarthy after finishing his brief discussion with Lemasters.

"Go ahead and get them into four firing orders. I've got to see a man about a horse." McCarthy was still feeling the effects of the contaminated ice as he quickly walked to the latrine at the rear of the zero range.

Sergeant Mooney raised the red flag on the pole, signifying the range was "hot." Heinz and Lemasters organized the 683rd into four equal ranks of firers. Each firer in the first firing order was given a piece of chalk, a #6 steel nail, and 12 white and 12 black half inch square target stickers.

"At ease everyone!" shouted Heinz. "Those of you in the front rank, remove your helmet and mark on the back with the piece of chalk, 'Number one, slash,' and then your firing point number. When you're done, hand the chalk to the person behind you. The second rank will mark their helmet 'Number two, slash,' and then their firing point number. Third rank, 'Number three.' Fourth rank, 'Number four.' Got it?"

"Yes, Sergeant!" responded the 683rd in unison.

"OK, listen up!" shouted Heinz, "The nail is for you to adjust your front and rear sites. Remember to adjust your sites like we told you in the bleachers. The stickers are for you to place over the holes in your target after you've finished firing all three rounds. When you're done, leave the nail and stickers for the next firer. Got it?"

Again the soldiers responded in unison, except for several who were looking around.

Heinz continued with his instructions to the firers.

"Here's how this is going to work," he said. "The first order will shoot first. The second order will be their coaches and ammo bearers. The third order will wait in the bleachers and the fourth order will be loaders at the ammo point.

"After the first order is done, they will be ammo loaders, the second order will fire, and the third order will coach, the fourth order will be in the bleachers. That's how the rotation will go. After you fire, you become a loader.

"Any questions?"

"Sarge, could you go over that again?" someone in the back yelled out.

"NO!" yelled Heinz, knowing it was on of the wise guys in his section.

"First order, to the firing line!" he yelled. "Second order, secure three magazines, one round each!"

The third firing order walked back to the bleachers, sat down and tried to relax and catch up on some sleep. The fourth order went over to the ammo point behind the range tower and began loading one round of ammunition in each magazine. It didn't take too long with more than 40 people at the ammo point, especially since First Sergeant Tisher was overseeing the ammo point operations.

Marshall came directly from Biggs' commanders' meeting and was in the back, watching and observing as McCarthy slowly walked from the latrine.

"Sir, you'll have to have someone else handle the range," McCarthy croaked. "I'm sick."

"What's wrong, Chief?" Marshall asked, seeing that McCarthy was sweating heavily and looking very pale.

"I've got a touch of dysentery, but I'll be all right," replied McCarthy.

"Chief, have a seat in the ¼-ton," Marshall said. "I'll have my driver take you to the Main Post health clinic so they can check you out."

"All right, Sir," replied McCarthy as he lumbered over to the jeep and had a seat. Marshall instructed his driver to take McCarthy to the Post health clinic and report back.

Marshall walked over to Lieutenant Smith and placed his hand on Smith's shoulder.

"Sean, you are now the zero range OIC," Marshall said. "Mr. McCarthy is going on sick call. Carry on."

"Yes, Sir!" replied Smith as he saluted his commander.

Smith quickly scrambled up the range tower ladder and stood on the front decking with bullhorn in hand.

"Firers, assume a good prone firing position!" Smith commanded from the range tower, watching the first firing order get ready in front of him. He now felt like he was in command of a vast army. This is great, Smith thought to himself as he looked around and took control of the zero range.

Mooney smiled at Smith and keyed the microphone on the radio to contact range control.

"This is zero range #6, permission to go hot, over."

Meanwhile, McCarthy uncomfortably bumped along toward Main Post.

"Private, pull over here. I need something to eat," said McCarthy as he spotted a PX shopette near the health clinic.

"Sure thing, Chief," replied the driver as he pulled into the parking area. McCarthy was famished. Everything he ate was going through him rapidly and leaving him hungry and sore at the same time.

He came back to the jeep with a box of glazed doughnuts. Two were already gone and he was munching on the third one as he sat down.

"Hungry, Chief?" the driver asked.

"Shut up and drive to the clinic," responded McCarthy as he downed the remainder of the third doughnut.

At the health clinic, McCarthy walked in and went up to the female corpsman, or medic, in charge of admitting.

"I'd like to see a doctor. I've got a bad case of dysentery," said McCarthy with a slight amount of pain in his voice.

The Army corpsman looked at McCarthy and saw his grayish color.

"Sure thing, Chief," she said. "Please have a seat. I'll let the doctor know you're here."

Despite the 50 or so soldiers of various rank in the clinic's waiting room, the Army physician immediately walked out to see the chief.

"Mr. McCarthy, I'm Doctor Alex Solon," the physician said. "Let's have a look at you in my office."

Both men exited the waiting room and walked into the doctor's examination room.

"Chief, we don't get too many warrant officers I think there's more generals than warrant officers on this Post," remarked Dr. Solon.

"You're probably right, Doc. Not too many of us in the Army nowadays," replied McCarthy.

"So tell me what happened, Chief," said Dr. Solon.

"I used some bad ice from the PX snack truck and got the runs immediately afterwards," replied McCarthy.

"Well Mr. McCarthy, you and about 45 other soldiers have the same problem," Solon said.

And just what is the problem?" asked McCarthy with a bit of alarm in his voice.

"It's dysentery caused by contaminated well water that the snack truck driver used," the doctor replied. "We've traced the ice to a small grocery store just down the road from the pig farm outside the Fort Knox main gate. You know where that is?"

McCarthy gagged.

Back at the range, the last firing order had come off the firing line and the zero range was closed down. Marshall was pleased with the amount of time taken to get everyone zeroed.

"Great job, Sean!" shouted Marshall as Lieutenant Smith exited the range tower.

"Thanks, Sir," replied Smith. "But it's Sergeants Mooney, Heinz and Lemasters that deserve all the credit."

Marshall smiled at his lieutenant and winked. He knew that his young officers were catching on. They were beginning to realize the NCOs were the heart and soul of the 683rd.

Heinz was getting the soldiers loaded up for the M16 qualification range as McCarthy and driver pulled into the zero range parking area.

"Hello, Chief. What'd the doctor have to say?" asked Marshall as he walked over and met Mr. McCarthy exiting the jeep.

"The doc told me to drink lots of Gatorade, take some Pepto and no more ice from the pogey bait truck." McCarthy had several large bottles of Gatorade in the back of the jeep that he picked up from the shopette, along with an empty box of doughnuts.

"Chief, I'll have the driver take you back to Mount Eden so you can rest," Marshall said. "The M16 range will be run by the range committee. No need for an OIC there."

"Thank you, Sir," replied McCarthy. "I can use the rest to catch up on my reading."

Marshall instructed the driver to take McCarthy back to Mount Eden and return to the range afterwards.

McCarthy and the driver immediately left the area and began their road trip back to Mount Eden Base Camp.

"Private, let's head toward the floating bridge," McCarthy said weakly. "I don't think I can handle the pig farm right now."

The driver headed through the Fort Knox training areas to the floating bridge. As they entered the woods, the air temperature dropped and became very comfortable. McCarthy was beginning to feel better as they made the turn and headed down the paved embankment to the floating bridge.

As they neared the bottom, McCarthy and the driver saw that the operators of the floating bridge had a deuce-and-a half stuck halfway across the river. McCarthy realized that the doughnuts he ate just made a shortcut through his intestines and wanted out. He looked over at the latrine, which was on the other side of the river from where they were.

"Private, give me your entrenching tool," said McCarthy.

"Sure, Chief. Here you go," replied the driver.

McCarthy exited the jeep and walked over behind some brush in the deeper part of the woods and began to dig a small hole in the ground. Time to leave my mark, thought McCarthy as he couldn't hold back any longer.

At the M16 qualification range, the 683rd trucks pulled into the parking area of Range 5. Marshall was already there, patiently awaiting their arrival. The zero range and the qualification range were only a quarter-mile apart.

Range 5 was the first in the Army to use the new computerized scoring system, which did not allow for any overly generous scoring. Marshall knew there was a possibility many soldiers would make the forced march from the range to Mount Eden Base Camp if they did not qualify.

Marshall asked the Range NCOIC a question.

"Sarge, would it be all right with you if our bolo firers were given another chance to qualify if we have enough time and ammo left?" he asked.

"No problem, Sir," the Range NCOIC replied. "I don't mind as long as I get home to dinner before 1800 hours."

Lemasters and Heinz were herding the 683rd soldiers into the bleachers as they continued to make their cattle noises, moving along in one large herd, which made everyone chuckle.

As they settled into the bleacher seats, the Range NCOIC walked over and introduced himself.

"I am Master Sergeant McDuffy, the Range NCOIC of the M16 qualification range," he said, his voice steadily growing louder. "You will not perform any unsafe acts while on my range! I will not see anyone with tired blood! I say again, I will not see anyone on my range with tired blood! Do you read me?" As he finished, McDuffy was shouting like one of the Army's most feared drill sergeants.

"YES, Master Sergeant McDuffy!" the 683rd personnel shouted right back.

McDuffy smiled as he received the 683rd response.

"Excellent!" he shouted back.

"You will obey all commands from the tower," McDuffy ordered the soldiers. "This is an automated weapons range. Each individual's score will be done by the Army's new scoring computer. That means you better hit your targets within the allotted time frame. I will tell you how many seconds you have to engage your targets. If they are not hit within that time frame, you will not get credit.

"A word of caution to all of you. If I see any unsafe acts committed on my range, you will be personally escorted from the firing line and placed in the bleachers!"

McDuffy turned to Marshall.

"Sir, give me five minutes and we can start with the first firing order," McDuffy said.

Marshall nodded his approval to Sergeant McDuffy and turned his attention to his soldiers sitting in the bleachers.

Captain Marshall waited a moment before he spoke while Master Sergeant McDuffy left to climb into the range tower.

"I've asked the good sergeant to give any bolo firers a second chance—and only a second chance—to qualify," Marshall said. "The computer scoring doesn't give you that advantage of counting a target as hit after the target drops back when the time runs out. That also means there is no need for scorers, but every firer will need a coach. Coaches, make sure you let your firer know where their shots are going when they miss the target.

"Third firing order will remain in the bleachers until it's the second firing order's turn to qualify.

"Fourth order will be ammo loaders and will then wait in the bleachers when the second order is firing. Everyone got the rotation picture?"

The assembled soldiers nodded their heads and said, "Yes, Sir," in a somewhat unified fashion.

"Any questions?" asked Marshall.

One of the soldiers in the back of the bleachers stood up and asked one.

"Sir, if we bolo and then bolo again on our second try, will we have to march back with Sergeant Lemasters?"

"Sir, let me answer that," Lemasters pounced forward from the side of the bleachers to respond to the posed question. "If'n you bolo twice, you 'n me are going to be marchin' all the way back to Mount Eden, and most likely double timin' some too. There ain't no reason for anyone here to bolo if you had listened to the instructions at the zero range and sighted your weapon properly. You understand?"

"Yes, Sergeant," replied the private.

Sergeant Bradford stood up in the back for a question.

"Sarge, what if we can't see our target because it's underneath a 'shadda' of a tree?" he asked with a slight grin on his face.

Everyone in the bleachers roared with laughter. They all knew about the "shadda" incident.

"All right, all right!" Lemasters said. "The Sarge makes a good point, even if he can't talk hillbilly too good."

"If'n you can't see your target, let your coach know. The Range NCOIC, he'll show y'all the targets one by one. If yer confused about which one is yours, or ya can't see it, raise yer hand. All yer targets will be shown to ya before ya fire."

Bradford gave Lemasters the thumbs-up gesture.

"First firing order to the firing line!" boomed the Range NCOIC's voice over the loudspeaker system.

"Coaches, secure for your firer from the ammo point four magazines, 15 rounds each," the voice continued.

The first and second firing orders began moving to their designated places. En masse, 40 soldiers walked over to their designated firing points and stood as they awaited further instructions from the tower.

"Firers, place your weapon on the stake to the right of your firing position, ejection port facing up!" the Range NCOIC commanded over the loudspeaker.

"Firers, enter your foxholes!"

The foxhole was a concrete pipe buried four feet into the ground vertically. Sandbags were in the bottom to stand on if the firer was short, or if rainwater filled the bottom of the foxhole.

"Coaches, proceed to your designated firing point and stand directly behind your firer!" The Range NCOIC had his commands down to a science, since he had done this daily for the past seven months.

"Firers, you may pick up your weapons and assume a good firing position by adjusting the sandbags in front of your firing position!"

All the firers were busy moving the sandbags around to help cradle their M16s and forearms for a comfortable and steady firing position.

"Firers, coaches, here are your targets!" boomed McDuffy's voice as he spoke clearly and loudly over the loudspeaker system.

"Fifty meters!" he shouted as a target silhouette popped up.

"One hundred meters!" Another target popped up.

"One fifty meters! Two hundred meters! Two fifty meters! Three hundred meters! Three fifty meters!"

All the targets were now exposed and in view. Each firer's lane was clearly marked by the lack of brush or grass growing in the front of the target, caused by previous hundreds of firers that missed their targets by shooting too low. Everyone was anxious and ready to go, with their earplugs tightly wedged into their ear canals.

The familiar warning from the range tower was issued to all inhabitants that may be loitering in front of the firing line.

"Is there anyone downrange? Is there anyone downrange? Is there anyone downrange?" Silence answered McDuffy's warning.

"Firers, the firing line is now secure!" he shouted. "You will be shooting a modified course C and will have 60 seconds to engage 15 targets at various ranges. Some targets will reappear after you hit them. Hit all targets in your lane that are standing.

"Coaches, give your firer one magazine, 15 rounds each. Firers, lock and load one magazine." The crisp sound of rounds being chambered by 40 M16s resounded along the firing line.

"Ready on the right?" the loudspeaker boomed. The safety NCOs on the right side of the range tower raised the white side of their safety paddles in the air. The safety officer looked at all his safety NCOs and saw all white paddles. He then raised his white paddle to the range tower.

"Ready on the left?" McDuffy asked. The safety NCOs on the left side of the range tower raised their safety paddles and showed the white side. One safety NCO raised the red side.

The safety officer saw the red paddle and raised his safety paddle as red, which signified that someone was not ready yet.

The slower soldier clambered to readiness, embarrassed to hold up the entire group. The safety NCO then turned his safety paddle over to the white side. The safety officer saw that and did the same. All was finally clear on the firing line.

"Firers, the firing line is now clear!" McDuffy yelled. "You may commence firing!"

Within a second, the targets began to appear and the 683rd first firing order was busy knocking down targets. The smell of burnt cordite was in the air as the M16 range roared to life.

"Cease fire! Cease fire! Cease fire!" McDuffy's voice boomed over the loudspeaker system. The 60-second interval had passed.

"Do I have any alibi firers?" McDuffy asked.

One safety NCO raised the red side of his safety paddle to indicate one of his firers had a problem. The safety NCO held up four fingers to convey to the range tower that the firer had four rounds left in the magazine due to a misfeed.

McDuffy gave a command.

"Alibi firers, watch your lane!" he yelled.

Targets began to pop up and the alibi firer shot his remaining four rounds.

"Cease fire! Cease fire! Cease fire!" McDuffy yelled. He barked the next set of instructions at the soldiers.

"Firers, place the selector switch on safe! Remove the magazine from your weapon and place it on the sandbag! Firers, place your weapon on the stake to the right of your firing position, ejection port up. Safety NCOs, check all weapons and make sure they are clear."

After one minute, McDuffy called out the next set of instructions from the range tower.

"Clear on the right?" he asked. All white-sided safety paddles were displayed by the safety NCOs and officers.

"Clear on the left?" questioned McDuffy. Again, only white-sided paddles were visibly waved in the air by the safety NCOs and officers.

"Firers, you may now exit your foxholes!" McDuffy yelled. "Pick up your weapons from the stake and assume a good kneeling firing position."

Soldiers did as they were told. McDuffy continued.

"Coaches, give your firer one magazine, 15 rounds each," he said. "Firers, lock and load one magazine, 15 rounds." The range again echoed with clattering as soldiers loaded their weapons.

"Ready on the right?" McDuffy asked, nodding at the white paddles. "Ready on the left?" he nodded at a second row of white.

"Firers, the firing line is now ready!" McDuffy shouted. "Watch your lane!"

Again, the eruption of M16s being fired at targets was thunderous.

"Cease fire! Cease fire! Cease fire!" McDuffy yelled, ending the chorus of gunshots.

"Any alibi firers?"

This time, everyone on the firing line had used up all his or her allotted ammunition.

"Firers, place the selector switch on safe!" McDuffy yelled. "Remove your magazine from the weapon and place it on the sandbag. Firers, place your weapon on the stake, ejection port facing up.

"Safety NCOs, check all weapons," McDuffy continued. "Clear on the right? Clear on the left?"

The safety NCOs once more waved white-sided safety paddles.

"The firing line is now secure!" McDuffy boomed. "Firers, pick up your weapon from the stake and assume a good prone firing position to the immediate right of your foxhole."

The soldiers on the firing line lay down on the gravel next to their foxholes and adjusted their body angles to their respective firing lane.

"Coaches, give your firer one magazine, 15 rounds each!" the loudspeaker boomed. "Firers, lock and load one magazine, 15 rounds."

McDuffy scanned the range for red paddles.

"Ready on the right? Ready on the left?" he saw nothing.

The firing line is now ready!" McDuffy yelled. "Firers, watch your lane! You may commence firing!"

Specialist Williams was ready and focused on her firing lane. She knew that she had a perfect score so far, and the shots that she thought she had missed had mysteriously hit the target. When the Range NCOIC gave the commence firing command, the first target she was aiming for was the 100-meter silhouette.

Before she could squeeze the trigger, the target went down. Confused, Williams took aim at the 200-meter target, which suddenly disappeared before she could get a shot off. Looking over to her left, Specialist Fran Peoples was angled slightly to her right and firing into her targets.

Thanks Fran, you're quite the friend, thought Williams as she looked back at her targets and began firing on the 300-meter silhouette. The target twisted to the right as it dropped, signifying a hit on the right shoulder. Not bad, thought Williams, as she had a couple extra shots to take care of any more targets still standing in her firing lane.

"Cease fire! Cease fire! Cease fire!" McDuffy's voice boomed over the loudspeakers.

Williams took the opportunity to look over at her friend and express her gratitude.

"Fran, you know you've been shooting at my targets?" she asked.

Peoples looked back and grinned.

"You're welcome girlfriend!" replied Peoples, who was an expert shot. She didn't mind boloing the first go round. She knew she could hit every target, and taking a second chance to qualify would be just fine with her.

McDuffy's voice over the loudspeaker boomed.

"Any alibi firers?" he asked.

All safety paddles were white.

"Firers, place the selector switch on safe!" McDuffy continued. "Remove the magazine and place it on the sandbag! Coaches, collect all empty magazines! Firers, place your weapon on the stake next to your foxhole, ejection port facing up! Safety NCOs, check all weapons!"

Even though the commands from the range tower became repetitious, the seriousness of the matter never changed. The troops were getting into a groove and the M16 qualification range was operating at what the Army likes to call peak efficiency.

After Master Sergeant McDuffy had gone through the safety checks that were on his clipboard, he was ready to start the last portion of weapons qualification. Out of the corner of his eye a dark object got his attention.

Looking to his left and downrange, he took his pair of binoculars and adjusted the focus wheel until the objects became clear and sharp. Three wild pigs were grazing just beyond the firing range boundary marker, about 400 meters from the firing line. The pigs had to be moved in order to get the range back online, and they didn't appear to be in any kind of hurry.

"Firing point number 16, do you see those pigs on the left side boundary marker approximately 400 meters away?" boomed Sergeant McDuffy's voice over the loudspeaker.

Both the firer and coach saw the pigs off in the distance and raised their hands in acknowledgment.

"I want you to fire several rounds to the right side of those pigs and kick up some dirt to scare them away," McDuffy boomed. "Can you do that?"

The firer gave McDuffy the thumbs up.

"All right, firing point 16, assume a comfortable firing position. Lock and load one magazine and commence firing."

Private Hudson drew a careful bead on the group of pigs and aimed five meters to the right. He slowly squeezed off the first round, which hit the embankment to the right side of the pigs and kicked up some dirt. It got their attention for several seconds, and they returned their attention to graze on the lush green grass.

"Firing point 16, give them a short four-round burst!" boomed the Range NCOIC as he began to get irritated with the unwanted intruders on his range.

Hudson placed the selector switch on full, took careful aim and slowly squeezed the trigger. A rapid burst of 5.56-mm ball ammunition went flying downrange toward the grazing herd of wild pigs. A small cloud of dirt was kicked up as the rounds hit the ground to the immediate left of the pigs. They decided it was time to get out of this rather strange area and moved back out of sight.

"Nice shooting, number 16," McDuffy acknowledged, as he watched the wild pigs disappear.

"All right firers, fun time is over!" McDuffy shouted. "Firers, take your weapon from the stake and assume a good sitting firing position. This will be your last chance to qualify! Aim and shoot carefully!

"Coaches, give your firer one magazine, 15 rounds. Firers, lock and load one magazine." A chorus of clicking answered McDuffy's order.

"Ready on the right? Ready on the left?" All the safety paddles were white. McDuffy exhaled.

"Firers, the firing line is now ready!" he shouted. "Watch your lane! You may commence firing!"

Peoples knew she couldn't hit all her targets and have enough to qualify. Time to help her buddy Pam, who seemed to be struggling trying to find a comfortable firing position. Spotting Williams' 300-meter target, Peoples squeezed her trigger and dropped the target. Looking at the 250-meter target, she again squeezed the trigger and dropped it.

Williams was now starting to fire at her targets and missed her first three shots at the 50-meter target. All three shots were too high. Peoples aimed at the base of the target and dropped it with her first shot. Williams looked over at Fran, then decided to return the favor by shooting the targets in Peoples' firing lane.

"Cease fire! Cease fire! Cease fire!" The firing stopped.

"Are there any alibis?" McDuffy asked. No red safety paddles answered his question.

"Firers, clear all weapons!" McDuffy barked. "Place the selector switch on safe and remove the magazine! Place your weapon on the stake next to your foxhole with the ejection port facing up! Firers, stand behind your firing position! Safety personnel, visually check all weapons."

Are we clear on the right? Are we clear on the left?" All paddles were waving the white side.

Round one was over. McDuffy shouted the final clean-up and safety instructions to the soldiers.

"Firers, pick up your weapon and keep it pointed up and downrange until ram-rodded by the two safety officers at the base of the tower!" he boomed.

The 40 M16 firers then picked up their weapons, faced the middle of the range, and began to slowly walk toward the base of the range tower. Both Lieutenant Smith and Lieutenant

Rodriguez were using cleaning rods, shoving them down the barrels of the firers' M16s as they reached the base of the range tower.

With the M16 bolt in the rear position, the cleaning rod was shoved down the barrel, which hit the spring-loaded bolt that was held by a latch. The force of the cleaning rod was enough to release the latch and allow the bolt group to go forward and push the cleaning rod out the barrel. If there was a round left in the firing chamber of the M16, the sound and feel would have been completely different and distinctive.

"Top, I've got to get over to the .45-caliber range," Marshall said to First Sergeant Tisher as he looked at his watch. "Whoever hasn't bolo'd from the first firing order should be sent back to Mount Eden to switch with those personnel holding down the field site."

"No sweat, Sir," Tisher replied. "John's getting the driver ready to haul the first firing order back as soon as they get cleared off the firing line."

"Don't worry. I've got it handled here, Sir. You just go ahead and spend some quality time with Colonel Biggs."

"Gee thanks, Top," Marshall said. He grinned as he signaled his driver to crank-over the engine on his ¼-ton jeep.

Marshall walked over to Lieutenant Rodriguez as he was clearing the last two firers.

"Rod, I'm taking off for the .45 range," Marshall said. "You're in charge."

"Roger wilco," replied Rodriguez. "We're ahead of schedule, and it looks like we'll have time to take care of any bolos."

"Sounds good, Rod," Marshall said. "Just let me know if there are any emergencies that come up. Otherwise, I'll see you either back here or at Mount Eden."

Marshall and his driver went off toward Range 7 as the remainder of the 683rd took its respective turn at the M16 range. The sun was shining brightly and directly overhead. *It's going to be another hot one,* thought Marshall as he and his driver enjoyed the scenic drive down Range Road.

As they pulled into the parking area of Range 7, Marshall felt something was amiss. Other than the Range NCOIC, they were the only ones there. Looking at his watch, they had another 45 minutes to go before the range went hot.

Marshall walked over to the safety tower to meet the Range NCOIC.

"Afternoon, Sir," the NCOIC said. "I'm Sergeant Mauer from the range committee. I'll be handlin' the range today." Marshall shook Mauer's hand.

"Thanks for being here for us, Sergeant Mauer," Marshall said. "We appreciate your help with the ranges."

"That's what we're here for, Sir," Mauer replied. "Just a question for you if I may."

"Please, go ahead," replied Marshall.

"Sir, where are your ambulance, corpsman, and safety personnel?"

Marshall suddenly realized what was missing.

"I'll check and see where the corpsman's at. Thanks, Sarge," Marshall said. "I've got some scrounging to do, which won't take too long."

Marshall headed back to his ¼-ton and informed his driver to head back to the M16 range.

As the ¼-ton headed back into the M16 parking area, Tisher saw his commander and walked over to him.

"What's up, Sir?" asked Tisher.

"Top, we need two safety NCOs and one ambulance with corpsman who hasn't showed up yet," Marshall replied.

"Sir, I'll get two safety NCOs for you, but I don't think I can get you another corpsman and ambulance," replied Tisher.

"Sir," the driver spoke up. "We passed another range that was starting to shut down."

Marshall was reading his driver loud and clear.

"Good idea," Marshall said. "Let's go visit that range and see what we can come up with. Top, send the two safeties to the pistol range ASAP. We'll meet them there in 10 minutes."

Marshall and his driver drove to the other range that was shutting down just in time to see the corpsman getting ready to leave.

"Excuse me, Corpsman. We need your help," Marshall said. He knew the corpsman could help if he was not scheduled elsewhere.

"If you have an extra 60 minutes you can be a life-saver—mine!" said Marshall. "Our corpsman for the pistol range is a no-show and we've got a group of 20 personnel that need to qualify. We're Reservists from Ohio and this is our only chance to qualify this year, if you can help us."

The corpsman looked at Marshall and smiled.

"Do you think you'll have enough ammo left over for one more firer?" asked the corpsman.

"I'm sure of it," Marshall replied with a beaming smile.

Marshall and his driver pulled into Range 7, along with the corpsman driving his ambulance. Two of the 683rd safety NCOs were already waiting in the parking area. Several of the group headquarters vehicles were parked nearby. The .45-caliber pistol firers had arrived. Specialist Dave Hullerd, the corpsman that generously volunteered to save the day, radioed his situation to his unit dispatcher, letting them know he would be busy for another hour or so.

"We owe you a big favor," Marshall said to Specialist Hullerd. "You've got an open invitation to visit our field site at Mount Eden and enjoy a great meal."

"What kind of unit are you, Sir?" asked Hullerd.

"We're a maintenance company. We can fix just about anything the Army's got," replied Marshall.

"Well, Sir, my directional signals are out," said Hullerd. "Maybe your people can fix 'em for me and we'll call it even."

"Consider it done," replied Marshall. "Bring your ambulance over any time. I'll have my people fix it for you."

The .45-caliber pistol qualification range operated perfectly. Sergeant Mauer had the firers break down into two firing orders. All fired their M1911 A1 .45-caliber pistols and qualified, including one life-saving Army corpsman.

The fourth firing order had just completed its turn at the M16 range when Marshall returned. The personnel that were on guard duty at Mount Eden were next, along with the bolo firers.

"Top," Marshall said as he walked over to Tisher. "How's it goin'?"

"Well, Sir, we've got only 16 people that bolo'd, and enough firing points to accommodate them, plus the personnel that just arrived from Mount Eden," Tisher said. "Looks like we'll be finished early."

Marshall pondered Tisher's comments.

"Top, if those 16 bolo firers don't qualify, it's seven miles back to Mount Eden and Sergeant Lemasters is going to make them remember every inch of it."

Tisher grinned.

"Oh yes, Sir," he said. "I've told 'em all after they got a bolo. Each one knows the score, and John is looking forward to a forced march back to Mount Eden."

Lemasters was smiling while standing next to Tisher as he overheard the comments.

The last firing order on the M16 weapons qualification range was finally winding down. All the firers were done and the safety NCOs were clearing the soldiers' weapons as they moved to the base of the range tower.

Master Sergeant McDuffy walked out of the range tower and handed Lieutenant Rodriguez the computerized score sheet of the firing points. Looking over the sheet, Rodriguez saw that there were five bolo firers for the forced march with Lemasters.

"Sergeant Lemasters, here you go," said Rodriguez.

"Thanks, Sir," replied Lemasters as he took the list and reviewed the firing points carefully.

"All right!" Lemasters yelled, excited for the march. "Last firin' order, I want the followin' people from these here firin' points to fall-in in front of me! Number 12, number 15, number 24, number 32 and number 35. Y'all bolo'd and yer ass is mine!"

The firers that failed to qualify twice were assembled in front of Lemasters with their weapons at sling-arms.

"Now I want you people to go up an' down the firing points and pick up any brass that ain't already been policed up," Lemasters ordered. "If I find any brass that ain't been picked up, we'll be double-timin' it back to Mount Eden. Hear me?"

"Yeah, Sergeant," was the disheartened and quiet response.

"What was that?" Lemasters asked the group.

"Yes, Sergeant!" the group responded, this time quite a bit louder and forceful.

"That's better," replied Lemasters. "Now git yer butts on the firin' line an' pick up any brass you see. Startin' at firin'

point one in a five-man-wide line, you're gonna check every point. Git goin'!"

The group slowly wandered over to the far side of the firing range, spread out in a five-man front, and began to search for overlooked spent brass cartridge casings, normally referred to as brass. Brass had to be turned in to the ammo point afterwards. The personnel at the ammo point did not want to see any unused boxes of ammunition being turned in. They only wanted the spent brass and unopened wooden cases of ammo.

"Top," Marshall said. "How many rounds of ammo do we have left over?"

Tisher looked over at the loading tables and walked over to take a closer look. Sergeant Mooney was at the loading table getting things ready for turn-in. Tisher saw there were only about 200 rounds left.

"Sir, we've got about 200 rounds left. Looks like we've got enough to load up 10 magazines," Tisher replied.

"OK Top," Marshall said. "Go ahead and load 'em up and shoot 'em off before Sergeant McDuffy closes down the range."

Tisher walked over to the range tower and told Sergeant McDuffy that there would be another 200 rounds to go downrange. Tisher asked if McDuffy would be so kind as to raise up all the targets on the range.

"Not a problem, Top," replied McDuffy. "Go ahead and fire 'em up when you're ready."

Marshall overheard McDuffy's approval of using the range to fire-off the remainder of the ammunition.

"Top, you and the others who haven't had a chance to qualify today take your turn at the firing line," Marshall said. "Sergeant Mooney and I will be the safeties. Besides, Sergeant Lemasters would probably like a little more company on the march back to Mount Eden."

"Sir, I didn't know you were a comic in civilian life," replied Tisher.

"All right you bolos! Time to start our little walk back to Mount Eden. Right...face! Double-time...march!" shouted Lemasters.

A few grunts and groans were heard as they began to trot down the road. The group headed down Range Road and slowly disappeared out of sight. Marshall watched his bolos move down the road. Knowing that the physical training test was going to be held the following morning, Marshall felt that the forced march might be too much of a physical strain on the soldiers, even though they had been warned about not qualifying on the M16 range.

After Tisher and the safety personnel fired, Marshall decided, they would pick up the bolo firers a few miles down the road. The embarrassment of failing to qualify twice was enough punishment for one person to take. No need to push it any further, thought Marshall.

Specialist Peoples was one of the last people to qualify since she had helped her buddy Pam Williams qualify as an expert—with a little help from her friends. Peoples had a score of 58 of 60 targets hit. Not bad, considering her first score of 14 hits and 46 misses. As she arrived at Mount Eden Base Camp, soldiers were already standing in line to turn in their cleaned M16s. She knew this was going to be her longest day, so she might as well give it her best.

"All right!" shouted Peoples. "Form a single file line at the back of the weapons trailer."

She unlocked the back door of the trailer and took the weapons register out of the drawer of the field desk inside.

"First man!" shouted Peoples as she looked down from her place on high.

The first soldier in the front of the line handed his weapon to Peoples for inspection. She grabbed the weapon, opened the ejection port cover with her fingernail and stuck her index finger into the breech.

"The breech's got too much carbon residue. Clean it again!" Peoples was in her realm.

The first soldier stayed in front of Peoples.

"Gee, Fran, I was hoping you could show me how to clean my weapon," he said with a wink.

Peoples shot him a hard look.

"If it weren't against Army regs, I'd slap you." She threw the M16 at his chest with enough force to knock him backwards.

"Wanna know what my score was today, soldier?" He shook his head. "Then clean your weapon again!" The soldier turned and walked away.

Peoples chuckled. Well, there's one more that won't bother me anymore, she thought.

Marshall instructed the last deuce-and-a-half driver to pick up the bolo firers and Sergeant Lemasters. Marshall followed the deuce to make sure that Lemasters followed his orders and didn't make them continue the forced march.

When all the bolo firers were picked up, Marshall told Lemasters to get into his ¼-ton jeep. Sitting in the back of the jeep was Tisher, who was glad to see that Lemasters hadn't run the bolos into the ground.

"John, how far did you double-time them?" asked Tisher.

"Shoot, Top," Lemasters said. "I'd have 'em run for three minutes an then I'd walk 'em for five. I don't think any of 'em broke much of a sweat."

Marshall turned around from his front seat.

"Sarge, I appreciate you taking them on a healthy march down Range Road," Marshall said. "I'm sure they'll never forget it and won't ever want to bolo again."

"Sir, I asked them soldiers why they bolo'd, and ya know what they told me? They told me that they never bolo'd before, and their weapons' barrels must be misaligned," remarked Lemasters.

"They might be right, Sarge," replied Marshall. "When I was at Bragg, we had a unit armorer clean all our weapons every month instead of issuing them out to the troops. He felt it would be faster and gave him something to do. What I found out was he used a cleaning rod and bore bush with an electric drill. It shined up the barrels nicely, but wore them out so badly that you couldn't hit the broad side of a barn after he cleaned them every month for 12 months."

First Sergeant Tisher was curious.

"So what happened?" he asked.

"After half the unit bolo'd at weapons qual, I had the small arms repair section check each M16 with a barrel erosion gauge. We had to replace over 100 barrels. A formal investigation took place and they found that the armorer used a hardened steel barrel brush instead of the brass brush that's Army issue. I think he's still in the Army working off the cost of replacing all those barrels."

"John, have those soldiers get their weapons checked by Peoples for barrel erosion," Tisher immediately remarked. "At least we can give them the benefit of the doubt."

As they headed toward the floating bridge, Marshall looked at his watch. The troops at the floating bridge quit at 1730 hours, and the time was now 1725 hours. As Marshall looked up, he saw the floating bridge personnel drive past them in the opposite direction on the way back to Main Post.

"Driver, might as well turn around," Marshall said. "We've got to take the road past the pig farm. That was the floating bridge personnel that just passed us."

The thought of driving past the pig farm on a hot day, or any day for that matter, was not a pleasant one.

At Mount Eden Base Camp, the dinner meal was being served. Soldiers were hungry and dirty from a day at the rifle range. Sergeant Emery had cooked up his special junk-food feast that wasn't on the Army's master menu. The cooks had made pizza, cheeseburgers, hot dogs, French fries and onion rings to satisfy the soldiers' cravings for junk food. The only thing missing was the beer and soda pop. Emery would only go so far to satisfy the soldiers' cravings. He didn't want to wind up in the military stockade.

Word of Emery's menu for dinner spread throughout Mount Eden Base Camp. The headcount was busy rejecting over 100 soldiers from different units trying to infiltrate the 683rd chow line. After a while, he gave up when all the 683rd personnel were fed. Emery's reputation as a master chef became common knowledge.

As the evening progressed, all the weapons were cleaned and turned in. Not one was missing and Marshall gave thanks.

"Another bullet dodged," he said to himself as he heard the report from Field First Sergeant Lemasters on the weapons inventory.

Peoples was told to check on the bolo firers' weapons in the morning and find out if there were any maintenance issues. If the weapons needed repair, that would give her and the small arms repair section of the armament platoon something to do. Everything else seemed to be in perfect order.

With evening setting in, Sergeant Nugot was doing some operator's maintenance on his newly-named 5-ton wrecker, the "Li'l Stinker." Leaning over the hood while he was checking the oil level on the dipstick, he spotted his little furry skunk friend hanging around the back end of the wrecker.

Nugot had an unopened package of peanut-butter crackers in his trousers and slowly got down from the front bumper. He opened up the pack of crackers, which were mostly crumbs, and poured them out into his hand. Walking slowly and closely to the ground, Nugot called out to his little friend.

"Come here, little buddy! See what Jimmy has for you."

The skunk saw Nugot coming toward him slowly and didn't run away, but backed up and raised his tail in a defensive posturing.

Nugot saw the skunk was ready to defend himself, so he sat down on the ground with his legs crossed and continued to hold out his hand and coax the skunk toward him. The skunk's curiosity and hunger were stronger than its sense of fear, and the skunk began to slowly walk toward Nugot's outstretched hand, filled with food.

The skunk stopped about three feet away and stared at Nugot, wondering what will happen next.

Nugot took a liking to his newfound friend, and began to softly talk to it.

"Hey, little buddy. Jimmy has some food for you. Here you go." He dumped the crackers onto the ground and put his hands on his knees and waited for the skunk to start eating, all the time talking softly to it.

The skunk took its cue and quickly walked over to the new pile of food on the ground that Nugot left. The skunk found the first morsel of peanut butter crackers to be excellent, and began to find Nugot's voice comforting and reassuring. The skunk finished the small meal.

"OK, little buddy. I'll have more for you tomorrow," Nugot told his little friend. "Now get along." He waved his hands in a gesture to let the skunk know it was time to leave.

The skunk got the idea and turned around and rambled off into the woods. Nugot hoped that the skunk would return the following day for more food. He was thinking that the "Li'l Stinker" wrecker needed a mascot.

Everyone in the 683rd had a long and tiring day. No night patrols or ambushes would be accomplished that evening. With the PT test coming up in the morning, Marshall decided to let his soldiers have a good night's sleep.

The PT test consisted of a four-mile course that had to be completed within 45 minutes. Marshall had considered letting everyone do the course individually, but that wouldn't bring the unit together as a team. The entire unit would have to do the four-mile course together, marching and running in unison, to have the impact Marshall wanted it to have.

As he was lying on his cot, Marshall was trying to figure out how fast the pace would have to be for everyone to finish the four-mile course together.

"Six miles an hour," Marshall murmured to himself. "That'll be a very fast marching pace or a double-time run. Better to use a combination of both." That would allow everyone in the formation to catch his or her breath and still do the course within the allotted time of 45 minutes.

"Top, we're going to do the four-mile course in formation," Marshall stated as Tisher was starting to drift off into sleep. The only response he got was light snoring.

Sergeant Tea piped in.

"That's nice, Sir," she said. "Do you want me to lead the formation tomorrow? I can be the gidon bearer."

"No Sergeant Tea, you've got more important things to care about," said Marshall. "Like making sure we know how much time we've got left as we head down the stretch toward the finish line. Have one of the soldiers with a medical profile drive my ¼-ton, and you'll ride along with the stopwatch. Meet us at the halfway point and then a mile away from the finish line so I'll know how much time we've got left."

"Sounds like a good plan, Sir," Tea said. "And I wasn't really volunteering to be the gidon bearer. I wanted to lead the run."

A.T. - DAY 7 (SATURDAY)

PT test today! It was the first thought that entered Marshall's mind as he rolled out of his cot and put on his tennis shoes.

"Top, time to rise and shine!" shouted Marshall as he headed out the tent flaps to get a cup of coffee from the 683rd's famous mess section.

Soldiers were already stirring, getting ready for morning formation. No breakfast would be served until after everyone had completed the PT test. Rumors had been circulating that everyone would have the rest of the day off after the PT test.

At 0700 hours, Field First Sergeant Lemasters blew his whistle.

"Formation!" he shouted.

The 683rd headed en masse toward the assembly area ready for the day. The soldiers were dressed in their PT uniforms: white T-shirts, tennis shoes, and olive drab trousers.

Marshall was now at the front of the formation.

"At ease!" he yelled.

The 683rd was ready to listen and gave the commander their complete attention.

"Today, we are going to do the Army's physical training test: the four-mile march," Marshall said. "Since we must complete the four-mile march within 45 minutes, it would hardly be justified to call it a march.

"We are going to all complete the four-mile march in formation," Marshall told the soldiers. He got some rather surprised looks from his troops in response. "If you must drop out of the formation, try and keep up. We will be marching and double-time marching to complete the four-mile distance within the allotted time. Depending upon how much time we have left, we may have to double-time the last mile. Our PT formation will be an eight-man front, so watch out for any potholes and rocks.

"I want everyone to finish and pass! After completion of the PT test, we will have breakfast and then another formation at 0900 hours for a shower run. You will have the rest of the afternoon to visit main post. Company, ten-hut!"

As soon as Marshall yelled "Company," the soldiers' heads and eyes went immediately to their respective fronts. After he yelled "ten-hut," in unison the soldiers all placed their right legs next to their left and their hands and arms were tightly brought to their sides.

Marshall was impressed at how well the 683rd soldiers had adapted to the field conditions and were actually enjoying their annual training experience.

"First Sergeant!" Marshall called out in a normal tone of voice. First Sergeant Tisher walked promptly up to the front of the formation and saluted his commander.

"Top, take charge of the unit," Marshall said. "Let's get 'em on the road!"

"Yes Sir," grinned Tisher as he took control of the formation.

"I want an eight-man front on the road," shouted the First Sergeant. "Fall out and fall in on the road!"

The 683rd quickly moved from the assembly area to the road, ready for the PT test. Sergeant Tea was in the ¼-ton jeep with the stopwatch, ready to begin timing the event.

Marshall was to the far right of the formation with the gidon bearer, and was ready to start the test.

"Right face! Forward march!" Marshall shouted.

The formation of 683rd personnel began marching in step toward the tent peg in the ground that signified the start and finish line.

As they crossed the start line, Marshall shouted.

"Double time…march!" Marshall ordered the troops.

The entire formation started jogging in step. The gidon bearer was in front of the formation and Marshall was to the immediate front and left, maintaining a good pace that wouldn't prematurely tire out the soldiers.

One of the NCOs in the formation began singing out a Jodi call, which everyone joined in and sang along. They chanted everything from "I wanna be an Airborne Ranger" to Marshall's personal favorite:

"I don't know but I've heard rumors, Captain Marshall wears pink bloomers!" The image of pink bloomers made everyone laugh and get out of step.

"Quick time...march!" Marshall shouted. His command brought everyone from a jog to a normal marching pace.

Lemasters began counting cadence.

"Hup, two, three, four! Your left! Your left! Your left! Right! Left!"

The time and distance quickly went by and the unit made the two-mile turn around in 20 minutes. Everyone was still in formation and no one had dropped out so far.

Marshall decided to lessen the length of double-time so the unit would have enough energy to finish under the 45-minute mark. As the unit marched, some of the soldiers were anxious to start the double-time pace.

"Are you ready to double-time?" Marshall shouted. Almost everyone in formation roared a grunt, signaling their response in the affirmative.

"Double-time...march!" shouted Marshall as the formation lurched forward.

Another NCO in the formation began his Jodi call, and everyone joined in. The distance and time seemed to go by effortlessly as they double-timed along the dirt road.

As they passed Sergeant Tea at the three-mile marker, she shouted out "31 minutes!"

The entire formation got the notion that they were well ahead of schedule.

Marshall quickly gave the "Quick time...march!" command and the formation slowed down to a marching pace. Everyone was in good spirits as Marshall began to increase the pace of the marching tempo. The Jodi calls became more and more creative, and all in the formation were glad to join along and respond to as they crossed the finish line.

"Forty-three minutes!" Tea shouted as the last soldier crossed the line.

Marshall marched the formation to the assembly area and gave them two commands: halt and left face. As the soldiers faced Marshall, he could see every face was beaming with satisfaction and pride. They had all passed the PT test together as a unit, and they did it under the 45-minute time requirement.

Marshall felt confident the 683rd had finally come together as team. Many of the soldiers were helping their buddies during the march to keep up with the formation by shouldering them on either side. It was a great display of teamwork, helping out a fellow soldier pass the test.

"At ease! Shake it off!" shouted Marshall.

"Give yourselves a hand! You make me proud! Fantastic job!"

The 683rd soldiers walked around the assembly area to get their breathing under control and relax their heart rates, just having completed the four-mile course at a very respectable pace.

"All right! Fall in!" shouted Marshall, after giving the soldiers enough time to assemble once more.

"Great job, everyone! You all passed your PT test!" Marshall announced.

Grunts and other sounds of satisfaction were heard in the formation.

Marshall continued announcements to the soldiers.

"Have a good breakfast so you won't have to spend too much money on food," he said. "Trucks will be leaving here at 1100 hours to take you to the Main Post. There you can enjoy the afternoon and shop, relax at the Enlisted and NCO Clubs, and take in all the wonderful things there are to do at Fort Knox.

"No one is allowed off main post—not even me—so let's stay on the Fort Knox Military Reservation. Use the buddy system and look after your buddy so they won't get into any trouble.

"Trucks will be returning from Main Post starting at 1600 hours. The last 683rd truck will leave the Main Post PX area at 1730 hours."

"We are expecting everyone back here for the dinner meal. Sergeant Emery tells me he's got fried chicken on the menu, so come back hungry."

"One more thing." Marshal had a final warning for his troops. "I don't want anyone getting into trouble while on Main

Post. We'll have one more formation before you're released. Fall out!"

The soldiers quickly dispersed back to their tents to get cleaned up and get ready for breakfast. Some were too hungry to get cleaned up and immediately ran to the chow line. Spending an afternoon on Main Post was a well-earned reward.

Marshall looked up at the sky, which was beginning to cloud over.

"Looks like we might get some rain, Top," he said as Tisher walked up to him after the formation.

"Sir, would you mind if I went to Main Post this afternoon?" Tisher asked. "I've got some things to get from the PX and I've got to give Peg a call."

"No problem, Top," replied Marshall. "As a matter of fact, would you have Peg call my wife? I'm sure she would be very grateful. Just have Peg call collect, and let my wife know I'm fine."

"I'll hold down the fort here while you and the troops relax and enjoy yourselves," smiled Marshall. "Make sure Sergeant Emery and his cooks get a chance to take some time off too.

"One more thing, Top," Marshall said. "Check in on Lieutenant Kiley and our troops working at Boatwright. I'm fairly sure they're already taking the day off. Just have her report to me this evening with an update on her situation.

"By the way, here's my wife's phone number." Captain Marshall wrote down the phone number on a piece of paper and added, "Lieutenant Kiley report to CO at 1900 hrs, ref: training."

First Sergeant Tisher got the to-do list from Marshall.

"Anything else you need, Sir?" Tisher asked.

Marshall thought for a moment,

"Top, just tell the NCOs to take care of the troops," Marshall said. "I don't want any unfortunate incidents to occur."

"My sentiments exactly," replied Tisher.

The breakfast meal was another hungry man's delight, and all the soldiers had their plates piled high with eggs, SOS, biscuits, sausage and home-fried potatoes.

Many civilians had never tried SOS, the Army's greatest recipe. The name was an acronym, derived from slop on a shingle, or what is technically termed as creamed beef on toast. The recipe was simple and quick. The cooks started by dicing up onions, placed in a skillet along with ground beef. They stirred the mixture until the beef was cooked. The fat was drained off and flour was added until completely absorbed by the cooked beef. Milk was the next ingredient, stirred in until the gravy appeared. Water would be added as necessary to thin out the mix, along with salt and pepper. The concoction was dumped onto toast or biscuits, topped with cooked eggs and served with coffee and orange juice. It still is a meal fit for a king or queen—or a hungry soldier.

Many came for another helping, knowing they might want to skip lunch and wait for dinner at Mount Eden Base Camp.

"Well, Commander, how did your PT test go today?" asked Colonel Biggs as he walked up behind Marshall while observing his soldiers at the chow line.

"It went well, Sir," Marshall replied. "Everyone completed the four-mile course within 45 minutes. We even had soldiers carrying other soldiers across the finish line. It was quite a sight, Colonel."

"Yes, I see," commented Biggs. "My staff informed me your unit did the entire four-mile course in formation. Is that right?"

"Yes Sir, it is," replied Marshall. "I felt that we were ready as a unit to accomplish something like that together"

"That is quite an accomplishment, Captain. Kudos to you and the 683rd."

"Thank you Sir," said Marshall. "It's been my goal to get the soldiers in the unit to function as a team, and now it's happening. It just took some difficult conditions in the field to do it."

Biggs smiled as he listened to Marshall speak. He reflected back on his own career and how he too had a similar experience. Biggs knew what qualities and characteristics it took to be a good leader. He saw those same qualities and characteristics in Marshall. Biggs excused himself and headed to the back of the chow line, which was beginning to diminish.

Lieutenant Burks walked over to Marshall with a smile on her face.

"Good morning, Sir," she said as she stopped for a short conversation.

"And a good morning to you, Lieutenant," Marshall replied. "How's the trailer inventory going?"

"Sir, that's what I was about to tell you," Burks said. "It's all done. I've just got the parts stocking list from our people and it's rather extensive. Sir, we should be able to support just about any type of repair mission we get out here."

"What about the obsolete parts?" asked Marshall.

"Sir, that list is fairly good size, and it will take a couple of deuce-and-a-halves to get it all turned in."

Marshall pondered the situation of obsolete parts. If the unit returned to Ohio with trailers full of old parts that had to be turned in and ultimately sent back to Fort Knox, then why not cut through the Army's red tape and turn the parts in while at annual training? That would save everyone time, material and money.

"Sarah, the property disposal office for our region is located here at Fort Knox," said Marshall. "I want you and Chief McCarthy to give the civilians a visit and see how we can get those parts turned in here while we're still on A.T."

"Yes, Sir. Sounds like a good plan of attack," replied Burks.

"When you and the chief visit the PDO folks, have them give you an example of what they want the turn-in documents to look like," Marshall cautioned. "They hate paperwork that's incorrectly done. Most times they'll just reject it and tell you to come back when it's done right."

Burks was all smiles.

"You got it, Sir," she replied. "I'll let Mr. McCarthy know the plan."

Burks excused herself and joined the end of the chow line as most of the enlisted personnel had already been through once.

"Sir, can I see you for a second?" asked Chief Farley as he walked over to Marshall.

"Sure, Chief," Marshall said. "What's up?"

"Sir, I've just got a call from the engineer unit," replied Farley. "Half of their trucks are broke. One's got a busted engine, three need new clutches, two need brakes, and one needs a new differential."

Marshall smiled.

"Sounds like we're in business for the rest of the week, doesn't it, Chief?" Marshall asked.

"Sure as hell does, Sir," replied Farley.

"Well, Chief," said Marshall, "I think it's time to get with group headquarters and Reserve Affairs. Looks like this will take some extra funding for those parts we won't have in inventory at tech supply."

"Sir, I'll check with McCarthy and see what they've got," Farley said. "Whatever we'll need, I'll draw up a list and start things going."

"Excellent idea, Chief. You've got my blessing," replied Marshall.

As the morning progressed, the soldiers of the 683rd prepared themselves for their trip to Main Post. It was a pleasure not having to wear the tactical field gear anymore since the tactical phase of the training was over. Putting on a clean uniform and shined boots meant a great deal to the 683rd soldiers. Most have been wearing the same uniform for days and many planned to visit the coin-operated laundry. Even though they were on an Army training facility, on Main Post they were expected to have a neat and clean appearance.

At 1100 hours, Lemasters blew his whistle.

"Formation!" he yelled. Soldiers scrambled into the lineup.

"Sir, the unit is formed," said Tisher as he held his salute while Marshall stood in front of him at the center of the company formation.

"Thanks Top," said Marshal. Tisher dropped his salute after Marshall returned it. First Sergeant Tisher walked to the side of the formation and allowed his commander to talk to the soldiers.

"At ease!" shouted Marshall.

"I want all of you to know that all your hard work and excellent efforts have not gone unnoticed," Marshall told the troops. "I appreciate everything you are doing. You all did an excellent job during the tactical phase.

"When you get back this evening, there will be a meeting with the officers and NCOs. The subject will be what is going to happen next week. To give you some insight, mission work is beginning to pile up and we'll be plenty busy working on equipment all next week."

Marshall finished his short speech.

"Have an enjoyable afternoon on Post. Relax and have fun. Keep up the great work and be back here before 1800 hours tonight. Everyone got that?"

A resounding "Yes, Sir!" was shouted in unison by the assembled formation of soldiers.

"Ten Hut! First Sergeant!" Marshall called and waited for Tisher to come back and take over the formation.

"Top, I want you to have that meeting with the NCOs on taking care of their soldiers while on Post," Marshall whispered to Tisher.

"Yes, Sir. That was the number one thing on my agenda," Tisher replied. "Damn, Sir, you're becoming a mind-reader."

Tisher grinned and saluted as Marshall walked over to the side of the formation.

"All right! Listen up!" yelled Tisher. "Like the Old Man said, I want all of you to have a great time on Post, not a wild time. Anyone found drunk will report to me for extra duty. Anyone found fighting on Post will report to me for extra duty. I want to meet with all NCOs after this formation. First truck will leave in 10 minutes. Fall out!"

The formation did an about-face and shouted "683rd!" It was music to Marshall's ears.

Within 30 minutes, the 683rd field site at Mount Eden Base Camp was nearly deserted. Everyone was on Main Post—except for Marshall, Lieutenant Rodriguez, Sergeant Tea, Sergeant Emery and several of the cooks who had already had spent some of their time off on Main Post. The afternoon was becoming hot and humid as the sun began to disappear behind the cloud cover. Rain was imminent as the day wore on.

Emery had made a special lunch for those manning the field site. After lunch, Marshall, Lieutenant Rodriguez, Staff Sergeant Tea and Emery settled in for a game of Euchre. It was a classical match-up of the officers versus the NCOs, and both Tea and Emery were masters of the game.

"Let's see now. That's five matches in a row we've won," mused Tea. "Sir, I don't know how you're gonna handle all this defeat."

"I'll do my best," smiled Marshall, knowing that as a team, Tea and Emery couldn't be beat.

"How about we switch partners?" asked Rodriguez. "No disrespect intended, Sir."

"None taken, Rod," replied Marshall. "I was just about ready to suggest the same thing."

Outside, a rather ominous loud buzzing noise was heard. The power generators were shutdown for periodic maintenance by a couple of the motor pool mechanics. This, however, didn't sound like a generator.

"Rod, please check that out," said Marshall, curious about strange noises near his area of operations.

Rodriguez briskly left the tent and walked up to the main road to observe what was happening. Moments later he returned with his gas mask on.

"Sir, it's the Post engineers spraying the area with pesticides!"

All in the tent took Rodriguez's cue and immediately went for their gas masks and put them on. The smell of pesticides already began to permeate the air.

Emery left to cover any open food stocks. Rodriguez went outside and shouted the gas attack warning to all those left in the field site.

At least this will kill off any chiggers in the area, thought Marshall as he and Tea began lowering the flaps of the shop office tent.

Within several minutes, the rain clouds opened up and a heavy rain hit the field site for 10 minutes. Small rivers and ponds of water began to run through the site, washing away any trace of the pesticides that were just sprayed.

"You know Sergeant Tea, maybe someone up there wants us to provide a good home for these chiggers here on Mount Eden Base Camp," mused Marshall.

Tea just laughed and shook her head in agreement. Rodriguez and Emery had returned to the tent in their rain ponchos ready for the next round of Euchre.

The rain ended as quickly as it began and cooled things off for a while as the group of card players enjoyed the remainder of the afternoon in the peace and serenity of Mount Eden.

As the afternoon passed, the soldiers began returning in regular intervals from main post. Sergeant Lemasters was one of the first to arrive and report to his commander.

"Sir, looks like y'all had some rain," Lemasters said. "Didn't rain a drop on Main Post."

"Sarge, it came down in buckets just after the Post engineers sprayed pesticide to kill off the chiggers," replied Marshall.

"Figures," said Lemasters. "It's hard to kill off them little blood suckers.

"Well, Sir," he continued, "thangs went well on Post. So far, no one's got inta any trouble that I know about."

Marshall was pleased to hear an update on his soldiers.

"That's good news, Sarge," Marshall said. "Let's hope it continues. Did you enjoy the Post?"

"Sure did, Sir," Lemasters said. "Went to the PX, and then went to the Patton Museum. Did ya know that Nazi General Erwin Rommel was a graduate of the Fort Knox Armor School? Shoot, Sir, that surprised the hell outta me."

"After that, I decided to go visit my money at the gold vault. Them fellers at the vault said it was just fine, but I'd need a higher security clearance to come in and see it in person."

Marshall really enjoyed Lemasters' sense of humor.

"Sarge, you were in the Marine Corps during the Korean War, weren't you?" Marshall asked.

"Sure was, Sir," Lemasters replied. "From Inchon to the Yalu River, me and Mac were fighting the commies for over two years."

"Got any war stories to tell?" asked Marshall.

Lemasters grinned from ear to ear.

"Where'd ya want me ta start, Sir?"

Lemasters relayed some interesting and frightening stories to a large group of soldiers that entered the tent while he delved into his memories of the Korean War. Like all old soldiers, they don't mind sharing their experiences with younger soldiers to give them a good understanding of what it's like to put in on the line for God and country. Old soldiers telling war stories is a tradition that shall go on as long as there are stories to tell and young soldiers to listen to them. Just about every soldier in the tent would ask questions during pauses in the storytelling as Lemasters would continue on from battle to battle and year to year, often describing in great detail of the exploits of the soldiers and Marines he served with. At no time did he ever give himself any credit for heroics. He was always giving thanks to those comrades he served with for coming through in the difficult and dangerous engagements and battles.

Before long, Lemasters had finished the Korean War and was about to start talking about the Vietnam War when the last truckload of soldiers pulled into the field site.

"Sarge, I hate to cut you off, but we've got to get a head count of the soldiers," said Marshall.

"Right, Sir. I'll handle it," replied Lemasters. "I'll continya' with Vietnam later on," smiled Lemasters as he headed out the tent to check on the soldiers.

Within 15 minutes, Lemasters had completed his informal head count and report to his commander.

"Sir, looks like we've got 100 percent accountability," Lemasters said. "Everyone is back in the field, and there was no problems on Main Post."

"Excellent news, Sarge," said Marshall. "Let's have a formation in 10 minutes. I'd like to have Top welcome everyone back and give them an update on activities tomorrow."

"Yes, Sir," replied Lemasters.

A loud whistle rang out as Lemasters shouted, "Formation!"

The 683rd soldiers all gathered at the assembly area and stood at attention while Tisher made some announcements and got an accurate headcount. All were present and accounted for.

"I wanna thank you guys for not getting into any trouble while on Main Post," Tisher said. "However, I have heard from some of the MPs that a couple of you were rather rambunctious at the Enlisted Men's Club. I'll be curious to know what went on there, if some of you want to enlighten me after formation."

An uncomfortable chuckle came from somewhere in the formation.

Tisher continued with the announcements.

"Tomorrow will be a non-denominational church service for those who would like to attend at 0900 hours at the shop office tent. Chaplain Dillon came all the way from Ravenna just to make sure his flock hasn't gone astray." Several soldiers in the formation couldn't help but let out a small burst of laughter.

The First Sergeant continued.

"Tomorrow after church services will be a full workday, so get ready for it. No more tactical training. It's all mission work from now on."

Tisher looked over to Marshall, who was standing off to the side of the formation.

"Sir, you have anything?"

"No Top, carry on," replied Marshall.

Tisher got his cue from the commander.

"Company! Ten-hut! Fall out!" he yelled.

The soldiers snapped to attention and did an about-face movement, then roared "683rd!" as they left to eat their evening meal, which smelled great even from the assembly area.

No one came up to First Sergeant Tisher after formation regarding the incident at the Enlisted Men's Club. As he walked over to Marshall, he saw Lieutenant Kiley's ¼-ton pull into the area.

"Sir, before Lieutenant Kiley has your ear, the incident at the Enlisted Men's Club is something I'm sure you'd like to hear," Tisher said, stopping Marshall. "Apparently, a couple of our female soldiers were getting harassed by several of the active duty soldiers. One of the active duty guys got a little too friendly and our gal decked him flat on his can."

"Don't tell me. Let me guess. Specialist Williams?" said Marshall.

"Right on target, Sir," replied Tisher. "She not only flattened him, the guy had to be carried out by several of his buddies. The MPs were called in because of the fighting in the club. Williams had several witnesses that saw the whole thing. She was within her rights and defended herself."

"Damn good soldier, that Williams," replied Marshall. "Did you have a chance to talk to her yet, Top?"

"Not yet, Sir. I was going to do that after chow," replied Tisher.

Lieutenant Kiley reported to Marshall.

"Sir, you wanted to talk to me about the training at Boatwright?" she asked.

"Sure do, Kathy," Marshall said, welcoming her back to the field site. "I'd like to discuss how well your people are being employed at Boatwright and if they are receiving meaningful training."

After several minutes of discussion, it was becoming evident that the 683rd personnel were working out so well, several civilian technicians at the Boatwright facility were putting in for vacation because their workload was taken care of by the soldiers of the 683rd.

"Well Kathy, it looks like things are going very well at Boatwright," commented Marshall.

"Sir, I've been told that the facility director may just put us in for a commendation," replied Kiley.

"That's very impressive. Keep up the excellent work."

"Now what's on the agenda for next week?" asked Marshall.

"We've got some more track and turret work scheduled, and there is some work that we can employ our recovery section at Boatwright for at least a couple days," Kiley replied.

Marshall looked at Farley, who was in the tent.

"Chief, how many personnel can we spare from the recovery section next week?" Marshall asked. "Lieutenant Kiley has some mission work for them at Boatwright."

Chief Farley pondered the request for several seconds.

"Sir, we can spare half of 'em over there during the day," Farley replied. "We'll need some of 'em here to handle wrecker operations, but if we really are in a bind, we can pull 'em out of Boatwright and put 'em to work out here."

"Sounds good to me," Marshall said. "How about you, Kathy?"

"Sounds great, Sir," replied Kiley.

Marshall smiled.

"You and Fred spend some time together today?" he asked.

Lieutenant Kiley grinned.

"Yes, Sir. We went shopping and then Fred took me to lunch, and then a matinee at the Post theater. I haven't had a decent meal at that mess hall we're eating at on post."

Marshall had heard of all the complaints from the soldiers and NCOs about the blandness of the food they were receiving.

"Why don't you have Fred take you to dinner out this evening at Sergeant Ralph's Taj Mahal of Mount Eden?" Marshall asked.

"That's exactly what I had in mind, Sir," Lieutenant Kiley said as she excused herself to find her husband.

Lieutenant Humphrey was sneaking about the 683rd perimeter, not wanting to be seen. His goal was to try and catch the 683rd doing something wrong, anything wrong. Behind the mess section, he was moving closer to have a look at how the rations were being stored, and thought he might be able to grab some oranges that were sitting on top of a large ice chest.

As he crept closer, one of the cooks came into view. Humphrey jumped into a large depression in the ground behind him that was freshly dug. As he squatted down not to be seen, he noticed his boots were sinking into mud. He realized by the smell he had just jumped into a freshly dug grease pit that the cooks had dumped the old vegetable oil in.

After waiting nearly five minutes crouched down in the grease pit, Humphrey finally emerged and found his boots and trousers were covered in muddy grease. His clean uniform and shinny boots were a mess and stunk of old cooking oil as he slowly crept back to his jeep that was parked a half-mile down the road.

Back at the tech supply area, Chief McCarthy was sitting in a patch of grass, relaxing and eating his dinner.

Sergeant Schmoot had found him and went over to speak with him.

"Hey Chief, how you feelin' nowadays?" Schmoot asked.

"A hell of a lot better than I did the past couple of days," replied McCarthy. "You know, Dennis, I think I've lost at least 10 pounds since we've been here."

"How's that, Chief?" asked Schmoot.

"Well, there's nothing to snack on," McCarthy replied. "That dysentery cleaned me out for a couple of days, and I'm not eating more than one serving at the chow line."

Schmoot smiled.

"You're definitely lookin' better today than you did for the past two days. But I wouldn't be sittin' in this grass too long, Chief. Those chiggers are pretty thick out here."

Chief McCarthy smiled.

"They don't bother me," he replied. "Besides, they sprayed out here. That should have killed them all off."

A.T. - DAY 8 (SUNDAY)

"Formation!"

Lemasters' yell roused the soldiers just like a rooster's crow wakes up all the people on a farm.

The 683rd soldiers slowly meandered to the assembly area as the morning sun was beginning to heat up the open ground. After all were assembled and called to the position of attention, First Sergeant Tisher received the headcount from the platoon sergeants and then gave the assembled mass of 683rd soldiers the day's agenda.

"Church services will be held inside the shop office tent right after formation. Those who do not attend will immediately report to your sections for mission work. Any questions?"

No one raised a hand or a voice.

"Company, ten-hut! Fall out!" Tisher shouted.

Eighty soldiers began to migrate toward the shop office tent for church service. Waiting inside was Chaplain Dillon, ready to receive his flock.

"Please come in. Let's begin to fill in the front rows first," said Chaplain Dillon. "Don't be shy. I'm not going to make you do any push-ups." He smiled and was pleased to see the tent filling up with soldiers.

"If you look on your chairs, I've placed a sheet of paper that has the words to the hymns we're going to sing," the chaplain said. "If you don't have a copy, please share with someone who does."

The crowd inside the tent was standing in the aisles since there were not enough chairs to go around. The heat inside the tent was beginning to build and several of the soldiers took it upon themselves to roll up the flaps and tent sides to allow the outdoor breezes to cool off the interior.

"OK everyone! Let us begin with prayer," said the chaplain as everyone inside the tent removed their hats and bowed their heads.

After the prayer was over, Chaplain Dillon continued the service.

"Let us raise our voices to the Lord and sing the hymn Closer to Thee, which is listed as the first hymn on your sheet."

He blew into a pitch pipe to give everyone the proper note to start off with and began to lead the singing. Without an instrumental accompaniment, everyone sang in their own key, and together it sounded horrible. The majority of the soldiers were unfamiliar with the hymn, and the others couldn't agree on what key the chaplain wanted the hymn to be sung in.

"Well, at least it sounded sweet in God's ears," Chaplain Dillon remarked after everyone was finished singing the hymn. Everyone in the tent began to laugh out loud and at themselves.

Undeterred, Dillon pressed on with more music.

"Let's try one that everyone here should know. Hymn number three, How Great Thou Art."

Again, the soldiers couldn't agree on the key and proceeded to harmonically butcher the hymn. Most of the soldiers couldn't help but laugh while they were singing, including Marshall and the chaplain.

"Thank you, everyone. That was enlightening," Dillon said after they finished singing. "I promise not to make you sing any more during the service." Everyone in the tent let out a roar of laughter. Chaplain Dillon felt their joy. These soldiers are great, he thought to himself as he began to conduct his sermon.

After 30 minutes of his morning message and words of encouragement, Chaplain Dillon concluded his service with a heartfelt prayer for all the soldiers in the field and the military. All that attended his service felt uplifted and glad.

Chaplain Dillon met with Marshall after the soldiers had left.

"Well, Dave, how's it going out here in God's country?" asked the chaplain.

"Not bad, Chaplain," Marshall replied. "We've been able to conduct some excellent training and the soldiers seem to be enjoying the experience. So far, we haven't had any unfortunate incidents. The only problems we've encountered have been the insect variety."

Chaplain Dillon smiled.

"I've heard about the chigger infestation you've got out here. Has that been taken care of?" he asked.

"Yes and no," replied Marshall. "The post engineers came out to the field site yesterday with their truck-mounted insect fogger. Right after they finished, the sky opened up and rained, washing all the insect spray away. Most of the soldiers are using pet flea and tick collars like the ones I'm wearing in my boot laces."

Chaplain Dillon looked at Marshall's boots in amazement.

"Do they work?" Dillon asked.

"Sure do. I haven't been bitten yet," replied Marshall.

The chaplain began scratching his right leg as he looked at Marshall's flea collars, and had a sickening feeling that he was a fresh meal for the local chiggers on Mount Eden. He raised his pant leg and saw a small red welt forming.

"Chaplain, I think you'll need some of this." Marshall pulled a small bottle of Army insect repellent from his pocket and gave it to the chaplain.

"Oh joy," remarked the chaplain.

"They're pretty hideous," remarked Marshall.

"Yes indeed," replied the chaplain.

The two continued their conversation about how the soldiers were doing in the field, and if there was anything that the chaplain could do for him or his soldiers.

"Just keep us in your prayers, Chaplain. That's all I can ask," asked Marshall.

"Absolutely," replied Chaplain Dillon as he winked an eye. "I'll be leaving today, and I'll let Colonel Finder know things are going well for you and the 683rd. I think everyone who attended the service this morning really enjoyed it."

"Thanks, Chaplain. I appreciate you coming all this way to hold worship services for the soldiers," said Marshall.

Both men shook hands as Marshall wished him a safe and pleasant journey. Chaplain Dillon left to visit Colonel Biggs and convey Lieutenant Colonel Finder's greetings.

Marshall knew the coming week would hold some big challenges for the 683rd to tackle head-on.

Meeting with Chief Farley was next on Marshall's agenda for the morning. Chief Farley had been completely absorbed in the logistical requirements of obtaining some special repair parts needed to fix several of the engineers' 5-ton dump trucks. The 683rd tech supply had come through with most of the required parts. Those parts tech supply did not have were referred to as high-dollar items, which included engines, transmissions, and axles. The purchase of high-dollar items had to be approved by higher headquarters, which slowed down the turn-around time for repairs to be made.

If the 683rd was lucky, the high-dollar items could be located and obtained on Fort Knox Main Post after funding was approved and released. Otherwise, the engineer reservists would have to leave most of their 5-ton dump trucks behind at Fort Knox for repair. The logistical nightmare of bureaucratic red tape and paperwork to get the engineer unit's equipment back—a situation no one wanted to come about—would ensue.

Marshall walked over to Chief Farley's desk and saw that he was in deep thought with a troubled look on his face.

"Chief, looks like you should've attended worship services this morning," said Marshall.

"You're right, Sir," Farley said. "I'm gonna need God's help to get these pieces of equipment repaired and back to the engineers."

"Fill me in, Chief," asked Marshall as he sat down in a chair next to Farley's desk.

"Well Sir, we've got two trucks that need new transmissions. One has a blown engine, and four have burned out clutches," replied Farley.

"Whoa," remarked Marshall. He knew from experience that engines and transmissions were big-ticket items, and not the kind of parts carried by tech supply. "Did you make contact with Reserve Affairs yet?" asked Marshall.

"Yes, Sir. I let them know what we needed," Farley said. "They'll get back to me tomorrow on the funding and availability of the engine and transmissions."

"Knox has a cannibalization point, doesn't it?" asked Marshall.

"Sir, I believe it does, but I wouldn't put much hope that they've got what we need," replied Farley.

"Well Chief, you've gotta have a little faith, if you know what I mean," replied Marshall.

Farley smiled at his commander. He liked his positive attitude about looking at problems and coming up with some possible solutions.

"Sir, if we get all the parts we need from Reserve Affairs and the cannibalization point, I'm buying you a steak dinner when we get back," replied Farley.

"Chief, I like my steak medium-rare," replied Marshall as he grinned at his shop officer. "I've got confidence the 683rd will get these vehicles fixed and back on the road before the end of A.T.," he said with a nod and a wink.

Chief Warrant Officer Farley looked at Marshall. This commander will do everything humanly possible to make things happen, he thought to himself.

Every large Army post had a cannibalization point that housed a collection of military vehicles and equipment deemed uneconomically repairable. Uneconomically repairable meant repairs would be more costly than the equipment was worth. The worth of the equipment was calculated by the amount of usage and life expectancy left. Every piece of equipment would be retired when the life expectancy limit has been reached.

The cannibalization point, or bone yard as it is commonly referred to, was a storage place located within a large fenced-in area where certain pieces of equipment still in the Army's inventory were sent. Those pieces of equipment were then stripped of parts by the Army unit mechanics needing hard-to-obtain or expensive repair parts. The bone yard became part of the Army's logistical supply system and had to operate within the existing parameters and guidelines.

As Marshall left the shop office tent, First Sergeant Tisher came up to him.

"Sir, I checked into that fight at the Enlisted Club," he said. "Williams told me what happened. She was defending herself like any good soldier would."

"Good to hear, Top," said Marshall. "Let her know nothing more is going to come of it. If it does, I'll handle it."

"One more thing, Top. You and the troops are in for a special treat during lunch."

"What's that gonna be, Sir?" asked Tisher.

"You'll see when you get to the serving line," replied Marshall.

It was approximately 1130 hours, and the noon meal was going to be served at 1200 hours sharp. Marshall began rounding up all his lieutenants. As they all were gathered up and encircled Marshall, he spoke to them.

"OK, everyone. It's time we all served our soldiers on the chow line." He saw some puzzled faces looking at him as he made the announcement.

"Ladies and gentlemen, we are going to serve chow to our soldiers, so let's all get down to the field mess and let Sergeant Emery know he's got us for an hour," Marshall said.

The group of 683rd officers all walked in unison to Sergeant Emery's mess area.

"Well hello, Sir. To what do I owe the pleasure of this distinguished group?" asked Sergeant Emery.

"Sarge, we're here to serve the noon meal," Marshall replied. "Go ahead and let the servers know we'll take care of the noon meal today. They'll still have to do the evening meal."

Emery looked at the commander with a puzzled look in his eyes.

"You sure you wanna do this, Sir?" he asked.

"Oh yeah," replied Marshall. "These soldiers need to know how much we appreciate them and the superb job they're doing out in the field."

"Well y'all roll up your sleeves, and let's get this serving line ready," Emery replied, grinning at Marshall's willingness to volunteer his services.

He dismissed the KPs and told them to come back after chow. This was the first time in Emery's military career that unit officers were going to help serve the meal to the soldiers in the field.

"Man, I wish your Captain Marshall was my commander," Sergeant Emery said to Sergeant Adkins. "He's really got his act together."

The soldiers of the 683rd began to filter in for noonday chow. All were pleasantly surprised to see their officers serving them from behind the serving line. Each lieutenant was smiling as the soldiers filed past and held out their mess kits for a serving.

"Hey L.T., what did you do to wind up on K.P.?" asked Sergeant Nugot as he passed through the serving line and held out his plate for a cheeseburger.

"I'm a volunteer, just like you," replied Lieutenant Burks with a smile as she continued serving the soldiers as they filed by her serving station.

Everyone was happy to see the 683rd Officer Corps, including Marshall, serve up lunch for the soldiers. Several asked if it was going to be a permanent change.

"Only on special occasions, like today," Marshall quickly replied.

As the chow line ended, the 683rd officers took their turn being served, this time by Marshall. Marshall was glad to see his officers enjoyed their brief KP duty and showed the soldiers that they would share duties, no matter how pleasant or unpleasant they were.

After all were served, Marshall walked over to Sergeant Emery.

"Sarge, I just want to tell you how glad we are to have you with us at Mount Eden. You've been a real lifesaver and a true morale booster. Thanks from all of us in the 683rd."

"Shucks, Sir. You don't have to thank me. The smiling faces on those soldiers is all the thanks I need," replied Emery. "Your soldiers are some of the finest I've seen in quite a long time. It's just an honor and a blessing to be out here in God's backyard."

Marshall grinned as he heard those words from Sergeant Emery. He knew Emery truly loved what he did in the Army Reserve.

It was time for Marshall to have lunch with Sergeant Emery and discuss some of the more mundane things like the "over & under report" that required each mess section to balance of the food budget and what was left to spend for the next week. If Sergeant Emery had spent too much on food per person, he would have to make it up by serving some lower costing rations, like pasta and potatoes. Marshall and Emery felt that was something they had to try and avoid, if possible.

"Sarge, what's the noon meal going to be tomorrow?" asked Marshall.

"Sir, I've got 200 rib eye steaks for tomorrow's noon meal," he replied.

"Please don't let that get out or we'll have everyone on Mount Eden coming for lunch," said Marshall.

Marshall looked at his watch and excused himself. Time to go over next week's training schedule with Lieutenant Stiles.

Walking back through the field site, Marshall spotted Lieutenant Stiles finishing up her lunch. He knew she was trying to avoid him as much as possible, but she couldn't escape this time.

"Come on, Lieutenant! Time to go over next week's training schedule," Marshall called. "Let's go over my copy at the CP tent."

Stiles slowly acknowledged her commander's orders, got to her feet, and walked with him to the CP tent.

Inside, Sergeant Tea was typing up some paperwork and spotted Marshall as he entered the tent.

"Well good afternoon, Sir," responded Tea as both officers entered the tent. "That meal you served up this afternoon was just one of the more enjoyable ones I've had in the field. I just wanted you to know that."

"Glad you enjoyed it," replied Marshall. "Did you get enough now that you're eating for two?" asked Marshall.

"Well, yes Sir," replied Tea. "You wouldn't want me to get too fat, now would you, Sir? I can hardly move around in all this heat. Does Sergeant Emery have any ice cream? You know Sir, I've just got this craving." Tea laughed as she finished. She truly enjoyed teasing all the soldiers, including her commanding officer.

"Sergeant Tea, if he does, I'll make sure some is brought up to you. If he doesn't, I'll make sure some is brought up to you," replied Marshall as he smiled at his admin NCO.

"Oh, you're so kind, Sir," replied Tea.

Marshall spotted First Sergeant Tisher outside talking to one of the soldiers and called to him.

"Top, our admin NCO needs some ice cream," Marshall said. "If Sergeant Emery doesn't have any, let him know he should get some for tomorrow and have my driver go to that little country store outside the main gate and pick up a pint."

The First Sergeant smiled.

"Hell, Sir, I was going to get some for myself," Tisher laughed.

Marshall nodded his head in agreement and went back into the CP tent.

"OK Sergeant Tea," Marshall said. "Your ice cream is on the way. You can thank Top for the special delivery when it arrives,"

He turned back to Lieutenant Stiles.

"Now back to the training schedule," Marshall said. "Let's look over this puppy and see what needs to be changed or amended."

Both Stiles and Marshall sat down and went over the training schedule for the next week. Many things would need to be changed, and Stiles made notes on her copy while Marshall took a close look at each day's events.

"Sir," said Stiles, "I'll make all these changes over at the shop office tent and hand-carry them to the group headquarters for Major Brown to sign off on them."

"That'll be fine" said Marshall. "Before you take it over, I'd like a copy to review and sign before you give it to him."

"You got it, Sir," replied Stiles.

Stiles excused herself from the CP tent and went up to the shop office to make changes to the training schedule.

Marshall noted that time was quickly going by as he looked at his watch. Tisher entered the tent with two pints of ice cream.

"OK Viv, which one do you want? Rocky road or French vanilla?"

"I'll take both, Top," she replied, trying to maintain a serious expression. Tisher saw through it.

"Rocky road or vanilla?" he asked again.

"Rocky road," she replied. "Did you bring me a spoon?"

Tisher's expression dropped to a frown. He knew there was something missing. Tea started to lecture him about the missing spoon.

Tisher smiled.

"You know, Viv, I thought I left my nag back home. Are you taking lessons from my wife?"

"Now, who you callin' a nag, First Sergeant?" Sergeant Tea asked with wry smile on her face. "Wait until I tell Peg what you just said! You'll be in the dog house for a week."

Both NCOs were enjoying their bantering conversation. It was as though they were keeping in shape for their eventual homecoming.

Marshall thoroughly enjoyed their debate as he pulled out two plastic spoons from the field desk.

"Here you go, kids," Marshall said. "Now, no more fighting and eat your ice cream in peace."

Everyone in the tent laughed as they began to enjoy their cold desert.

Stiles appeared several hours later with a copy of the revised training schedule for Marshall to look over. As he reviewed it, he noticed Stiles had made all the changes they had discussed, and even placed additional training in some of the time slots that were vacant.

"Looks like you've plugged in some classroom training on Thursday afternoon. Hope we have time for it," said Marshall.

"Well Sir, if we don't, it's not going to hurt us. We can always reschedule," replied Stiles.

Marshall gave his approval.

"Okay, looks good to me. Go ahead and walk it through."

Stiles turned with a smile on her face and walked away. She was pleased that Marshall didn't make her redo the training schedule again.

As she was walking up the path toward the group headquarters area, Lieutenant Humphrey was walking down the hill toward Marshall. Marshall looked out the open tent flap and noticed Humphrey walking toward the CP tent wearing his tactical field gear, including his steel pot.

Marshall walked out to greet him.

"Well hello, Lieutenant," Marshall said. "What brings you out into the field on such a lovely Sunday afternoon?"

"It's the only day I've got that I'm not bogged down with paperwork that's piled up on my desk," replied Humphrey.

"Yeah, I know what you mean. It always seems when you work one pile of requirements down, another pile takes its place. It just never seems to end," said Marshall.

"Tell me about it," replied Humphrey with a sad and tired look.

"So, would you like to see what's going on?" asked Marshall.

"That's why I'm here, Captain," replied Humphrey rather dryly.

The two began with the 683rd mess section area and worked their way through the motor pool to the automotive platoon and service section. Everyone was gainfully employed, working on equipment or some fabrication requirements to repair vehicles and equipment.

"Looks like you've got some jobs in shop," Humphrey noted. "Can we take a stroll over to the shop office?"

"Let's go. This way," directed Marshall as the two men walked up the hill to the shop office tent.

Chief Farley was going over the job orders on his field desk when both walked in.

"At ease!" Farley shouted as he spotted both officers walking into the tent.

"Afternoon, Chief," said Marshall. "You remember Lieutenant Humphrey, our evaluator?"

"Sure do, Sir. Welcome to the 683rd shop office. Please have a seat. Would you like some coffee?" asked Chief Farley.

Humphrey said yes, and a cup was quickly brought by one of the 683rd shop office clerks.

"Sir, would you like me to give you both a mini briefing of what's happening with our maintenance mission?" asked Farley.

Marshall grinned visibly and nodded as he watched his professional shop office staff begin to conduct an unscheduled briefing for the evaluator. After 10 minutes of presentations from the NCOs and Chief Farley, Humphrey was impressed with how the maintenance mission was being handled.

"Any questions, gentlemen?" Farley asked after the presentations were over.

"No Chief, I think you've covered everything thoroughly," remarked Humphrey. "Looks like you've got things handled out here."

As Humphrey and Marshall left the shop office tent, both men had sized each other up fairly well during their brief encounters. Humphrey knew that Marshall was a knowledgeable unit commander, but was still holding an inner a grudge about Marshall's reference of him being a rookie. The insult would be repaid, if Humphrey could help it. However, Humphrey also knew Marshall was not easily rattled.

"I'd like to do some unescorted observations, if you don't mind," Humphrey said to Marshall.

"Go right ahead. Let me or my people know if you need anything," replied Marshall as he watched Humphrey walk away.

Over at the recovery section, Sergeant Nugot finally got the skunk to eat from his outstretched hand. The skunk didn't seem to fear Nugot, and readily accepted the tasty handouts that Nugot was glad to give. Before long, Nugot was petting the skunk, who seemed to enjoy this human's attention and soothing words.

"You're my little buddy, aren't you?" whispered Sergeant Nugot as he got the skunk to lie in his lap and gently stroked the skunk's fur. The young skunk was thoroughly enjoying the newfound friendship and slowly closed his eyes and began to nap. Nugot had a new pet that was hoping he could take home from the field. The only trouble would be to convince his wife to keep it.

"Yes, Sir! You're gonna be our new mascot. You're gonna be called Stinker from now on," whispered Nugot. He didn't want to alarm his new pet and realized a trip to the vet would be in order when he brought Stinker back home.

Sergeant First Class Baxter walked by and saw Nugot with a skunk in his lap. Being a farmer in his civilian occupation, Joe Baxter had some fairly bad experiences with skunks and decided not to cause any undue alarm that might cause the skunk to defend himself. He motioned to Nugot he wanted to see him, without the skunk.

Nugot gently picked up the skunk from his lap, rubbed the skunk's head, and placed him on the ground.

"There you go, little buddy," Nugot cooed. "I'll see you later."

The skunk looked at Nugot for several seconds, saw the other soldiers standing nearby and decided it was time to leave.

As the skunk rambled off into the deep woods, Baxter got in front of Nugot.

"What the hell is wrong with you?" Baxter asked. "Besides stinking up the whole place, that critter could be rabid. Did ya ever give much thought to that, Nugot?"

Nugot grinned at his section sergeant. He knew Stinker was not going to be a problem, other than the obvious problem of being a skunk.

"Sarge, that's our new mascot," Nugot said. "Don't worry. He's not gonna stink up the place. I'm thinking of taking him home with me."

"You're gonna what?" exclaimed Baxter.

"I'm gonna make him my pet," replied Nugot.

"Listen Nugot, that's contrary to Army regulations," Baxter said, thinking quickly. "You find me something in the Army regs says that it's okay to keep wild animals as pets and I'll let you keep 'em. If you can't, you ain't gonna make that skunk into a pet. Hear me?"

"Yeah Sarge, I hear ya," replied Nugot. Nugot knew that Stinker was going back home with him no matter what Baxter said.

A short while after Baxter left, Stinker's curiosity and hunger brought him back to Nugot, who was working on his wrecker. Stinker spotted Nugot while he was standing on the front bumper checking the engine oil level.

"Hey li'l buddy! How you doin'?" asked Nugot as he slowly climbed down. He didn't want to make any sudden moves that could startle the skunk.

Nugot wiped his hands with the rag he had in his back pocket and reached into his shirt for a cracker he had saved.

"Want some more?" Nugot extended his hand toward the skunk and held the cracker as he kneeled down to show his new offering.

Suddenly, Lieutenant Humphrey walked into the area and came upon Nugot and the skunk. "

What the hell you got there, Sergeant?" asked Humphrey in a loud voice.

"Sir, I wouldn't move too suddenly or shout," Nugot said, standing up and saluting Humphrey. "This little guy might think you're after him."

"Shoo! Shoo!" yelled Humphrey as he stomped his foot, trying to scare the little creature.

The skunk turned, aimed and fired. Lieutenant Humphrey was hit directly by the little skunk, who immediately scampered into the thicket of brush behind the 5-ton wrecker.

The stench was everywhere and Humphrey became overwhelmed with nausea as he walked away from the area trying to get a breath of fresh air. Nugot went inside his tent, brought out a can of deodorizer he had bought at the PX, and began to immediately spray the area. Luckily, the wind blew most of the stench into the woods. The residual skunk smell was soon eliminated with Nugot's can of deodorizer spray.

Humphrey climbed into his ¼-ton jeep, started the engine and quickly left the area. His first thoughts were to get into a shower as soon as possible. He realized his field gear was soaked with the odor, which would not come out for a very long time.

At the CP tent, Marshall was looking over some of the reports that Sergeant Tea had prepared for the coming week. He had to sign each one as Tea finished another and handed it to him.

"You know, Sergeant Tea, my pen is going to be out of ink pretty soon," remarked Marshall.

"Don't you worry none, Sir. I've gotta whole box of 'em right here in my desk. You got spoons, I got pens," Tea remarked with a slight giggle in her voice.

Marshall smiled and continued his proofreading of the letters and correspondence as Lieutenant Stiles entered the CP tent.

"Sir, I just heard from Major Brown that General Markel will be in the area tomorrow," Stiles said.

"Thanks for the heads up, Lieutenant," replied Marshall.

He knew that Major General Markel was a decent man and a well-respected commanding general of the 83rd Army Reserve Command. His command philosophy was to let his commanders do their jobs and help them out when required.

"Have you ever met General Markel?" asked Captain Marshall.

"No Sir, I haven't," replied Stiles.

"Well, you're in luck," remarked Marshall. "General Markel is one of the most decent generals you'll ever have the pleasure of meeting. He's not one of those who tries to intimidate soldiers or throw his weight around and growl at everyone. He's a down-to-earth individual who was an enlisted man before he became an officer."

"I didn't know that," said Stiles.

She would get to meet the general the following day and get to know him firsthand.

She suddenly remembered to give Marshall his approved copy of the training schedule.

"Here, Sir. I almost forgot," she said, handing him the training schedule. "Major Brown looked it over and signed off on it. Looked good to him."

"Thanks Lieutenant," Marshall said. "Good job. Keep it up."

Stiles thanked Marshall and excused herself from the CP tent. Marshall looked at this watch and realized it was 1730 hours.

"Sergeant Tea, it's time for chow."

"That's great news, Sir!" Tea replied. "Me and baby are starving. Could you do me a favor and give me a hand gettin' up, Sir? My feet and ankles are startin' to swell in all this heat."

"Not a problem, Sergeant Tea. My wife had the same thing happen to her when she was pregnant."

Marshall gave Tea a hand getting to her feet and made sure she was all right before she walked down to the mess area. Marshall put the word out that Sergeant Tea did not have to wait in line, and could walk right up to the headcount and get served immediately. She appreciated the extra courtesy.

Tea was enjoying her time away from home. However, she did miss her daily dose of television soap operas.

At the chow line, Marshall spotted Tisher and called him over.

"Top, we've got General Markel coming over for a visit tomorrow," Marshall said.

"What time do you think he'll be over?" asked Tisher.

"My guess is he's gonna be coming in around 1100 hours and will visit our area around noon. Better have Sergeant Emery put something good on the lunch menu," replied Marshall.

"No need, Sir," said Tisher. "He's got steak on the menu for the noon meal."

Marshall smiled and shook his head.

"Oh yeah, I forgot about that," Marshall said. "Well, Top, the general's gonna have a hard time believing that we eat like this normally out in the field. Just between you and I, don't tell Sergeant Emery about the general's visit until right before noon chow. I'll invite General Markel to dine with us if he arrives before noon."

Tisher agreed. No need to get everyone worried about the upcoming visit.

"Top, just make sure the sections are busy if he does come in. I don't want him to see many of our soldiers not training," mentioned Marshall.

First Sergeant Tisher nodded his head in agreement.

"Well Top, anything going on personnel-wise?" asked Marshall.

"Nothing that I can't handle, Sir," replied Tisher. "Most of the soldiers seem to be heavily employed with mission work. They had plenty of tactical training during the first week to keep them well occupied. Most seem glad to be out here, which baffles the hell out of me."

"Yeah, me too, Top," added Marshall. "At least they're so busy they don't have time to complain. When they do, they're too tired and settle down in the evening for a good night's sleep."

Tisher agreed, and saw Sergeant Lemasters walking over to them.

"Hello John!" Tisher called out. "What's up, Field First Sergeant?"

"Ya hear that Nugot's gotta pet skunk?" asked Lemasters.

"No John, but that doesn't surprise me," replied Tisher. "You know what they say about birds of a feather."

Both Marshall and Lemasters laughed at the reference made.

"I had a pet skunk when I was a young 'un back in the hills," Lemasters said "My momma said if'n I got sprayed, I'd have ta stay in the barn until the stank wore off. That skunk never sprayed me, but got the dog a couple of times. Shoot, that ole hound dog became good friends with that skunk after a while." Lemasters story captured the attention of both Marshall and Tisher.

"What happened to the skunk, John?" asked Tisher.

"It up and ran off with another skunk one day," replied Lemasters. "Jest 'bout broke my heart, too. Seems like it enjoyed my company, but it had to go back to the wild sooner or later. I'd see it now and again when I was workin' out in the garden or fixin' thangs in the barn. It would just wander in with a friend or two and look for a handout. After a while, I never seen it again."

As Lemasters finished his story, Nugot was spotted in the chow line. Tisher walked over to him and asked him about his new friend. Both were grinning and laughing during their conversation.

Tisher returned to Marshall and Lemasters .

"He's hoping to make the skunk his pet and bring it back to his wife," Tisher said. "I asked him, 'What about the smell in the apartment?' He said; Let the skunk get used to it like I did."

Both Lemasters and Marshall were laughing so hard they almost lost their balance. The soldiers in the chow line looked at their commander and first sergeant and chuckled to themselves. They all were glad to see the bosses were openly having a good laugh.

Tisher's face grew a bit serious.

"He also told me the skunk just sprayed our evaluator, Lieutenant Humphrey."

Marshall had to sit down. He was laughing so hard he could hardly stand up. Just seeing the image of Humphrey getting sprayed and the first sergeant's serious demeanor was too much for Marshall to try and maintain his military bearing. As much as he tried to maintain his composure, Marshall was wiping the tears from his face while his shoulders were shrugging from the laughter he was trying to hold inside, but to no avail.

When the soldiers had overheard what had happened with Lieutenant Humphrey and the skunk, they also began to laugh openly.

After the laughter had subsided, and Marshall finally was able to talk without laughing when he spoke, he remembered an unrelated question.

"Top, did your wife call my wife?"

Tisher got an embarrassed look on his face.

"Sorry, Sir. I forgot."

"No problem, Top. I'll give her a call when I go onto main post tomorrow," replied Marshall. He thought to himself that he'd better remember or there wouldn't be much of a homecoming when he got back.

The evening came quickly upon Mount Eden Base Camp. The sound of the generators and the occasional banging of metal on metal was heard within the company area as equipment was being repaired. After 2100 hours, Marshall put the word out that everyone should get some rest and start to work after morning formation.

Marshall decided to check in with his shop officer and see what was facing them in regards to the 683rd's maintenance support mission. As he walked over to see Chief Farley, Marshall couldn't help but notice that the evening sky was cloudless. Looks like we're in for another beautiful evening, he thought as he entered the shop office tent.

Chief Farley was reviewing some Fort Knox Regulations when Marshall appeared through the tent flaps.

"Evenin' Sir," Farley said. "Care for a cup of coffee?"

Marshall smiled and nodded in the affirmative as he walked over to the coffee maker, grabbed an empty mug, and helped himself. Chief Farley had already looked over the jobs that were scheduled on the 683rd production control board and came up with a plan of attack for the following day.

"Sir, if we can't get the parts to repair all the 5-ton dump trucks, one needs to be sacrificed as the hangar queen so we can strip parts off it to fix the other two."

Marshall sat down with his cup of coffee, had a few sips and pondered the idea for a moment without making a snap decision.

The Army had always frowned upon controlled substitution, or cannibalization of a piece of equipment. Normally that was a decision made by higher headquarters; it was not within the realm of choice for a maintenance company. Only in times of war—or clearance from higher headquarters—could that ever be suggested, much less done.

"Chief, you know as well as I we'll never get permission to do that. You don't want to risk your career, much less mine," Marshall said. "We'll find out what Reserve Affairs can do for us. Remember, Knox does have a cannibalization point. Let's see how many hard-to-get parts you'll need before you make an official visit."

The stars were bright against the moonless night sky as Marshall gazed up at the vast expanse and saw the Milky Way. The starlight was bright enough that a flashlight wasn't needed. It was one of those moments to savor and enjoy. Feeling a bit small and insignificant when he looked out to a tiny portion of the universe, Marshall began to hum a song as he made his way to his CP tent.

Time to put the day behind him. Tomorrow would be another challenging day.

A.T. - DAY 9 (MONDAY)

"Captain Marshall, I'd like you to accompany me to meet General Markel," remarked Colonel Biggs as he ate his breakfast at the officers' dining table under the trees by the far end of the mess section area.

"Yes, Sir. Be glad to," Marshall replied. "Will the general be dining with us in the field?"

"Possibly," replied Biggs. "The general will be in the Mount Eden area for the afternoon, then departing around 1500 hours."

Marshall looked at Biggs.

"I'll inform my personnel," Marshall said. "Please excuse me."

Marshall left Biggs so he could let Sergeant Emery know the possibility of a VIP having lunch with the 683rd.

"Steak still on the menu, Sarge?" asked Marshall.

Emery winked his eye at the commander.

"What kind of gravy you think the general would like?" Emery asked.

Marshall smiled.

"Anything that you make, Sarge," he replied. "Just don't forget the steak sauce."

Marshall walked over to First Sergeant Tisher, who was keeping an eye on the soldiers.

"Top, get a hold of Lieutenant Rodriguez and let him know we've got General Markel coming into our area," Marshall said. "When he gets here, I want each lieutenant to give the general a briefing on his or her area of responsibility. Make sure Rod briefs the general on the unit layout, and Stiles briefs on the training that's been conducted. Have Chief Farley give General Markel a rundown on what's in the shops and what we expect for the rest of the week."

"No problem Sir," replied Tisher. "I'll toss in a few other briefing topics if the need arises."

"Sounds good, Top," replied Marshall. "I leave it in your good hands."

Marshall finished eating a quick breakfast since Biggs was waiting for him by the 683rd shop office tent.

"Captain Marshall, are your people prepared to brief the general?" asked Biggs.

"Yes, Sir. I believe they are," Marshall replied. "The first sergeant will put the word out to prepare a briefing for the general by noon. They should be ready by then, Sir."

"Excellent," replied Biggs. "Well, Commander, let's go. You can ride in the back of my jeep."

"Yes, Sir," said Marshall as he quickly jumped into the back of Biggs' ¼-ton.

As they were pulling out of the 683rd area, the driver asked Biggs which direction they should travel to get to the airfield.

"Let's hope the floating bridge is still in operation," Biggs said. "I'd hate to have to bring the general out here by way of the pig farm."

The driver took a right turn onto the dirt road that led to the floating bridge. Their luck was good—they found the floating bridge in operation and no one was being ferried across as they arrived.

"Looks like a good omen, Colonel," said Marshall.

"Let's hope it holds for the rest of the day," replied Biggs as they exited the jeep and the driver pulled the ¼-ton onto the pontoons of the floating bridge. The floating bridge operators showed their military courtesy and saluted the officers as they ferried the ¼-ton jeeps across the river.

Once on the other side, the small convoy headed toward the Army airfield to meet General Markel's plane. As they pulled into the airfield, Marshall noticed a twin-engine Beechcraft with the 83rd Division patch on the tail. The general was early.

"Sir," said Marshall, "I believe the general is already here," as he pointed to the tail of the aircraft parked on the airstrip.

Biggs had an anxious look on his face as the group quickly walked into the airfield terminal. Standing in the middle of the small terminal was Major General Claude Markel, smiling as the group from Mount Eden Base Camp approached. Biggs was the first to salute and report to the general, who grinned and asked how things were going out in the woods of Mount Eden. Colonel Biggs told him all was fine and introduced Marshall.

Before Marshall could salute, General Markel grabbed the captain's hand and shook it vigorously.

"Captain Marshall, I've heard some good things about you," Markel said. "Glad to finally meet you."

"Thank you, General. Glad to finally meet you as well, Sir," replied Marshall.

Markel looked around the terminal and at his watch.

"It's after 1030 hours and the bar is open," Markel said. "How about a drink?"

Marshall smiled at the general.

"Yes, Sir. Who's buying?" Marshall asked.

Biggs was shocked and speechless, while Markel laughed.

"I'll buy the first round, Captain," Markel said. "I can see we're going to get along just fine."

The group walked over to the luncheon area and sat down to order some drinks before heading to the field site.

Biggs was relieved to see Markel was in a good mood and not offended by Marshall's remark. Markel was very interested in Marshall and what the 683rd was doing. The staff officers that accompanied the general silently listened to the conversation as the commanders were having their chat.

After the drinks were finished, they all left the terminal and got into the ¼-ton jeeps. The drivers were patiently awaiting their orders.

"Okay driver, let's head to Mount Eden by way of the floating bridge," commanded Biggs. The general sat in the front seat of the second jeep, which now had a red placard with two white stars on it, signifying that this was the ¼-ton jeep of a major general. Marshall rode in the back of the general's jeep along with the general's aide de camp.

The general's jeep was the lead vehicle as they went back to Mount Eden. Marshall was the tour guide as the general was asking questions along the way. After they crossed the river using the floating bridge, Marshall told the general about the other route that went past the pig farm.

The general laughed out loud.

"Captain, you're making me homesick," Markel said. "I was born and raised on a pig farm. Matter of fact, I teach several courses at Ohio State on livestock husbandry."

Marshall grinned at the general.

"Sir, I'll have the driver take you the other way around on your return trip if you like," he said.

"No Captain, that won't be necessary," Markel laughed.

The jeeps finally reached the field site of the 683rd and parked in the shop office area. Several of the 683rd officers were waiting to greet the general as he arrived.

After the introductions were finished, General Markel had a question.

"Your mess section serving chow?" Markel asked.

"Yes, Sir," Lieutenant Rodriguez piped in. "Chow will be served in 5 minutes, and we've got enough for you and your party, Sir."

"Good," remarked Markel. "I understand you've got Sergeant Emery out here in the field."

Marshall was surprised to hear that the general knew of Sergeant Emery.

"Yes, Sir, but he hasn't made anything too special for lunch," Marshall said.

Markel and his party briskly walked down to the mess section and met with Emery.

"Sergeant Emery, good to see you again!" exclaimed the general.

"Good to see you again, General Markel," replied Emery. "Had I known you were comin', I'd have prepared something a little more special."

"What ya got on the menu, good Sergeant?" asked Markel.

The servers pulled the foil off the serving trays to expose the noon meal to the general and his staff. Steaks, baked potatoes, green beans, corn on the cob, corn bread, tossed garden salad, fresh fruit salad and assorted pies for desert.

"Sarge, did you serve this up special for me?" asked Markel.

"Oh no, Sir," replied Emery. "I'd had this on the menu since last week. I kinda' figured that we'd be cutting back on rations after Monday, so we might as well splurge early and serve the spaghetti later in the week."

Markel was very pleased to see how well Emery had been planning and preparing the meals for the soldiers.

"How many did ya plan to feed today?" asked Markel.

Emery looked back at the general.

"With y'all eatin, that'll make 255 for the noon meal. We're feedin' the MPs and the group HQ too."

Markel grinned as he held out his plate and was served by the soldiers in the serving line.

"Colonel, looks like you've got things handled well out here," Markel said to Biggs. "Didn't you bring a mess section?"

Biggs was a bit flustered at the general's question.

"Well, yes we did, General, but two of the cooks are on bed rest," Biggs replied.

Markel smiled.

"What a stroke of luck for you," he said to Biggs.

"Indeed, Sir," replied Biggs. "The good commander here felt it was his duty to keep his group headquarters well-fed while our cooks recuperated."

General Markel and his staff waited for the 683rd soldiers to go through the chow line, while he and Biggs talked over the status of the other units in the field at Mount Eden. The officers' dining table was all prepared and set with linen tablecloth and linen napkins. The officer's mess kit, complete with stainless steel flatware and plates, was finally being utilized instead of the standard paper plate, and plastic forks and knives.

Sitting down at the table, the officers noticed that the table was at an angle from the slope of the hill it sat on. As some placed their plates on the table, they found themselves grabbing after their baked potatoes as they began to roll off their plates. Some were not fast enough and a few baked potatoes rolled onto the ground. The mess servers saw what was happening and brought over some baked potatoes that were already halved to prevent them from rolling. Marshall was amused to see more than one of the VIPs chasing after their moving vegetables.

"So Captain Marshall," announced Markel," have you given much thought to where your next annual training location should be?"

Marshall was quick to answer. He had thought long and hard about what the next phase of annual training should be for the 683rd.

"Sir, the 683rd has some hard-to-train specialties which we can't train on in the field," Marshall replied. "I've got some fire control instrument personnel that are vital to our wartime mission, as well as some track and turret mechanics that need to be instructed on the newest equipment the Army has recently fielded. We can't get that kind of training unless we attend formalized instruction at Aberdeen Proving Grounds."

"What about the rest of your people?" asked Markel.

"General, we could have a split A.T.," Marshall replied. "Those who don't need to attend training at Aberdeen could attend A.T. wherever the Army needs us."

The general looked over at one of the members of his staff and said.

"You got that, Steve?" Markel asked.

"Yes, Sir. Duly noted," his aide de camp replied. "I don't think that will be a problem. The company commander will have to prepare a special A.T. request when the unit returns to home station. We can process the request with your endorsement through channels and make it a reality for next training year."

The general smiled at Marshall.

"Captain, you've got your wish," he said. "Just do as Steve says and we'll take care of it for you."

Marshall smiled at the general.

"Thank you, Sir," he said. "I'll make sure the request is typed up and on your desk before our next drill date."

As they continued to enjoy their noon feast, the 683rd officers had excused themselves from the table and went up to the shop office tent to finalize their briefings for the general.

"General," said Biggs, "I hope you've enjoyed your meal with the 683rd folks. I know you'd like to see their area of operations and look over the other units as well."

The general looked up and smiled at Biggs and Marshall.

"Yes, I would like to see your field layout, Captain Marshall," he said. "Why don't we take a stroll and look it over?"

Marshall got up from the table and led the way. The general was impressed to see every maintenance section busily at work. He would stop and ask a few questions of the soldiers and NCOs. The answers he received were impressive. All the soldiers were getting meaningful training and enjoying their A.T. experience at Mount Eden Base Camp, despite the summer heat and insects.

"General, we've got a briefing prepared at the shop office tent for you," said Marshall as he led the way to the shop office.

"That won't be necessary commander. I can see you've got everything well squared away. It's time I bother some of the other units out here. You take care and keep up the good work." The general shook Marshall's hand and left with Biggs and his entourage in tow.

Marshall walked into the shop office tent and looked at the scared faces of his lieutenants.

"You're in luck," Marshall said with a small grin on his face. "The general's time is limited and your briefings have been postponed. However, I'd like to hear what you've got to say.

"Rod, you're up. Give me your briefing. The rest of you, have a seat until it's your turn. I will correct you if you make mistakes in presentation. OK, first batter."

Lieutenant Rodriguez began his briefing by diving right into the subject.

"Whoa, Rod," remarked Marshall. "The first thing you've got to do is introduce yourself and your subject to the VIP in front of you. You then give a brief synopsis or outline of your subject that you're going to cover. Then ask if there is anything in particular the VIP may not want to hear or skip over. Got it?"

Lieutenant Rodriguez nodded his head in agreement.

"OK," said Marshall. "Go ahead and start over. This goes for all of you in the room. Be as professional and as courteous as possible."

Rodriguez began all over again. This time he did as instructed.

At the end of his briefing, he asked, "Sir, do you have any questions on my presentation?"

Marshall smiled.

"No Rod, you did an excellent job," he replied. "OK, next presenter! Front and center, post!"

Everyone in the tent was ready and prepared this time. Rodriguez had led the way for the others to follow. The rest of the briefings were done perfectly. Marshall was very pleased to see his officers learning so quickly.

"OK everyone," said Marshall after the last presentation had finished. "Be prepared if General Markel has a change of heart and wants to be briefed by you. Just hang loose until he departs the area."

An hour later, Biggs entered the shop office tent to see Marshall. Luckily, First Sergeant Tisher spotted Biggs as he walked in and shouted "Ten hut!"

Marshall sprang to his feet and reported to Biggs.

"Sir, hope everything went well with General Markel's visit," Marshall said.

"Yes, he did find a few interesting things with some of the other units, but we won't get into that," Biggs replied without showing any emotion. "He was impressed with your operations, however."

Marshall was keenly interested in what Biggs had to say and gestured to the colonel to have a seat at the front of the briefing area.

"So what are your people doing now?" asked Biggs as he spotted the 683rd junior officers sitting in the chairs.

"Sir, I'm having them give me the briefings they had prepared for the general," replied Marshall. "I thought it best for them to give me their presentation and afterwards I'd critique them. We're just about done. Would you like to have them give you a briefing, Sir?"

"That would be appropriate," said Biggs. "By the way, the general wanted to express his thanks for the excellent meal that Sergeant Emery prepared."

"Thank you, Sir. I'll inform Sergeant Emery," replied Marshall.

The assembled group took turns giving their briefings to Biggs as he sat quietly and soaked in all the information the young 683rd lieutenants presented.

After the lieutenants had given their briefings, Colonel Biggs had a question for Marshall.

"So what news do you have regarding the equipment needing repair in your shop?" Biggs asked.

"Mr. Farley, could you give us a rundown on what's going on in the shops for the colonel?" Marshall replied.

"Be glad to, Sir," replied Chief Farley as he stood up from the rear of the seated group and moved to the front to present his briefing. "Good afternoon, Colonel Biggs, I'm Chief Warrant Officer Jim Farley, the shop officer of the 683rd Maintenance Company.

"At the present time we have eight vehicles in our shops for repair. Of these eight vehicles, six belong to the engineer outfit. Repairs needed for the engineer vehicles range from replacement of clutches to replacement of engines, transmissions and differentials."

Biggs was amazed when he heard the extent of the repairs that were needed, and interrupted Farley's briefing.

"What is being done to secure the repair parts?" Biggs asked.

Farley was quick to answer.

"Sir, I've made a special visit to the Reserve Affairs Office and contacted your headquarters regarding the funding to obtain these high-dollar parts," he said. "Reserve Affairs said they'll have an answer for us by tomorrow. Your headquarters is working with them as well."

"What is your back-up plan if funding doesn't come through?' asked Biggs.

Marshall was ready for that question and answered Biggs directly.

"Sir, we've discussed that particular scenario last evening and have come up with a couple of ideas," Marshall said. "If we get the funding and parts in time, we can complete the repairs and have all the vehicles ready to make it back to home station in Ohio.

"If we get partial funding, or parts aren't readily available, we'll fix what we can and tow the remainder back with us to Ohio."

"If little or no funding is available, we will have to leave the equipment here at Fort Knox for repairs. Or, with your permission, we can use controlled substitution to get as many fixed as possible and tow the rest back to home station."

Biggs pondered the information in his mind.

"I'm glad you've brought me up to date on this situation," he said. "I'll have my staff make some inquiries to 83rd Headquarters and get this funding as fast as possible. Can your people get these vehicles fixed in time?"

Farley jumped back into the conversation.

"Sir, if we can get the parts within the next two days, I can assure you most of the equipment will be in drivable condition for the trip back to home station," he said.

Biggs gave a serious look to Chief Farley.

"That's a pretty large undertaking, Chief."

Farley smiled with confidence.

"Sir, we love a challenge and I know our people can do the job if we've got the parts," Farley replied.

Marshall was pleased to see the confidence in his shop officer.

"Colonel, I have faith in my people," Marshall said. "We'll get the equipment fixed and ready for the trip home. All we'll need are the parts."

"Commander, I must say your confidence is invigorating," Biggs said. "I'll have my people stay on top of this situation and obtain the funding and parts for your unit. Carry on."

Biggs stood up and shook both Farley and Marshall's hands, then quickly departed the shop office tent. Marshall smiled at Farley as the rest of the junior officers relaxed and sat back down in their chairs.

"Well, we've just made a big commitment to the boss man and I know we're not going to let him down, right?" Marshall looked around the room at the eyes of all his junior officers.

"Yes, Sir," was the overall response from his officers.

"Chief, when these parts start arriving, I'd like you to start planning on around-the-clock shift work to get these vehicles up and running," Marshall said.

"No problemo, Sir," Farley replied. "Matter of fact, I've already got the first automotive section using the one truck with the blown engine for controlled substitution."

Marshall smiled at the chief.

"You know you're supposed to get permission from the higher command channels before you start doing that," Marshall said.

"Yeah, I know Sir, but it's highly unlikely we're going to get an engine in time," Farley replied. "So do I have your permission, Sir?"

Marshall chuckled and shook his head in disbelief.

"Sure, go ahead. What have I got to lose, besides my command?"

"Great," replied Farley. "I really didn't want the automotive section to re-install the transmission and trans-axle they just took off the new hangar queen."

Marshall looked at Farley and rolled his eyes in amazement. He stood still for several seconds.

"You are going to install the other parts on the hangar queen when we get them, right?" Marshall asked.

"Oh yes, Sir," replied Farley. "I don't want to have a stripped vehicle loaded with the new repair parts in the bed being towed back to home station. They'd have my butt in a sling for sure."

"Yeah, mine too," said Marshall.

Both men discussed the new game plan for the vehicles in the shops while the junior officers went back to their sections to oversee their respective maintenance operations.

"Chief, let's you and I go visit the shops and see how things are progressing," said Marshall.

Both men departed the shop office tent and walked down to the first automotive maintenance tent.

Sergeant First Class Lufton was overseeing a maintenance team that was removing components from the engineers' 5-ton dump truck. As Farley and Marshall entered the tent, Lufton walked over and greeted both officers.

"Welcome to our little world, gentlemen," greeted Lufton. "We've just about got all the components out of this bad boy and are having them hauled over to second auto. They've got the other two 5-ton dumpers with the bad trannie and differential."

Marshall surveyed the situation.

"Do you have all the tools you need?" he asked.

"Oh yes, Sir," Lufton replied. "It's a good thing you made us bring everything. We'd be in a world of hurt right now if we hadn't. I didn't think we'd be using the transmission jack or the hydraulic press, but they sure came in handy."

Farley jumped into the conversation and began to inform Lufton of what Biggs and the Reserve Affairs Office was doing to procure the needed repair parts and components.

"Sounds good Chief" replied Lufton. "I sure hope they can get us the parts before Friday. By then it'll be too late to make any meaningful repairs."

"I hope so too," replied Marshall. "We've just stuck our necks out pretty far by doing this," referring to the controlled substitution and making a vehicle into a hangar queen.

The three men continued their discussion, which included a visit to the cannibalization point on Main Post the following day.

"Sarge, I'd like you and Chief Farley to visit the cannibalization point in person tomorrow," Marshall said to Lufton. "I don't want to take the word of some civilian clerk who doesn't really give a hoot about our situation. All the parts we need should be there."

"Right on, Sir," replied Sergeant Lufton.

Marshall and Chief Farley checked the second automotive shop to see how the other pieces of equipment were coming along. Sergeant First Class Heinz greeted both men and showed them the work being done on the other two 5-ton dump trucks.

"We should have these up and running by tomorrow, as long as we don't find anything else wrong with 'em," said Sergeant Heinz.

"Sarge," interjected Farley, "you better have your men check the clutch wear on those trucks. I've got a gut feeling you'll see they don't have much clutch left."

"Will do, Sir," replied Heinz.

"Tech supply has enough clutch kits to fix all those 5-tons," said Farley. "Have your people check 'em out when they've got the other components replaced."

"Gotcha, Sir," replied Heinz as he walked over to one of the NCOs supervising the repairs.

"Well, Chief, I believe things are going in the right direction," said Marshall. "I just hope that Colonel Biggs can come through for us."

Farley looked at his commander with a slight grin on his face.

"Don't worry, Sir," he said. "The worst thing that can happen is that we'll only have the hangar queen left to tow back to home station. If you look at the alternatives, they would have to leave their trucks here at Knox for repair at the convenience of Boatwright, and nearly every Army Reserve unit has a lower priority than the active duty units on post. They wouldn't get their equipment repaired and back within a year if we leave it here, Sir."

"Chief, you're right," replied Marshall. "Let's just hope we get lucky at the can point tomorrow."

"Sergeant Lufton and I'll be there as they open up in the morning," replied Farley. "We'll see what they've got to offer."

Both men knew it was a crap shoot, but the odds of finding what they needed at the Knox Cannibalization Point were better than what they could find in the Army supply pipeline. It would take weeks for large components and assemblies to be released for shipment. Bureaucracy was standard operating procedure for all large organizations. The Army was no exception.

After Farley and Marshall left the maintenance sections to continue with their work, the mess section was serving the dinner meal. Soldiers were lining up for chow and Marshall thought it would be a good time to get with his junior officers and go over the schedule of events for the coming day.

As Marshall stood on the rise of ground immediately in front of the mess serving area, Lieutenant Kiley approached.

"Good evening, Sir," she said. "Thought I'd drop by and get you updated on what we've got going on at Boatwright for the remainder of the week."

"Glad to see you, Kathy," replied Marshall. "How are they treating you and your folks at Boatwright?"

Lieutenant Kiley was both serious and confident of herself as she answered the question.

"Sir, we've received excellent training so far, but if it begins to fall off or slow down, I'll pull the sections out of garrison and bring them to the field for the remainder of A.T.," she replied.

"OK," replied Marshall. "So, what's on the agenda?"

"We need a 20-ton crane operator from the recovery section, "said Kiley. "Boatwright has some equipment that has to be off-loaded from railcars. The only qualified person at Boatwright is on emergency leave this week."

Marshall thought of Sergeant Bitsko as the only qualified operator the 683rd had in the field.

"Kathy, I'm sure that Sergeant Bitsko would enjoy working at Boatwright for a couple of days. He's the best 20-ton crane operator we got. You want him?"

"Oh yes, Sir. That would be wonderful," replied Kiley. "I could also cross-train a couple of personnel that aren't too busy at the shop if time allows."

"I'll have Sergeant Baxter informed of the mission on main post for Sergeant Bitsko," said Marshall. "I don't think there'll be a problem. By the way, have you eaten dinner yet?"

"Not yet, Sir. That's one of the reasons I came out here. I needed to have a decent meal to start the week off right," replied Kiley, "And I also came out here to see Fred."

Marshall smiled and spotted Sergeant First Class Fred Kiley walking toward them.

Alarm bells suddenly went off in Marshall's head. He realized he had not called his wife since he had been at Fort Knox. He spotted his driver finishing up his meal and signaled to him to come over.

"Get my jeep ready," Marshall said to his driver. "We're going to Main Post."

First Sergeant Tisher walked over as he saw Marshall having a brief conversation with his driver.

"Going to call the wife, Sir?" asked Tisher.

"Yeah Top," replied Marshall. "I suddenly remembered."

Tisher grinned as he looked over his commanding officer.

"Sir, I don't want you to get into any trouble while you're on Main Post, so I'm comin' along to watch over you."

"Top, I appreciate your company," replied Marshall. "Let's go." They started walking up the hill to the ¼-ton jeep.

When they both got to the jeep, Tisher waved Sergeant Lemasters over to see him.

"John, the Old Man and I are goin' into main post to make some phone calls. Take charge," commanded Tisher.

"Aye aye Sir," replied the ex-marine, showing his old ways as he saluted the first sergeant and Marshall simultaneously.

"Sergeant Lemasters," said Marshall. "Please inform Sergeant Baxter that Sergeant Bitsko has a 20-ton crane mission at Boatwright starting tomorrow. He is to report to Lieutenant Kiley this evening for instructions. She's here right now eating chow."

"Yes, Sir," replied Lemasters. He excused himself and made his way back to the mess area.

"The floating bridge personnel are gone for the day. Better go by way of the pig farm," said Marshall to the driver.

The ¼-ton took a left turn onto the dirt road and headed toward the paved county road that led to the Fort Knox main gate. The odor from the pig farm was strong that evening and Marshall was glad that he hadn't eaten dinner. The stench hit them like a wall.

After they made it through the wall of stench, Tisher leaned over from the back seat and shouted, "Hungry, Sir?" and chuckled as Marshall shook his head.

As they passed through the main gate, Marshall instructed the driver to head toward the PX, where there were plenty of pay phones on the outside wall of the shopping complex. Marshall realized during a normal training day, hundreds of trainees would be lined up to use the phones after they were released from training. Hopefully the trainees were still eating dinner and the phones would be available.

As they approached the PX, they passed a large phalanx of trainees marching in formation toward the pay phones. The driver pulled up next to the pay phones as Marshall and Tisher got out of the ¼-ton and headed directly to the two nearest phones. Within three minutes, more than 200 soldiers were waiting in a neat line to use the phones. Their drill instructor would time their phone calls to three minutes each.

Marshall called his home phone collect, but no one answered. She's probably over her folk's house, he thought as he gave the operator the number for his in-laws. After several rings, his mother-in-law answered the phone.

"Hi Mom! It's Dave."

His mother-in-law was happy to hear from her favorite son-in-law, and asked a few basic questions like how are you, how's the weather, when you coming home, are you eating well, having a good time, and so on.

Before Marshall could ask if his wife was there, his mother-in-law asked if he would like to speak with Linda.

"Sure," Marshall calmly said. Marshall tried to be as calm as possible since he had an audience of young trainees within ten feet of him.

"Hi Daddy!" a little voice shouted over the phone. He felt overwhelming joy as his 3-year old daughter spoke to him on the phone. "I miss you, Daddy!" she said as Marshall began to feel tears welling up in his eyes.

"I miss you too, Pumpkin," he replied. "Are you taking good care of Mommy while I'm gone?" he asked.

"Uh huh! Mommy and I went to Sea World yesterday and we saw Shamu and then we watched the fireworks show," replied Marshall's daughter.

"That's great, Honey! We'll go there again as soon as I get back, OK?"

"OK Daddy. Here's Mommy."

"Hi, Stranger. I thought we wouldn't be hearing from you until you got back," his wife said jokingly.

"Sorry, Honey," replied Marshall. "Things have been rather busy out here in the field and I haven't had a chance to get to the phone until now."

"Oh, that's all right. I kinda figured you'd be busy minding your soldiers," she replied.

Marshall was very fortunate to have an understanding wife that had also been an Army nurse. She knew that the company commander's first responsibility was to the mission, and secondly to his soldiers. The family was on the lower end of the priority list when you put on the uniform.

Marshall and his wife talked for several minutes and each updated the other regarding the goings on.

"I'll see you on Saturday at 5 o'clock. Bye Honey. Love you," Marshall said, hanging up the phone.

Marshall felt relieved that he finally got a hold of his wife and spoke with his daughter. He felt he was re-energized and ready to take on any new obstacles in his path. He looked over and saw Tisher waiting for him in the ¼-ton, but the driver was gone.

Marshall walked over and sat in the front seat.

"Top, you need anything from the PX?" Marshall asked.

"Naw," replied Tisher. "I don't need to spend any more money in there."

Marshall spotted a T-shirt vendor on the sidewalk and walked over to check out his wares. Looking through the pile of T-shirts, he spotted one featuring the ordnance bomb—the symbol of the Army's ordnance branch, of which the 683rd was a part.

"How much if you placed the unit designation on a T-shirt?" asked Marshall.

"Fifty cents," the vendor replied.

"How much for 200 shirts, ranging from small to extra large, with '683 HEM Co' on them?" Marshall asked.

The vendor took out a calculator and figured out the total.

"Eight hundred dollars, which includes a 20-percent discount."

"Can you have them ready by Friday of this week?" Marshall asked.

The vendor quickly said yes. Marshall then pulled $400 out of his wallet and gave it to the vendor as a down payment on the tee shirts. He also started to give the vendor information, including the quantities of each size.

Tisher looked at Marshall after the deal was completed.

"Sir, you don't have to do that," Tisher said.

Marshall looked at him.

"Top, has anyone ever done something like this for these troops?" he asked.

"No, Sir. You'll be the first," replied Tisher.

"Well Top, it's about time that we show our appreciation to the soldiers. I'll ask the officers for a donation when we get back to the field. I don't expect much from some of them, but I think it's time that we do something like this."

Tisher was baffled at his commander to spend that much money out of pocket for the soldiers. It would take Tisher two weeks to earn that kind of money at his civilian job, and he just witnessed Marshall parting with $400 as though it was nothing.

Despite the way that it looked, $800 was a big sum of money for Marshall. He was a generous man, and sometimes a little too impetuous for his own good. This act of generosity would have a positive impact on the soldiers of the 683rd—one they would remember for the rest of their lives.

The driver came back from the PX with two cartons of cigarettes in a plastic sack and climbed into the driver's seat.

"Sorry if I made you wait a long time, Sir," he said as he stashed the bag of cigarettes in the back.

"No problem," replied Marshall. "You just cost me $800."

Tisher laughed out loud as the driver gave the commander a puzzled look.

"Back to Mount Eden Base Camp before I have to visit the gold vault for a loan," said Marshall. The realization of what he had just done began to sink in. Oh well, Marshall thought to himself. People waste that much gambling on the ponies. This is an investment in my people.

As the ¼-ton with Marshall and Tisher was making its way back to Mount Eden, Sergeant Nugot was playing with his pet skunk. The skunk had become so tame that Nugot could pick it up and carry it around with him. The recovery section now had a new mascot. For the time being, Sergeant "Road Kill" Nugot would no longer try to live up to his nickname. He had found a new respect for the animals of the wild, both living and dead.

"Hey Sarge, can I ask a favor of you?" requested Specialist Tony Cutnoff. "Can you leave that skunk outside the tent tonight? That thing started licking my nose last night when I was sleeping."

Nugot smiled.

"He likes you, Tony," Nugot replied. "He won't do that with just anybody."

"Yeah, right," Cutnoff replied sarcastically. "I'm honored."

The ¼-ton with Marshall and Tisher pulled into the company area as twilight was beginning to appear. The vehicle came to a stop and the driver locked up the steering wheel. Marshall and Tisher decided to take a slow walk around the perimeter of the 683rd area.

"Top, when does the unit fund money need to be picked up?" asked Marshall.

The First Sergeant pondered for a few seconds.

"Sir, I believe we can draw that money any time after tomorrow," Tisher said. "I'll have to look at the Fort Knox regs on that to make sure, but whomever you've selected as the Class A agent is supposed to do it."

Both men continued their walk of the company perimeter. Marshall tried to remember whom he selected as the Class A agent.

"I believe Lieutenant Stiles is our Class A agent," remarked Marshall as he continued to observe the perimeter and look for anything out of the ordinary. "I signed a stack of unit orders before A.T. that Sergeant Tea gave me to look over, and I believe that Stiles is our delegated agent."

Every unit had a payroll officer—or Class A agent—that would pick up the unit's payroll from the Army's finance office on Main Post. When Marshall was a Class A Agent on active duty, the payroll was made up of checks and currency. The Class A agent would have the soldier sign the check, then pay them in cash. After pay call was concluded, all checks and leftover cash would be returned by the Class A agent to the finance office. There, the finance office clerks would carefully account for the cash and checks that were initially withdrawn and returned. The Class A agent was responsible for making sure everything was accounted for to the last penny. The Army's payroll system now consisted of checks that were made out to each soldier, whether they had a checking account or not.

When are we supposed to draw the payroll, Top?" asked Marshall.

The first sergeant pondered that for a moment.

"We can draw the payroll on Friday, Sir. Half of the soldiers will take the check home with them, and the other half will want to cash it so they can buy some stuff at the PX to take home."

"Let's make arrangements for the soldiers to do some shopping at the PX on payday. We've got to let the bank on post know that our people may be cashing their paychecks for cash and money orders. I also want you to put the word out in formation that the Class 6 store—you know, the one that sells alcohol—is off limits to those below the rank of sergeant."

Tisher smiled.

"Sir, that won't go over with the soldiers."

"Top, I don't think we should allow our young soldiers to indulge themselves with alcohol while in our care. Do you?" replied Marshall.

"No, Sir. If they are going to buy some booze, they'll get it on their own," said Tisher. "At least we can inform them of your, I mean our, policy."

"Let's not put out the word about payday and the restrictions on the Class 6 store until Friday morning," remarked Marshall as they continued to walk the perimeter of the 683rd area. "Our people are pretty clever and I'm fairly certain that whatever they want to buy - they'll get, no matter what we say," said Marshall with a wry smile as they continued their perimeter walk.

"By the way Top, how are your chigger bites?"

"Ever since I started wearing the flea collars in my boot laces, those little buggers haven't bothered me," the first sergeant calmly replied. "Even the sores have healed up. The flea collars worked."

"I'm glad to hear that, Top," replied Marshall. "Anyone else getting bit up by chiggers or fire ants?"

"From our sick call rosters, the chiggers and fire ants aren't bothering our people any more, now that we've put the word out not to leave food in trash cans and to use the insect repellent. Sir, if you've noticed, nearly all of our soldiers are using the flea collars, except for Chief McCarthy. From what I understand, his legs look worse than mine did."

"Why hasn't he done anything to prevent that?" Marshall asked.

"He's cheap, Sir," replied Tisher. "If the Army won't provide it, he won't take money out of his pocket to buy it."

Marshall was troubled by McCarthy's situation. If a Reservist were incapacitated during annual training, he or she would remain on active duty receiving pay and benefits until he or she were recovered or medically discharged from the service.

"Top, I'm going to have Lieutenant Burks see that Mr. McCarthy reports for sick call tomorrow."

"Sir, you can't make someone report to sick call unless you give 'em a direct order," replied Tisher.

As soon as he said that, Marshall smiled at his first sergeant and nodded his head.

"Exactly. I'll have Lieutenant Burks give that crusty warrant officer a direct order. That'll really piss him off," Marshall said.

Tisher laughed out loud as they continued their walk.

"Sir, you keep that up and the troops are gonna love you," replied Tisher.

"Hell Top, I just hope I can earn their respect," said Marshall.

First Sergeant Tisher grinned at his commander. He didn't have to say a thing. He already knew that the soldiers of the 683rd had a company commander they would follow, no matter what.

Satisfied with their walk about the perimeter, both men head toward the mess area to help themselves to the soup that Sergeant Emery always had ready for anyone who wanted an evening snack.

"What's cookin', Cookie?" asked Tisher as he approached the kettle of soup on the serving line at the mess area. Sergeant Adkins smiled and greeted Marshall and first sergeant.

"Evenin' Sir, Top. We've got split pea and ham tonight. Made it myself usin' Sergeant Ralph's special recipe."

"Hot damn!" replied Tisher. "That's my favorite."

Both men got large cups and began drinking them slowly, blowing the steam off the surface of the soup to cool it off.

"Man is that good, Lonnie," said Tisher as Marshall agreed by nodding his head.

"So how's things goin' down here near the bottom of the hill?" asked Tisher as they all sat down at the officers' dining table and enjoyed the evening.

"Top, I've learned more here in one week than I've learned my entire military career as a cook," replied Adkins. "My cook's helpers are also getting pretty sharp. We'll have a functional mess section when we return to home station."

Marshall was pleased to hear that Adkins was confident that he could apply the newly learned skills when they all returned to Ohio.

"Sarge, how many personnel are you still short in your section?" asked Marshall.

"Just two, Sir," Adkins replied. "If what Vivian tells me is correct, I should have a completely manned section by September. All we'll need is a mess hall."

"You know Sarge, I've been thinking about that," said Marshall. "There must be an old mess hall on the arsenal somewhere."

"There is!" replied Adkins eagerly. "I've been in it when the civilians who run the arsenal have the deer hunters' safety briefing. It's a nice big one that's been moth-balled for years."

"You mean to tell me that the civilians who run and maintain the arsenal have had this mess hall in their back pocket for years and haven't given it over to the Reserves?" said Marshall with a touch of anger in his voice.

"Sir, the civilians at the arsenal aren't going to hand over the mess hall unless they receive orders directing them to do so," replied Tisher.

"Top, I do believe we've got a friend in the commanding general of the 83rd. A letter of request through channels is all we need to do to get that mess hall," Marshall said. "It will have to be well written with good justification for the mess hall, but I strongly believe that justification will not be a problem. The catered meals are a nice convenience, but it doesn't help train your section, does it Sarge?"

"No, Sir," replied Adkins. "The catered meals don't do us any good as far as training, and my cooks would enjoy working in their MOS instead of just serving chow."

"Sarge, I promise you I'll do everything I can to secure that mess hall for this unit when we get back to home station," Marshall said with confidence. "First thing, however, will be to take a good look at it and see what needs to be fixed up. Can we get in there and take a look around?"

Tisher pondered the question for a moment.

"If we tell the head civilian that we're interested in using it, I don't see any reason why they wouldn't let us in to look around."

Marshall was mentally forming a plan of attack.

"OK, here's how we'll go about getting the mess hall. Before we write a letter of request, let's make sure the facility is useable and the utilities are all available. They may have shut off the steam lines and gas lines to it. Any big repairs may not be funded by the command, so we'll have to be fairly specific about the condition of the facility in our letter. Sergeant Adkins, I'll let you spearhead the inspection of the facility. Take whomever you need from the unit to get a feel for what we can do in-house, and what will have to be jobbed-out to bring the mess facility into full operation. Put it in writing and we'll draft up a request through the command channels to the 83rd."

"Yes Sir!" replied Adkins with a huge smile on his face as he stood up and saluted.

Marshall smiled and returned Adkins' salute.

"Sarge, I can't promise you it will definitely happen, but I'll give it my best try," Marshall said.

"Sir, I couldn't ask for more," replied Adkins. "I really appreciate your involvement."

"You got it, good Sergeant," smiled Marshall as he sat back down and enjoyed the rest of his soup.

By Christmas, the 683rd would be eating out of their new mess hall, built in 1942.

While they were discussing future plans with the 683rd mess section, Private Hudson was helping himself to a cup of soup. He had been evicted from his tent again as Peoples and Kayrule were enjoying each other's company.

"Evening, Sir. Evening, First Sergeant," said Hudson as he walked by.

First Sergeant Tisher looked at Hudson.

"Hudson, I've noticed you've been having soup every night. You getting enough to eat, Soldier?"

"Yeah, Top. I just love this soup," he replied as he walked over to a tree and sat down to slowly eat his evening snack.

While Marshall and Tisher began talking about other areas of training and mission work, Chief Farley walked down to join them.

"Good evening, Chief," said Marshall as he walked over to the table and sat down with his hot cup of homemade split pea with ham soup.

"Good evening, Sir, Top. What's going on?" asked Farley.

"Oh nothing much," replied Marshall. "The First Sergeant and I were just talking about how the troops were going to have the afternoon off on Friday to go onto Main Post and shop after they get their paychecks, and how we were going to take over the mess hall facility at the arsenal."

"You're kiddin' me!" said Farley. "You know that mess hall was shutdown after the Vietnam War. I believe it's on the demolition list. You better hurry and try and save it or the cooks will be serving chow from a mess tent on the foundation of that old mess hall."

"Thanks for the heads-up," said Marshall. "I'll make sure I expedite the request when we get back to home station. By the way, who in the unit knows all about construction?"

"The only one I'd trust is Sergeant Lufton," replied Farley. "He's got a small construction business on the side and did some work on my house. He does good work."

Adkins was still in the area and overheard the conversation. Marshall looked over to Adkins and nodded.

Adkins nodded his head in agreement.

"Yes, Sir. I'll talk to Sergeant Lufton first thing in the morning."

The three at the table changed the conversation to the situation at-hand. Marshall was concerned about the growing maintenance requirements and amount of equipment that might fill the shops if the other units they were supporting continued to have breakdowns.

"Chief, with the present backlog we've got, can it all be repaired by Friday?"

Farley was quick to answer.

"Sir, if there are no more catastrophic breakdowns like a blown engine or transmission, we should be able to handle anything that comes in and have it ready before Friday."

"What about clutch jobs for our engineer buddies?" asked Marshall.

"Sir, we're so good at rebuilding clutches, we can have them in and out within two hours," Farley said. "It's a damn good thing the sections brought all their equipment, otherwise I couldn't say that."

"Well Chief, here's to good luck with your visit to the bone yard tomorrow," said Marshall. They toasted each other with their cups of soup and departed company for the evening.

The tree frogs were croaking loudly as the twilight faded into darkness. The generators were humming along as the sections used them up to power up their light sets installed in their maintenance tents and section tents. Some of the sections were working on the job orders they received that day and were on the second shift of personnel. The unit didn't have to worry about noise and light discipline, now that they were in the non-tactical phase of training out in the field.

Marshall mused to himself about how well the 683rd had adapted to life in the field, no matter if they were in a tactical mode or not.

"You know Top, we've got a great bunch of soldiers in the 683rd," Marshall said as they both walked toward the CP tent.

"Yes Sir, they are," replied Tisher. He was glad that the Old Man knew how to work with the NCOs and warrant officers of the unit.

The first sergeant had seen many commanders come and go, and he was so glad that Marshall came to the 683rd. It made his job as first sergeant much easier and much more rewarding. He didn't have to keep an eye out for the commander, like he did for the others before Marshall.

A.T. - DAY 10 (TUESDAY)

The morning air felt crisp and cool as Sergeant First Class Lufton and Chief Farley were driving to Main Post to check out the Fort Knox Cannibalization Point. Due to the early hour, the floating bridge crew would not arrive in time to ferry them across, which left them no choice. The pig farm route was the only way in to Main Post that early in the morning.

Both Lufton and Farley did not seem to mind the stench as they focused their minds on the more important matters at hand. The bone yard would either fulfill their parts needs, or they would have to make other plans. That would involve a great deal of effort and jumping through hoops, as Chief Farley would say, to get the engineer unit's 5-ton dump trucks repaired on time.

Chief Farley was a bit angry at the motor sergeant of the engineer unit. He warned him about how their drivers were abusing the equipment and the motor sergeant politely told him to mind his own business. Now the tables were turned and the engineers' motor sergeant was pleading with Chief Farley to get their equipment repaired as soon as possible. The engineers' A.T. mission of clearing brush and repairing the Mount Eden Training Area road network had come to a standstill due to the arrogance and ignorance of one man.

Chief Farley also had some requisition forms partially filled out for the repair parts needed to fix the 5-ton dump truck that had become the hangar queen.

"Are you sure the bone yard is next to the property disposal office?" asked Lufton.

"Yeah, I'm sure," replied Farley. "I've been down here a couple of times when I was the motor sergeant of the 661st Transportation Company. We used to come down here and get parts after we'd drop off some obsolete equipment at PDO."

The two men continued their drive through the Fort Knox Main Post area, careful to watch for soldiers marching in the streets. Farley directed Lufton to take a shortcut through the post residential housing area. It looked like any residential neighborhood, except all the houses were built with red brick.

"Hang a left at the stop sign," Farley directed. "It'll be another 200 meters, then hang a right."

Within several minutes, they had arrived at the Fort Knox Cannibalization Point. The hand-painted sign at the front showed a large black kettle boiling on an open fire. Inside the kettle were trucks, jeeps and tanks bubbling to the surface. The cartoon character Beetle Bailey was stirring the kettle with a wrench, and Sergeant Snorkel stood by his side, ready to kick Beetle in the backside.

Both Farley and Lufton climbed out of the ¼-ton jeep after they parked close to the cannibalization point office. The office was an old wooden-sided structure that was the size and layout of a one-story orderly room.

When they walked into the office, a young enlisted soldier was reading a Playboy magazine, not aware that he had company.

Chief Farley smiled.

"That's for later, Private!" he yelled.

The young soldier looked up and was embarrassed to be caught by surprise.

"Yes, Sir! What can I help you with, Chief?" the young soldier blurted out as he jumped to his feet.

"We need to know if you've got these parts in stock," replied Farley as he handed the clerk the requisitions. "While you're checking the stock numbers against your stocking list, Sergeant Lufton and I want to take a look around. OK with you?"

"Oh, no problem Chief. Make yourselves at home," replied the clerk as he took the paperwork from Farley.

The two men walked out the back door of the office and walked through the open gate of the chain-link fence with barbed wire on top to see what the bone yard had in its inventory.

As they walked through the gate, the entire cannibalization point opened up into an orderly and well-spaced junkyard. Old and obsolete vehicles, as well as newer demolished ones, were placed in homogenous groupings. Equipment that was too badly damaged to repair was stripped of its main assemblies and components. The components and assemblies were placed on wooden pallets and concrete cinder blocks next to the stripped chassis.

"Chief, I think we've found our parts. There they are," Sergeant Lufton said to Chief Farley when they arrived at the 5-ton truck area.

"Yep, them's the ones," replied Farley as he took out his small green notepad out of his shirt pocket and began writing down the parts location in the bone yard. "Looks like we've got an engine that's in pretty good shape. Help me with the tarp," said the chief as they examined the engine a little closer.

"Yep, they've plugged the intakes and exhausts to keep the moisture out. Except for the cracked water pump housing, this just might work out fine," replied Lufton as they placed the tarp back over the engine.

The two headed back to the office to see what the clerk had found.

"Sir, I've got all you need except for the engine," responded the clerk as Farley and Sergeant Lufton walked up to the counter.

Chief Farley smiled.

"You've got a 5-ton multi-fuel engine sitting on a pallet. It's just what we need."

"Oh, that's got a broken water pump cover, Chief," said the clerk.

"Tell you what, good Private," said Farley. "I've got a truck with a busted engine. I'll swap it out with the one out there, take off the parts and make a good one out of it, and bring the busted one back for rebuild."

"Chief, if you bring in the busted one, I'll let you take the one out there on the pallet," said the clerk.

"Deal!" replied Chief Farley. "I'll have my people over here within a couple of hours to swap engines."

"As for the other parts, hold onto those requisitions until I get the funding source codes for you. I'll be back with a couple of deuces and a wrecker to get the parts and swap engines."

"No problem, Chief. I'll be here until 1600 hours," said the clerk as he sat back down and got back to reading his Playboy.

As Sergeant Lufton and Chief Farley walked out of the cannibalization point office, Lufton was excited.

"Man, are we lucky or what?" he said.

"Yeah, we sure are," replied Farley as they jumped into the jeep and drove off to the 683rd field site.

The cannibalization point had all the parts available to get the 5-ton dump trucks repaired. All that was needed was funding for the parts. They returned to Mount Eden Base Camp and told Captain Marshall the news.

Marshall smiled.

"We've got the funding too," he said. "Colonel Biggs just called over and said the 83rd has given the funding request its highest priority. They're also looking high and low to find an engine."

Farley grinned back at the commander.

"Sir, tell 'em we also found a replacement 5-ton multi-fuel engine at the bone yard for free. We just got to swap a few parts on it and it should run."

"That's great, Chief," replied Marshall. "When can we get the parts?"

Sergeant Lufton jumped into the conversation. He too, wanted to share in bringing the good news.

"Right now, Sir," Lufton said.

Marshall was thrilled to hear of the success his people had in locating the needed parts. If the parts had been ordered through regular channels, it would have taken months for the parts to arrive.

Sergeant Lufton returned to his section area and told the mechanics to pull off the needed parts from the broken engine, which was already bolted to a metal-framed engine stand. They were going to load the engine, stand and all, on the back of a deuce-and-a-half, take it to the bone yard and swap it out for another. They also loaded up a broken trans-axle and a transmission for turn-in at PDO.

Things were going well for the automotive maintenance sections that day, and the maintenance techs were anxious to start the rebuilding process on the stripped 5-ton dump truck in the shop. They had already replaced seven clutches and were working on two more. The engineer unit was very happy to get their 5-ton dump trucks back so quickly, and their drivers that had helped the 683rd automotive repairmen fix the trucks realized the error of their ways. They would be very careful in the future. No more burned-out clutches if they could help it.

The parts the 683rd so desperately needed were found and received within three hours of Chief Farley and Sergeant Lufton's visit to the Fort Knox Cannibalization Point. The engine at the bone yard was in perfect working order and installed in the dump truck that afternoon. The truck was back on the road before evening and all the soldiers of the 1st automotive section were very proud to have accomplished a difficult job in so short a time.

To celebrate, the service section stenciled "683rd Hangar Queen" in black paint on the newly resurrected 5-ton dump truck.

The 683rd jubilation was short-lived as more trucks began to enter the shops. Colonel Biggs' and Captain Marshall's advice to the other company commanders to closely check all vehicles before returning home became apparent. The automotive sections would be busy fixing everything from bad brakes to burnt-out clutches. The mechanics didn't care. Work made the time go by quickly, and boredom was never a problem.

As the afternoon wore on, Marshall went over to see Lieutenant Burks at the tech supply section.

"Hello, Lieutenant," Marshall said. "What's happened to Chief McCarthy? I haven't seen him since he left for sick call this morning."

Lieutenant Burks was a bit flustered by the commander's direct question.

"Oh, I'm sorry, Sir. I meant to tell you they admitted the chief to the hospital. Apparently his chigger bites were pretty bad."

Marshall shook his head in disbelief. All the pain and discomfort Chief McCarthy had gone through with his recent bout of dysentery and now this. He didn't feel too sorry for him since the chief had brought both conditions upon himself, drinking soda pop with contaminated ice and not applying enough insect repellent to ward off the chiggers.

Marshall decided it was a good time to give McCarthy a visit at the hospital and see if he needed anything.

"Sarah, do you want to come along with me and give the chief a visit?" asked Marshall.

"That's OK, Sir," replied Burks. "Just let him know that we're doing fine out here and hope he returns to the field soon."

Marshall grinned at his lieutenant.

"I'll pass that along when I see him," Marshall said.

Marshall asked her about the status of the obsolete parts turn-in at PDO and the remaining stock of needed repair parts. All was reported to be going well, and no problems were anticipated with the obsolete parts turn-in.

Tech supply still had a sufficient quantity of parts to take care of most of repairs that were entering the shops. Chief Farley and the shop office personnel were maintaining an open channel of communications with tech supply, identifying which parts were needed for each job coming into the shop office. The tech supply platoon was responding quickly with the needed parts. Marshall knew tech supply was now providing superb support to the A.T. mission.

The 683rd engine was firing on all eight cylinders. Even Sergeant Schmoot was doing an excellent job as the platoon sergeant, helping to organize and direct efforts. The section had finally come together due to the assistance of some excellent soldiers from the 646th Supply Company and Burks' emerging leadership skills.

Marshall left the tent and headed over to the CP tent to see First Sergeant Tisher about Chief McCarthy's condition. A visit to Ireland Hospital was in order.

"Sir, I've got some personnel issues to handle with the group S1," replied First Sergeant Tisher when asked if he would like to accompany Marshall and visit Chief McCarthy in the hospital. "Why not take my field first sergeant? I'm sure John would love to see Mr. McCarthy confined to a hospital bed." Tisher was smiling as he made his suggestion.

Marshall chuckled to himself as he heard his first sergeant's recommendation. Tisher had little respect for McCarthy, and was glad to know he would be out of his hair—or what was left of it—for a while.

"Top, I can see you're a man who doesn't like to mince words," Marshall said. "I'll get Sergeant Lemasters and go pay our stricken warrant officer a visit. Anything you need from the PX?"

Sergeant Tea jumped into the conversation.

"Sir, if you don't mind, would you bring me some of those Krispy Kreme glazed doughnuts? I just been havin' this awful craving."

"And you, Top?" asked Marshall.

First Sergeant Tisher smiled.

"Make mine a dozen cinnamon-raisin. I got a craving too."

Marshall picked up the field phone and rang up the 683rd switchboard operator and asked them locate the field first sergeant. After several minutes, the field phone rang back at the CP tent. Sergeant Lemasters was on the line. Sergeant Tea answered the phone and instructed him to meet Captain Marshall for an unscheduled trip to main post. She also told Lemasters what needed to be picked up at the PX shopette when they made their return trip.

"OK Vivian, I won't ferget yer doughnuts. Tops' neither," Sergeant Lemasters replied as he hung up the field phone and made his way to the motor pool to dispatch the headquarters ¼-ton jeep. The MPs were still doing their roadside spot checks, so Sergeant Lemasters made sure everyone in the 683rd was dutifully being dispatched from the motor pool before they started up their vehicles.

Sergeant Lemasters drove toward Ireland Hospital on main post with Captain Marshall in the passenger seat.

"Sir, how come you don't get yerself a military driver's license?" Lemasters asked.

Marshall kept his focus on the road ahead.

"I'm old Army, Sarge. If I need to get somewhere, I've got a driver assigned. In an emergency, I can drive," Marshall said.

"By the way, I do have a military driver's license."

"Shoot, Sir. I kinda figured ya did," replied Lemasters, slightly flustered. "I was jist testin' ya."

The floating bridge personnel were still on duty and the trip to the hospital took less than 15 minutes. The hospital was the standard gray concrete eight-floor hospital design that the Army constructed during the mid-sixties on most of the large military installations. The hospital was engineered to be functional, practical, and be structurally sound for at least 40 years.

After checking at the front desk, Marshall and Lemasters found that Chief Warrant Officer Kenneth McCarthy was in Room 423, on the fourth floor.

"Hello, Chief," said Marshall to McCarthy as he entered the private hospital room. "How are you coming along?"

Chief McCarthy had the sheets lowered to mid-thigh and his legs were covered with antiseptic and bandages.

"They're taking pretty good care of me," replied McCarthy. "They had me on my stomach patchin' up the other side about 10 minutes ago. Looks like I'll be here for another couple of days."

Marshall looked at his warrant officer's legs and noticed there wasn't much the chiggers missed.

"Chief, how far up do those bites go?" asked Marshall.

"I've got 'em up to my waist."

Marshall was somewhat surprised.

"Chief, why did you ever let it get that bad?" he asked.

"Sir, had I known I was getting bit up this bad, I would've taken a bath in insect repellent. I didn't feel a thing until I started itching on Sunday. I kinda knew I was in trouble then and started using a whole bottle of that clear nail polish, but it didn't do any good."

Lemasters extended his greetings to the chief.

"The fellers in yer section said to get yer big ole butt back out there or they'd leave ya at Mount Eden," Lemasters said. "They really miss ya, Chief."

The old warrant officer chuckled out a "yeah, sure." He knew that Lemasters was trying to cheer him up.

"Chief, tech supply is doing a great job," Marshall interjected. "You've taught them well."

McCarthy seemed to take some comfort in what Marshall told him.

"Sir, how's the maintenance mission going?" McCarthy asked.

"Chief, the jobs are being completed as we speak. Chief Farley went to the bone yard this morning and found all the big-ticket parts we needed. Everything is going better than expected. We've got the funding from the 83rd and the jobs are flowing through the shops."

Marshall looked at his watch, realizing that the floating bridge personnel would be leaving in less than an hour.

"Chief, I know they'll take good care of you here. We'll check in tomorrow to see how you're doing. Just rest easy. Is there anything you need?" asked Marshall.

"Yes, Sir, there is one thing," McCarthy said. "Could you go to the PX and get a can of insecticide and have one of my section personnel spray all my clothes in my laundry bag and field gear? I don't want to be bringing any chiggers back with me."

Marshall grinned.

"You bet, Chief," he said. "We'll stop at the PX and pick up a can. You know, you must taste pretty good to those chiggers. They almost made you their entrée."

Lemasters and McCarthy all had a good chuckle as they parted company.

"Sir, I've got a full can of Raid in my foot locker," said Lemasters as they walked down the hospital corridor toward the stairs. "Let's git them doughnuts fer Top and Vivian quick so we kin git back before the floatin' bridge soldiers leave fer the day."

Marshall respected Lemasters and his ideas. He also didn't want to go past the pig farm if he could avoid it.

After their short visit to the PX shopette, Marshall and Lemasters found the floating bridge personnel sitting in their vehicles, anxiously waiting to finish their day. The enlisted men groaned and climbed out of their jeep as Marshall and Lemasters drove onto the floating pontoons. One man climbed into the deuce-and-a-half, started the engine, and put the truck into reverse.

The cable that was attached to the front bumper of the deuce-and-a-half passed through a pulley that was attached to a concrete piling on the side of the hill. The cable was routed across the river and through another set of pulleys on another concrete piling on the opposite shore. The same cable came back across the river and was attached to the opposite end of the floating bridge. The sides of the floating bridge had guide cables, which were anchored to concrete buttresses on both sides of the river. These were in place to keep the bridge from floating down stream with the current.

Captain Marshall grinned at Sergeant First Class Lemasters.

"Let's hope they don't snap the cable while we're in the middle of the river," Marshall said.

Lemasters nodded in agreement as they were being pulled across the river. When they reached the opposite shore, the floating bridge was still being pulled.

Marshall and Lemasters simultaneously shouted out "Whoa! Whoa!" but it was too late. The deuce driver didn't realize the floating bridge had reached the opposite shore and the extra tension on the cable ripped off the mounting shackles. The bridge would be out for a while.

"I'll have my people fix it for you!" Marshall shouted to the floating bridge personnel on the opposite shore.

"That's okay, Sir. We'll handle it," one of them shouted back.

As Lemasters drove the ¼-ton jeep off the floating bridge and onto the concrete ramp, Marshall climbed back in.

"I bet they did that on purpose," Marshall said. "They wouldn't mind taking a day off cause the bridge is out, and we'll have to suffer by driving by the pig farm."

Lemasters reassured his commander.

"Sir, I'll have the service section out here tonight fixin' the bridge," he said. "It'll be done like a bunch of work-hungry elves in olive-drab out here waitin' fer somethin' ta do."

Marshall laughed as they drove back to the 683rd field site.

"Sarge, that sounds like a great nickname for the service section. Elves in olive drab. Let's stop on by their area and let 'em know they've got a top priority mission tonight."

"Yes, Sir," replied Lemasters with a large grin as he drove through the tree-lined dirt road toward Mount Eden Base Camp.

Sergeant Emery and his crew were preparing for the evening meal as the rain clouds began to come through the area. The sky opened up and a deluge of rain came thundering down on the Mount Eden area. As Marshall and Lemasters pulled into the 683rd area, they were relieved that they put the canvas top up before the rains came.

Marshall sat in the jeep.

"Sarge, do you think we should wait it out?" Marshall asked.

Lemasters looked out at the sky.

"Sir, if this rain continues like this, we'll be needin' paddles pretty soon," Lemasters replied.

Almost immediately, the downpour lessened. It stopped within two minutes. It rained two inches of water within 10 minutes. Puddles of standing water were everywhere on the flat areas of Mount Eden, and several of the woodchip-covered paths through the 683rd field site were now washouts and gullies.

Marshall got out of the jeep and surveyed the area while he walked over to the CP tent with two boxes of doughnuts. Sergeant Lemasters went to his tent to get the can of Raid and spray McCarthy's laundry bag filled with dirty clothes and his field gear. Being the thoughtful NCO, Lemasters also sprayed the chief's cot and sleeping bag.

Not wanting to keep the chief's dirty laundry filled with dead chiggers, Lemasters took all of Chief McCarthy's clothing and gear to the 928th S&S Company laundry section to have it washed and cleaned. The chief's clothes and gear would come back the next day clean and pressed. The only problem with a field laundry section was they had a bad habit of breaking nearly all the buttons on the trousers and shirts after they had starched and pressed the fatigue uniforms. That was typical of any Army field laundry unit. Broken buttons were a distinct possibility.

Lemasters made a special visit to the 683rd Service Section tent and spotted Sergeant First Class Joe Baxter eating his dinner.

"I got a mission for y'all, and the Old Man wants it high priority!" Lemasters said.

"What ya got, John?" Baxter asked.

"Them floatin' bridge idiots tore the shackles off the pontoon," said Lemasters. "Y'all need to have your people get their portable welder fired up. Better have 'em take their swimmin' trunks too. Ain't no way to cross the river unless you swim. The cable's on the other side of the river."

"Shoot John, that sounds like fun," Sergeant Baxter replied. "As long as that rainstorm didn't make the river rise too much, that should be an easy one. Thanks! I've been waitin' for something to do."

Joe Baxter grabbed his hat and walked out of the tent and yelled for several soldiers to report to him immediately. The floating bridge would be ready by morning, thanks to the service section's elves in olive drab.

Lemasters decided it was a good time to have some chow and headed toward the mess area.

Marshall and First Sergeant Tisher were standing at their usual spot watching the chow line get shorter and shorter. They were talking about McCarthy's condition when Lemasters joined the conversation.

"Top, you shoulda seen the chief," Lemasters said. "He looked like an extra-large pizza on white linen with all them chigger bites."

Both Tisher and Marshall burst out laughing at Lemasters' accurate description of the well-bitten warrant officer.

After they collected themselves Marshall continued.

"He's going to be quite sore for the next couple of days. We should have him back by Friday. I think I'll have him stay at the barracks on Main Post and have his gear brought to him. I don't want him to get bitten again. The next time might prove fatal."

"Good idea, Sir," replied Tisher. "I'd rather keep him out of our hair as well."

Lemasters couldn't resist the opening Tisher gave him.

"Top, you ain't got no hair for him ta get in ta," Lemasters said.

"OK John, get your butt in that chow line," commanded Tisher.

"Aye aye, Sir," was Lemasters' grinning response as he walked to the end of the line.

Marshall smiled. Looking at the balding first sergeant he said, "Well, at least you can keep him out of my hair."

"Sir, may I speak frankly?" Tisher replied.

Marshall had a broad smile.

"No. Get in line, First Sergeant. I'm getting hungry too."

Both men smiled and walked down to get their supper. They could feel that everything was going well.

Lieutenant Stiles was standing in the chow line as Marshall walked over next to her.

"Lieutenant Stiles, did you know that you are the Class A agent for the 683rd?" Marshall asked.

"Yes, Sir. Why do you ask?" she replied with a little confusion in her voice.

"You're going to pick up the unit fund check from the Post finance office tomorrow after 1000 hours," Marshall replied. "You'll need a copy of your unit orders and the paperwork to get the 683rd's unit fund monies."

"Sir, do you know how much the amount is going to be?" asked Stiles.

Marshall smiled.

"It should be around $50. No need for an armed guard."

"Can I carry a sidearm?" asked Stiles anxiously.

"No, Lieutenant," responded Marshall. "That won't be necessary. You will need a sidearm and guard when you pick-up the 683rd payroll on Friday morning at the same time, 1000 hours. Those funds will be dispersed in the form of individualized checks."

"OK, Sir. I'll be ready tomorrow," Stiles replied. "I'll see Vivian after supper and get the paperwork for the unit fund money."

"Sounds good," said Marshall.

Both were ready for their supper as they arrived in front of the serving line. Spaghetti with meatballs and tossed salad was the main course for the evening. Sergeant Emery was balancing out the cost of meals before the end of the week was out. Marshall and Emery had discussed what they felt should be the last meal served in the field. They decided it should be a feast for the soldiers, and Emery was going to make sure it was within the budget he was given.

Lieutenant Humphrey was observing the unit from the top of the hill by the fixed latrine. The evening air temperatures were starting to become more comfortable as he decided to join the 683rd chow line and have some dinner, as well as sample a field-cooked meal for the 1-R unit evaluation report.

"Lieutenant Humphrey, welcome back," said Captain Marshall as he saw Humphrey approach.

"Good evening, Captain. Hope you've got enough chow left over for me."

Marshall took a quick glance over to the serving line and saw there was enough.

"Looks like they do," Marshall said. "Hope you enjoy our excellent field cuisine."

Sergeant Emery and his cooks had prepared his secret spaghetti sauce recipe that made most Italians homesick. He got the recipe from one of his chefs that was born and raised in Tuscany. The sauce was so delicious, it could make a meal of broom straw taste great—as long as there was enough sauce on it. Also on the menu was homemade garlic bread, Caesar salad, meatballs, meatball sandwiches, and assorted pies and pudding for desert.

Humphrey filled his plate with Sergeant Emery's spaghetti and meatballs, garlic bread and Caesar salad, and helped himself to seconds and thirds as he wolfed down the dinner.

"How's the food?" asked Marshall as he saw Humphrey load up his plate for a third time.

Humphrey was a bit embarrassed.

"Captain, this is the best spaghetti I've ever ate in my entire life," Humphrey replied.

Marshall smiled.

"Well, you can tell that fine NCO standing right over there how much you like it," Marshall gestured toward Emery. "He just might invite you to his restaurant for a free meal next time you're in Youngstown."

Sergeant Emery overheard the conversation and walked over to Lieutenant Humphrey.

"I'm glad you're enjoying the dinner, Lieutenant. You're always an invited guest at Ralph's Taj Mahal, whether it's in Youngstown or Mount Eden."

"Sarge, this is absolutely great," Humphrey said. "Like I said before, I've never had better."

Sergeant Emery smiled. The evaluator's compliment meant a great deal to him.

"Thank you, Sir. You come again, anytime."

Lieutenant Humphrey got up from the table and realized he had eaten so much, he didn't feel like doing anything else but relaxing and watching some TV at his bachelor's officer quarters. The Cincinnati Reds were playing the New York Mets, and Humphrey was a big Mets fan.

"Captain Marshall, I just came to sample the chow. My compliments," Humphrey said. "Well, if you'll excuse me, I've got some work to do at my quarters. Good night, Captain."

Marshall bid him farewell and watched him walk up the hill. As Lieutenant Humphrey drove away in his ¼-ton jeep, he could still smell the skunk odor from the other day that lingered on the canvas fabric of the seat covers. The smell was present, but not overpowering.

Humphrey was quickly coming to the pig farm area and stepped on the gas pedal to get the stench over with as quickly as possible. Suddenly, the farmer pulled out of the farm in front of the jeep, slowly driving a tractor with a trailer of feed. Humphrey stepped on the brakes and sighed. He had to endure the stench since he could not pass the tractor due to oncoming traffic.

After three minutes that seemed like an eternity, the farmer pulled his tractor off the road and Humphrey was able to speed up and pass. Finally some fresh air, he thought to himself as he began to relax and enjoy the evening drive.

His ¼-ton began to slow down as the engine sputtered and suddenly died. Coasting to a stop, Humphrey looked at the fuel gauge, which read empty. He ran out of gas. Luckily, he had a full can of gasoline strapped on the back of the jeep, and climbed out of his driver's seat to refill his gas tank.

While unstrapping the fuel can, the wind changed direction. The pig farm stench came back to overwhelm Humphrey. Holding his breath, Humphrey decided to just put in a gallon or two of gas and refill at the motor pool in the morning.

Back at Mount Eden, Specialist Williams and Specialist Peoples were doing an inventory check of all the weapons in the weapons trailer.

After they had completed the count, Peoples locked up the trailer and both women sat on the trailer steps for a breather.

"You hear that Road Kill has a pet skunk?" Peoples asked.

"Yeah Fran," Williams replied. "But that didn't surprise me. Nothing he does surprises me."

Peoples smiled and looked at Williams.

"So girlfriend, found anybody that interests you yet?"

Williams grinned and took her time responding,

"Besides those jerks at the Enlisted Club?" she asked.

Peoples giggled.

"Neanderthals who somehow got in the Army don't count," Peoples said.

"Well, Tony Cutnoff's rather cute and unattached," Williams said, shyly smiling. "He complimented me on my score at the rifle range."

Peoples laughed.

"You mean our score!"

"Yes, our score," replied Williams. "He hinted that he'd like to take me to the movies on Post if we get payday activities. How about you?"

Peoples smiled.

"I've been rather busy with Johnny Kayrule lately, if you know what I mean."

Williams looked at her.

"Yeah Fran, I think I do."

A.T. – DAY 11 (WEDNESDAY)

Sergeant Bob Bitsko of the recovery section was busy operating a 20-ton crane that belonged to the Boatwright Maintenance Facility. Lieutenant Kiley had requested his attachment at Boatwright to assist in offloading railcars at the railhead behind the vast civilian maintenance facility located on the Fort Knox Main Post area. His civilian counterpart who operated the 20-ton crane had a family emergency and left the previous day, leaving 12 rail flatcars that were fully loaded and parked behind Boatwright to be offloaded. The containers on the railcars held components and repair parts needed to keep the large Army post operational. Sergeant Bitsko had inadvertently become a significant factor in overall military preparedness of Fort Knox and the United States Army.

Bitsko's experience with the 20-ton crane went back to his early days in Vietnam at Camron Bay, were he was assigned as a longshoreman at the harbor. The 20-ton crane was small enough to maneuver through the dock areas and help load and offload cargo onto vessels that came into port. The fixed cranes at the port facility were occasionally knocked out by enemy mortar fire, and the 20-ton crane was the back-up system to get the ships' cargo moved. Bitsko became very comfortable in the operator's seat and knew every control and capability the 20-ton crane possessed. He knew how to gently work each knob and lever and could move the boom with ease as he raised and lowered the cargo attached to the ball and hook. It was as though the machine became part of him. He was its master who could make it do anything he wanted to.

As Bitsko was enjoying a peaceful morning in the operator's control cab section of the 20-ton crane, a loud crashing noise came from behind him on the paved street in front of the rail yard.

An Army 10-ton tractor had just had an accident with a civilian car. The civilian car ran a stop sign as the 10-ton tractor was going through the intersection. The car was partially crushed under the tractor. The occupant of the civilian car was alive, but trapped inside with the doors and windows crushed. The driver of the tractor was shaken up as a crowd gathered around the accident site.

Bitsko shut down the 20-ton crane and ran over to see if he could lend any assistance. When he arrived at the site, it was clear to him that the 10-ton tractor had completely straddled the civilian car and the driver of the civilian car was trapped inside the crushed car.

As the MPs arrived on the scene and sized up the situation, Bitsko spoke to the MP in charge.

"Hey Sarge, I've got a 20-ton crane a couple hundred yards from here," Bitsko said. "I was just off-loading some railcars. I've got the cables and snatch blocks to attach to the tractor's bumper shackles, and I'll lift it off the car and set it down wherever you want."

The MP looked at Bitsko like he had just heard a voice from heaven.

"Sarge, go get your crane and bring 'er over here," the MP said. "I'll get traffic moved back for you."

Bitsko didn't have to be told twice, and ran toward the parked 20-ton crane.

The crane roared to life as Bitsko prepared to move the large contraption over to the accident site. He placed the boom in the travel position, retracted the outriggers, and got the main engine started. In less than three minutes, Bitsko was moving to the accident site.

Within five minutes, Bitsko had the crane positioned and anchored. The cables, spreaders and snatch blocks were all ready to go. He climbed into the crane's control cab and fired up the hoisting engine. He lowered the ball and hook with the spreaders and snatch blocks as the MPs attached them to the 10-ton's bumper shackles.

After he got the thumbs-up from the MPs, Bitsko reeled in the slack and raised the boom gently. Tension was placed on the main cable and onto the spreaders. The entire assembly began to groan from the weight as Bitsko engaged the cable reel.

Slowly, the 20-ton crane lifted the tractor off of the civilian car. The assembled crowd began to cheer. Within seconds, the tractor was lifted eight feet above the ground as Bitsko skillfully swung the boom to the left. He set the tractor back onto the ground 20 feet away from the crushed car.

The MPs gave Bitsko the thumbs-up signal that everything was good as he lowered the cable to allow some slack on the spreaders that were attached to the lifting shackles. Several soldiers in the crowd detached the lifting hooks from the tractor lifting shackles, and Bitsko was able to place the crane's main boom back into the travel position.

The Fort Knox Fire Department Rescue Team was on the scene with the jaws-of-life and began to cut the car's door pillars. Within five minutes, the occupant was placed on a stretcher and loaded into an awaiting ambulance. Bitsko had already moved the 20-ton crane back to the rail yard and returned to the accident scene to see if he could be of any more assistance.

"Sarge, what's your name and outfit?" the MP asked Bitsko. Bitsko gave the MP all the information for the official accident report, which would be filed later that morning.

"You know, Sarge, because you were here with your crane, that person has a very good chance to be around to thank you in person," said the MP.

Bitsko smiled.

"I'm just glad that I could help, Sarge," Bitsko said. "Maybe it was my turn to be someone's guardian angel."

"Well, you sure were," replied the MP sergeant as he smiled and shook Bitsko's hand.

Bitsko felt pretty good about what he had just accomplished and returned to the rail yard. He resumed unloading the railcars, not thinking too much about what had just happened. He decided it would be a good idea to pay a visit to the civilian that was in the accident after duty hours. He hoped that she would be OK and discharged from the hospital in a few days.

As the morning wore on, Bitsko noticed there were three civilians in the rail yard. They waved their arms at Bitsko to stop and come down from the crane cab.

As he climbed down from the crane, Bitsko saw a general walking toward him. What on earth did I do now? He thought to himself as he tried to spruce himself up and button up his shirt he had unbuttoned because of the heat.

"Sergeant, are you the one that operated the crane and saved the life of the passenger in that accident a couple of hours ago?" the general asked.

"Yes Sir, that was me," replied Bitsko, not knowing if he was going to get a good chewing out or a handshake from the general.

"Son, I'm General Marski," he said. "I wanted to personally thank you for saving my niece's life."

Bitsko was greatly relieved to see the general was grateful and not angry with him for leaving his assignment behind to assist at the crash scene.

"General, I'm glad I could help," Bitsko said. "I was operating the crane when I heard the accident."

"Well son, we're all in your debt," Marski said. "I just want you to know how grateful we are that you're here. I understand you're a Reservist."

"Yes Sir," replied Bitsko. "I'm a member of the 683rd Heavy Equipment Maintenance Company. We're at Mount Eden Base Camp supporting the engineers and we've got some people training at Boatwright."

"Well I'm glad you were Johnny-on-the-Spot with my niece, young Sergeant. God bless you, Son," said the general.

"Here, I want to introduce you to these folks over here." The general had his hand on Bitsko's shoulder as he turned and walked over to the three men standing about 10 feet away.

"Gentlemen, this is the young man that saved my niece," said the general as the three men smiled and introduced themselves as reporters for both the local newspaper and the TV station in nearby Elizabethtown.

They began asking Bitsko questions, and he was glad to answer them. Most of the questions focused on his background in the Army and his civilian occupation. When they asked him about the Army Reserve unit he was in, he was proud to tell them all about the 683rd.

After they were done getting their story from Bitsko, he invited them all to the Mount Eden Base Camp field site. Bitsko's invitation extended to the post commanding general as well, who was very pleased to accept.

The general had Bitsko join him in his staff car as the reporters followed. Bitsko thought it might be a good idea to update General Marski on the condition of the floating bridge.

"Sir, the floating bridge is back in operation," Bitsko said. "Our service section fixed it last night."

The general was surprised to hear that.

"Son, I heard this morning that it would take our people a week to fix it," he said.

Bitsko grinned.

"Oh no, Sir. Our CO gave us the mission last night," Bitsko said. "He doesn't like to drive past the pig farm on the way to and from Main Post."

The general laughed out loud.

"Son, no one likes to drive past that damned place," he said. "I wish I could shut that place down, but the pig farmer's family has owned that farm for generations.

"Sergeant, your commander sounds like he's got his head screwed on right. I'd like to meet him. Tell me more about your unit."

As the driver headed toward the floating bridge, Bitsko told the post commander about the 683rd and how they were fully immersed in their mission work. The general seemed to be very curious about the 683rd and their mission at Mount Eden Base Camp. It seemed odd to him that of all the training areas available at Fort Knox, the Reserve Affairs office would allocate Mount Eden to the units of the 83rd Army Reserve Command from Ohio. General Marski seemed to remember someone telling him it was an old impact area around the turn of the century.

At the 683rd field site, Lieutenant Stiles reported to Marshall after she returned from the Main Post finance office.

"Sir, I've picked up the unit fund check," she said. "It's a whopping $58!"

Marshall gently nodded his head.

"That's enough to buy a horseshoes set and maybe a volleyball and net," he said. Marshall took the check and endorsed the back of it.

Marshall looked at Sergeant Tea and Lemasters.

"How about both of you go to the PX today and see what you can buy with this?" Marshall said. "Sarge, how about you type up a memo that gives you the authority to cash it at the bank."

"No problem, Sir," replied Tea. "I'll be glad to spend the unit's money."

While everyone was enjoying the conversation at the CP tent, the field phone rang. Marshall picked up the phone and gave his call sign. "Honcho one."

"Sir, we've got a general in the area with some reporters at the shop office tent," the field switchboard operator said.

"Thanks," replied Marshall. "I'm on my way."

Marshall looked over at Lemasters.

"We've got a general and some VIPs in the area," Marshall said. "Make sure that Colonel Biggs is notified and try and get a hold of Top. Let him know that they're in the shop office tent.

"Lieutenant Stiles, get all the officers and advise them they may have to give an impromptu briefing."

"Yes, Sir," replied both Stiles and Lemasters.

Marshall smiled at Tea.

"It's show time," Marshall said as he left for the shop office tent.

At the shop office tent, the general had already introduced himself to Chief Farley and sat down to see how things were going. As Marshall walked into the tent, he spotted the general and walked over to report to him.

The general stood up and Marshall walked over and gave him a crisp salute and held it.

"Captain Dave Marshall, commander of the 683rd Maintenance Company, Sir," he said.

General Marski saluted back.

"Nice to meet you, Commander," Marski said. "I'm here at your Sergeant Bitsko's invitation. This fine young soldier just saved my niece's life."

"Sir?" queried Marshall as he looked over at Bitsko with a puzzled look on his face.

The three reporters took their cue and began to inform Marshall and everyone present in the tent of Bitsko's fast actions, which saved the general's niece.

As the reporters were just about finished with the story, Colonel Biggs walked into the tent and immediately reported to the general. The post commander was happy to see Biggs. Both men exited the tent and walked through the 683rd field site as the general explained what was going on and why he and the reporters were there.

Biggs had already met General Marski during the first week of annual training, which was proper military protocol when a visiting unit came to an active duty post. It was standard operating procedure for the highest-ranking officer of the visiting unit to pay their respects the post commander.

"You hear about miracles happening to other people. Well, sometimes they happen to you," said General Marski. "I've got to get back to the hospital to check and see how my niece is doing. They've got her in surgery right now and my wife is probably worried to death about why I'm not there with her."

"It's good to see you again, Colonel. I want you to have dinner with the wife and I on Thursday at 1900 hours. Can you arrange that?"

Biggs saluted the general.

"Thursday at 1900 hours it is, Sir," Biggs said as General Marski motioned to his driver to get the staff car started.

Even though the reporters were still asking some questions about Bitsko and the 683rd, they saw the general leaving and decided to follow. They already had their big story for the evening news and tomorrow's headlines.

Biggs walked over to Marshall.

"Captain Marshall, your people continue to surprise me," Biggs said.

"Sir, I hope they continue to do so, and pleasantly," Marshall responded. "The soldiers deserve all the credit. This is one fine unit."

Biggs concurred.

"Yes it is, Commander. Keep up the good work."

Marshall snapped a salute as Biggs departed the 683rd area. Biggs knew that every Army Reserve unit had good personnel. It took a knowledgeable commander to nurture their potential and make it happen.

Bitsko was a bit bewildered with all the attention he had just received as Marshall walked over to him. Marshall extended a handshake to Bitsko.

"Well done, Sarge," Marshall said. "You've brought some excellent praise upon yourself and this unit."

"Thank you, Sir. It wasn't really anything special," replied Bitsko.

Marshall smiled at the Sergeant's humble response.

"Go ahead and grab some chow. I'll have someone take you back to Main Post so you can get back to work."

Bitsko smiled and thanked his commander. That's exactly what he wanted to hear: eat some good chow and get back to work in his 20-ton crane doing what he loved to do.

As Bitsko left to get in line for noon chow, Marshall, Sergeant Tea and Sergeant Lemasters joined the unit officers walked in the shop office tent.

"Well, it looks like you people have dodged another one. The General just left to go back to Main Post," said Marshall, observing the looks of relief on his lieutenants' faces.

"Sir, I was hopin' that someday I might be able to give my briefing to some VIPs again," Lieutenant Rodriguez said.

"Don't worry, Rod. You'll have plenty of opportunities," Marshall responded. "Just make sure the others are as ready as you are."

Things began to settle down in the 683rd area after the VIPs and Biggs left. Marshall walked over to Lemasters.

"Sarge, you all right?" Marshall asked. "You look kind of worried."

"Shoot, I'm all right, Sir," he said. "I'm just a bit worried about Vivian. She's gettin' kinda crabby in this heat."

"Where is she now?" asked Marshall.

"She's piggin' out again at Sergeant Emery's Mess Hall. Heck, she's eating for three, not two!" replied Lemasters.

"Sarge, I want you to take good care of Vivian when you're on Main Post," replied Marshall. "If she's not feeling well, take her to the hospital, OK?

"I also want you to pay a visit to Chief McCarthy and give me an update on how he's doing and when he's going to be released.

"And one more thing. Take the 683rd hero for a day back to the rail yard."

"Aye aye, Sir," replied Lemasters as he saluted his commander and walked over to get Tea for their trip to Main Post to spend the unit fund money.

Marshall was still standing in the shop office tent.

"Sir, you want an update on what's goin' on in the shops?" asked Chief Farley.

"Great idea, Chief. Fill me in," replied Marshall.

Farley went over the job status of each piece of equipment and how many they had already fixed and were awaiting customer pickup. The numbers were impressive. Fifteen jobs already completed, five more in shop and three more waiting shop. All jobs were projected to be finished by the following day.

"Chief, this is very good news," said Marshall. He was very pleased to hear the 683rd shops were cranking out completions as fast they were coming in.

"Has the word gotten out to all the units that we're not accepting anymore turn ins after tomorrow morning?"

Farley smiled.

"Sir, we're not taking anymore jobs after 1900 hours tomorrow, unless it's an emergency."

"Sounds good, Chief," said Marshall.

Sergeant Lemasters, Sergeant Tea and Sergeant Bitsko were headed toward the floating bridge and Main Post in one of the 683rd ¼-ton jeeps. The floating bridge personnel saw them as they approached the river crossing, and pulled the pontoon bridge over to their side.

After they got the jeep onto the pontoon platform and were pulled over to the other side, the personnel from the floating bridge crew saw that they belonged to the 683rd by the bumper number on the jeep.

"Sarge, we were all hopin' to have the day off until your people fixed our bridge," one of the soldiers sarcastically told Lemasters.

Lemasters decided to get into the soldier's face.

"Why, you bunch a sad sacks!" Lemasters yelled. "Y'all better be glad you ain't in my unit or I'd chew ya up and spit ya out fer a comment like that. Ya sit on yer butts and fish all day and ya call that solderin'?"

Sergeant Tea saw Lemasters face turning red and decided to intervene.

"Come on Sarge. You're scarin' the baby," Tea said, touching Lemasters' arm. "Let these boys alone so they can go back and play."

Tea's words had a calming affect on Lemasters. The bridge personnel were glad to see her calm him down. Lemasters just growled, got back into the driver's seat, and started the jeep's engine.

Before they left, Lemasters gave the bridge crew another warning.

"Y'all had better take good care of this here bridge," he said. "The general knows what's goin' on around here and your butts are all on the line."

As the jeep climbed the embankment and disappeared from sight, the bridge crew went back to their fishing, wishing they had the day off.

Sergeant Bitsko was dropped off at the rail yard so he could get back to work in the 20-ton crane, while Lemasters and Tea headed toward the PX. A small commercial bank was next to the PX and both Lemasters and Tea cashed the check.

They went into the PX, got a shopping cart, and began their search in the sporting goods section. They found that they had enough unit fund money to buy a horseshoe set and the volleyball and net and proceeded to the checkout register. Lemasters also had some money from the 683rd shop office coffee fund collection to supplement the unit fund money.

As he was paying for the merchandise, Tea had a sudden urge to go to the bathroom.

"Sergeant Lemasters, will you hurry up?" Tea asked in a hushed whisper. "I've got to go pee!"

Lemasters was surprised to hear that.

"Hold on, Vivian. I'm almost done," he said, counting the loose change to pay for the merchandise.

"Oh John, darling, our child and I can't wait much longer, so would you hurry it up so I can PEE?" said Tea. Lemasters became flustered as he counted the change.

"Ma'am do you have a bathroom here?" Tea asked the cashier as she shifted her weight from foot to foot.

"Sure honey," replied the cashier. "Just go through the double-doors by the shoe racks in the back of the store and turn to your left."

"Thank you," said Tea as she shuffled off to relieve herself.

Lemasters looked at the cashier.

"She ain't my wife," he said.

The cashier smiled at him and rang up the sale.

After Tea returned from her trip to the PX bathroom, Lemasters was visibly upset.

"Vivian, you are the most irritatin' female I've ever had ta work with. That's the last time you and I are gonna be shoppin' together."

Tea could not stop laughing.

"Oh, hush up Sergeant Lemasters, and take me home to Mount Eden." They both walked out of the PX and Tea was still trying to hold back her laughter.

"Well, aren't you going to hold my hand while we cross the parking lot?" Tea asked, teasing him.

Lemasters just rolled his eyes.

"Shut up, Vivian, and git you and yer unborn youngun's tail in the jeep," Lemasters said. "Time to go visit Mr. McCarthy."

They climbed into the jeep and headed toward Ireland Army Hospital.

At the hospital parking lot, Tea slowly climbed out of the jeep. Lemasters locked up the steering wheel with the chain and lock, which was standard on all military vehicles.

Two Army nurses were going on duty for their eight-hour shift and saw Tea in the parking lot as she tried to ease the pain in her back after she had climbed out of the passenger seat in the Jeep.

One of the Army nurses walked over to Tea.

"Sergeant, are you near your due date?" she asked.

Tea looked at the nurse with a bit of surprise.

"Oh no, Ma'am. I'm not due for a while. I'm trying to get the soreness out of my back," Tea replied. "It's been bothering me lately. We're just here to visit one of our warrant officers that got all bit-up by chiggers."

"Ohhh, we heard about him," the nurse said. "Why don't you come with me? I work in the pre-natal clinic. Let's give you a check-up while you're here, and maybe you can get some physical therapy for your back."

Lemasters was listening to the conversation.

"Ma'am, be my guest an take her off my back fer a couple hours," he said. "Maybe you kin admit her fer a couple days instead. I won't mind."

Tea looked at the nurse with a smile.

"Now isn't he the sweetest thing?" Tea asked.

All three walked toward the main entrance to Ireland Hospital. Lemasters told Tea that he would visit Chief McCarthy while she got a check-up. They made arrangements to meet in the lobby in two hours, which would be enough time for Tea's check-up.

Lemasters took the elevator to the fourth floor. As he walked into McCarthy's room, an orderly and a nurse were applying new sterile dressings to McCarthy's backside.

"Hello Chief," said Lemasters. "Nice ta see yer good side again."

McCarthy was in no mood for company.

"If that's you Lemasters, get the hell outta here," McCarthy snarled.

The nurse looked over at Lemasters and then to McCarthy.

"Is that any way to talk to someone who came all the way up here to see you?" the nurse asked. "You better lighten up, Mr. McCarthy, or we may have to do a couple of special procedures on you." She winked at Lemasters. The nurse was nearly done working on McCarthy and pulled the bed sheet over his backside.

The nurse spoke to the orderly in Spanish. The orderly nodded his head and responded, "Si, Si, Senora."

Lemasters looked a bit surprised as the orderly left the room.

"Doesn't he speak English?" Lemasters asked.

The nurse smiled.

"We get our orderlies from the medical units on a rotation for six weeks. A few of our corpsmen come from Puerto Rico. When they enlist, the Army hopes that by the time they get assigned stateside, they'll be speaking fluent English. Some take longer than the others, especially if there are other Latinos in their unit. Eventually they come around and catch on to the language."

Lemasters grinned.

"Well Ma'am," he said, "it's a good thing you speak Spanish."

The nurse smiled at Lemasters.

"Sergeant, are you from Mr. McCarthy's unit?" she asked.

"Yes Ma'am, I am," replied Lemasters.

"Mr. McCarthy can be discharged on Friday if there are no other complications," the nurse said bluntly. "He's on antibiotics to counter any infection. I don't recommend that he goes back to the field."

"Yes Ma'am," Lemasters replied. "We were planning to pick him up on Friday evening 'cause we're leaving Saturday morning for Ohio. He'll be ridin' a chartered bus back, so he kin relax and stretch out."

The nurse looked at the chief.

"Mr. McCarthy, you will remember to take care of all those areas that haven't healed yet and take your medication as prescribed," she said.

McCarthy was trying to keep his voice as calm as possible and not show his anger.

"Yes, Nurse, I will," he replied.

The nurse left the room as Sergeant Lemasters sat down on the chair next to the bed.

"Well, Chief, everyone says hey and hope yer on yer feet soon," Lemasters said. "The Old Man wants ya to know everythin' is goin' jist fine in tech supply. They're doin' a fantastic job out thar in the field supportin' the mission."

McCarthy turned his head on the pillow toward Lemasters.

"Sergeant, thanks for the visit," McCarthy said. "Now would you mind gettin' the hell outta here? Tell the Old Man I'll be OK for the trip back home."

Lemasters knew he wasn't one of McCarthy's favorite people to talk to and took the hint.

"All right Chief. We'll see ya later."

Lemasters began to walk out the door. He decided to leave the chief a little gift for his rudeness by breaking some wind he had been building up inside.

"Was that me?" Lemasters said in mock horror. "Excuse me, Chief."

"Get the hell outta here!" McCarthy shouted as Lemasters left the room.

Serves the bastard right, thought Lemasters as he walked toward the elevator.

As Lemasters exited the elevator on the ground floor, he spotted Sergeant Bitsko heading toward the information desk. Lemasters decided to see what Bitsko was up to.

"Well, well, hello thar, Sergeant Bitsko. Didn't we drop you off at the rail yard? What brings ya here?" Lemasters said. "If'n ya want ta see Mr. McCarthy, he's in a pretty bad mood right now."

"Hey, Sarge," said Bitsko. "I got done with the offloading so I thought I'd check up on the general's niece I helped out this morning."

"Don't let me stop ya," said Lemasters, "I've got some time ta kill waitin' for Vivian."

"What's wrong with Vivian?" asked Bitsko.

"Oh nothin'," replied Lemasters. "She's decided to get a check-up while she's here. No harm in that, 'cept'n I've got ta wait on her fer another hour or so."

Bitsko realized he would need a ride back to Mount Eden.

"Sarge, I'm gonna need a ride back to the field, so why don't you hang loose for a little while? I'll be back soon and wait with you for Vivian."

Lemasters nodded his head in agreement and smiled as he decided to take a seat in the lobby and read a fishing magazine.

Bitsko was asking about the general's niece at the information desk when General Marski walked into the lobby and spotted him.

"There you are," said Marski as he walked over to the information desk and shook Bitsko's hand. "How about I introduce you to my niece?"

"Yes Sir, that would be great," replied Bitsko. "I was just checking on her condition."

"She's doing just fine," said Marski. "And she's been asking about her knight in shining armor. Just follow me, Son." The general smiled, put his hand on Bitsko's shoulder, and led him down the hallway to the recovery room.

Inside one of the recovery rooms, a lovely young woman was lying on a hospital bed with her arm in a cast and a few minor cuts on her face and scalp.

"Hi Nichole," the general said as they entered the room. "Are you feeling well enough for a little company?"

"Sure, Uncle Mike. Please come in," she said in a soft voice that sounded like she just woke up from a pleasant dream.

"Honey, this is the young man that saved your life. Go ahead son, introduce yourself," said the general.

"Hi, I'm Bob. How are you feeling?" asked Bitsko in a thoughtful and polite voice.

"Oh, like a truck ran over me," replied Nichole as she smiled and started to chuckle. "Oh, it hurts when I laugh," she said. "I better try and be more serious."

"I just came by to see how you're doing and hope you're gonna be on your feet soon," Bitsko said.

"Thanks," said Nichole softly. "I'm supposed to check out of here tomorrow, right Uncle Mike?"

"You bet darlin'," replied the general with a grin as he looked at his niece's condition with both gratitude and despair.

"The doc says you'll be fine in a few weeks. No scars and ready to go back to college in the fall."

Bitsko was a bit curious.

"Where do you go to school?" he asked.

"I'm going to be a senior at Kent State," she said. "I'm majoring in journalism."

Bitsko couldn't believe his ears.

"I'm going to Kent State, too," he said. "I'm finishing up my master's in biology. Maybe we'll run into each other."

"Nichole, you take care, honey. I've got to get back to my headquarters," the general said. "It looks like you two have a lot to talk about. I'll be back after dinner to see you, okay?"

His niece nodded and blew him a kiss as the general smiled and winked back at her.

The general then placed his hand on Bitsko's shoulder.

"I don't know how to thank you enough," General Marski said. "God bless you, Son." General Marski turned and walked away as Bitsko and Nichole struck up a mutually interesting conversation.

Lemasters was finished with his third magazine when Tea walked into the waiting area of the lobby and took a seat next to him.

"Been waitin' long for me?" asked Tea as she relaxed in the soft chair next to Lemasters.

"Naw," replied Lemasters looking at his watch. "Now we're waiting for Bitsko while he's visitin' that gal he rescued this morning."

"So how's Mr. McCarthy doing?" asked Tea.

"He's full of piss and vinegar as usual," replied Lemasters. "Maybe we should leave him here. The son of a bitch threw me outta his room while I was visitin'. That no good, arrogant old fart."

After he said that he started to chuckle, which caught Tea's attention.

"What's so funny?"" she asked as she saw Lemasters chuckling.

"I left the old fart with an old fart," said Lemasters chuckling.

Tea didn't catch the meaning as Bitsko appeared.

"Sorry to keep you guys waiting," Bitsko said. "How's it goin', Sergeant Tea?"

"I'm fine, Sergeant Bitsko," replied Tea. "How's the general's niece doing?"

"Oh, she's fine. She's very fine," replied Bitsko. "She's going to Kent State. I'm sure I'll be seeing her this fall."

Tea looked at Bitsko and thought to herself, this boy's in love.

"All right you two, let's git back to Mount Eden. Them chiggers is hollerin' for their dinner," said Lemasters.

The threesome walked out to the parking lot and got into the ¼-ton jeep. It was 1600 hours, and little time was left before the floating bridge would be closed for the day.

Marshall was talking with Farley in the shop office tent when Lieutenant Kiley walked in to update the commander on the status of training at Boatwright.

"Hello Sir, Chief," said Kiley to both men as she sat down in one of the steel folding chairs next to them. "I bring you good news."

Marshall smiled.

"That's what I like to hear," he said. "What's going on Kathy?"

"Sir, the training for all sections has been excellent and things are starting to wind down now," she replied. "By tomorrow evening, we'll be finished with all the jobs at Boatwright and ready to come back to the field."

"That won't be necessary just yet," Marshall quickly replied. "I want your people to remain on Main Post until Friday, then come to Mount Eden that evening. The barracks you signed for have to be cleaned and turned back into Post Housing before we leave."

Kiley had a surprised look on her face.

"Do we have to have it inspected?"

Marshall smiled and nodded his head.

"And it has to shine like new," he added.

"Looks like we've got some serious cleaning to do," replied Kiley. "I'm going to have Sergeant Huddle get things going in the right direction as soon as I get back."

"Pay day activities will begin at 1200 hours on Friday," Marshal said. "I'm giving all the unit personnel the afternoon off to cash their checks and buy whatever they want at the PX. I want you to advise your personnel that we don't want to see our young people spending their hard-earned money on booze."

"What about the NCOs?" asked Kiley.

Marshall grinned.

"They can do whatever they want to do," he said. "I just don't want any alcohol consumed in the field or on the way back to Ohio."

"Looks like Fred and I won't have that beer we've been looking forward to," Kiley replied.

"Me too," Chief Farley added.

Marshall looked at both of them.

"You can go to the club and enjoy the afternoon on Friday. I'm sure they'll be glad to serve you. Just have your designated driver with you for the return trip," Marshall said.

"Now, let's get back to coordinating the turn-in of the barracks. Chief, do you have a copy of the post regulations?"

Farley found his copy of the Fort Knox Post Regulations in his field desk. Detailed procedural guidance for all visiting units was given, which is what they were looking for.

"I believe this reg will describe in great detail everything you need to do," remarked Marshall. "Do you need a copy of this reg?"

"Yes Sir, I sure do," replied Kiley.

"Take it," replied Marshall. "We've got another copy at the CP tent that Vivian is using. That reminds me, anyone here seen Sergeant Tea lately?"

As soon as Marshall asked about Tea, the jeep with Sergeant Lemasters, Sergeant Tea and Sergeant Bitsko pulled into the field site. Marshall spotted them as they arrived, since the side flaps of the shop office tent were rolled up to allow the summer breezes to come through. Lemasters and his passengers were exiting the jeep as Marshall walked over to see what they had bought at the PX.

"So what did you get for us?" asked Marshall.

Lemasters took out a volleyball from the bag and tossed it to the commander.

"Got a net fer it too, Sir," replied Lemasters as Bitsko carried a box with the horseshoes game.

"So how's Chief McCarthy doing?" Marshall asked.

Lemasters grinned.

"That old fart's just as mean and ornery as ever," he said. "The nurse said he'd be okay to travel by Friday. He's takin' some medicine ta help reduce the infection. He's still a mess. They got 'em laying on his stomach now."

"I'm glad he's riding the bus back. He'd be miserable in the convoy," mentioned Tea.

"All his gear and clothes have been cleaned, right Sarge?" Marshall asked.

"Oh yes, Sir," Lemasters replied. "I made sure them boys in the 928th laundered his stuff twice."

"That's great, Sarge," replied Marshall. "I want you to make sure his bus ride back is as comfortable as possible. He's going to be very sore and irritable."

Lemasters grinned.

"Sir, he's always been like that."

"Just take good care of him, Sarge," Marshall said with a grin. "I don't want the chief to have to do anything but ride the bus back home."

"Sir, I'll take good care of the old timer," said Lemasters confidently.

Evening chow was being served as Tisher walked over to the group talking by the shop office tent.

"You guys took a heck of a long time to cash a check and see Mr. McCarthy," Tisher said.

Tea explained what had happened with their visit to the hospital and the visit to the pre-natal clinic.

The first sergeant grinned.

"So how's our baby doing?" Tisher asked.

"Just fine, Top," replied Tea. "As a matter of fact, they tell me everything is perfect. I even got a massage for my back."

"Maybe I'll come along with you next time. My back's been bothering me too," said Tisher with a broad smile on his face.

The group began walking toward the mess area as they handed the recreational gear to several soldiers that had already finished eating their evening meal. Within minutes, the clanging of horseshoes was heard above the noise of the generators. Soldiers were playing volleyball by the time Marshall was done with his supper.

Over at the service and recovery platoon, Specialist Cutnoff was playing with what he thought was Nugot's pet skunk, Stinker.

As Nugot walked over to climb into his 5-ton wrecker for a recovery mission that was just given to him, he called out to Cutnoff.

"Tony, let's go. We've got to haul another engineer dumper to the shops," Nugot said.

"OK, Sarge. Let me just put your pet skunk back in the tent."

Cutnoff climbed into the wrecker as Nugot started the engine. A small skunk head peered out of Nugot's unbuttoned shirt and looked at Cutnoff curiously.

"Hey Sarge, if that's your skunk, what skunk did I just put in our tent?" asked Cutnoff.

Nugot put the wrecker into gear and smiled.

"Beats the hell outta me."

They begin their short journey to the engineer field site. Cutnoff kept worrying about the wild skunk he just put in his tent.

Stinker seemed to enjoy the ride and crawled out of Nugot's shirt. Nugot gently grabbed Stinker and put him between the back of the seat and his neck for a better view. As they drove down the dirt road, Nugot noticed his new pet was thoroughly enjoying the adventure.

When they arrived at the engineers' field site, Nugot gently placed Stinker inside his empty duffel bag in the cab of the wrecker so he wouldn't run away.

Within 10 minutes, Nugot and Cutnoff were heading back to the 683rd with another truck in tow.

At the shop office, Chief Farley had his tech inspectors waiting for the truck to arrive. Their job would be to assess the damage and what was needed for repairs. When Nugot pulled in, the inspectors began going over every part of the truck. Within five minutes they concluded that the clutch needed replacing, and it also needed new brakes on the front end.

The engineers' motor pool NCO was there to write up the paperwork. As the paperwork was being submitted, the front wheels were off the truck and the brakes were being replaced. The clutch would be replaced before nightfall. The 683rd mechanics had the repairs down to a fine art, and looked forward to taking some time off and relaxing.

As the sun disappeared over the trees, some of the soldiers of the 683rd were playing volleyball and horseshoes while others were waiting their turn. The evening shift was busily working on the jobs in shop, doing what they loved to do—fixing things.

Everyone at Mount Eden Base Camp knew that there were only a few days left before they could go home. Marshall was well aware of that fact, and wanted to make sure that everyone kept busy doing mission work or training. Sitting around waiting for time to go by was the worst thing a soldier could experience.

Marshall and Tisher were making their nightly rounds and noticed Private Hudson enjoying some of Sergeant Emery's bean with bacon soup. He had become a regular nightly customer after Peoples and Kayrule evicted him from the half-shelter every evening.

The 1st and 2nd Automotive Platoons were still busy fixing the engineers' trucks, which continued to flow through the maintenance shops with worn-out clutches or bad brakes. The standard routine maintenance of oil changes, replacement of filters and tires was done by the engineers' motor pool. The big repairs were accomplished by the 683rd, and the engineers were so glad the 683rd was there.

The remainder of the 683rd was fast asleep, resting for the new day coming. All had made adjustments to sleeping on the ground in their sleeping bags and made their sleeping areas as comfortable as possible, using the natural materials in the woods of Kentucky to their advantage.

Despite all the hardships everyone faced, they were all able to adapt and overcome, just as Captain Marshall had told them to. The 683rd was now a confident, can-do unit. Proud to serve their country and show all they were capable to perform their mission—and any mission that would be thrust upon them.

A.T. - DAY 12 (THURSDAY)

Captain Marshall walked over to the shop office tent, stifling a yawn as he opened the entrance flap and entered.

"Mornin' Chief. How's shop operations going?"

Chief Farley smiled and pointed to the production control board mounted on an easel on the side of the tent.

"Sir, we've got eight vehicles awaiting pick up, and only two are in the shops. Both should be done before evening."

"Excellent news, Chief," replied Marshall. "Colonel Biggs gave the 683rd some praises this morning at the commander's meeting. Apparently everyone at Mount Eden is 100 percent operational, vehicle-wise, and ready to roll on Saturday morning. I told him that we would have our maintenance contact teams available during the convoy phase in case of any breakdowns.

"Unfortunately, for that very reason, we'll also be the last to leave Mount Eden."

Farley smiled at the commander.

"Sir, from my experience, you won't see any broken down trucks or vehicles on the way back," he said. "These soldiers are taking real good care of them now, and every motor pool is checking every piece of rolling stock over very carefully. I'd be really surprised if we come across any breakdowns on the way back home."

"I hope you're right, Chief," Marshall said with a smile. "I don't think anyone here wants to have a slow journey on the way back home."

"Sir, you remember how long it took to get here," stated Farley. "Well I can guarantee you it won't take but maybe eight hours to get back, if that."

Marshall was glad to hear his shop officer was confident about a rapid trip back to Ohio, and smiled.

"Got anything that I need to know about or look into?" Marshall asked.

"No Sir, I've got everything handled here," replied Farley.

Marshall gave him the thumbs up and walked toward the CP tent to talk with First Sergeant Tisher.

He saw Lieutenant Stiles walking by and asked her to join him and talk about some training for the afternoon.

"Deb, it looks like we might need some formal training for some of the troops this afternoon," said Marshall. "What do you have slotted in the training schedule?"

"Sir, this afternoon we've got decontamination training with Sergeant Bierce as the primary instructor. I picked up 100 training decon packets from my secret admirer at group HQ."

"Major Brown had some extras, did he?" Marshall grinned and said. Stiles smiled coyly in response. "Good work, Lieutenant," said Marshall. "I think I'll be there for the class if nothing comes up or gets in the way. Where is it going to be held?"

"If the weather holds, we'll have it in the shade near the assembly area, right after noon chow."

Marshall continued his journey to the CP tent as Lieutenant Rodriguez walked up to him.

"Sir, we've got a bit of a problem," Rodriguez sheepishly said.

Marshall, not wanting to slow down, looked at his lieutenant.

"How so, Rod?" he asked.

"Did you have a chance to talk with the unit armorer, Specialist Peoples?" asked Rodriguez.

"No I haven't, Rod. Why don't you enlighten me while we take a stroll over there," replied Marshall. They both changed direction as Marshall turned to his lieutenant for more information.

"Sir, I think it would be better if I showed you," said Rodriguez.

Marshall was trying to figure out exactly what was the problem that had Rodriguez so worried. As they approached the weapons trailer, Specialist Peoples was sitting on the trailer steps, looking at her boots and waiting for the commander to arrive.

"Specialist Peoples, show the commander what you just showed me," said Rodriguez as both men came to the back of the weapons trailer.

"Sir, we've got some problems with the crew-served weapons as well as some of the M16s," responded Peoples. "I checked for barrel erosion on each M60. I'm going to have to send them all in for new barrels. Looks like they've been reamed with an electric drill and bore brush. The lans and grooves are just about completely worn out. About 10 of the M16s are the same way."

Marshall listened intently to what Peoples had to say. He knew all about weapon systems.

"Good job, Specialist Peoples," Marshall said. "We'll start turning them in for repair or replacement once we get back to home station in Ravenna. Have you started the maintenance request paperwork?"

"Yes, Sir. I'm a little rusty at it, but I'll type it out when I get my hands on a typewriter," replied Peoples.

"Stop by the shop office and see if they can help you out with that," said Marshall as he turned to leave the area. "Rod, anything else for me?" asked Marshall.

"No Sir, that was it," Rodriguez said.

Marshall smiled confidently and continued his journey to the CP tent.

As Marshall entered the CP tent, Tisher was talking with Sergeant Tea.

"Howdy. Sir! Just two more days and a wake up to go!" said Tisher.

"Top, if I didn't know any better, I'd believe you actually want to leave this garden spot of Fort Knox, Kentucky," said Marshall with a touch of sarcasm in his voice.

"I'm startin' to get a touch of homesickness," replied Tisher.

"Well Top, I've got the cure for you. Let's take a trip to the post hospital and drop in and see our favorite warrant officer," said Marshall.

"Okay Sir, I'm ready to take my medicine," said Tisher. "Let's go. I'll drive. No need to submit our driver to any unnecessary punishment." Marshall enjoyed the way Tisher made light of the differences he had with McCarthy.

As both men climbed into the jeep, Marshall cautioned him.

"You better get the dispatcher to write you down as the driver," said Marshall. "We don't want to get pulled over on Main Post by a roadside spot check and get our vehicle impounded, now do we?"

"Yeah, yeah, you're right Sir," replied Tisher.

"Hey Chief, who's working dispatch this morning?" Tisher yelled to Chief James.

"That'll be Jessie, Top," replied Chief James as he walked by.

Tisher got out of the jeep grumbling and walked over to the Motor Pool tent with the vehicle log book to get the jeep dispatched properly. After several minutes, he came out of the motor pool tent with the green log book tucked under his arm and climbed in the jeep.

"All done, Sir. I hope you're happy," said Tisher in a whimsical manner.

"Top, I'm just thrilled to death. Let's go."

"Which way, Sir? floating bridge or pig farm?" asked the First Sergeant with a grin.

Marshall pondered the question.

"We don't have our gas masks with us," Marshall said. "Let's take the floating bridge, shall we?"

Tisher was keeping the same grin.

"Good choice, Sir, good choice," he said.

As they headed down the dirt road to the floating bridge, a cloud of dust kicked up from the road. Marshall noticed that the brush along the side of the road was covered in road dust, just waiting for another rainstorm to wash it all off. As they neared the floating bridge, the bridge crew was busy fishing.

"Man, I wish I had a job like that," Tisher remarked. "It must be nice to fish all day and get paid for it. Plus get three squares a day and a warm bed to sleep in."

Marshall agreed with the first sergeant.

"Yeah, maybe they should put these guys on a recruiting poster."

Both men couldn't help but laugh at the absurdity of the picture it painted in their minds. Join the Army and fish all day long – eat three great meals, sleep in your own bed, and get paid for it. What could be better?

As the bridge crew brought the floating bridge pontoon over to Marshall and Tisher's side of the river, Lieutenant Burks' tech supply section pulled in behind them with loaded deuce-and a halves.

"Top, looks like the tech supply section is ready to turn in all those old parts," Marshall remarked.

Tisher looked at his commander with a grin.

"Yeah, and I'm glad as hell they're behind us," Tisher said. "I've already swallowed my yearly allowance of road dust since I've been out here."

Marshall knew exactly what he meant and agreed.

"Yep, me too. Let's make sure we don't catch them in front of us on the way back."

As they pulled their jeep onto the floating bridge, the bridge operator told them to move the vehicle all the way forward so they could load a deuce and a half on as well. The floating bridge tipped upwards slightly as the deuce was driven on. The operator gave a shout with a hand signal to the cable operator, who then began driving the floating bridge-towing deuce up the hill on the opposite bank.

The first sergeant was talking with Sergeant Schmoot who was in the deuce as they were being pulled to the opposite shore.

"Dennis, we're gonna check on Mr. McCarthy," Tisher said. "Anything you want to pass on?"

"Just let him know I'll be stopping by to see him after we turn these parts in to PDO," replied Schmoot.

"I'm sure he'll be glad to see you," replied Tisher in a sincere voice.

As the floating bridge reached the shore, the 683rd personnel climbed back into their vehicles and drove onto the exit ramp. Schmoot waited for the other tech supply deuce and a half as Marshall and the first sergeant topped the hill and sped off to Ireland Hospital.

"Maybe I can get a back massage like Vivian did," remarked Tisher. "You can pay your respects to McCarthy and I'll see if I can schmooze one of the nurses."

"Good luck, Top," replied Marshall. "I'm married to an Army nurse and I never get a back rub, much less a massage." The first sergeant grinned.

"That's because you're married to her," he said. Both laughed as the jeep proceeded down the dirt road to the paved intersection about a mile away.

Back at the floating bridge, the other tech supply deuce had made it across the river. The bridge operator took a long look at the deuce.

"Hey Sarge, you know you've got two inner flats on that vehicle?" the operator asked.

Schmoot walked down to look at the deuce and shook his head in disgust.

"Thanks," Schmoot said. "We'll fix it when we get back to Mount Eden."

The bridge operator told Schmoot something he wasn't expecting to hear.

"Sarge, we're not allowed to transport any vehicles that are not in condition code B unless it's an emergency," he said. "You'll have to go the long way around to get back to Mount Eden. Sorry."

Schmoot wasn't going to argue with the man. The drivers had to accept the situation as they climbed back into their deuces.

"OK everyone," said Schmoot. "Let's head to PDO."

It was becoming a very hot day, and they were not looking forward to passing the pig farm on the way back, but they had no choice. Schmoot was decidedly upset with the driver of the other deuce for not checking his vehicle over a little more carefully.

Ireland Hospital was not very busy in the lobby area as Marshall went to the information desk. Tisher decided to visit the emergency room waiting area and ask the receptionist about getting a back massage.

On the fourth floor, Marshall made his way to Chief McCarthy's room. McCarthy was lying on his back, watching a sports show on TV.

"Hello, Chief! How's it going?" asked Marshall.

"It goes well, Sir. Thanks for asking," replied McCarthy cheerfully. The chief's legs were covered with large gauze bandages.

"So what's the prognosis?" asked Marshall. "Are they going to let you outta here on time?"

McCarthy was busy watching the sports news and gave Marshall a brief answer.

"They're going to discharge me Friday night."

Marshall was amused to see the chief more focused on the TV than him.

"I'll have a jeep waiting for you when they discharge you. Just keep on healing up and take it easy. I'll see you on Friday. By the way, Sergeant Schmoot will be dropping in to pay you a visit."

Marshall left the room and check with the nurses' station on the floor.

"Could you tell me what time you'll be discharging Mr. McCarthy on Friday evening?" asked Marshall.

"What time would you like to pick him up, Captain?" the nurse behind the desk asked.

"1900 hours would do just fine," replied Marshall. "I'll have a driver up here to escort him."

"1900 hours will be fine," the nurse replied. "We'll have him ready for you."

Marshall thanked the nurse and took the elevator down to the lobby area to meet up with Tisher. As he exited the elevator, Tisher was waiting for him in the lounge area.

"Well Top, did you get your massage?" asked Marshall.

The first sergeant laughed as he pulled out a pack of matches.

"I went to the ER to see if there were any of our troops waiting there. Didn't see anyone so I went up to the receptionist and asked him about seeing someone for a back massage. He told me that if I wanted a good one at a low price, to check out this place and he gave me this book of matches."

The book of matches was an advertisement for the Oriental Massage Palace, and its address, phone number and hours of operation were on the cover.

"Go ahead and open it up," Tisher said. Marshall did. Inside the book of matches was a color photograph of a nude model in a suggestive pose.

"We're not going to take you there no matter how bad your back is aching, Top," replied Marshall as he handed the book of matches back to him with a smile.

"Oh, c'mon Sir! My back's been really aching today," pleaded Tisher half-heartedly.

"Top, you're homesick, remember?" Marshall said as if he were admonishing a little child for doing something wrong.

"Gee whiz, Sir, you never let me have any fun," replied Tisher as he chuckled and acted out the roll of a spoiled little child. "Maybe I'll give them a visit during payday activities," he said as his eyes lit up.

"Just don't drive a military vehicle over there or be in uniform," said Marshall. "The MPs are always looking for military personnel to be at the wrong place during duty hours."

The two men headed out the main entrance of the hospital and decided to drive over to the PX and make a call home to their wives. It was always a good idea to let loved ones know that they'd be home soon and what time they'd be there.

Marshall made sure that his wife would meet him at the Reserve Center at the Ravenna Arsenal at 1700 hours on Saturday.

After finishing their phone calls to home, Marshall had another idea.

"Top, let's go check on our Boatwright folks' barracks here on post," Marshall said. "They should have some of the personnel getting the barracks cleaned up for turn-in."

"Righto, Sir," replied Tisher as they climbed into the jeep. "They're over in the old section of the post, just about a mile and a half from here."

The two drove off toward the old billeting area of Fort Knox that was built during World War II. Rumor had it that during the war, a completed barracks was built every fifteen minutes. That was made possible due to the standardization of all Army barracks floor plans. All World War II-style Army barracks were identical from the outside. Only the interiors were changed to suit the occupants' requirements.

The barracks the 683rd personnel were staying in were being cleaned from top to bottom as Tisher and the commander walked in. All the bedding was stripped and the mattresses were rolled up. The floors were mopped and a buffer was being used on the second floor to buff up the wax. Tisher walked over to the latrine to see how things were progressing there. Latrines were normally the first area the inspectors looked at. The shower room was the hardest to keep clean, and two men were busy with scrub brushes washing down the walls with disinfectant cleaner.

"Hiya, Top. Wanna lend us a hand?" asked one of the soldiers as he spotted the first sergeant.

"Nah. You're doing a good job. Keep it up!" replied Tisher.

Marshall spotted Lieutenant Kiley coming from the adjacent barracks building.

"Hello, Kathy! How's everything going?" asked Marshall.

"Sir, we should have the female barracks done within the next hour. This one should be done soon. I've got the Post housing inspector coming over at 1600 hours to turn these back in if they pass," replied Kiley.

"Well Kathy, if they don't pass the turn-in inspection, your people will have to stay here and keep on cleaning until they do," said Marshall.

"Yes Sir," replied Kiley. "I've made my people aware of that. I don't think they'll want to do have to do it all over again, so they're doing it right the first time."

Marshall smiled.

"Then I'll see you and your people at Mount Eden for evening chow," he said.

Marshall and Tisher gave Kiley some words of encouragement and climbed back into the jeep.

"Top, speaking of getting things ready for turn-in, I'm positive that all foxholes and fighting positions have to be filled in and the area has to be closely policed for any trash in our training area."

"Yes Sir, it sure does," replied Tisher. "I'm going to have my field first sergeant take care of that when we get back to Mount Eden."

"By the way, Top, have you seen or heard from our evaluator lately?" asked Marshall.

"Oh no, Sir," replied Tisher. "He hasn't shown up for a while. Maybe he's sneaking around again while we're not looking. Vivian would have mentioned it to me if he had visited the area and we weren't there."

They drove off toward Mount Eden through the dirt roads and training areas. Tisher had become reacquainted with the back roads of Fort Knox. When he was a younger man, he went through basic training and AIT at Fort Knox.

At Mount Eden, Lieutenant Humphrey had arrived with his finished 1-R evaluation of the 683rd Maintenance Company.

Sergeant Tea greeted him

"Sir, the commander and First Sergeant went to the main post hospital," Tea said.

Humphrey's face was a bit bewildered.

"Are they both all right?" he asked.

"Oh yes, Sir," Tea replied. "They went to see one of our warrant officers that got all bit up by chiggers. From what I hear, he's a real mess."

"Oh, I see," replied Humphrey. "Yes, the chiggers are bad out here. I received several bites myself the last time I visited."

"Sir, next time you come out this way, try using a flea collar laced in between your boot laces like mine," replied Tea, pointing to her boots.

"Do they work?" asked Humphrey.

"They haven't bit li'l ole me," replied Tea in her southern belle voice.

"Sir, if you'd like to wait for Captain Marshall, I'm sure he'll be back within the hour," she continued.

"Thank you, Sergeant Tea, but I've got to get back to my unit. Please make sure your commander gets this." Humphrey handed the 1-R evaluation report to Sergeant Tea.

"Yes Sir, I will," replied Tea. She noticed a foul odor emanating from Humphrey as he spoke.

"Sir, pardon me for asking, but did you get sprayed by a skunk?"

Humphrey was a bit chagrined by the question.

"It still smells, does it?" he asked.

"Well, I've got a very sensitive nose, Sir, and it seems to be a little more sensitive now that I'm expecting," Tea replied.

Humphrey's expression turned sour and as he turned to leave.

"Just make sure Captain Marshall gets that. Thank you."

"Yes Sir, I'll let him know," said Tea as Humphrey walked back to his Jeep.

The First Sergeant and Marshall pulled into the 683rd training area about 30 minutes after Humphrey departed Mount Eden for Main Post.

"Top, drop me off near the tech supply CP tent," Marshall said. "I want to let Lieutenant Burks know when Mr. McCarthy is going to be ready to check out of the hospital on Friday."

Tisher slowed down and headed toward the tech supply section CP tent.

"Thanks, Top," Marshall said. "Now behave yourself and don't let the soldiers know about your planned pay day activities."

The First Sergeant grinned.

"I won't say nothing if you won't," he said.

Marshall played along and winked as he climbed out of the jeep and headed toward the tech supply CP tent to see Lieutenant Burks.

Inside, he found Burks reading over some of the repair parts inventory reports.

"Hello, Sir. I didn't see you come in," said Burks as Marshall walked over and sat down by Burks' field desk.

"Hello, Sarah," Marshall replied. "I just got back from the hospital and checked in on Mr. McCarthy. He'll be ready to checkout at 1900 hours on Friday. Have one of your soldiers there on the fourth floor to greet him and escort him out of the hospital. He should be able to handle the bus ride back home. Sergeant Lemasters will be the NCOIC for the bus trip back."

"OK Sir. I'll take care of that. Is there anything else?" asked Burks.

"Yes there is," Marshall said. "How did the parts turn-in go?"

"So far so good, Sir. Everything we had identified to be turned in was loaded onto the two deuces."

Marshall had more to smile about. 683rd Tech Supply would have more room inside their trailers to work in. The other intangible benefit was they did not have to waste fuel to haul tons of old obsolete parts back to Ohio.

Marshall caught up with Tisher while he was talking to Lemasters about filling in the foxholes and fighting positions. Field First Sergeant Lemasters was giving Tisher one of his many salutes.

"You got it, Top," Lemasters said. "I was gonna have a police call right after evenin' chow and one tomorra' after formation."

"Sounds good, John," replied Tisher as Marshall walked up. The men stopped talking.

"Don't let me interrupt," Marshall said, smiling.

"Sir, you can always interrupt. You're the boss," remarked Tisher with a grin.

"So, what's the agenda for the remainder of the day?" asked Marshall, looking at Lemasters for some kind of answer.

"Sir, we jest completed the decon trainin' that Sergeant Bierce put on," Lemasters said. "Ya missed a darn good class, if I may say so, Sir. That boy knows what he's talkin' bout. Everyone there got somethin' out of it.

"Most of the sections still have some mission work to clear out. Seems there were a few emergency jobs that jest popped up while you was out."

Marshall nodded his head, acknowledging what Lemasters had said. He looked at his watch and saw that it was 1530 hours.

"Thanks, gents," Marshall said. "I think I'll take a stroll over to the shop office."

"Sir, before ya go, ya might want to see Vivian. We got the 1-R from the evaluator," said Lemasters.

Marshall changed direction and headed toward the CP tent.

As he entered the CP tent, Marshall saw Lieutenant Stiles sitting on his cot reviewing the 1-R unit evaluation report.

"Excuse me, Sir," Stiles said, slightly embarrassed. "My curiosity got the best of me."

Marshall noticed that she wasn't smiling, which was not a good thing to see from his training officer while reviewing the evaluation report.

"So, how did Lieutenant Humphrey rate us?" asked Marshall.

Stiles handed him the 1-R.

"Everything was either a 2 or a 3 Sir," replied Stiles. This meant the unit was doing an average or below average job in all areas of training.

"I don't see how Lieutenant Humphrey could have given this kind of rating," remarked Marshall. "But I'm not going to allow this rating to be final! This is not an accurate, nor unbiased rating of this unit!"

Marshall looked over the 1-R in detail and saw that Humphrey had observed the unit on six separate occasions. Some of the observations where during the hours of darkness when only the guards were awake.

"I believe we should share this information with the first sergeant," mentioned Marshall.

"Sir, I'll get him," Tea said. "I think he's over at the shop office tent."

"Thanks, Sergeant Tea," replied Marshall as he sat down on his cot. Marshall knew this evaluation would have to be shared with Colonel Biggs, who held the 683rd in higher regard than Humphrey.

"Deb, you did a good job handling the training and training schedule," said Marshall as he gave the 1-R back to Sergeant Tea.

"Thank you, Sir," Stiles said. "Everything went so well. I don't understand why that creep would do this."

Marshall smiled.

"I think I know why our rookie evaluator did it," he said.

Marshall had known this might happen after his first meeting with Humphrey at Major Brask's office. Humphrey was getting even. Marshall knew it was time to throw down the gauntlet. This would be done quickly and through the proper channels.

Tisher walked into the CP tent. Marshall opened his mouth to speak, but Tea broke the bad news.

"Top, we got a less-than-satisfactory rating from our evaluator, Lieutenant Humphrey," Tea said.

"That's what I just heard through the grapevine, Viv," replied Tisher. "John told me what we got."

Marshall looked over to Tisher with a serious look.

"I'm going to pay Colonel Biggs a visit. I'm going to get things started on rebutting this piece of crap before the troops find out what Humphrey has done. I'll make sure Colonel Biggs sees this. Maybe he can help us get this reversed."

"I'm with you, Sir," replied Tisher.

Outside the tent, Marshall reiterated to Stiles his next plan of attack. He left the 683rd field site and walked over to Colonel Biggs' headquarters. Walking into the large GP medium tent, Marshall spotted Major Brown at his field desk going over some paperwork.

"Sir, I was wondering if Colonel Biggs is in the area," Marshall said.

Major Brown looked up from his bifocals and smiled as he saw Marshall standing in front of him with a look of concern and urgency on his face.

"Sure is, Dave," Brown responded. "Why don't you grab yourself a cup of coffee and I'll let Colonel Biggs know you're here to see him."

Marshall forced a smile and headed over to the coffee pot to fix himself a cup on a hot July day.

"Captain Marshall, what brings you here to our neck of the woods?" asked Colonel Biggs as he walked into the tent and spotted Marshall.

"Sir, I'd like to go over the 1-R we just received from our evaluator."

"By all means," replied Biggs as he signaled Major Brown to join in the impromptu meeting. Marshall handed the 1-R over to Biggs without saying a word. Biggs and Brown were looked over the 1-R together, shaking their heads in disbelief at what they read.

After they both carefully reviewed the document, Colonel Biggs removed his reading glasses, looked down at the floor of the tent and then looked at Marshall.

"Thank you for bringing this to my attention. There seems to be a great difference of opinion from what my staff and I feel about the 683rd and what your evaluator thinks. I'll look into this, Commander. In the meantime, continue to march with what you're doing."

Marshall was silent the entire time, knowing that Biggs would be his best ally in righting what they felt was an obvious injustice.

"Yes, Sir," Marshall replied. "Our people have not been advised of what has happened. I'm concerned about a letdown in morale if word does get out about this low-balled rating that Lieutenant Humphrey gave us."

Biggs smiled at Marshall.

"Not to worry, good Commander," Biggs said. "It's my turn. I'm having dinner this evening with someone who might be able to help."

Marshall thanked Biggs and saluted. It was time to get back to the 683rd and continue to march, as Colonel Biggs had recommended.

Things inside the 683rd were going smoothly as the tech supply deuces pulled into the area. Sergeant Schmoot went into the tech supply tent and reported to Lieutenant Burks.

"Ma'am, we turned in all the obsolete parts at PDO without any problems," Schmoot said.

"Very good, Sarge," replied Burks as she looked over the turn-in documentation she received from Schmoot.

"Mr. McCarthy sends you his regards, also Ma'am," Schmoot went on. "And he said he appreciated the fact that you didn't come to the hospital to visit him."

Burks was a little surprised to hear that remark. Schmoot went on to clarify what he said.

"Ma'am, what I mean is Mr. McCarthy is partially naked because of all the dressings they had to put on him. He's got chigger bites all over his legs, thighs, buttocks and groin area," Schmoot said.

Burks smiled at Schmoot.

"I'm sure Mr. McCarthy will be glad to see me when he's got all his clothes on," she said.

"Yes Ma'am," replied Schmoot. "He's not in a very good mood right now."

Burks looked at Schmoot.

"Is he ever?" she asked. Not wanting the conversation to end, Burks asked Schmoot another question.

"Is there anything else I should know?"

Schmoot thought for a couple of seconds.

"Yes Ma'am, there is," he said. "We've got two flats on one of the deuces that's got to be fixed ASAP."

"Well, carry on Sergeant," replied Burks in a calm and understanding voice.

"Yes Ma'am," replied Schmoot as he exited the tent.

At the shop office tent, Marshall was going over the production control board with Chief Farley. Marshall was carefully looking over the status of the new emergency jobs that came in while he was out visiting Mr. McCarthy.

"So what do you think, Chief? Will the shops finish these jobs by morning?" asked Marshall.

Farley was confident in his answer.

"Sir, we've got the parts on hand, and the mechanics have the know-how to get these fixed. I'd say these should be completed by morning if all goes well," he said.

Marshall stroked his chin looking at Mr. Farley. Judging by the amount of work in the shops and the fact that the personnel were more than eager to work on the equipment, Marshall felt that the last-minute dumping of broken down vehicles by the supported units would be a true test of how well the 683rd could perform.

"Chief, this is a real test that I think the troops will not only pass, but excel at," Marshall said.

Marshall was right. Before noon on Friday, all vehicles would be repaired and awaiting pick up by the units who dumped them off. Marshall made a mental note to bring up the subject of dumping at the next morning's commanders' meeting with Colonel Biggs and staff.

As Marshall exited the tent and walked over to the automotive shop tents, he saw that all the mechanics and technicians were busy working on equipment. Marshall conversed with the NCOs and soldiers, making sure everything was going smoothly and seeing if they needed anything.

The only comment the soldiers had was to make sure that Sergeant Emery had some late-night chow available for the night shift. It was going to take everyone working all night to get the jobs done before noon Friday.

There were a couple of requests for beer and chips. Marshall replied that he'd get some soda pop and chips from the local country store down the road. He also warned them not to put any ice in their cups and reminded them of what happened to Chief McCarthy. McCarthy's story got a laugh from several of the NCOs.

Walking back to the CP tent, Marshall spotted Tisher.

"Top, I've got to make a soda pop and chip run to the country store," Marshall said. "Does Sergeant Tea need any ice cream?"

"Let's go, Sir," Tisher said. "I was just about to make a special trip for her."

Both men jumped into the jeep and headed off to the country store, which was past the pig farm. The wind was coming out of the north, which was kind enough to keep the stench off the paved road as Marshall and Tisher went quickly past.

Marshall and the first sergeant returned with six cases of pop and 10 bags of chips. Tisher returned with two half-gallons of rocky road ice cream: one for him and one for Sergeant Tea. Sergeant Vivian Tea was going to be very contented that evening.

Colonel Biggs had arrived at Brigadier General Marski's residence on Main Post at 1850 hours, 10 minutes ahead of schedule. The general's house was easy to find. The post commander of Fort Knox had the largest and most beautiful house in the residential area, with a large and perfectly landscaped lawn and garden.

Marski greeted Biggs at the door before he could reach for the doorbell.

"Welcome, Cliff! Come on in," Marski said. "Can I get you something to drink?"

"Iced tea would be fine if you have that, Sir," replied Biggs as he entered the general's house.

"You're in luck, Cliff. My wife makes the best sweet tea on Fort Knox," boasted Marski as they entered the kitchen.

Mrs. Marski was still in her Army nurse's uniform when Biggs entered the kitchen, wearing the rank of colonel on her white uniform lapel. She smiled, offered a handshake to Biggs and presented him with an iced tea in a large glass tumbler.

"Nice to finally meet you Cliff," replied Colonel Marski.

"The pleasure is all mine," replied Biggs.

Mrs. Marski looked at Biggs.

"We had one of your warrant officers on the fourth floor just covered in chigger bites," she said. "I believe his name was McCarthy. Do you know him?"

Biggs smiled.

"Why, yes. He's one of the technicians in the 683rd Maintenance Company," Biggs said, taking advantage of the shift in conversation. "General, you remember Captain Marshall?"

"Sure do, Cliff," Marski said. "He's the commander of the fine unit and that fine young NCO, Sergeant Bitsko, who came to Nichole's rescue."

"How is your niece doing, General?" asked Biggs with a look of concern.

"She'll be out of the hospital on Monday, right honey?" said General Marski as he looked over to his wife to confirm the good news.

"That's what the doctors are saying, Mike," she replied.

General Marski looked at Biggs as they sat across from one another on the patio.

"Colonel, before we sit down for dinner, I'd like to get any unfinished Army business out of the way first. That way we can talk about other important matters like if Ohio State will be in the Rose Bowl with Michigan this year."

Biggs smiled.

"I don't know about Michigan, but you can bet on Ohio State being there."

Marski laughed.

"You didn't know I played for Michigan, did you Cliff?"

Spotting the large banner with a blue M with the gold edges hanging on the wall, Biggs smiled.

"No, Sir," Biggs said. "Did you know I played linebacker for Ohio State in 1957?" He lifted his hand and showed his Rose Bowl Ring to General Marski.

Marski laughed out load again.

"Colonel, I played halfback in '57 for Michigan. Do you remember that game?"

"Like it was yesterday," replied Biggs. "Let me see," reminisced Biggs. "We were down 0 to 14 at halftime. Coach Woody Hayes came into the locker room and gave us his patented motivational speech, which I'll never forget.

"We then went back out onto the field and scored 31 unanswered points and went straight to the Rose Bowl to meet Oregon for the title, which we won."

General Marski was smiling and nodding his head.

"And the Ohio State linebackers put me on my can the rest of that game," Marski chuckled. "You were probably one of 'em, Cliff."

"Maybe so, General," Biggs replied.

"Well, it is a pleasure to meet an old adversary after all these years," replied Marski. "Now getting back to Army business, anything you'd like to discuss?"

Colonel Biggs handed the 1-R evaluation report of the 683rd to General Marski.

"Sir, I believe you should have a look at this," Biggs said. "Me and my staff do not agree with the evaluation the unit was given. They are a superior unit and the evaluator is way off the mark with regards to this evaluation. He's a newly commissioned officer with no experience. He shouldn't have been assigned as the 683rd's evaluator."

"Hmmmm. Looks like a young lieutenant needs to meet his commanding general in the morning," Marski said, looking at the comments and numerical scores the 683rd was given and concurring with Biggs. "This boy doesn't know what he's doing. This will be fixed before the unit leaves. I'll see to it."

"Now, tell me about that game with Oregon for the championship."

A.T. - DAY 13 (FRIDAY)

The morning chow line moved past the serving area cheerfully and quickly. The only 683rd soldiers missing were those that trained at Boatwright. They had failed their first barracks inspection and had to clean the barracks a second time. If all went well, they would be at Mount Eden before noon.

The soldiers of the 683rd were only one day away from leaving the field and returning home to their loved ones and friends. Soldiers were tired from working the long hours to repair broken down vehicles, but satisfied with the fact they would receive their pay that afternoon. Payday was going to help raise unit morale immensely.

From his past experience, Captain Marshall knew there was nothing more depressing to a soldier than a paycheck and no opportunity to spend it. Payday activities was an event that every soldier looked forward to. It was their reward for a job well done.

Friday was going to be a very busy day for all members of the unit. The jobs in the shops had to be completed by noon, and after they returned from payday activities it would be time to strike all the 683rd tentage and start loading for the trip home.

The only thing that worried Marshall was the turn-in of all training areas and barracks the unit had signed for. If the field site or barracks was not acceptable to the Fort Knox civilian inspectors, the 683rd personnel would have to stay and fix whatever was found wrong and schedule another turn-in, adding to the delay of going home. All this and more was going to be divulged at morning formation.

Sergeant Lemasters blew his whistle loudly and shouted.

"Formation!"

The 683rd soldiers quickly fell into formation at the assembly area within two minutes.

As was the custom, First Sergeant Tisher conducted the first portion of the formation. After the accounting of all personnel, he went over the day's events.

"We're gonna have a police call right after formation, and I want every square inch of this training area to be completely groomed," Tisher said. "All drainage ditches around the tents will be filled in and raked smooth. All fighting positions better be filled in and the ground around it to be brought back to its original condition. All half-shelter tents will be taken down and packed away. Except for the shop office tent, all platoon CP tents will be taken down, cleaned and loaded. Maintenance tents will be disassembled and packed on the vehicles. The noon and dinner meals are going to be C-rations. I hope ya'll enjoyed Sergeant Emery's cooking."

A loud cheer and clapping erupted after Tisher finished his sentence.

"Just make sure you let the cooks and Sergeant Emery and Atkins know how much you appreciated their cooking," Tisher continued. "You all look like you gained a few pounds while you were out here roughing it." Many of the soldiers began to chuckle.

"For those going back on the convoy, you'll receive two additional C-ration meals tonight for the trip home tomorrow."

The 683rd soldiers cheered and whistled, knowing they were getting close to going home.

"You'll receive your Army paycheck after the noon formation from Lieutenant Stiles. At noon formation we'll give you more details on what's needed to be done before we can leave. Company! Atten…hut!"

Everyone in formation snapped to attention as Marshall took over the formation from Tisher.

"Stand at ease!" said Marshall, using his command voice.

"Soldiers of the 683rd, you have done well," Marshall said. "You've accomplished a great deal of training and proved to all that you know how to soldier. I am proud of each and every one of you."

"Because of that fact, and because Lieutenant Stiles has placed it on the training schedule, all of you may partake in payday activities." Smiles and grins were evident throughout the formation.

"I've made arrangements for the bank next to the PX to cash your paychecks so you may do some shopping at the PX. Let me just add something here. No contraband will be brought back to home station. That includes items from the Class 6 store." Several frowns were observed from the soldiers.

"Check with your section leaders or the first sergeant if you have any questions on that," Marshall said, ignoring the dirty looks from several of the soldiers. "I highly recommend that you safeguard your pay, and take only what you will need in cash for the next two days. You can mail yourself a cashier's check that the bank can prepare for you.

"Finally, we want you back in the field before1600 hours this evening. There is still a lot of work to do before we can depart the area. Company! Ten hut!"

Tisher walked briskly up to his commander and saluted.

"Top, take charge of this great company," said Marshall as he returned the first sergeant's salute and walked off to the side of the formation.

Tisher grinned as he gave instructions for the personnel of the 683rd.

"Fall out for police call!"

A resounding grunt was heard as the soldiers did an about-face movement and began to assemble around Field First Sergeant Lemasters as he took charge of the 683rd for their first of many police calls of the area.

Cleaning up the Mount Eden training area the 683rd occupied was not an easy task. The area covered more than 20 acres, including woodlands and open field areas. The soldiers began to form a single line stretching for more than 150 yards across.

At Lemasters' command they began to slowly walk forward, picking up trash and any man-made objects off the ground. Anything that wasn't formed by Mother Nature was removed and placed in garage bags as they moved along through the training area.

As the entire formation reached the boundary line of the 683rd training area, they repeated their movement toward the original starting point, picking up more trash and debris that others had overlooked.

While combing the field site, Lieutenant Kiley and the entire section that trained at Boatwright entered the field site area. Marshall saw Kiley climbing out of her jeep and went over to see how the turn-in of the barracks went.

"Welcome back to Mount Eden, Kathy," said Marshall.

"I'm so very glad to be here Sir," she replied in an exasperated voice. "You won't believe how picky those people can be when you try to turn something in on this post."

Marshall was curious. Kiley began to tell of her ordeal the past day.

"The inspectors were looking at every little thing. If they found any sand in between the grooves of the rubber treads on the steps, they'd give you a gig. Any powder residue from cleaning the latrine floors or walls, that's a gig."

Marshall grinned.

"So how many gigs did you get on the men's and women's barracks?"

"Fourteen total," replied Kiley.

Marshall looked serious.

"What happened that ticked them off so much?"

Kiley wasn't ready for that kind of question, and had to think for several seconds before asking.

"I had Sergeant Huddle go over to the housing office to let them know the barracks were ready for turn-in."

Marshall was silent for a while and then remarked softly.

"Kathy, maybe you should have gone there yourself," he said. "I don't think Sergeant Huddle can schmooze them as well as you can."

"Well Sir, they've got two really clean barracks on Post right now," Kiley said.

"I'm sure they really appreciate that, too," said Marshall.

"So what else is new? How was the overall training from Boatwright?"

Kiley's face broke into a big smile as she opened her briefcase and pulled out an official-looking folder.

"Sir, I think you'll enjoy reading this," she said as she handed the folder to Marshall.

Inside the folder was an official letter of commendation signed by the director of maintenance of the Boatwright Maintenance Facility. The letter of commendation went on to praise the 683rd personnel for their outstanding work and support of the maintenance mission of Fort Knox, Kentucky.

"Well congratulations, Kathy!" Marshall said. "Looks like they've appreciated the good work your folks have done while our folks were learning to fix the new weapons systems the Army's got in inventory. Great job!"

"Thank you, Sir. We've really got some got soldiers in this unit," replied Kiley.

Marshall was quick to reply.

"And all it takes is a good officer to recognize that fact and bring that quality out of them," he said. "Again, excellent job to you and your people."

The remainder of the morning the 683rd personnel were as busy as ants, scurrying around taking down tents, removing power cords for the light sets, taking down the field phone wires from the trees, striking tents, filling in drainage ditches, raking areas clean, and loading trucks. It was a sight to behold. The mess section was also cleaning up and packing their equipment and gear into their deuce-and-a-half. A large coffee pot and a cooler filled with punch was left for the soldiers to use.

Marshall came over to the mess section to see Sergeant Emery.

"Hello, Sarge," Marshall said. "Do you need any additional assistance or extra personnel to help you load up?"

"Oh no, Sir. I think we've got this handled, but I do appreciate the offer," replied Emery.

"Sergeant Emery, the behalf of the 683rd I just want to let you know how much we appreciated you and your personnel from the 646th," Marshall said. "I can't remember a time when I've heard so many soldiers say how much they enjoyed the food in the field. You've certainly made our annual training mission so much easier and enjoyable. I just wanted to thank you personally."

Emery was smiling.

"Sir, it was my pleasure and honor to work with you and your people," he replied. "It was one of the best times I've ever had in the field, and your Sergeant Atkins is one fine NCO."

"Well Sarge," replied Marshall, "I don't want to steal you away from the 646th, but if you ever are in need of a new home, the door of the 683rd will always open for you and your personnel. You've been a great help to us and I'm sure Sergeant Atkins has learned so much from you this A.T."

Emery smiled.

"Sir, thank you for those kind words," Emery said. "I will always remember this A.T. fondly."

Chief Farley was going over the paperwork for the jobs that had been finished during the night. Six trucks were waiting to be picked up by their owning units. All were fixed by the 683rd mechanics on the night shift.

"Chief, you've done a marvelous job out here in the field, and I wanted to thank you personally," said Marshall as he sat down in a folding chair at the side of Farley's field desk.

"Captain Marshall," Mr. Farley replied in a serious tone of voice, "I've served with many company commanders in my time. I've seen a lot of 'em come and go. Sir, I just wanted to say that I appreciated you not getting in my way as the shop officer, and letting me run things my way."

Marshall was used to back-handed compliments.

"Mr. Farley, I was also a shop officer, and the commander was always looking over my shoulder, telling me what to do," he replied. "I resented it, and I resented him. I vowed if I were a commander, I'd let my shop officer run the shop operations until he proved to be incapable of doing an adequate job. Chief, you proved to be more than capable long before we left for A.T."

Mr. Farley smiled. He knew this commander had faith and confidence in his abilities and graciously accepted his commander's praises for a job well done.

Changing the subject to the tasks at hand, Marshall asked a question.

"Tell me, Chief, how do we stand on jobs in shop right now?"

Farley kept his smile.

"Sir, all jobs are done," he said. "Any that come in now will have to be towed to home station unless it's for a minor repair, and minor repairs are supposed to be done at their unit motor pools."

Marshall was glad to hear that all jobs had been done.

"At the commanders' meeting this morning, Colonel Biggs said he might be stopping by for a visitation at our afternoon formation. Chief, I believe he's got something up his sleeve," said Marshall with a grin.

Both men turned the conversation to new maintenance requirements. Both came to the conclusion all new maintenance requirements would be handled by the 683rd Maintenance Contact Teams.

Lieutenant Stiles walked in to speak with the commander.

"Sir, just wanted to let you know that I'm leaving to go to the finance office to pick-up the paychecks," Stiles said.

"Carry on, Lieutenant," replied Marshall. "Who's your payroll guard?"

"I've got Specialists Williams and Peoples accompanying me, Sir," replied Stiles, looking anxious to depart.

"Loaded and ready for bear?" asked Farley as he spotted her holstered pistol with loaded magazine on her web belt.

"Okay Deb, I'll see you when you return. Safe trip," said Marshall as Stiles exited the shop office tent and climbed into her jeep. Williams was her driver and Peoples rode in the back seat.

Marshall looked at Mr. Farley.

"So when do you want to strike your tent?" Marshall asked.

Farley looked around at the tent then walked outside and squinted as he looked at the sky.

"Sir, you never know what the weather's gonna be around here when you're up on a mountain. One minute it's a beautiful, clear and sunny day. The next, it's raining cats and dogs. I'll keep my tent up as a shelter until first light tomorrow morning."

"Sounds like a good idea, Chief," replied Marshall.

Outside, the sections were busy tearing down and packing up their tents and camouflage nets. The maintenance tents took longer to strike because of their aluminum framed rib sections.

Each section was held together by cross-members and fasteners, and had to be taken apart piece by piece. Specialist Jessie Dweedle was enjoying the moment, climbing on top of the rib frames. Chief James watched him carefully since Dweedle had the reputation of being accident-prone.

"Jessie, be careful when you unfasten that top support," cautioned James as he supervised the disassembly of the motor pool maintenance tent. "I don't want to have to bring ya home in pieces."

Dweedle was having more fun than he could have imagined.

"Don't worry none about me, Chief! I'll be all right," Dweedle called as he walked on top of the ribbed structure to the next section to assist in removal of the next rib frame.

James was not as confident as Dweedle was up in the air. Luckily, Dweedle's guardian angel was on duty that morning, watching over him as he walked 14 feet up in the air with reckless abandon.

Sergeant Lemasters walked over to the motor pool area and saw Dweedle on top of the ribbed sections and shook his head.

"That fool's gonna break his neck someday," Lemasters said to himself.

He spotted Mr. James and pulled him aside.

"Chief, Top wants ta know if everyone has pulled motor stables this mornin' and if we've got anymore flats need fixin'?" Lemasters said.

"Well, I'm glad you asked, Field First Sergeant," said James. "Everyone tells me they're good to go, except for tech supply's two inner flats. We gave 'em two new tires and haven't received the bad ones yet."

"OK Chief, thanks. I'll check with Sergeant Schmoot and find out what's goin' on," replied Lemasters as he began walking toward tech supply.

Lemasters walked over to the tech supply area and found three soldiers busily working on replacing the flat inner tires on their deuce-and-a-half. The men had both outer tires removed and the back end of the deuce was jacked off the ground.

Lemasters saw Sergeant Schmoot supervising the detail.

"Sarge, when do ya' expect yer people will be done?" Lemasters asked him.

Schmoot looked over to Lemasters.

"If all goes well, it shouldn't take more than a couple of hours," Schmoot replied.

Lemasters looked at his watch and noted that it was already 1120 hours.

"OK, Sarge. Jest remember, payday is coming purty soon." Schmoot grinned.

"Aye, Field First Sergeant! Were doin' the best we can!" Schmoot said in his best Scottish accent.

Lemasters didn't watch TV very often. The imitation of the character Chief Engineer Scott from the television series "Star Trek" didn't register with him.

Soldiers began to open their boxes of C-rations for lunch, and the trading began. Different variations of C-rations among the soldiers included chicken loaf, turkey loaf, chicken and noodles, ham and eggs, ham fried, beans with meat balls in tomato sauce, beans with franks in tomato sauce, ham and lima beans, beefsteak with potatoes and gravy, turkey or chicken boned in broth, and pork loaf. Some soldiers didn't like the ham and lima beans, while others didn't like the eggs and ham. Nearly everyone wanted the beans and franks C-ration meal. Unfortunately, when it had aged in the can, the franks disintegrated once they were in your mouth with little or no consistency. The beans were rather bland, not sweet like the store-bought baked beans everyone was accustomed to. When C-rations were over ten years old, all the canned meat tasted like ham, which tasted pretty good if you were hungry.

In order to open a C-ration can, one needed a can opener. To solve that dilemma, the Army developed the P-38 can opener. After eating a dozen C-rations, a soldier would become fairly proficient with the P-38 can opener. There were usually two or three P-38s that came with every case of C-rations.

The P-38 was small and had a pivoting cutter blade that would fold against the steel handle. The size of a P-38 was maybe an inch and a half long. It had a hole on the bottom of the flat handle that allowed it to be placed on a key ring or on your dog tags. Many found out that the blade would open up when it was carried in their pocket and stab them in the thigh.

One could always tell who the "Old Soldiers" were in the field. They were the ones with a P-38 on their key rings or dog tags, and had small puncture wounds on their thighs or chests.

The discarded cardboard boxes and empty cans made quite a large pile of scrap material and litter after everyone had eaten, which necessitated additional police calls through the area.

Marshall was at the CP tent with Sergeant Tea. The CP tent and the shop office tent would be the last ones to be taken down. Tea needed help opening up her C-rations. Marshall promptly obliged her, using his personal P-38 on his key ring.

"Here you go, Sergeant Tea. One can of turkey loaf," he said, handing her the opened can with the lid still attached and bent out of the way.

"What do you have, Sir?" asked Tea as she looked at the open can and was a bit reviled by the coagulated grease at the top of the can.

"Hmmm. Looks like I've got beans and franks," Marshall said. "Would you like to trade?"

Tea's eyes lit up and she shook her head in the affirmative several times as she handed back the can of turkey loaf.

"I have to warn you, Sarge, sometimes those beans and franks don't taste as good as they look," replied Marshall.

He opened the can of beans and franks, took a spoon, and scraped off the top layer of grease and fat.

"Here you go, Sergeant Tea," Marshall said, handing her the can. "Bon appetite, which means 'good eating' in French."

"Sir, I'm Cajun," said Tea. "Bon appetite a vous!"

She began to spoon the beans and franks into her mouth.

"Oooh, you're right, Sir," she said. "These franks kinda crumble in your mouth, but they still taste good."

"Glad to hear," replied Marshall. "You know, this turkey loaf is one of my favorites, but it doesn't compare to one of Sergeant Emery's meals, does it?"

Tea agreed. Everyone in the field had been spoiled by Sergeant Emery's cooking. The 683rd would have to eat several more meals of C-rations to allow the mess section adequate time to pack up their equipment and get ready for the convoy home.

While they were busy opening their C-rations, Lieutenant Stiles appeared in the tent and sat down with her briefcase.

"Hi, Sir," she said. "There was no problem getting the checks. Everyone in the 683rd got one."

"That's good news, Deb. Did you eat yet?" asked Marshall as she sat down in one of the vacant steel chairs.

"No Sir, not yet," she replied.

"You go ahead and eat," said Marshall. "We'll have formation afterwards and you can set up a pay desk in the shop office tent. All the soldiers will report to you for their paychecks, OK?"

"Sounds good to me, Sir," replied Stiles as she opened up her box of C-rations and began to look around for a can opener.

"Don't these things come with a pull-tab?" she asked.

At 1300 hours, Lemasters blew his whistle for formation. The 683rd soldiers quickly appeared and lined up in their respective sections in orderly rows.

Tisher was in front of the formation and received a quick "all present and accounted for" headcount from each section. He then turned the formation over to Marshall.

"At ease!" Marshall shouted. All the soldiers took a relaxed posture with their feet apart and their hands behind their backs.

"This afternoon, we will be having payday activities," he said. Every face in the formation broke into a smile.

"You will sign for your paycheck from Lieutenant Stiles at the shop office tent. The procedure will be to report to the paymaster, salute, and then show your ID card. After you receive your paycheck, the deuces will be leaving for the PX after each is filled.

"Soldiers will line-up in alphabetical order. Rank is immaterial. Any problems with pay must be brought to Sergeant Tea's attention.

"You will have approximately three hours to enjoy pay day activities. Deuces will return to Mount Eden from the PX at precisely 1600 hours. Absolutely no one will be allowed to go off post, and everyone here knows what areas are off-limits. If you don't know what is off-limits, check with your section sergeants."

Marshall spotted Colonel Biggs approaching with several members of his staff, and knew it was time to bring the unit to attention.

"Company, atten…hut!" Biggs walked up behind Marshall as he did an about-face movement to greet his boss.

"Sir, Captain Marshall and the 683rd reports," said Marshall as Biggs returned his salute.

"Have your soldiers stand at ease, commander," replied Biggs.

Marshall did another about-face movement and gave at ease command to the formation. Biggs then stood next to Marshall and began to speak to the entire unit loudly and distinctly.

"Soldiers of the 683rd, my staff and I want to congratulate all of you on a job magnificently done here at Mount Eden Base Camp," Biggs said. "The support rendered during this annual training period was far above what was expected or anticipated. The tactical phase of your training was superbly done. Every VIP that came into your area was highly impressed that a maintenance company of this size was performing the mission so professionally. You are all to be highly praised and congratulated for your outstanding efforts."

"The 683rd was voted by my staff as the best unit in the field," Biggs finished, holding a trophy over his head. "The training, service and support, and food service was the finest we've ever experienced in the field. Congratulations and keep up the excellent work."

Biggs handed the large trophy to Marshall.

"Congratulations, Captain Marshall," Biggs said. "You've done a remarkable job."

Marshall was not only surprised, but also a bit speechless as he received the praises and trophy from Biggs. He knew he had to say something, and with as much grace as possible, he did.

"Sir, on behalf of the 683rd, I would like to thank you for this honor," Marshall said. "Everyone in the unit worked very hard and learned a great deal during this annual training period. We appreciate this very much, Sir."

Biggs smiled.

"It is our pleasure, Commander," he said. "You may carry on."

Marshall snapped to attention and held a salute to Biggs as he and his staff departed the area.

Marshall turned around with the trophy in hand and raised it over his head.

"683rd, this is for you!" he shouted.

Everyone in the formation cheered and clapped. After a short while, the clapping and whistling subsided, Marshall continued.

"When I took command of the 683rd in January, I don't think anyone here had an idea of what we could do together and accomplish as a team," he said. "Now you know! Give yourselves a hand!"

The clapping and cheering started again as every face was smiling, knowing that they had a part in making the A.T. a great success.

"Top, do you have anything to add for these great soldiers?" asked Marshall.

"No, Sir," Tisher answered. "I think you've covered it all."

Marshall grinned.

"Now for some well-earned payday activities! Company, ten...hut! Fall out for paycall!"

Everyone in the formation did an about-face and shouted "683rd!"

Marshall was very glad to see the soldiers were in a great mood as they all began to line up alphabetically at the shop office tent.

Lieutenant Stiles was setting up the desk inside. Her goal was to get the soldiers their pay as quickly as possible. First Sergeant Tisher and Sergeant Lemasters were assisting Stiles and helped keep the paycall an orderly process, walking up and down the single-file line of soldiers and making sure everyone was in the correct alphabetical order. It all went smoothly as Stiles and Tea handled each soldier that reported for pay.

"Sir, would you like to get paid?" asked Stiles after everyone else had collected their A.T. paychecks.

"Ma'am, Captain Marshall reporting for pay," he said, walking up in front of Stiles' desk, snapping to attention, and holding a salute.

Stiles enjoyed Marshall's adherence to military protocol. She returned his salute.

"Sir, please sign here and here," she said, showing him two records of receipt with his name printed on each.

After he had done so, Stiles handed him his paycheck and with a pay statement showing all the details of the pay and the deductions.

"Thank you, Ma'am," said Marshall as he saluted her again. "So who's left, other than Mr. McCarthy?" asked Marshall.

"Everyone got their check, Sir," Stiles said. "I'm going to the hospital to give Mr. McCarthy his and then I'm going to turn the documentation in to the finance office."

Marshall smiled.

"Don't forget to enjoy payday activities as well. You've earned it," he said.

Stiles smiled back.

"Thanks, Sir. I appreciate that," she said. "Being the paymaster is OK. Everyone gives you a lot of respect."

Stiles left the shop office tent and yelled to Williams to be her jeep driver for the trip to Main Post. The rest of the unit was busy getting aboard the last of the deuces and pulling out to go to Main Post for payday activities.

Mr. Farley and Mr. James decided to stay behind to keep any eye on the field site.

"Top, you and I have to see a man about some T-shirts today," Marshall mentioned to Tisher.

"Oh yeah," replied the First Sergeant. "Maybe he didn't skip town with your deposit after all."

Marshall smiled.

"See if Sergeant Lemasters wants to go in with us," Marshall said. "Maybe he'll convince you not to go to that massage parlor."

"Hell, Sir," Tisher said laughingly. "I'll be the one holding him back from going."

They both had a good chuckle about the matter and found Lemasters supervising the last of the personnel to load up in the deuce.

"John, get in the back of the jeep. I'll see if Vivian wants to go," said Tisher.

"She better not embarrass me again!" remarked Lemasters as the first sergeant walked to the CP tent.

"I heard that remark, Sergeant Lemasters!" shouted Tea as she emerged from the tent, ready to go.

"I'm ready, Top," she said sweetly as she walked slowly to the jeep. Marshall got out of the front passenger's seat, tipped the seat forward, and helped Tea climb into the back of the jeep.

"Hello darlin'. I'm ready to go shopping now," said Tea as she sat down next to Lemasters.

Lemasters grinned.

"Vivian, you're somethin' else," he said.

"I know, John. Let's just keep this between you and I. Tyron doesn't have to know," Tea teased as Tisher started the engine and began driving toward the floating bridge.

The floating bridge operators were not overly pleased to see more 683rd personnel pull up onto their waiting area to cross the river. They had been ferrying trucks across the river for over an hour straight without stopping.

As Tisher pulled the jeep onto the floating pontoon bridge, he talked to the operator.

"Had a busy day, Soldier?" Tisher asked.

The private just shrugged his shoulders and signaled the other side to begin pulling them across.

"Fishin's been pretty lousy today, Top," he said as the pontoon was being pulled across the water.

"Hmm. That's too bad. Why aren't they biting?" asked Tisher.

The private just shrugged his shoulders a second time.

"Don't know," he said. "Haven't had a bite all day."

As they reached the other side of the river, Tisher gave the private a pearl of wisdom.

"If you caught fish all the time, it wouldn't be called fishin'. It'd be called catchin'."

The private smiled as the First Sergeant drove the jeep off the pontoon and headed up the hill to the paved road.

The jeep pulled into the PX parking lot and Marshall spotted all the 683rd deuces parked in the far corner. They stopped in front of the PX to let Tea exit from the back of the jeep.

"Thank you, Sir," Tea said as Marshall let her out.

"Now John, darlin', get down from there and escort me as a proper gentlemen should," Tea said teasingly to Lemasters.

"Vivian, I ain't no gentleman. I work fer a livin'," replied Lemasters as a major and a lieutenant colonel walked past Tea, looking at Lemasters with one eyebrow raised.

"Dang it, she's done it again," said Lemasters as he climbed out of the jeep to escort Tea into the PX.

Tisher and Marshall couldn't hold back and laughed out loud as Lemasters and Tea disappeared into the PX.

Marshall spotted the T-shirt vendor displaying his assorted shirts on the outside of the PX. With his wallet in hand, Marshall walked over to the vendor who recognized him immediately.

"Captain Marshall, I'm glad to see you," the vendor said. "Everything is ready and the shirts look great."

Marshall opened one of the boxes marked 683, and pulled one out to see it closely. The vendor was right, the shirts looked great. "683rd HEM CO" in bold, red letters was placed right over the top of the ordnance branch symbol.

"Let's see," said the vendor. "That'll be a balance of $400 you owe on the shirts."

Marshall reached into his wallet, pulled out four $100 bills, and handed them to the vendor.

"Nice doing business with you, Captain," said the vendor as he began stacking the boxes of T-shirts on top of his vending table. "I threw in a few extra for you just in case," he said as he continued stacking the boxes.

"Thanks. I'm sure my soldiers will love 'em," replied Marshall as he began carrying the boxes to the jeep.

"Are those the T-shirts, Sir?" asked Tisher as Marshall dropped off the first four boxes in the back of the jeep.

"These are the ones," replied Marshall. "I think I've got enough money left for a hamburger. I just paid the vendor last of my emergency money. I sure hope my wife will understand when I get back home," Marshall said, trying to re-justify the fact he just spent a fairly large sum.

"Don't worry, Sir," replied Tisher, trying to keep a straight face. "If she kicks you out, you've always got a place to stay at the Reserve Center."

"Funny, Top. Very funny," responded Marshall as he held up an extra-large tee shirt for the first sergeant. "Here you go Top, this should fit you pretty good."

Tisher immediately took off his Army fatigue shirt and cap, removed his white T-shirt, and put the new one on.

"Hey, they look great Sir!" said Tisher as he modeled it for the commander. "Maybe I should give this one to Viv. How many more extra larges do you have?"

Marshall couldn't resist the opening Tisher gave him.

"I've got enough to mop up all of your blood that will be spilled when you give Sergeant Tea an extra-large T-shirt."

Tisher couldn't help but chuckle at the Old Man's quick wit. "You're right, Sir. You better hand 'em out," Tisher said.

Marshall went back to the vendor's table several times to load the additional boxes of T- shirts into the back of the jeep. While he was walking back fully loaded with boxes, several enlisted men took the opportunity to salute Marshall to see what he would do. Marshall smiled and nodded at the soldiers.

"Carry on, men. Carry on," he said from behind the boxes.

While the first sergeant and commander were waiting on Lemasters and Tea, Lieutenant Stiles was paying a visit to Mr. McCarthy at the Army hospital nearby.

"Hello, Mr. McCarthy. I come bearing gifts," announced Stiles as she walked into his room. Mr. McCarthy was having his legs and thighs examined by the Army nurse to see how well the bite marks were healing.

The nurse smiled at her.

"Would you give me a minute, Lieutenant? I've got to check Mr. McCarthy over and see how he's healing." Mr. McCarthy was lying on his stomach, thoroughly disgusted in his current condition and position with a female officer coming to visit.

"If you need any assistance, I'm a fourth-year nursing student," Stiles said. "I'll be taking my state boards next month."

The nurse finished examining Mr. McCarthy, pulling the bed sheets over his exposed backside.

"Thank you, but I'm done," she replied. "You can inform your commander that Mr. McCarthy will be discharged as scheduled on his chart later today."

"Sure thing," replied Stiles as she smiled and looked at Chief McCarthy.

"Chief, I've got your paycheck. I just need your signature."

McCarthy suddenly changed his mood and became more upbeat.

"Well, glory be! Uncle Sam didn't forget about me. Where do I sign?"

Lemasters and Tea had walked out of the PX with Tea giggling and Lemasters angrily shaking his head. As they got to the jeep, Tisher looked at the pair.

"Now what?" he asked.

Tea was still giggling.

"I asked Sergeant Lemasters to give me his opinion on some maternity dresses that I wanted to try on. He sure does have a good eye for clothes."

Lemasters was shaking his head in disgust.

"She did it to me again, Top. Right in front of everyone, she came sashayin' out of the dressing room sayin', 'Well, what do you think, honey? Should I try on some lingerie, too?' I tell ya Top, she's got it in fer me."

Lemasters suddenly noticed all the new cargo loading down the vehicle.

"What's goin' on with all these here boxes in the back of the jeep?" he asked.

"It's my gift to the 683rd," Marshall replied.

Lemasters opened a box and pulled out a T-shirt.

"Hot damn, Sir! These here are nice," Lemasters said. "You givin' these out to all the soldiers?"

Marshall just nodded his head with a slight grin on his face.

"Mighty kind of ya, Sir," replied Lemasters.

It was another lovely day in Kentucky. The sun overhead had no clouds to hide behind. Tea was enjoying the ride and kept up her harassment of Lemasters with an occasional, "Sergeant Lemasters, now keep your hands to yourself!" or "Quit crowdin' our baby."

Both the First Sergeant and commander enjoyed her amusing outbursts and Lemasters denial of any wrongdoing as they headed back to the Mount Eden field site.

They arrived back at the 683rd field site and noticed there was nothing going on. No sound of generators, no clanging or banging of metal. Just the sweet summer sounds of blowing wind, chirping birds and restless grasshoppers.

Over at the commanding general's office, Second Lieutenant Humphrey was reporting to see General Marski.

"Sir, Lieutenant Humphrey reports!"

Humphrey was visibly nervous, and had reported to the general approximately 15 feet away from the his desk.

General Marski returned his salute and shook his head.

"Lieutenant, let's try that again," Marski said. "Next time, stop in front of my desk a little closer."

"Uh, yes Sir," replied Humphrey. He stepped out of the general's office and reported to him again, this time stopping within three feet of the general's desk.

"At ease, Lieutenant." Marski said. He started his inquisition.

"How long have you been in the Army, Son?"

At Mount Eden, Chief James and Chief Farley were relaxing on lawn chairs they bought earlier at the PX and sipping on some cold soft drinks. Marshall began unloading the back of the jeep and carrying the boxes to the shop office tent. He returned with two T-shirts in his hands for both of the unit's hard working warrant officers guarding the field site.

"Here you go, gents," said Marshall. "I had these made up especially for you. Actually, especially for you and 198 others, to be exact."

Both Farley and James took the T-shirts and thanked Marshall.

"Sir, I think you better give me an X-large," said Farley as he looked at the size.

"You got it, Chief," replied Marshall as he took the shirt back and went back to the tent for another. I hope I ordered enough of the extra-large size, he thought.

"What are these for, Sir?" asked James with an inquisitive look on his face.

"I thought we should reward all the soldiers of the 683rd for the outstanding job they've been doing in the field this A.T.," replied Marshall.

"How much did these set you back?" asked Mr. Farley.

"I got a great deal on the shirts, Chief," Marshall said. "I was hoping to get some donations from all the officers and really show how much we appreciated the work the NCOs and enlisted personnel did out here."

"Well Sir, this musta cost you a small bundle," said James. "Here's $20 from me."

"Me too," replied Farley as he pulled a $20 bill from his wallet.

"Thanks, gents. Now I can say these T-shirts are a gift from the officers," Marshall said. "I was counting on a $20 donation from every officer in the unit."

"Here, Sir. Here's another $20 for Chief McCarthy," said Farley. "I'll make sure he gives me his 20 bucks as soon as he gets his triple X-large backside out of the hospital."

"Thank you, Chief. Now I can take the wife out to dinner when I get back," replied Marshall.

Marshall decided to arm himself with several boxes of T-shirts and started passing them out to the soldiers that had remained at the field site. Everyone was pleased and grateful after they received his or her T-shirt. As every deuce-and-a-half returned from the PX, every soldier was given his T-shirt when he got off the back of the truck.

Within a couple of hours, the T-shirts were almost gone and the morale of the unit was sky high. Work on loading up for the return trip home continued, but at a slower and more cheerful pace. Some had bought portable radio/cassette players at the PX and began playing them loudly as they worked and enjoyed their music. Music ranging from rock and roll to rhythm and blues was blasting loudly throughout the field site.

As evening approached, the sky remained clear. Within 30 minutes of the order to strike and pack all remaining tentage was given, they were all packed and loaded up.

The 683rd field site was given another police call and the remaining trash and debris was picked up and placed into large plastic bags.

Lieutenant Rodriguez was busy lining up the trucks for the convoy back to Ravenna. Every vehicle had a chalk number on the door and bumper to identify what serial it was in, and in what order the vehicle would be in the serial.

Sergeant Johnny Burkette, who had been mostly invisible during the two weeks in the field, was ready to go with his fuel tanker deuce. He had been refueling unit vehicles all day, making sure every vehicle in the convoy's fuel tank was filled. His fuel pods were refilled and he was anxious to get back to the Flats in Cleveland and enjoy the nightlife as a bartender he so dearly loved and missed.

McCarthy returned to the field site, dressed in Army sweatpants and a hooded sweatshirt, with white socks and new tennis shoes.

"Chief, you look like you're ready for PT," said Lemasters as he greeted the chief.

"Yeah? Well why don't you drop and give me 50," replied the crusty warrant officer.

"Glad to see yer in good spirits, Chief," smiled Lemasters as he walked away shaking his head.

Marshall walked over to the jeep where Mr. McCarthy remained motionless.

"Welcome back, Chief," he said. "Here's a welcoming present for you." Marshall handed a XX-large T-shirt to McCarthy.

"What's this all about?" he asked with a bit of suspicion in his voice.

"Everyone in the field gets one, Chief," smiled Marshall as McCarthy held it up and looked at it.

"Chief, I think it might be a good idea if you would stay in the jeep until the bus arrives at 0700 hours tomorrow," Marshall said. "The way the chiggers seem to be attracted to you, walking around the area may not be such a good idea."

"OK by me," replied the Chief. "So when does the convoy leave?"

Marshall looked at him.

"0800 hours. We're the last unit to leave Mount Eden," Marshall said. "I don't think I'll be able to keep these troops here any longer than they have to be. A civilian from Post will be here at 0700 to clear the field site.

Marshall called over to Lemasters.

"Sergeant Lemasters, would you have someone bring Mr. McCarthy's gear to him so he won't have to walk through the area to get it?" asked Marshall.

"Sure thing, Sir," Lemasters replied. "I'll have one of the tech supply people bring it over right away."

"Chief, I want you to know that Sergeant Lemasters personally made sure all your gear was cleaned and laundered—even your sleeping bag," said Marshall. "There shouldn't be any chiggers hiding in them."

Within 10 minutes, Mr. McCarthy was reunited with all his field gear and duffel bags of clothing.

Marshall had Tisher hold an evening formation. The soldiers were told to keep the area clean, when to expect the field site to be inspected, and when the bus and the main convoy would depart.

In order to facilitate a quick departure at 0800 hours, they were told to be ready with rakes and shovels to fix anything that the inspector found wrong with the site. The first sergeant then told everyone to get a good night's sleep. Tomorrow was going to be a long day.

Later that evening, Marshall had an impromptu meeting with all the officers and NCOICs. The topic was rewarding the soldiers for outstanding performance.

"Many of you and your soldiers deserve recognition," said Marshall. "I want to make sure that happens. I want to see recommendations-for-award paperwork from every section on my desk next drill. If you need help preparing the paperwork, see Sergeant Tea for assistance. We've got a lot of very good people in this unit and I want to make sure they are recognized for their efforts during A.T."

Everyone at the meeting was pleased to hear Marshall's thoughts and would comply with his request. Rewarding excellence was always a great motivator.

Over at the recovery section area, Sergeant Nugot fed his pet skunk Stinker some of the C-ration crackers and peanut butter he had saved. Stinker was a very contented little skunk that took a liking to Nugot.

Nugot purchased a flea collar for Stinker, who didn't like wearing it and would pull it off with his rear feet. The fleas didn't like it either and left Stinker to find other more friendly habitats. Stinker would not stray far from Sergeant Nugot and became an affectionate pet in a very short time.

As the sun began to set over Mount Eden Base Camp, soldiers used their rain ponchos to curl up in to get a few hours of sleep on the ground. Others slept in the cabs of their trucks or in the backs of the deuces. Peoples and Williams slept in the weapons trailer, which could be locked from the inside.

Peoples had been too tired the last two days of A.T. for any midnight romances with Specialist Kayrule. She had made up her mind this was her last hurrah with the Army and the Army Reserve. She felt worn out, like she had burned her candle at both ends during A.T.

The evening passed into the wee hours of the morning. The 928th, which was located across the dirt road from the 683rd, had built a large bonfire and continued to party all night long. Twice, First Sergeant Tisher had to walk across the road to tell them to keep it down a little. The 928th commander and first sergeant were sound asleep on cots, using their Army-issued earplugs, oblivious to what their soldiers were doing.

Dawn was coming fast, and the lack of sleep had little effect on the soldiers. Everyone was ready to go home.

A.T. - DAY 14 (SATURDAY)

Lemasters didn't have to blow his whistle that morning. Everyone in the 683rd was excited to be leaving the field and couldn't wait for sunrise.

Vehicles from the other Army Reserve units began leaving Mount Eden Base Camp and passed by the 683rd field site honking their horns. They too were excited to be going home.

The bus arrived an hour early, which was a very good omen for all those waiting around with nothing to do.

"All right you bus people, get yer gear together and begin loadin this here bus!" yelled Lemasters.

Within 10 minutes, the soldiers who were designated to ride the bus had their gear loaded and were on the bus. Chief McCarthy had a row of seats to himself in the back of the bus, while Lemasters stationed himself at the front.

"Sarge, we'll see you at the Reserve Center," Marshall said. "Nobody's to be released until we get the entire convoy back at the Reserve Center and all the weapons offloaded and secured."

Sergeant Lemasters gave his commander a wink of acknowledgement and an "Aye aye, Sir."

The bus departed the field site while the remainder of the personnel in the convoy watched, wishing they could be on the bus and leaving Mount Eden Base Camp.

As the bus departed the area, the civilian inspector from the post pulled into the 683rd field site to look at the condition of the training area. First Sergeant Tisher escorted the inspector as a detail of eight soldiers with rakes and shovels followed closely behind them.

The inspector, like most of the civilians that worked on Fort Knox, was retired military and enjoyed the military life. The added benefit was collecting a monthly retirement pension check for military service and a regular paycheck as a full-time

U.S. government civilian employee. These ex-military civilians knew what soldiering was all about.

Within 20 minutes, the inspector gave the field site his OK and left the area.

"Top, did the inspector find anything?" asked Marshall.

"He said the area looked OK," replied Tisher.

Marshall acknowledged Tisher's remarks.

"Are we ready to go, administratively and every other way?" Marshall asked, glancing at his watch. It was 0715 hours.

The first sergeant smiled.

"Sir, we're as ready as we'll every be," he replied.

It was command decision time for Captain Marshall. Should we wait until 0800, while every unit has departed Mount Eden more than an hour ago? That could lower the soldiers' morale, even though it's the unit's window of departure. Or should we leave now and get a head start since we are the furthest unit from Fort Knox?

It didn't take long for Captain Marshall to make up his mind. That was what being a commander was all about.

"TOP!" shouted Marshall.

"Yes, Sir," replied Tisher.

A broad smile came to Marshall's face.

"Let's get these vehicles fired up and rolling toward Ravenna!" he said

"Yes, Sir!" replied Tisher with the same broad-faced smile. The first sergeant blew his whistle loudly to get everyone's attention.

"683rd fall in for formation!" he yelled.

As the soldiers assembled, Tisher put out the good news: they were leaving early. As the soldiers cheered, Tisher turned the formation over to Marshall.

"I've decided we're going to leave a little earlier than scheduled," Marshall said. "Lieutenant Rodriguez will be in charge of departure times for each convoy serial after each serial departs. A convoy speed of 55 miles per hour will get us back home fast enough."

"Everyone here knows how long it took us to get out here, so let's not have any problems down-shifting when you're going up hills. I don't want to arrive at the Reserve Center after midnight, and neither do you. I want everyone to have a safe trip."

"When we get back to the Reserve Center, the first item of business will be to offload the weapons trailer and place all weapons in the vault. After all weapons are accounted for and secured, you will be released."

A cheer went up from the formation.

"For those who do not have vehicles that are securable from the outside, park them in the shops and begin off-loading them next drill," Marshall said.

Smiles were very visible from all the NCOs who were hoping Marshall would say just that.

"Company, ten…hut! First serial, prepare for departure! Fall out," Marshall shouted.

As Marshall was walking to his ¼-ton jeep, Lieutenant Humphrey pulled into the area. He parked his ¼-ton next to Marshall's jeep.

"Sir, please accept my apologies for the first 1-R I gave you," Humphrey said sheepishly. "I didn't know how to prepare and rate a unit properly. Here's the revised one."

Marshall was momentarily speechless. He was glad to see Lieutenant Humphrey apologize and at the same time revise his overall rating of the 683rd's performance in the field.

"Thanks, Lieutenant," Marshall said. "Why the change of heart?"

Humphrey was looking rather embarrassed as he explained himself.

"Sir, you were right. I shouldn't have been your unit's evaluator," he said. "Like you said at Major Brask's office, being a newly commissioned officer with little or no experience, they should have found someone with more rank and experience than me."

Marshall was reviewing the 1-R, which now had mostly ones and a few twos.

"Well, I must say, this is more like it," said Marshall. "Lieutenant, this is appreciated. Good luck to you."

Humphrey gave Marshall a salute, which was returned.

Marshall walked back to Lieutenant Stiles.

"Put this in your briefcase after you've had a chance to review it," Marshall said.

He walked back to his ¼-ton jeep and gave the nod to Lieutenant Rodriguez.

Rodriguez came over and gave the commander the okay to leave.

"OK, Sir. Have a safe trip," Rodriguez said. "We'll see you back in Ravenna."

With a map in hand, Marshall had his driver begin to move onto the dirt road.

As the other vehicles followed the ¼-ton jeep, Lieutenant Humphrey noticed the mud flaps on several of the trucks had a characterization of him being sprayed by a skunk. As the drivers passed by Humphrey, one of the deuces hit a mud puddle, which splashed onto Humphrey as he watched the trucks depart.

The drivers blew their horns simultaneously as they left the Mount Eden field site, signifying their renewed joy in payback and departure.

The first serial drove down the two-mile long dirt road that dead-ended into the paved road. As the convoy began to form up behind the jeep, Marshall told his driver to slowly get up to the speed limit. The pig farm was stinking in all its glory as the convoy passed through the area.

Marshall shouted to his driver over the engine and transmission noise.

"I'm glad we won't have to pass by here anymore," he said.

His driver nodded in agreement as they made their way to the intersection near the main gate of Fort Knox. Instead of taking their normal left turn toward Post, the driver turned right toward their destination home.

The road opened up into a four-lane highway within a short distance and 55 mph became the convoy speed. Everyone in the convoy had no problems keeping up.

Marshall looked at his map and checked the location of the next refueling point: Kings Mills, Ohio, which was approximately 250 miles away. With the information they learned on the way down to Fort Knox, Chief James and

Captain Marshall had determined all the vehicles in the convoy would require only one fuel stop.

The ¼-ton jeeps did not have the same fuel mileage range as the larger trucks in the convoy, which meant there was a possibility of running out of gas before the refueling point was reached. As long as the jeep was driven gently, reaching the refueling point should not be a problem. Every ¼-ton jeep in the convoy had a full five-gallon fuel can strapped on the back bumper, just in case.

Sergeant Burkette's fuel tanker deuce had departed at 0500 hours to meet the first elements of the Mount Eden convoys at Kings Mills. Burkette was partying all night long with the soldiers of the 928th and did not get any sleep. He felt he could get his rest while waiting at the refueling point for the convoys to arrive.

The units going to Columbus and Dayton had enough fuel in their deuce-and-a-half trucks to make the trip on one tank. The jeeps in those convoys would stop and get gassed-up at a civilian gas station. Sergeant Johnny Burkette's only customers would be the 928th and the 683rd.

Chief James had calculated that both fuel pods filled with diesel should be able to top off every 928th and 683rd truck. Ten jerry cans—5-gallon fuel cans—filled with MOGAS—gasoline—should take care of all the ¼-ton jeeps.

The distance from the Kings Mills refueling point to Ravenna was within the driving range of all the convoy vehicles with a full tank of fuel. Burkette could relax for a couple of hours before his first customers would arrive.

All the 683rd convoy serial elements were on the road, heading north toward Ohio. The speed limit was easily maintained and often surpassed as the convoy drivers were excited and anxious to get home at a decent hour. The previously encountered problems of slow convoy speed, lack of driver experience, blown tires and bad weather were gone. Every driver felt he or she could handle the truck like an expert, and driving 55 mph or faster was not a problem.

Civilians driving by the convoy would honk and wave to the soldiers, which was warmly received by the 683rd personnel. They enjoyed the recognition and would often honk their horns and wave back, thanking them for their show of support. One of the young boys in the back seat of a car gave the convoy drivers a salute, which brought a smile to their faces.

Marshall wondered what all the honking was about when a car passed his jeep and the little boy in the back seat saluted. Marshall returned the salute. The little boy smiled as the car pulled further away.

Going down the big hill on I-71 heading north to the Queen City of Cincinnati was much easier than it had been two weeks earlier when they had to go up the killer hill. The 683rd convoy made its way rapidly going through Cincinnati on I-71, and it soon neared Kings Mills and Sergeant Johnny Burkette's mobile gas station.

Burkette was snoozing soundly as the 683rd pulled into the designated refueling point at Kings Mills. Marshall had the jeep pull well past the fuel truck as the rest of the convoy serial pulled next to it. Marshall noticed Sergeant Burkette hadn't moved; he was still sound asleep. Marshall signaled to the driver of the first deuce and a half to honk his horn.

With a blast from the deuce's air horn, Burkette woke from his deep slumber with a start.

"Welcome to Johnny's Gas Station, y'all," he mumbled, climbing down from the cab of the truck with a grin on his face.

He and Specialist Kayrule began refueling the deuces as Marshall's driver went over and brought back two jerry cans of gasoline.

Within 15 minutes, all vehicles of the first serial were refueled. They began to pull out onto the highway as the second convoy serial of the 683rd pulled in for refueling. When it came to refueling, Burkette was as proficient as he was a bartender. He made sure he got his customers refilled as fast as possible.

Nugot was in the third serial, the last serial of the convoy. Everything had been going well. There were no breakdowns or problems on the road. One vehicle had a problem with water in the fuel filters, but the automotive contact team had already repaired it and got it back on the road within ten minutes.

Stinker was enjoying the ride and the cool breeze as he sat on Nugot's shoulder looking out at the passing cars and scenery. Some of the cars that passed by caught a glimpse of Stinker and thought it wasn't a real skunk until Stinker would move. Nugot had placed a leather collar and leash on Stinker, to prevent him from wandering. Stinker enjoyed chewing on the leash, and Nugot had to re-tie it a couple of times before he reached the Reserve Center.

When Nugot's serial reached the refueling point, Specialist Cutnoff was glad to get out of the wrecker and get away from Stinker, who still had a bit of skunk smell on him. As Nugot took Stinker for a walk near the bushes, the other soldiers at the refueling point gave him a wide berth. Stinker was not yet "fixed."

As the convoy continued its way north past Columbus, the traffic was light for a Saturday afternoon. They were making excellent time, and with any luck should arrive at the Reserve Center in Ravenna before 1700 hours.

Marshall looked at his watch and then checked the map to reconfirm his estimated time of arrival. The weather remained perfect, and maintaining the convoy speed of 55 mph had become a difficult task. Before long, the convoy was doing 60 mph with Marshall in the lead vehicle at the wheel of his jeep. At that speed, every nut and bolt on the jeep was rattling, but Marshall didn't care. He also wanted to arrive early.

When the convoy was nearing the town of Ashland, Burkette's fuel tanker deuce passed the convoy. Burkette's fuel pods were empty and he didn't want to be the last vehicle to arrive at Ravenna.

The pace of all three serials of the convoy was much faster than their trip to Fort Knox two weeks prior. All the 683rd convoy serials were close together and Marshall decided to contact Lieutenant Rodriguez, who was positioned in the last serial, on the radio.

"Rod this is Captain Marshall, over," he said as he keyed his handset on the newly repaired AN/VRC-46 radio.

"Sir, this is Rod, over," the radio crackled.

"Rod, what mile-marker are you at?" asked Marshall.

"Wait one, Sir," replied Lieutenant Rodriguez. After 15 seconds, he responded.

"Mile-marker 192," Rodriguez said. The last serial of the convoy was two miles behind the first serial.

Marshall began to grin.

"Rod, looks like we'll all arrive at Ravenna together," Marshall said. "No need to slow your serial down. Drive safe."

"Roger that, Sir," replied Rodriguez.

The convoy continued its pace toward home—Ravenna, Ohio. The traffic had remained light and the cars that passed continued to honk and wave, welcoming their soldiers back.

At the entrance gate to the Ravenna Army Ammunition Plant, the gate guard waved Sergeant Burkette through. The Reserve Center building was 100 yards away from the entrance.

Burkette parked his deuce and decided to take a nap, telling Kayrule to do the same.

Ten minutes later, the 683rd convoy had arrived en masse. The gate guard just waved every vehicle through. The convoy was home and everyone had arrived safely.

The bus had arrived 30 minutes earlier, giving those soldiers a brief amount of time to relax.

The 683rd was reunited, and ready to do more soldiering.

Tisher put the word out that there would be a formation in 10 minutes. Almost everyone in the convoy had to use the latrine first. The line stretched out the Reserve Center door as every toilet fixture in the center was utilized, including the portable one near the gate guard shack. Those who couldn't wait found relief outside the Reserve Center wherever they could.

"Formation!" shouted Lemasters as he blew his whistle.

Tisher put the word out to the soldiers standing in formation. All radios would be turned in to the commo NCO. All soldiers had to turn-in their gas masks to Sergeant Bierce. All trucks with securable doors could be parked in the parking lot adjacent to the headquarters building. All trucks and vehicles with non-lockable doors had to be parked in the shops. Everyone had to help unload the weapons trailer first. Another formation would follow for final dismissal.

The weapons trailer was backed up to the side door of the Reserve center as the arms room vault was opened inside the center. A line of soldiers formed from the weapons trailer to the arms room vault as Specialist Peoples and Specialist Williams worked together to hand the M16s to the first soldier in line.

Sergeant Mooney was inside the arms vault receiving the weapons in butt-number sequence, filling up each rack inside the vault. Within ten minutes all the weapons were off-loaded and inside the vault. All weapons were accounted for.

The radios were disconnected and brought into the commo room, where Sergeant Mooney took them in.

Sergeant Bierce received all the gas masks in the NBC room. Everything was accounted for, which meant no searches would need to be conducted and everyone could leave after final formation.

Chief James organized the drivers of the non-lockable trucks to convoy down to the shops, where the vehicles could be stored inside a secured building. One deuce-and-a-half had to be off-loaded so the drivers could get a ride back up to the headquarters building.

Within 30 minutes, all the soldiers were ready for final formation.

First Sergeant Tisher gave his familiar shout.

"Fall in!" he yelled as the soldiers of the 683rd lined up in their sections.

Not wanting to waste time, Tisher handed the formation over to Captain Marshall.

Feeling rather worn out from the drive, Marshall's words came out slowly and his voice was deep from a lack of sufficient sleep.

"I want to congratulate all of you on an outstanding job during A.T., the convoy back home, and the off-loading of equipment," Marshall shouted. "I want to personally thank all of the NCOs, officers, and enlisted personnel for all your superb efforts."

"This is an A.T. that you will all remember and can reflect back on with great pride," Marshall continued. 'It was one of those moments that will bring a smile to your face as you go through life. You were all part of a team effort that successfully accomplished every mission, every obstacle that was thrown at you. You have proven to me, yourselves, and to all that you can perform your duty as a soldier, anywhere, anytime."

"I am proud of all of you. See you next drill. Company dismissed!"

The entire 683rd did an about-face movement and shouted in unison, "683rd!"

The soldiers were all weary and smiling. They were grateful that everything had gone their way and glad to have successfully overcome a difficult annual training period. It was time to go home to their families and friends. They had proven to everyone the 683rd knew how to soldier.

Marshall sat on the steps waiting for his wife to pick him up at the Reserve Center. All the soldiers had departed as he sat, reflecting back on what had just happened during the past two weeks. He mused to himself he had accomplished what he had set out to do as the commander of the 683rd Heavy Equipment Maintenance Company. He brought out their professionalism and espirit de corps.

The 683rd was now a highly talented team of soldiers that would continue to grow and develop into one of the finest units in the Army Reserve. Marshall had successfully slain the beast that had lurked about in the shadows of the 683rd.

Marshall was reminiscing as his wife pulled into the Reserve Center. Linda Marshall was a very lovely woman that Dave Marshall felt lucky to have married.

She got out of the car.

"Hello stranger," she said in her sultry voice. Marshall's 3-year old daughter was walking next to her.

"Go ahead. It's Daddy," Linda Marshall said.

Little Megan Marshall stood staring up at father who looked rather tired and haggard, not having shaved that morning. She took a few steps closer at her mother's urging, and then realized it was her father. She rushed into his waiting arms and hugged him as tightly as she could.

Tears of joy began to flow from Dave Marshall's eyes. A scene repeated millions of times in the past, present and will be in the future. This is what serving his country was all about, and he was home.

THE END

EPILOGUE

The drill date in August came three weeks after the 683rd returned from Mount Eden Base Camp. Recommendations for letters of commendation and awards and decorations began to pour in to the 683rd Orderly Room. Sergeant Tea had counted 46 for the soldiers of the 683rd and the attached members of the 646th Supply Company.

All requests had to be carefully reviewed by First Sergeant Tisher and Captain Marshall. Most of the requests for awards and decorations would have to be forwarded to higher headquarters for approval. Marshall and Tisher wanted to make sure those personnel recommended for an award would receive the proper one befitting their performance. Each request would pass the careful scrutiny of the 683rd Commander and First Sergeant.

Some requests would have to be downgraded and many had to be rewritten. The critical factor was the wording of the recommendation and the facts. Fixing flat tires was not considered exemplary performance; it was good job performance worthy of a letter of commendation. Going above and beyond the normal standards of duty performance was what higher headquarters was looking for, and Marshall and Tisher wanted to make sure those requests that went forward had a good chance of being approved.

The members of the 683rd came back from annual training as a better unit. They were now a team and attending weekend drills was something they looked forward to. The 694th Maintenance Operations Section, headed by Major Breedlow, was obtaining new mission work for all the sections within the 683rd.

The 1st and 2nd automotive platoons were traveling to the civilian maintenance shops and working on jobs at those locations. This eliminated the problems of the past. If the 683rd could not finish the job on the weekend, the civilian technicians would finish it up when they returned to work during the week.

The track and tank turret sections were drilling with the National Guard Armor Brigade and providing maintenance assistance.

The service section was busy fixing torn canvas and machining new parts and widgets, and the armament platoon was repairing the 683rd weapons from A.T.

Tech supply was busy every drill filling parts requisitions.

The mess section finally got a mess hall and more cooks. From then on, all meals were prepared and served by Sergeant Adkins in the newly refurbished 683rd Mess Hall.

As time went on, more missions for all the other sections within the 683rd were augmented.

Captain Marshall placed more responsibilities on the younger officers. The young lieutenants of the 683rd had developed into excellent junior officers. They began to learn how to be an effective leader, which was the normal progression at company level.

As the years passed, Colonel Biggs was promoted to brigadier general. Two years after receiving that promotion, he was promoted to major general and commanded the 83rd Army Reserve Command, headquartered in Columbus, Ohio.

As for the members of the 683rd, Lieutenant Burks, Stiles and Smith graduated from college and went on active duty.

Of the three, Smith returned to the 683rd as a Reservist.

Stiles became an Army nurse.

Burks stayed on active duty and was stationed in Korea.

Lieutenant Rodriguez was promoted to captain and was reassigned to the group headquarters in Cleveland.

Kate Kiley was promoted to first lieutenant and became the 683rd Shop Officer.

Chief Farley had to retire earlier than he wanted, due to his health.

Fran Peoples left the military when her service was up. She continued using both her brains and beauty to her advantage and graduated from law school with honors. After several years as one of Ohio's top criminal prosecutors, she was elected judge of the Common Pleas Court.

Pam Williams became a sheriff's deputy in a rural Ohio county. She opened up a shooting range in a field next to her house and could outshoot anyone—except, of course, Fran Peoples.

Sergeant Nugot's wife loved her husband's new pet. Stinker turned out to be a girl skunk and shared his wife's love for primping and, of course, perfume.

Sergeant Bitsko and General Marski's niece Nichole fell in love when school started at Kent State University that fall. They married after graduation. Bitsko returned to Fort Knox many times after A.T. 1982, but was always the general's guest.

Chief Murphy joined a weight loss program and lost over 100 pounds in a year.

The full-timers were rotated to new duty stations throughout the Army. Chief Jones was transferred to Red Stone Arsenal and retired a year later. Sergeant Penny became an Army recruiter in Cleveland. Sergeant Mooney was promoted and was reassigned to Kaiserslaughtern, Germany, where he worked in the G4 section of the 21st SUPCOM Headquarters.

Sergeant Tea was promoted and transferred to the Pentagon in Arlington, Virginia. She later became a sergeant major and worked in the Army Material Command section.

First Sergeant Bill Tisher stayed on as the first sergeant of the 683rd. After four years, he retired and lived with his wife in a cottage on Lake Erie, fishing and enjoying life's small rewards.

Sergeant First Class John Lemasters stayed on until he was no longer allowed to attend drill. He wanted to serve longer, but he had reached mandatory retirement age. He moved to Morgantown, West Virginia and served as the post commander of the local VFW.

Captain Marshall stayed on for three years as commander of the 683rd. The subsequent annual training events in 1983 and 1984 were just a memorable, but all the members of the unit agreed that nothing would ever come close to their experiences at Mount Eden Base Camp in 1982. All would take pride as they would reflect on the accomplishments and what took place amidst the hardships of the mission and Mother Nature. They were all proud to have participated in an event they would fondly remember for the rest of their lives.

Marshall stayed in the Army Reserves, and was promoted to lieutenant colonel, and became the battalion commander ten years later. He promised himself he would someday write a book about what happened that year so he could share it with all that enjoy a good story.

The men and women that comprised the 683rd came from all walks of life to better themselves and serve this great nation. The 683rd Maintenance Company shared a common bond with other units within the Army.

Those whom fill the ranks of these units are cross-sections of what makes America great, and the envy of the entire world. People from different backgrounds and walks of life come together with a common purpose and mission: making a better tomorrow for themselves, their loved ones, the United States of America, and the future of this world.

"It may be laid down as a primary position, and the basis of our system, that every Citizen who enjoys the protection of a Free Government, owes not only a proportion of his property, but even of his personal services to the defense of it."

—George Washington

ARMY BRANCHES

ADJUTANT GENERAL's CORPS: Personnel and administration.

AIR-DEFENSE ARTILLERY: Missiles, rockets and radar systems.

ARMOR: Tanks and tracked vehicles.

ARMY MEDICAL SPECIALIST CORPS: Doctors, surgeons, veterinarians, etc.

ARMY NURSE CORPS: Established in 1775. Became an official branch in 1901.

AVIATION: Rotary and fixed wing aircraft with their own maintenance and logistics.

CHAPLAINS: Ordained ministers representing all faiths.

CIVIL AFFAIRS: Provides multiple civil services in occupied or liberated areas.

CHEMICAL CORPS: Caretakers of some very nasty stuff.

CORPS of ENGINEERS: Builders, designers, and fighters.

DENTAL CORPS: Dentists and their technicians.

FIELD ARTILLERY: Artillery, cannons, howitzers and rockets.

FINANCE CORPS: A soldier's best friend. The Army's payroll and accounting system.

INFANTRY: The soldiers that fight the battle at close interval.

JUDGE ADVOATE GENERAL's CORPS: Legal branch of the Army.

MEDICAL SERVICE CORPS: Hospital and medical administrators.

MILITARY INTELLIGENCE: Provides national and tactical intelligence.

MILITARY POLICE CORPS: Provides security, traffic control, prison and POW compounds.

ORDNANCE: Ammunition, maintenance of equipment, testing of weapon systems.

QUARTERMASTER: Issues food, fuel, water, clothing, equipment.

SIGNAL CORPS: Provides communications assets to all levels within the Army.

SPECIAL FORCES: The Army's elite fighting force.

TRANSPORTATION CORPS: Hauls just about everything the Army needs.

U.S. ARMY MILITARY RANK STRUCTURE

The Army's rank structure has three distinct areas: enlisted, non-Commissioned officer, officer and warrant officer.

ENLISTED

PRIVATE (PVT): The first rung on the ladder of military rank. One who enlisted would be a Private (PVT). He or she would enter basic training, and learn the basic skills of soldiering and become a soldier. After successful completion of basic training, a newly designated soldier would attend advanced individual training (AIT). This phase of training is more refined to the soldier's military occupational specialty (MOS), the military job assigned during period of enlistment.

PRIVATE SECOND CLASS (PV2): After successful completion of AIT, the enlistees would normally be promoted to Private Second Class (PV2).

PRIVATE FIRST CLASS (PFC): Honor graduates of AIT would normally be promoted to Private First Class (PFC). Those PV2s normally were eligible within six months to be promoted to PFC. All promotions came with an increase in pay.

SPECIALIST FORTH CLASS (SP4): After one year as a PFC, the soldier was eligible for promotion to SP4 (which used to be the rank of corporal) if he or she met the criteria: good job performance, staying out of trouble, leadership skills, physical requirements, and a unit position vacancy to be promoted into.

NON-COMMISSIONED OFFICERS

Non-commissioned officers, hereafter referred to as NCOs, are the enlisted soldiers that come up through the ranks. NCOs possess the leadership and skills to perform their MOS and instruct it as well.

SERGEANT (SGT): Wears three chevrons or stripes and is considered the first NCO rank. They usually hold the position of team/crew leaders and are considered a junior NCOs required to attend the basic NCO course (BNCO), a formalized leadership course to prepare them for advancement.

STAFF SERGEANT (SSG): Three chevrons and a rocker underneath the chevrons. SSGs normally lead a squad of 8 to 11 soldiers, depending upon the type of position and branch they serve in. The have successfully completed BNCO and must attend advanced NCO course (ANOC).

SERGEANT FIRST CLASS (SFC): Two rockers under the chevrons. They normally serve as platoon sergeants, second in command to the platoon leaders and/or on staff positions at higher headquarters. Normally they have 14 years of experience and are experts in their fields of military endeavor.

MASTER SERGEANT (MSG) and FIRST SERGEANT (1SG): After serving twenty or more years in the military and having successfully completed all required NCO courses and academies, an enlisted soldier may become a MSG or 1SG. Their rank is three rockers below three chevrons. The 1SG's rank has a diamond centered between the chevrons and the rockers. The MSG rank does not. 1SGs are the ranking NCOs in a company-sized unit and work closely with the company commander. MSGs are normally found in battalions and higher headquarters units in administrative/technical positions.

SERGEANT MAJOR (SGM): The highest NCO rank and normally found in battalion-sized headquarters units or higher. After completing the sergeant major academy, these NCOs are considered the Army's finest, having worked their way up from PVT. At battalion level, their main concerns are the soldiers within the assigned companies and their welfare.

COMMAND SERGEANT MAJOR (CSM): Their duties are similar to those of the MSG and 1SG, and normally found in higher-level headquarters.

OFFICERS

SECOND LIEUTENANT (2LT): Officers start at second lieutenant and are referred to as commissioned officers. They receive a commission from the President of the United States and Congress. Commissions are earned through the U.S. Military Academy, Reserve Officer Training Corps (ROTC) offered at some colleges, or Officer Candidate School (OCS). During wartime, battlefield commissions are sometimes awarded. The 2LTs go through their basic branch course, where they learn skills required within their respective branches (Infantry, Armor, Cavalry, Artillery, Air Defense, Special Forces, Aviation, Military Police, Engineer, Signal, Ordnance, Chemical, Military Intelligence, Transportation, Finance, Adjutant General, Quartermaster, Judge Advocate General, Medical, and Chaplain). After completion of their basic branch courses, it's off to the advanced course where the 2LTs learn more specific information and training in their chosen fields. After assignment to a unit, the 2LT becomes a platoon leader, in charge of 40 or so personnel within the platoon. The platoon is made up of four or five squads, consisting of enlisted personnel, a few SGTs, one or two SSGs and one SFC, known as the platoon sergeant. The platoon sergeant helps coach and advises the young 2LT on how to effectively lead the platoon. A good 2LT will listen to the seasoned NCO's advice. Decisions are made by the 2LT platoon leader, who is ultimately responsible for everything that happens, both good and bad.

FIRST LIEUTENANT (1LT): After a couple of years, the 2LT may be promoted to first lieutenant (1LT). Assignments for 1LTs can range from being the executive officer (XO), which is second in command of a company, to being a battalion staff officer, working in operations and intelligence, supply and logistics, or personnel administration.

CAPTAIN (CPT): The next rank is captain and assignments range from command of a company to staff officer within a battalion headquarters. Serving as a company commander can be one of the most rewarding or career-ending assignments for an officer. No one ever comes away from a command position unscathed.

MAJOR (MAJ): If the CPT survives his or her tenure, this is the next rank up the ladder, and the rungs on the ladder begin to be more difficult to obtain. This rank is for seasoned officers who have served in numerous positions of command and staff, and have attended all required military course including Command and General Staff College (C&GS). The duty assignments for a major include XO of a battalion, and to staff positions on group or brigade level headquarters or higher.

LIEUTENANT COLONEL (LTC): Those fortunate enough in their military career to have made it thus far may serve as a battalion commander, which oversees five to six company units. After years in command and staff positions, these are seasoned officers in their late thirties and early forties that have made the military their career of choice.

COLONEL (COL): After completing the Army War College (one year in length) and having impeccable ratings and evaluations received throughout the entire military career, the officer with superior intellect, conduct and character may be promoted to COL if the position is vacant and needing to be filled. Needless to say, the rungs of the ladder of rank are very far apart at this level. A COL may command a regiment or group, which consists of several or more battalion-sized units with troop strength over two thousand personnel. The responsibilities are awesome.

BRIGADIER GENERAL (BG): One star, and normally commands a brigade or is XO of a division or serving as a high-level staff officer. Brigade commands are very limited and are composed of several groups or regiments.

MAJOR GENERAL (MG): Two stars, and normally commands a division (i.e. 82nd Airborne, 1st Infantry) many up of many brigades, or the XO of an Army Corps.

LIEUTENANT GENERAL (LTG): Three stars, and commands an Army Corps (i.e. XVIII Airborne Corps) consisting of multiple Army divisions, or assigned to the Pentagon. The rungs of the rank ladder are now in the ionosphere.

GENERAL (GEN): Four stars and is currently the highest officer rank within the Army. During WWII, generals were in command of an army (i.e. 1st Army, 2nd Army, 3rd Army). Armies consisted of multiple corps, tailored to conduct warfare in specific geographical areas of the world.

GENERAL OF THE ARMY: Five stars, and this position has not been used since General Omar Bradley. If this position is ever used in the future, the United States has a very, very big war on its hands.

CHIEF WARRANT OFFICER

The Army realized it needed skilled technicians to fill a void in those highly technical areas. This included pilots as well as technicians. Most warrant officers are found in maintenance and aviation units, with some in personnel and administration. These technicians were normally senior NCOs that have excelled in their area of expertise. Aviation warrant officers are trained helicopter pilots. Warrant officers normally do not hold leadership positions, which frees them up to train others in their field of expertise. They do have authority over all enlisted and NCO personnel within their assigned positions. A 2LT outranks a warrant officer, even though the warrant officer may be old enough to be the lieutenant's parent or grandparent.

CHIEF WARRANT OFFICER-1 (WO1): Rank is designated as a silver bar with one black square centered in the middle.

CHIEF WARRANT OFFICER-2 (WO2): Rank is designated as a silver bar with two black squares centered in the middle.

CHIEF WARRANT OFFICER-3 (WO3): Rank is designated as a silver bar with three black squares centered in the middle.

CHIEF WARRANT OFFICER-4 (WO4): Rank is designated as a silver bar with four black squares centered in the middle.

CHIEF WARRANT OFFICER-5 (WO5): Rank is designated as a silver and black bar with four white squares centered in the middle.

MICHAEL M. POINSKI
BIOGRAPHICAL INFORMATION

The author was born in Paris, France while his father was stationed in Paris, France after WWII. His father was one of the many U.S. Army soldiers in the initial amphibious assault of Omaha Beach on June 6th, 1944.

Raised in Ohio, he attended public schools and graduated from the University of Akron with a BA and an Army R.O.T.C. commission. Married 1972, both the author and his new bride served on active duty in the Army at Ft. Bragg, NC. His wife became an Army Nurse while he was a second lieutenant platoon leader of a maintenance company. Both left active duty in 1976 for civilian careers.

In 1980, he joined the U.S. Army Reserve and became a "Citizen Soldier". He was promoted to captain and was assigned as the S1 (adjutant & personnel officer) of the 693rd Maintenance Battalion in Ravenna, OH. In 1982, he received a new assignment, commanding officer of the 682nd Maintenance Company, also located in Ravenna, OH.

In 1986, Michael was assigned as the S2/3 (operations & intelligence officer) of the 693rd Maintenance Battalion. Shortly afterwards, he was promoted to major and reassigned to the 2077th USAR School, in Cleveland, OH as the training officer. In 1990, was reassigned as the maintenance operations officer of the 693rd Maintenance Battalion and in 1993, was promoted to lieutenant colonel and became the battalion commander of the 693rd Maintenance Battalion, retiring in 1997 with 24 years of military service.

WA